*Assessing Adolescents in Educational,
Counseling, and Other Settings*

T0347362

# Assessing Adolescents in Educational, Counseling, and Other Settings

Robert D. Hoge
*Carleton University, Ottawa, Canada*

Routledge
Taylor & Francis Group

NEW YORK AND LONDON

First published 1999 by Lawrence Erlbaum Associates, Inc.

This edition published 2015 by Routledge
711 Third Avenue, New York, NY 10017, USA
2 Park Square, Milton Park, Abingdon, Oxon OX14 4RN

First issued in paperback 2015

*Routledge is an imprint of the Taylor & Francis Group, an informa business*

Cover design by Kathryn Houghtaling Lacey

**Library of Congress Cataloging-in-Publication Data**

Hoge, Robert D.
Assessing adolescents in educational, counseling, and other settings /
    Robert D. Hoge.
        p.   cm.
        Includes bibliographical references and indexes.
    ISBN 0-8058-3094-4 (alk. paper)
    1. Teenagers—Psychological testing. 2. Youth—Psychological testing.
        I. Title.
    BF724.25.H64    1999
    155.5'028'7—dc21                                          98-41565
                                                                    CIP


ISBN 13: 978-1-138-00317-0 (pbk)
ISBN 13: 978-0-8058-3094-1 (hbk)

# Contents

# Preface

The goal of this book is to explore the role of standardized psychological assessments in the treatment of young people in educational, counseling, forensic, and other settings. A basic argument is that standardized assessments provide a better basis for assessing individuals than the informal and unsystematic procedures commonly used in schools, agencies, clinics, and practitioners' offices, and that in turn, more valid assessments lead to better decisions about possible courses of action. This argument is more fully developed in the coming chapters.

Why focus on the assessment of adolescents? First, adolescence is a distinct development period and youths in the teen years display somewhat different risk and need factors than younger and older groups. We know this from experience and from a large body of theory and research on adolescent development. Second, most texts and handbooks on psychological assessment either concentrate on adults or lump together younger children and adolescents. In both cases, there is a relative neglect of assessment issues specific to adolescents.

The book is directed toward three audiences. The first group includes mental health professionals involved in the conduct and interpretation of psychological assessments of adolescents. This group is composed primarily of psychologists, but other professionals such as psychiatrists, social workers, educators, and child care workers are sometimes involved as well. The second group includes professionals who may be required to use the results of psychological assessments in their decision making. School principals, youth court judges, and managers of residential treatment facilities are three exemplars of such professionals. This book should help them understand the purposes and procedures of psychological assessments, as well as the associated strengths and weaknesses. The third group includes developmental researchers interested in adolescents. They may benefit from the review of standardized assessment tools presented in the book.

## ACKNOWLEDGMENTS

Some of the research on which this book is based has been supported by funds from Health Canada's Strategic Fund for Children's Mental Health, the Ontario Ministry of Community and Social Services, and Carleton University. I also wish to thank Lynda Robertson and Marlo Gal for their assistance in the preparation of the manuscript. As well, I am grateful for the excellent editorial support provided to me at Lawrence Erlbaum Associates by Susan Milmoe, Kathryn Scornavacca, and Teresa Horton. Finally, I wish to extend gratitude to the many students, colleagues, and family members who have supported my work over the years.

# 1

## *Introduction*

This book is based on three key propositions. First, the effectiveness of any educational, therapeutic, or counseling intervention depends at least in part on the quality of the assessment on which it is based. For example, a decision to provide a youth with a program of behavior modification treatment for depression would be appropriate to the extent that it reflects the actual emotional state of the youth and other characteristics that would affect his or her reactions to this treatment. Similarly, the ultimate success of a decision to counsel a youth to follow an academic stream in secondary school will be limited by the accuracy of the initial assessment of the student's aptitudes and interests.

Second, standardized psychological assessments and structured diagnostic procedures are more likely to yield valid information about an individual than the informal and unsystematic assessments so often employed in clinical, counseling, and educational settings. There is certainly a role for experienced clinical judgments in the treatment of clients, but, as I try to show in later sections of the book, standardized psychological assessments provide a firmer and more defensible foundation for diagnostic and decision-making activities.

Third, assessment tools and procedures should be appropriate for the individual being assessed. I have chosen in this book to focus on the assessment of adolescents because I believe that this group often exhibits characteristics and circumstances that set them apart from children and adults. Further, these unique features mean that, in many cases, assessments and interventions appropriate for younger and older age groups may not be indicated. This point is reinforced in the discussion of theory and research on adolescence that follows.

## DEFINING ADOLESCENCE

The terms *adolescent* and *adolescence* are ubiquitous in our language, and we use them with absolute confidence. However, closer examination reveals a great deal of ambiguity in their meaning, and, in fact, historians and social scientists have argued for a very long time over alternative definitions of the construct.

The word *adolescence* derives from the Latin *adolescentia*, which refers to the process of growing or growing up. It does not have any referent to an age range in Latin, but the *Oxford English Dictionary* indicates that it first appeared in English in the middle of the 15th century as a term referring to a young man. The current use of the term to refer generally to the teen years apparently evolved from that time.

We do generally refer to the teen years as the period of adolescence and a youth in that age range as an adolescent. However, establishing more precise criteria for defining this developmental period is quite difficult.

One approach to definition is in terms of physical development. In this case the beginning of adolescence is said to correspond to the onset of puberty when primary and secondary sexual developments make their first appearance. This process is guided by hormonal changes and accompanied by other significant physical changes. I show later in this volume that the physical events associated with the progress toward sexual maturity do have important consequences for the development of youth during the early years. On the other hand, there are some problems with using these physical changes to delimit the period of adolescence. First, there is considerable variability both between and within the genders with respect to the period of onset of puberty. Menarche, for example, may appear as early as age 9½ in some girls and as late as age 16½ in others. Further, the age of onset of puberty is generally about 2 years earlier in girls than boys. Second, delineating the end of the adolescent period by the achievement of sexual maturity is not particularly meaningful. Most young people achieve sexual maturity before what we would consider emotional maturity. Third, many of the psychological processes popularly associated with adolescence do not relate in any direct fashion to the onset or achievement of sexual maturity. For example, the beginning of dating behavior, typically associated with early adolescence in Western society, sometimes appears before any signs of sexual development.

A second approach to definition of adolescence is in terms of singular psychological processes that appear to mark a transition from childhood at one extreme to adulthood at the other. Certainly there are popular assumptions in this regard. Thus, the onset of adolescence is presumably marked by efforts to achieve independence from adult influence, to form a stable identity, to develop a gender role, and by other processes and events thought unique to this age period.

There are some problems with this approach as well. One difficulty is that there is no real agreement over the nature of these psychological processes. Rather, as I address in chapters 2 and 3, a variety of hypotheses have been advanced. This variety makes it nearly impossible to develop an explicit definition of adolescence purely on the basis of psychological processes. A second difficulty is that the psychological approach has tended to ignore the operation of historical and social forces. We now know that this is a mistake. It is clear that the psychological experiences of youths (and even their physical development to some extent) are very much affected by their social environment. The dynamics of home, school, and community have a very direct impact on the course of their psychological development:

> Adolescence (or the broader category of youth) can be fully understood only when viewed within the life course and its historical setting. Each generalized stage, or age category, is constructed from norms and institutional constraints that establish a basis for identity and specify appropriate behaviors, roles, and timetables. (Elder, 1980; p. 6)

This also means that the nature of the adolescent experience will vary across time and across cultures. Therefore, the search for a universal psychological definition of adolescence is complicated.

In spite of these reservations, I show in chapters 2 and 3 that continuing efforts are being made to discover and analyze physical and psychological processes particularly relevant to youths in the teen years. For the purposes of this book, then, the term *adolescence* will generally be used to refer to the period from 11 to 19 years of age, but we must keep in mind the limitations associated with any efforts to generalize across all youths within that age range.

## NATURE OF THE ASSESSMENT PROCESS

We tend to take for granted assessment activities, but it should be understood that they underlie all decisions about individuals and the quality of our assessments places limits on the effectiveness of our decisions. These issues are explored in chapters 4 and 5, but some introduction to the main points is appropriate.

The assessment process involves three steps: (a) the collection of information about an individual, (b) the translation of that information into an inference or judgment, and (c) the use of the inference or judgment as the basis for a decision. The inferences or judgments are often referred to as *assessments* or *diagnoses*. These are sometimes expressed in qualitative terms as, for example, where diagnostic categories such as attention-deficit-disordered, severely depressed, or developmentally delayed are employed. In other cases the judgment may be expressed in quantitative terms. Thus, the youth is characterized as above average in mathematics aptitude or at the 30th percentile with respect to an index of conduct disorder. In still other cases the judgment is expressed in terms of a predictive category. For example, the youth is judged at high risk for delinquent behavior, at moderate risk for academic problems, or with a high likelihood of succeeding in a program for the gifted.

Varying levels of structure may be imposed on both the information collection and inferential components of the assessment process. In many applied situations both the information collection and diagnostic processes are based on informal and unsystematic procedures, and are referred to as clinical assessments or diagnoses. An example would be a school psychologist who informally examines a boy's work, consults with his teacher, and diagnoses him as learning disabled. Another might be a therapist who conducts an unstructured interview with a client and diagnoses depression. The information is being collected in these cases through informal procedures, and the inference or judgment about the client is based on an intuitive process utilizing the clinician's education and experience.

The alternative is to base the information collection and diagnostic processes on standardized psychological assessments. The latter may be defined as instruments or procedures with (a) fixed stimulus, response, and scoring formats (b) that yield quantitative scores and (c) for which normative and psychometric data are available. These are also sometimes referred to as *objective* or *psychometric assessments*, although some ambiguity is associated with those terms.

An example of a standardized assessment would be the use of a standardized intelligence test to collect information about cognitive performance and provide a quantitative index of cognitive potential. The latter represents the inferential or judgmental phase of the process. The use of a standardized teacher rating measure to collect information about classroom behavior and form an inference about behavioral pathology is another example. The information is being collected and the inference or diagnosis formed in these cases through standardized procedures.

It should be recognized that the line between clinical and standardized assessments is not always entirely clear. Clinical assessments may be based in part on standardized assessment tools. For example, mental health professionals will often utilize both informal and standardized sources of information in arriving at a psychiatric diagnosis. On the other hand, standardized psychological assessments may entail the exercise of more or less clinical judgment. An inference that a youth with a score of

135 on the Wechsler Intelligence Scale for Children–III (Wechsler, 1991) is significantly above average in cognitive ability relative to a standardization group requires relatively little clinical judgment. The use of the score to derive a specific diagnosis or to project future performance may, however, require a measure of clinical judgment. Similarly, combining scores from multiple standardized measures usually depends on subjective procedures, although in some cases we have available statistical or actuarial procedures for this purpose. These issues are explored in more detail in chapter 5.

The final step in the assessment process is the translation of the judgment into a decision. Thus, the youth judged at high risk for delinquent behavior is placed in a residential setting; the person judged as high in math aptitude is placed in a special enriched class; or the severely depressed youth is provided a psychotherapeutic treatment. This phase, too, can exhibit more or less structure. In most cases the actual decision is made by the clinician or counselor on the basis of the diagnosis. However, as we will see, there are now some efforts to develop standardized statistical or logical formulas for directly translating diagnoses into decisions. An example is use of an empirically derived formula to derive a risk classification for a youthful offender and to link that directly with the level of custody to assign him or her.

## THE IMPORTANCE OF STANDARDIZED
## PSYCHOLOGICAL ASSESSMENTS

The first assumption stated at the beginning of the chapter was that the quality of decisions about clients depends very directly on the validity of the assessments on which the decisions are based. There is ample evidence from the clinical literature that many inappropriate decisions have been made on the basis of invalid assessments of clients' characteristics and situations. For example, countless adolescents have been misdiagnosed and inappropriately placed in opportunity classes for the developmentally delayed, secure custody facilities for youthful offenders, or treatment programs. Conversely, many others have been deprived of needed services through inadequate assessments.

The second assumption was that standardized psychological instruments and procedures are more likely to produce valid and useful information than the informal and unstructured clinical procedures so often used in applied settings. The arguments in favor of this assumption are developed through this book, but an overview of the major points is appropriate here.

The third assumption was that assessment instruments should be appropriate for the individual. As shown in later chapters, there is a growing body of increasingly sophisticated standardized assessment tools and procedures for adolescents. These apply to the whole range of aptitude, personality, attitudinal, and environmental attributes of interest in applied assessment situations.

There are, to be sure, limits on the reliability and validity of these instruments, but significant advances are easily documented. In clinical assessments, on the other hand, there is generally no psychometric information available. Further, as we see in chapter 4, where direct comparisons have been made between clinical and standardized assessment procedures, the latter have nearly always proven superior.

The issues of consistency and control of bias arise in clinical assessments. Industrial psychologists have long argued in favor of the use of standardized assessment and selection procedures in job hiring situations. These procedures help ensure that applicants are treated consistently and that individual biases and prejudices do not confound the selection process. The same point could be made with respect to many of the decision situations involving adolescents, whether they involve streaming into academic programs, placement in special classes, or referrals to residential or custodial settings.

Finally, operational definitions of standardized psychological assessments are available. There is sometimes ambiguity and controversy over the constructs assessed by tests and other measures, but at least the bases for the assessment are explicit because they are represented in the content of the measure. In clinical judgments, there is generally no such information. This is an important consideration from the point of view of understanding and justifying our judgments and decisions.

The emphasis thus far has been on the benefits of improved assessment procedures for the individual client. It should also be clear, though, that the use of standardized assessments and structured diagnostic procedures can also provide positive gains in the management of system resources. Schools, hospitals, juvenile justice systems, and community-based services are all concerned with the optimal use of resources. I try to show later that this is best achieved where service delivery decisions are based on accurate assessments of the needs and circumstances of the client.

Various cautions regarding the use of standardized psychological assessments are given in the following chapters, but several caveats need to be noted at the beginning.

First, we must acknowledge that there are areas in which effective standardized assessment instruments have not been developed; here we are forced to use more subjective methods of assessment. One example is the assessment of risk for suicide. Although efforts to provide some screening tools have been made, clinical judgments still form the main bases for these risk assessments.

Second, we must emphasize that the application of psychological assessments usually requires special training and experience. The level of expertise required varies rather widely, but there are an unfortunate number of misdiagnoses arising from the use of the measures by unqualified individuals. The various ethical guidelines that have been developed regarding psychological assessment are reviewed in chapter 5.

Third, we must point out the danger that the use of standardized psychological assessments and structured diagnostic procedures might limit the opportunity for the exercise of professional discretion. There is a serious issue involved here. Although I have argued that standardized assessment tools are preferable to the more clinical procedures, they are still imperfect instruments, and ultimate decisions about clients must rest with the responsible educator, clinician, or service provider. I develop this point further in a later chapter in my discussion of what is referred to as the professional override principle.

## TYPES OF PSYCHOLOGICAL INSTRUMENTS AND PROCEDURES

There has long been a tendency to equate psychological assessments with psychological tests. In fact, most of the standard textbooks on assessment include the term *test* prominently (or exclusively) in their title. To some extent this practice reflects reality: There is, in fact, a heavy dependence on tests and self-report inventories in applied settings. This is illustrated in Table 1.1, which is based on a usage survey of clinical psychologists who work with adolescents. It can be seen that standardized tests (e.g., Wechsler Intelligence Scales, Minnesota Multiphasic Personality Inventory, Beck Depression Inventory) and projective tests (e.g., Rorschach Inkblot Test, Kinetic Family Drawing) are heavily weighted in the listing.

Although the frequency listing in Table 1.1 is undoubtedly accurate, there are two cautions to be observed in interpreting those data. First, the survey was conducted with clinical psychologists, and, hence, it does not include other types of practitioners who work with adolescents. It is likely that these other practitioners—school psychologists, vocational counselors, and mental health professionals who are not psychologists functioning in mental health and juvenile justice settings—might employ other types of assessment tools. Second, as I try to show later, these alternative measures are catalyzing some of the most exciting developments in assessment. They include judgmental measures such as ratings and checklists, standardized interview schedules, and various types of measures of

TABLE 1.1
Frequency of Use of Assessment Instruments
With Adolescents (in Order of Usage Frequency)

Wechsler Intelligence Scales
Rorschach
Bender–Gestalt
Thematic Apperception Test
Sentence Completion
Minnesota Multiphasic Personality Inventory
Human Figures Drawing
House–Tree–Person
Wide Range Achievement Test
Kinetic Family Drawing
Beck Depression Inventory
Millon Adolescent Personality Inventory
MacAndrew Alcoholism Scale
Child Behavior Checklist
Woodcock Johnson Psychoeducational Battery
Peabody Picture Vocabulary Test
Conners Behavior Rating Scale
Developmental Test of Visual-Motor Integration
Reynolds Adolescent Depression Scale
Children's Depression Inventory
Vineland Adaptive Behavior Scale
Vineland Social Maturity Scale
Roberts Apperception Test
Benton Visual Retention Test
Piers–Harris Children's Self-Concept Scale
Stanford–Binet Intelligence Scale
Personality Inventory for Children
Peabody Individual Achievement Test
Halstead–Reitan Neuropsychological Battery
High School Personality Questionnaire

*Note.* Adapted from "Psychological Test Usage With Adolescent Clients: 1990 Survey Findings," by R. P. Archer, M. Maruish, E. A. Primhoff, & C. Piotrowski, 1991, *Professional Psychology: Research and Practice, 22.*

environmental factors. The standardized psychological tests are extensively reviewed in this book, but an effort is also made in succeeding chapters to show that the range of instruments and procedures available for assessing adolescents extends considerably beyond psychological tests.


## ORGANIZATION OF THE BOOK

My major goal in writing this book was to provide the reader with a comprehensive review of instruments and procedures for assessing adolescents. The focus is on standardized psychological assessments, and an

effort has been made to include instruments that are accessible to practitioners and that are the subject of current research activity. A second
goal was to describe the effective use of psychological assessments in
educational, clinical, counseling, and organizational settings and offer
some guidelines for the conduct of optimal assessments.

The book has been divided into three parts.

## Part I

The two chapters in this section provide an introduction to contemporary
research and theory on adolescence.

*Chapter 2.* This chapter begins with an overview of the various aspects
of adolescent development of concern to psychologists, which is followed
by an overview of traditional theories of adolescent development and a
discussion of some of the more recent trends in theory and research. The
chapter is obviously not a comprehensive treatment but lays the conceptual foundation for the subsequent consideration of assessment.

*Chapter 3.* The focus of much assessment activity is psychological
impairments and problematic behaviors, and this chapter introduces issues in identifying and treating behavioral, social, and emotional problems of adolescence. The first sections of the chapter discuss definitional
concerns, later sections review various intervention models appropriate
for use with adolescents.

## Part II

The two chapters in Part II provide an introduction to the selection,
utilization, and evaluation of assessment instruments and procedures.

*Chapter 4.* This chapter reviews some of the basic concepts in psychological assessment. It describes the assessment process and various bases
for characterizing instruments and procedures, and discusses the major
bases for evaluating psychological measures—reliability and validity.

*Chapter 5.* This chapter extends the discussions in the preceding chapter to a variety of professional and practical issues. It includes overviews
of the various uses of assessments and their usual contexts, and a review
of the major ethical issues that arise in assessments. It describes current
ranking about standards for the conduct of assessments and provisions
for regulating the profession.

## Part III

The five chapters in Part III lay out the assessment instruments and procedures.

Readers should note, first, that the review of instruments is not designed to be comprehensive. I have made an effort to include assessment tools that are widely available and that are the subject of current research and evaluation activity. Each instrument is briefly described, and a summary of information about its psychometric properties is presented. References to more detailed discussions of research on the instrument are then provided.

Two cautions relating to the reviews are also important. First, many of the instruments and procedures in question are protected by copyright and should be used only with the explicit permission of the copyright holder, whether a commercial publisher or the test author. Sources are identified in the chapters. Second, administration, scoring, and interpretation of the instruments and procedures require varying levels of training, experience, and certification. Some instruments are freely available and their use involves no special skills. Others require higher levels of expertise, and some may be utilized only by certified psychologists or other mental health providers. This issue is discussed in more detail in chapter 5.

*Chapter 6.* This chapter presents a variety of standardized instruments designed for assessing aptitudes and achievement levels. They include the major individual and group IQ and achievement tests appropriate for use with adolescents as well as more specialized aptitude tests such as the Differential Aptitude Tests, the Bender Visual Motor Gestalt Test, and the Scholastic Aptitude Test.

*Chapter 7.* This chapter reviews structured personality tests appropriate for use with adolescents. They include general measures of personality, self-concept, and specific personality domains.

*Chapter 8.* This chapter deals with interview and observation measures. Although my primary concern in the book is standardized measures, I begin the chapter with a discussion of the clinical interview, because it so often forms a part of assessment activities. Presentations of recently developed standardized interview and observation schedules suitable for use with this age group follow.

*Chapter 9.* This chapter presents behavioral ratings and checklists. They include a wide variety of instruments for use in collecting behavioral information from adolescents and parents, teachers, clinicians, and other observers. The foci of the measures range from general social competence and emotional pathology to measures of specific concerns, relating, for example, to suicidal potential, eating disorders, substance abuse, and conduct disorders.

*Chapter 10.* This chapter reviews a variety of measures of cognitions, attitudes, beliefs, and interests, discussed under the following headings: (a) attitudes, values, and beliefs; (b) cognitive states; and (c) career and academic interests.

*Chapter 11.* This chapter describes a variety of composite and environmental measures that do not fit easily into the preceding categories. They are divided into the following groups: (a) neuropsychological assessment batteries, (b) adaptive functioning measures, (c) parent and family functioning measures, and (d) broad-based risk measures. The latter include measures with particular relevance to forensic settings.

*Chapter 12.* This chapter recapitulates the instruments reviewed in the previous chapters, discusses the strengths and limitations of standardized psychological assessments and structured diagnostic procedures in applied settings, and offers a set of practical and research recommendations.

# I

*AN INTRODUCTION TO CONTEMPORARY RESEARCH AND THEORY ON ADOLESCENCE*

# 2

*The Analysis of Adolescent Development*

The effective utilization of assessments requires a clear understanding of the constructs being assessed. This is true whether we are trying to assess level of cognitive functioning, need for autonomy, or risk for suicide. It follows that any attempt to develop tools or procedures for assessing adolescents must be based on an understanding of adolescent development. It is in this sense that theory and research regarding adolescent behavior become so important.

This chapter presents, first, an overview of different aspects of adolescent development that have been the focus of concern and the various environmental influences on development. This is followed by a review of the major types of theoretical efforts relevant to adolescent development, including both traditional theories of development and some of the more recent theoretical advances. The intent of the discussion in this chapter is to provide background to an understanding of the various problems associated with adolescent development to be discussed in the following chapter and the subsequent review of tools and procedures for assessing adolescents. The reader is referred to Compas, Hinden, and Gerhardt (1995), Crockett and Crouter (1995), Jackson and Rodriquez-Tome (1995), and Lerner (1993) for extended discussions of this literature.

## DESCRIBING ADOLESCENT DEVELOPMENT

Many efforts to analyze adolescent behavior have focused on describing the course of development. These efforts are of interest from a scientific perspective, but they are also valuable to parents, teachers, clinicians, and youths in providing a gauge against which to evaluate the progress of individual adolescents. The descriptions are also important for developing and selecting assessment tools. The intelligent use of assessments depends on a full understanding of the characteristics and needs of the youth being assessed.

Before giving an overview of descriptions of development, it is useful first to identify some recurring issues underlying these descriptive efforts.

One issue concerns whether development is best characterized as a continuous, seamless process or as a process that occurs through qualitatively distinct stages of development. The former view predominates in the various learning theory orientations in which the development of the organism is represented in terms of the gradual accumulation of more and more complex responses. The latter view is represented in both the psychoanalytic and cognitive-developmental perspectives in which the development of the individual is characterized in terms of passage through qualitatively distinct stages of development. It should be clear that neither continuity nor discontinuity is inherent within development; rather, these represent different means for conceptualizing development. Both are capable of contributing to our understanding of the developmental progression.

A second recurring issue in these descriptive efforts concerns the stability of development. There are some characteristics that seem to exhibit a fair bit of stability over the life span. For example, young children motivated to engage in high levels of physical activity generally display similar levels as adolescents and adults. There are other characteristics, though, for which the level of stability is more debatable. One example is intelligence, as the extent to which individuals show consistency in intelligence levels across the life span continues to be a point of controversy. Another behavioral characteristic that is the object of considerable attention in this regard is aggressive or other antisocial behaviors. What is the likelihood that the highly aggressive 8-year-old will continue to show aggression in adolescence and adulthood?

A third issue in these descriptive efforts concerns consistency across individuals in the course of development. To what extent do adolescents share a common developmental experience? Application of a common label, *adolescence*, to this developmental period reflects an assumption that there are some commonalties to this age period. Further, popular stereotypes reinforce the image of consistency. Thus, all adolescents are assumed to experience emotional turmoil, conflicts with parents, and risk-taking behaviors. As shown later, though, research often does not support this view. In fact, adolescents exhibit considerable variability with respect to cognitive, social, personality, and physical functioning. This variability is even more dramatic when we contrast the experience of adolescents from different gender, cultural, and ethnic groups. This does not mean there are not consistencies in development over this period, but it does suggest that generalizations should always be viewed with some caution.

A fourth related issue that has received attention in this literature concerns secular trends in development. This refers generally to downward shifts in the age at which developmental transitions occur. One of the most dramatic of these trends has occurred in the age of onset of puberty, with a dramatic drop in the age of menarche since the mid-19th century. Secular trends have been observed, though, in nearly all aspects of adolescent development, including the ages at which individuals complete schooling and leave home.

A fifth issue arising in this descriptive work concerns the definition of normal or normative development. This is an extremely important issue because so much of our treatment of adolescents (and their feelings about themselves) revolves around judgments about the normality of their development and behavior. I address this issue in more detail in chapter 3, but I note two points here. First, atypical development generally reflects departures from patterns exhibited by a particular sample of individuals, and the definition may not be relevant to other individuals. For example, a commitment to academic achievement may be the norm for students from middle-class suburban communities, but that commitment may have little relevance for a student from another community, and, further, an absence of the commitment may not signify a problem. Second, it is important to make a distinction between atypical development and problematic development. Some youths exhibit gender identity behaviors different from those of the average (or even majority) of adolescents; whether that represents a problem, though, depends on other considerations. Similarly, a high percentage of youths exhibit dangerous risk behaviors; however, the fact that such behaviors are common among adolescents does not necessarily mean that they are not problematic.

The development of the individual represents a complex gestalt of biological, cognitive, social, and personality characteristics advancing through a complex social environment. Descriptive efforts have, however, traditionally focused on the analysis of individual facets, and the following represents an outline of some of the major themes that have emerged in those facets. The integration of the different aspects of development and efforts to understand the forces acting on development are considered in later sections on theoretical developments and a discussion of problems of development is dealt with in chapter 3.

## Biological and Physical Development

Changes in the height and weight of the individual increase rapidly during infancy, increase more gradually during the middle years of childhood, and then show accelerated development during the teen years. During the 2 or 3 years of the adolescent growth spurt, gains of 2 to 4 inches in height and 10 to 15 pounds in weight are not uncommon. The timing of this growth spurt is not highly predictable, showing considerable variability across individuals and across gender: In general, height, weight, and musculature develop earlier in girls than boys. This spurt terminates sometime in adolescence and is generally followed by minimal changes in stature until growth is completed in late adolescence. Of some significance, too, is the fact that growth of overt physical features is somewhat uneven during the adolescent years, with hands and feet developing at a faster rate than arms and legs.

Another feature of physical development concerns the development of sexual features and the reproductive system. This is one of the most significant aspects of adolescent development and it is associated with many facets of the social and personality functioning of the youth.

The sequence of development in the sexual maturation of boys and girls normally results in complete sexual maturity around the age of 13 for girls and 15 for boys. However, there is considerable variability across individuals in the timing of this sequence. There is considerable evidence for a secular trend in the maturation of sexual functioning. Tanner (1991) estimated that age at menarche has dropped by approximately 3 to 4 months every 10 years over the past 100 years. This trend is reflected both in earlier sexual maturity and a generally faster rate of physical growth.

Another aspect of physical development concerns the activity of the endocrine system; that is, the system of glands producing hormones and the neural structures that regulate their activity. The most critical of the endocrine glands in physical maturation is the pituitary, which appears to regulate other glands and also produces a growth hormone that directly stimulates growth and development of cells. The adolescent growth spurt and the development of the primary and secondary sexual features is apparently governed to a great extent by the release of hormones from the pituitary gland, in turn, stimulating the production of estrogen in girls and testosterone in boys (Tanner, 1989). Both the onset and conclusion of puberty are governed in large part by this system.

This brief overview of the course of physical development leaves open several important issues. The first issue concerns the way in which the different aspects of physical development—physical growth, sexual development, and hormonal activity—relate to one another. A second related issue concerns the ultimate determinants of this physical development. The course of physical development is governed to some extent by genetic programming. However, the mechanisms of that programming and the involvement of environmental influences remain important topics. A third issue concerns the way these aspects of physical development interact with social and emotional development.

## Cognitive Development

The evolution of cognitive functioning is a second aspect of development that has long been a focus of attention. Very generally, *cognition* refers to the mental processes used by humans to acquire knowledge and solve problems. The major components of cognition include perception, attention, memory, and information processing. An understanding of these cognitive processes is important in comprehending adolescents' interactions with their environments. It is also important for the creation and selection of assessment instruments.

There is a wide array of developments taking place in the general field of cognitive psychology, but three lines of analysis are particularly relevant to issues in the assessment of adolescents; these derive from structural developmental models, psychometric models, and social cognition models.

*Structural Developmental Models.* Included in this category are models designed to describe the sequence of development of basic cognitive processes. The most prominent example is represented in the descriptive framework presented by Piaget (1950; see also Flavell, 1963, 1985), which represents an effort to characterize the nature of perceptual and cognitive processes at various points in the developmental sequence.

The model represents the cognitive maturation process in terms of passage through qualitatively distinct stages of development. The most important of these stages for adolescence is the period of formal operational thought. Individuals are assumed to reach this stage sometime during early adolescence. Its most significant feature is that the individual now acquires an ability to process information in purely abstract terms and to reason logically. This represents a significant advance in the adolescent's ability to acquire knowledge and solve academic problems. The movement to this period of formal operational thought is also believed to have important implications for an adolescent's conceptualization of self and perception of social phenomena.

There are a number of points of controversy relating to Piaget's descriptive framework that bear brief mention. First, as mentioned earlier, the representation of development in terms of passage through qualitatively distinct stages has been questioned by some, who suggest that development is simply not that orderly. A second related point is that individuals may show considerable variability across tasks in level of cognitive functioning. Thus, an adolescent may be capable of formal operational thought in some areas of cognitive activity but not others. Third, some critics have suggested that Piaget's representation of the nature of thought during adolescence is too simplistic. One expression of this view is represented in Broughton's (1983) hypothesis that there are actually two forms of formal operational thought that emerge during adolescence, with early and late forms differing in the quality of abstract thought exhibited. A fourth limitation of Piaget's analysis particularly relevant to the subject matter of this book is that relatively few efforts have been made to translate the descriptive framework into practical assessment instruments. The psychometric approach has had much more of an impact on the way in which cognitive processes are assessed.

*The Psychometric Approach.*  Unlike the previous approach, descriptions of cognitive development in this case have been derived empirically from analyses of cognitive behavior. The earliest efforts in this case derive from the work of Galton, Binet, and Spearman (see T. B. Rogers, 1995, for a review). The approach has been tremendously productive in the sense of producing a wide range of practical assessment instruments (see chap. 6).

On the other hand, until recently the approach has not yielded particularly useful frameworks for describing actual cognitive processes. Most of the descriptive efforts have been based on some conceptualization of constellations of general and specific cognitive abilities, but the efforts have generally provided little information about the actual nature of cognitive activities or the way in which they may evolve over the life span.

There are, however, some recent developments deriving from this tradition that may be viewed as more adequate descriptions of cognitive activity during the developmental sequence. One of these is represented in Sternberg's triarchic theory of intelligence (Sternberg, 1985, 1988), which characterizes intelligence in terms of three components: context, experience, and information-processing skills. The model essentially asserts that any description (or assessment) of intelligent behavior should take account of (a) of the context in which the behavior is exhibited, (b) the individual's experiences with the task, and (c) the actual information-processing activities brought to bear on the task. The latter part of the analysis is particularly important because it represents an effort to describe the processes underlying cognitive activity.

The second of these developments is represented in Gardner's theory of multiple intelligences (Gardner, 1983, 1993). The core of this model is the identification of a set of seven distinct types of intelligence (see Table 2.1). The major contribution of this model is its considerable expansion of the scope and functions of intelligent behavior. It thereby serves as an important corrective to the very narrow definition of intelligence represented in traditional models. This can be particularly relevant in attempting to characterize cognitive processes in adolescents; the realms in which they utilize these are very broad indeed.

TABLE 2.1
Gardner's Multiple Intelligences

| Type of Intelligence | Description |
|---|---|
| Linguistic | Competence in the comprehension and use of language |
| Spatial | Ability to accurately perceive visual-spatial relations and to operate on those relations with both visual and symbolic stimuli |
| Logical-mathematical | Capacity to think logically and systematically; ability to manipulate abstract symbols |
| Musical | Sensitivity to pitch, melody, and other aspects of music; ability to form rhythmic patterns; capacity to perform music |
| Body-kinesthetic | Ability to effectively combine gross and fine motor skills to accomplish physical tasks and for artistic expression |
| Interpersonal | Capacity to accurately interpret social cues provided by others and to act appropriately and effectively in social situations |
| Intrapersonal | Ability to accurately interpret one's own emotions; capacity to cope effectively with problems and stresses |

*Note.* Based on H. Gardner (1983). *Frames of Mind: The Theory of Multiple Intelligences.* New York: Basic Books.

Although the latter two developments are encouraging in broadening the conception of cognitive activity represented in traditional psychometric models, two limitations should be noted: The analyses of the postulated processes remain incomplete at present and the models have not been fully translated into practical assessment instruments. In fact, all of the intelligence and other aptitude tests described in chapter 6 derive from earlier work within the psychometric approach.

*Social Cognitions.* Cognitive activity encompasses all aspects of information processing, whether that information concerns sorting a set of blocks according to color, shape, and size; solving an algebraic equation; or attempting to infer the motives of someone who has injured another person. The latter, though, represents a rather special case of cognitive activity because it involves the processing of social cues. *Social cognition* refers generally to the way in which individuals reason about themselves and their social worlds. Because this is such a critical aspect of development, it has evolved to some extent as a separate area of cognitive development analysis.

Two separate lines of analysis have evolved in social cognition, one representing a structural developmental perspective evolving out of cognitive-developmental theory and the other an information-processing perspective. The latter traces its lineage back to earlier work on social intelligence and human problem solving.

The structural developmental perspective originated from Piaget's descriptive framework, described earlier. It is represented most notably in the work of Flavell (1963, 1985), Kohlberg (1969, 1984), and Selman (1980). This work has focused specifically on descriptions of the development of moral reasoning and social perspective taking.

Piaget (1965) made the initial efforts to apply his description of the course of cognitive development to the development of moral reasoning, but Kohlberg (1969, 1984) considerably expanded the analysis and evolved a six-stage model that presumably describes the sequence that individuals go through in achieving higher levels of maturity regarding moral judgments. Stages 3, 4, and 5 are most typical of the moral reasoning of adolescents, and those stages are briefly outlined in Table 2.2.

Although the descriptive framework developed by Kohlberg has been immensely influential in generating research and has had some influence on the development of interventions for conduct-disordered youth, its practical applications have been somewhat limited. Some assessment tools relevant to the framework, however, are noted in later chapters.

Another area of activity within this approach has focused on social perspective taking. This work may be traced back to Piaget's (1965) earlier work on egocentrism in young children, but the most notable recent work has been stimulated by the work of Selman (1980). The goal of this work is to describe the way in which perspectives about the self and others evolve over the life span. Selman proposed a number of stages that are linked with Piaget's stages of cognitive development. Three of these stages are relevant to the adolescent period, and they are outlined in Table 2.3.

The second approach represented in the analysis of social cognitions is based on information-processing constructs. The primary concerns in

TABLE 2.2
Stages 3, 4, and 5 of Kohlberg's Model of Moral Reasoning

---

Stage 3: Conformist or "Good Boy, Good Girl"
   This is the first stage in the Conventional Moral Reasoning Level. Moral actions are primarily directed by a concern for the opinions and expectations of others. Moral behavior is that which pleases or helps another individual.
Stage 4: Social-Maintaining Morality
   This is the second stage of the Conventional Moral Reasoning Level. It represents a more abstract view of moral behavior. In this case the individual's moral cognitions and actions are guided by a conception that observing moral rules and procedures is important from the point of view of preserving social order.
Stage 5: Social Contract
   This represents the first stage of the Postconventional Moral Reasoning Level. Moral reasoning in this case involves a recognition that moral rules and procedures are social creations and, hence, somewhat arbitrary. The emphasis is now on the functions served by the rules.

---

*Note.* Based on L. Kohlberg (1969). Stage and sequence: The cognitive-developmental approach to socialization. In D. A. Goslin (Ed.), *Handbook of Socialization Theory and Research.* Chicago: Rand McNally.

TABLE 2.3
Stages 2, 3, and 4 of Selman's Levels of Social Understanding

Stage 2: Self-Reflective Level (8–10 years)
Individual understands that others may have different interpretations of situations than they do and are able to adopt the perspective of another person. However, they cannot simultaneously consider both their perspective and that of another at the same time.
Stage 3: Mutual Level (10–12 years)
The individual can now consider things from both their own and the other's perspective, and they recognize that the other can do the same. They can also adopt a "third-party" perspective whereby they can observe both themselves and the other from a disinterested position.
Stage 4: Social and Conventional Level (12 and older)
The "third-person" perspective is now generalized, and the behavior of the self and of others is understood in terms of the social context in which it appears. Interactions are now understood as being guided by social rules.

*Note.* Based on R. Selman (1980). *The Growth of Interpersonal Understanding.* New York: Academic Press.

this literature are with descriptions of the processes individuals utilize in analyzing social situations and regulating their own social behavior. This has become an extremely active area of research because of rapid advances in cognitive psychology and developments relating to cognitive behavior modification interventions. Chapter 10 details how this work has led to the creation of some important assessment tools.

The basic framework for this type of analysis was established by Spivack and Shure (1974; see also Shure & Spivack, 1978), focusing on cognitions operating at several points in the social problem-solving process: identifying a situation as problematic, generating alternative solutions, anticipating potential consequences of the alternatives, and selecting and implementing a course of action. Another component of the analysis involves the processing of social cues. The identification of a social situation as problematic depends, for example, on the interpretation of cues provided by another.

Although much of the work within this approach has focused on younger children, there have been some significant applications at the adolescent level. One example may be found in the work of Dodge (1993; Dodge, Price, Bachorowski, & Newman, 1990), in which the social problem-solving activities of highly aggressive adolescents are characterized as limited with respect to the generation of alternative solutions to problematic situations and by an inability to assess the consequences of different courses of action. The cognitions of these adolescents are also characterized by what Dodge termed a *hostile attributional bias;* that is, a tendency to overestimate the harmful intentions of others.

A related line of research concerns the analysis of beliefs and attitudes and their relevance for behavior (Slaby & Guerra, 1988). Bandura (1989), for example, demonstrated that beliefs about self-efficacy constitute important determinants of behavior. Similarly, Hoge, Andrews, and Leschied (1994), Guerra (1989), and others have shown that attitudes toward antisocial actions do, in fact, mediate those actions.

Although these information-processing analyses of social cognitions have produced some important findings, two general criticisms should be noted. First, and in contrast to the structural-developmental approach, these models have generally not reflected a developmental focus. Thus, little attention has been paid to the way in which these skills and capacities evolve (or fail to evolve) over the life span. Second, the approach in many cases has been oversimplified because links among the various components have not been fully explored. Still, some important developments in the treatment of social dysfunctions have derived from this work, as have some useful assessment instruments, which are explored in later chapters.

## Personality Development

Personality is a ubiquitous term in psychology that is not easily defined. Very generally, *personality* refers to more or less stable attributes of the individual represented as traits, dimensions of temperament, or distinctive behavior patterns. Although there is considerable controversy over definitions of the construct personality, there is general agreement that personality constructs may represent useful means for describing and analyzing the behavior of individuals.

There is a vast literature on personality and social development and countless systems have been developed for describing the developmental processes. It is sufficient here to present an outline of the various areas of analysis relevant to adolescent development and assessment. The focus is on descriptions of normal development. (Problematic forms of personality and social development are discussed chap. 3.)

*Identity Development.* One of the most fascinating aspects of development through the childhood and adolescent years is the way in which the individual evolves a sense of self and of self in relation to others in the social environment.

Two key concepts in the analysis of identity development are the self-concept and self-esteem. The *self-concept* refers in very general terms to the image we hold of ourselves. It has also been defined as a theory of the self: "It is a theory that the individual has unwittingly constructed about himself as an experiencing, functioning individual, and it is part of a broader theory which he holds with respect to his entire range of significant experience" (S. Epstein, 1973, p. 407). *Self-esteem* refers to the evaluative component of the self-concept; it refers, in other words, to the extent to which individuals place a positive or negative value on the way in which they perceive themselves.

There are a number of issues that have been raised in the literature concerning the self-concept. The first relates to the way in which self-concept and self-esteem evolve over the childhood years. The most prominent example of an effort to describe this developmental process is found in the work of Erikson (1963, 1982) and those who have extended his theory (e.g., Marcia, 1989). This framework represents an effort to describe the crises or conflicts that characterize the effort to develop a sense of self at various points in the life span. Erikson's descriptive model postulates eight distinct stages of development of the self, but it is the fifth developmental stage—identity versus role confusion—that is most relevant to the analysis of adolescent functioning. This stage represents the transition between the period of late childhood in which the child is primarily concerned with developing a sense of competence (industry vs. inferiority) and the succeeding period (intimacy vs. isolation) in which social relations constitute the primary focus of concern. This stage of identity versus role confusion represents the phase in which the individual is evolving his or her self-concept, particularly his or her social and occupational selves. Erikson viewed the adolescent as preoccupied with working out a sense of selves, particularly within the peer context.

Although Erikson's descriptive framework has been extremely influential in our perception of adolescent development and has had some impact on clinical treatment of adolescent problems, the theory has had relatively little impact on the development of practical assessment tools.

The second issue raised in connection with self-concept concerns definition. Bracken's (1996) and Byrne's (1996a) recent books show that there remains considerable controversy over definitions of the self-concept and self-esteem. One key question concerns the meaningfulness of a concept of global self-concept or self-worth. Most researchers today seem to favor a multidimensional construct in which a number of independent dimensions of the self-concept are represented. Shavelson, Hubner, and Stanton's (1976) hierarchical model of the self-concept was one of the earlier versions of this type of concept, shown in Fig. 2.1. As discussed later, these definitional issues have important implications for assessment of the self-concept.

*Personality Traits.* Another approach to the analysis of adolescent functioning involves the use of personality trait constructs. The reference in this case is to enduring characteristics of the individual. Introversion, need for achievement, and sociability represent examples of the type of construct found in this approach. A wide range of assessment tools appropriate for use with adolescents have been developed from models of

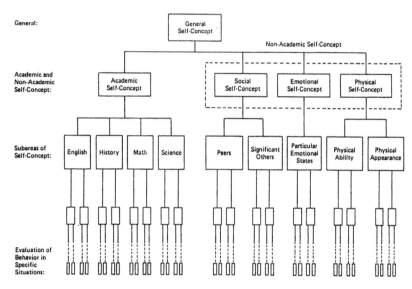

FIG. 2.1. Hierarchical model of self-concept. From R. J. Shavelson, J. J. Hubner, & G. C. Stanton (1976). Self-concept: Validation of construct interpretations. *Review of Educational Research, 46,* 407–442.

personality. Three major sources of these models may be identified: the theoretical, clinical, and empirical.

Theoretically derived descriptions of personality may be traced back to the writings of Freud (1938), with significant later contributions from Jung (1933), Sullivan (1953), Fromm (1965), and Erikson (1963, 1982). These descriptions generally are based on developmental stages, with each stage of personality treated as qualitatively distinct from the others. Erikson's (1963, 1982) previously discussed description of the development of self-identity over the life span represents an example of this approach. Generally this approach has not had a great impact on contemporary assessment tools.

A somewhat different type of theoretically derived personality construct is represented in the work of theorists such as Allport (1968), Eysenck (1982), and Murray (1938), with a focus on identifying dimensions of personality rather than explicating the dynamics of personality development. Many of the standardized personality tests in use today derive from this theoretical tradition.

The clinical approach represents a second means for the development of personality constructs. The constructs in this case are derived from the experience of clinicians and they generally reflect aspects of disordered development. The most notable applications of this approach may be found in the *Diagnostic and Statistical Manual of Mental Disorders* (4th ed.

[*DSM–IV*]; American Psychiatric Association, 1994), the World Health Organization (WHO) system, and the Group for the Advancement of Psychiatry (GAP; 1966) system. These represent efforts to identify and define various forms of personality disorder utilizing constructs such as anxiety, depressive disorder, and attention deficit hyperactivity disorder. These have been influential in developing diagnostic systems and many assessment tools have been derived from them.

Empirical procedures constitute the third means for developing personality constructs. These have generally employed either factor analysis or the criterion group strategy to derive personality constructs from empirical data. An example examined later is the adolescent version of the Minnesota Multiphasic Personality Inventory. The personality dimensions represented in that test (e.g., defensiveness, social introversion) derive from an analysis of data on the characteristics of large samples of individuals.

It is also worth noting that some of the most recent advances in the development of personality constructs and assessment tools represent efforts to combine the theoretical and empirical strategies. The five-factor model of personality (Costa & McCrae, 1988) is representative of these efforts, and the NEO Personality Inventory (McCrae & Costa, 1987) and the Basic Personality Inventory (Jackson, 1996) are examples of practical instruments developed through the combined procedures.

*Behavioral and Emotional Functioning.* Another approach to the analysis of what we have broadly termed personality may be found in efforts to analyze behavioral and cognitive processes as they relate to social and emotional functioning. These efforts have derived from applications of learning theory principles to complex human functioning, notably through the earlier theoretical efforts of Bandura (1977, 1986) and Rotter (1982).

The emphasis in this type of analysis is on patterns of observable behaviors and the cognitions, beliefs, or attitudes that underlie these behaviors. Researchers working within this approach have generally been concerned less with the dynamics behind behaviors than have those working within the traditional personality trait approach. For example, instead of attempting to analyze the underlying dynamics behind aggressive behaviors, the concern in this case would be describing the pattern of aggressive behavior exhibited by the individual, the circumstances under which these behaviors occurred, and, perhaps, the cognitions associated with the behaviors.

This approach has led to the development of a wide range of assessment tools. Later chapters include many examples of the observational schedules, self-report ratings, and behavioral checklists developed within this approach for assessing dimensions of behavior and cognition. It should also be noted, though, that the line between the traditional personality trait approach and the behavioral approach is often blurred and in many ways the two are merging, at least in the development of assessment tools.

## The Ecology of Development

The preceding discussion may give the impression that the development of youth in different areas occurs in a vacuum. This is, of course, not the case. Rather, development proceeds in the context of complex, reciprocal interactions between characteristics of adolescents and forces within their environments.

In the mid-18th century, philosophers such as Rousseau and Locke were analyzing the way in which the child's environment shapes his or her development. Among contemporary scholars, though, it has been Bronfenbrenner (1979, 1986) who has been most influential in demonstrating that human development cannot be fully understood without taking account of the environment within which the individual is functioning.

Table 2.4 contains an outline of the four nested structures within which human development takes place according to Bronfenbrenner's analysis. These range from the microsystem representing the characteristics of the adolescent to the macrosystem that represents characteristics of the larger culture in which the individual is functioning. The following sections provide brief introductions to the most important of these environmental contexts.

TABLE 2.4
Outline of Bronfenbrenner's Ecological Model of Development

The Microsystem
This refers to the immediate context in which the experience occurs. It is the dynamic system in which the youth's behavior is affected by his or her environment and that environment in turn is affected by his or her actions. Interactions with parents, peers, and the school environment constitute the most important microsystems for adolescents.

The Mesosystem
This represents the level at which the various microsystems connect with one another. Of interest in the case of adolescents, for example, is the way in which experiences with parents relate to experiences with peers. The course of development is viewed as optimal where positive links are established among the mesosystems.

The Exosystem
Aspects of the youth's environment that do not impact directly but may have indirect effects. The quality of parents' marriage, the parents' work experiences, and the economic state of the community are examples of exosystem factors.

The Macrosystem
The most global level of the environment reflecting the cultural or subcultural context in which the other systems function. This represents the source of values, attitudes, and beliefs that influence the treatment of the youth in the various systems.

*Note.* Based on U. Bronfenbrenner (1979). *The Ecology of Human Development.* Cambridge, MA: Harvard University Press.

*The Family.* Any effort to describe the family environment in relation to the developing youth must begin with the observation that families represent immensely complex entities. We are dealing first with individuals (mother, father, children, grandparents, etc.) with their own histories and their own characteristics, stresses, and needs. Added to this are the often complex relationships among individuals within the system (mother–father, parent–grandparent, sibling–sibling, parent–child). Further adding to the complexity is the fact that family is, as Minuchin (1974) expressed it, a system moving through time. As we have seen, the needs of children are changing quite drastically as they enter and proceed through adolescence, putting special pressures on the parent. On the other hand, the world confronting the parent is also altering, as they may be adjusting to middle age, coping with career changes, and dealing with aging parents. Because of these considerations, and in spite of the fact that progress is being made in the analysis of family systems (see, e.g., Belsky, Lerner, & Spanier, 1984; Conger, Patterson, & Ge, 1995; Tolan & Gorman-Smith, 1997), there remain many unanswered questions about the role of the family in the development of the child.

Despite these limitations, it will be useful to outline the aspects of family functioning that are the objects of research before introducing the various assessment tools relating to the family.

Analyses of the developmental history and the characteristics of parents constitute a first important focus of inquiry. The parents' history of abuse, mental status, social attitudes, stresses, coping capacities, and substance abuse difficulties are just a few examples of the types of variables that have been explored in relation to the development and functioning of the adolescent.

Parent–adolescent relationships constitute a second focus of concern in this area. Most of the attention has been on analyses of the parents' treatment of the adolescent and efforts to assess this treatment and develop interventions for improving the treatment have a long history. The relevant dimensions of parenting in these analyses generally relate to aspects of communication, expressions of warmth and acceptance, expectations, and the degree of control exercised over the adolescent. These efforts have traditionally been based on a unidirectional model in which parent behavior is viewed as impacting on the youth, but more recent efforts have acknowledged the reciprocal nature of parent–child relationships (Belsky, 1981).

*The Peer Group.* There can be no doubt that peers play an increasingly important role in an adolescent's development. The youth's self-identity; his or her social, academic, and political attitudes; relationships with parents; and behavior are all profoundly affected by relations with peers.

Probably the most extreme expression of peer group influence may be found in the effects of gang membership; all aspects of members' attitudinal and belief structures and their behavior are dictated by the peer group context.

Analyses of peer group influences have typically made a distinction between two modes of influence. The first line of inquiry is based on the influence of close friendships. Research has shown clearly that these friendships can play a critical role in the development of an adolescent's attitudes and behaviors. The second line of inquiry has focused on acceptance by peers in the adolescent's school or community. This research has shown that the individual's experience of acceptance or rejection can have an impact on his or her self-concept and other aspects of personality.

Because psychology has traditionally focused so narrowly on the individual, the role of the peer group in both normative and abnormal development has been relatively neglected. However, the critical role of peers is being increasingly recognized in theories of adolescent development and in the development of intervention strategies.

*The School.* Just as the peer group forms an increasingly important influence on the socialization of individuals as they enter and proceed through adolescence, the school also assumes an increasingly important role. The primary influence of the school is in the acquisition of academic skills and knowledge, but its influence extends far beyond academic matters. It is in this context that much peer group experience occurs, and, hence, this is an environment in which social attitudes and social problem-solving skills are developed. Beyond this, though, the school functions as part of what Bronfenbrenner (1979, 1986) referred to as the *macrosystem*; that is, its role in transmitting the values, attitudes, and customs of the larger culture to the young person.

Because the school plays such a critical role in development, it is also the context in which many problems of development originate or, at any rate, express themselves. Academic underachievement, delinquency, social rejection, and negative self-concept are all problems that may be associated with the school environment. The school also represents a useful venue for introducing interventions designed to address these problems and, for this reason, assessments focusing on the school environment assume considerable importance.

*Other Institutional Settings.* Many adolescents come into contact for varying periods with other types of institutions, including foster homes, group homes, medical facilities, psychiatric facilities, and correctional institutions. These, too, are capable of having a significant impact on development. Although their role in development has been largely neglected, increasing theoretical attention is being paid to these institutions and some beginning efforts are being made to assess their characteristics.

*Other Environmental Influences.* The outline of Bronfrenbrenner's analysis presented in Table 2.4 makes clear that there are other influences in the adolescent's environment. These include television and other media, church, and other community-based groups (e.g., scouts, athletic teams). However, with the exception of the media, these influences on socialization have received little attention in research and have little impact on assessment activities.

## THEORIES OF ADOLESCENT DEVELOPMENT

The preceding discussion has provided an overview of the different facets of adolescent development and the various contexts in which that development takes place. That picture of development, however, is incomplete in two senses. First, it does not reflect the fact that development in the different areas is connected. For example, the development of a self-concept cannot be fully understood without an understanding of the biological changes associated with puberty. Second, the purely descriptive efforts provide no information about the causes of development. Why, for example, do many youths exhibit a strong desire to achieve autonomy from their parents during this period?

These are the kinds of issues addressed within the theories of development. These theories represent a set of assumptions about human development, a framework for organizing empirical data, and a basis for generating additional hypotheses regarding developmental processes. The theories sometimes deal very broadly with development and behavior. For example, B. F. Skinner's (1953) behaviorist theory was designed to explain a very broad range of human functioning. Other models provide for a focus on more narrow aspects of development. Piaget's (1950; see also Flavell, 1963) cognitive developmental theory, for example, focuses more narrowly on cognitive development, and other theories provide even more specific focus on, for example, the development of conduct disorders or problems of substance abuse.

Three general cautions should be noted before I discuss these theoretical developments. First, the term *developmental theory* is misleading in some cases. Strictly speaking, developmental theories are those that posit different processes at work at different points in the life span. Piaget's cognitive development theory is a true developmental theory in that it represents progress toward cognitive maturity by passage through qualitatively distinct stages of development, with different forces operating on development at each stage. Other theories relevant to the analysis of adolescent behavior lack this developmental focus. For example, social learning theorists posit that the forces affecting aggressive behavior in the 4-year-old are the same forces affecting that behavior in the 14-year-old. This distinction has some implications for the way we view the behavior of adolescents and for the development of intervention strategies and assessment tools.

A second caution is that much research in child and adolescent psychology is presented as atheoretical in nature; that is, it is either purely descriptive in intent or not tied to any particular theoretical orientation. The same applies to some intervention strategies and assessment tools that appear not to derive from any single model of development, although this view is deceptive. All research, interventions, and assessments reflect a set of assumptions about human behavior and it is important to be sensitive to that point.

A third caution relates to limitations associated with current theories of adolescent development and behavior. Although the various models have presented us with important insights into the behavior of adolescents and significant theoretical advances continue to be made in this area, all of the models are incomplete in some sense. As yet, we do not have conclusive answers about the forces shaping adolescent development.

Our view of adolescent development and most of our research and assessment efforts have been guided by a relatively small group of theories. These traditional theories continue to exercise considerable influence in the field, but there are some important recent shifts in theoretical focus that are beginning to have an impact on our thinking about adolescent development. I begin with a brief introduction to the traditional theoretical orientations and then review some of the more recent developments.

**Traditional Theories**

There are a number of different ways of categorizing psychological theories relevant to adolescent development, but I deal with them in terms of the following categories: psychoanalytic, learning and behaviorist, cognitive-developmental, humanistic, and ecological.

*Psychoanalytic.* The psychoanalytic orientation developed out of the writings of S. Freud, and his writings have had an immense influence in past thinking about child development and efforts to treat mental disorders. The influence of this approach has waned considerably in contemporary child psychology, but Freud's writings continue to have some important indirect influences.

S. Freud (1938) emphasized an instinctual or biological orientation to the understanding of personality and social development. The major instinct in these aspects of development is the sexual instinct, and Freud viewed development proceeding in terms of distinct stages of development, with each stage representing a different type of conflict with the sexual instinct. Freud also emphasized the importance of the unconscious and the role of repression in explaining problems of adjustment. The therapeutic technique developed by Freud, *psychoanalysis*, involves attempting to discover evidence of conflicts within the unconscious that are finding expression in current neuroses or other expressions of maladjustment.

The most important extensions of Freud's theory to the analysis of adolescent development and behavior were made by A. Freud (1958) and Erikson (1963, 1982). A. Freud emphasized the importance of defense mechanisms in the understanding of adolescent behavior. She postulated that many of the stresses and problems of adjustment exhibited during adolescence reflected unresolved attachment to parents dating from earlier in childhood. Erikson's contribution was to translate Freud's theory into a framework for describing the evolution of an identity or sense of self. Erikson also deemphasized the importance Freud placed on the sexual instinct and postulated that personality is shaped by forces operating throughout the life span rather than only during the earlier years of childhood.

These developments within psychoanalysis have been very influential on our view of children and adolescents. Psychoanalytic approaches to the treatment of dysfunctional development have also been widely used in the treatment of childhood and adolescent disorders. However, the psychoanalytic approach must be considered out of fashion in contemporary psychology, and its influence is more indirect than direct.

*Learning and Behaviorist.* This represents a second group of theoretical orientations. It encompasses a variety of theories, but this is a group of theories that traditionally has shared certain features. First, all of these theories have emphasized the role of environmental experiences in development and have assigned a lesser role to genetic explanations. Second, these theorists have generally encouraged a focus on observable behaviors and have avoided the use of inferred constructs reflecting underlying dynamics. Third, theories within this approach have usually rejected the stage concept and have preferred to represent development as a seamless or continuous process. Finally, the experimental method, particularly laboratory experiments, has been the preferred method of study for learning theorists. In recent years many working within this behaviorist tradition have become more flexible in their approach, and these traditional positions have been compromised at times.

The major branches of learning theory include behaviorism, radical behaviorism, social learning theory, and cognitive social-learning theory. It is the latter type of theory that has probably had the greatest influence in the analysis of adolescent behavior and the writings of Bandura (1986) and Mischel (1984) have been most instrumental in developing the orientation.

Cognitive social-learning theory emphasizes three kinds of processes. The first is cognitive processes. An essential assumption of this group of theories is that humans are basically cognitive beings; that much of their interaction with the environment is guided by beliefs, attitudes, memories, etc. The second process is that observational learning constitutes an important means by which the individual acquires new behaviors. The third process is that behavior is explained in terms of reciprocal determinism; this is the notion that the interaction between individual and the environment is a two-way street: Social forces do have an impact on the individual, but the individual also influences the environment.

Both social learning theory and cognitive social-learning theory have had an immense impact on our understanding of adolescent behavior. Also, as we will see, they have had a significant impact on strategies for dealing with dysfunctional behaviors and for the development of assessment tools.

*Cognitive-Developmental.* This orientation developed out of the theoretical and empirical work of Piaget (1950; see also Flavell, 1963). Piaget's structural developmental model of cognitive development has already been noted, as have efforts to apply the model to descriptions of moral development and the development of social cognitions.

There are also explanatory constructs represented in cognitive-developmental theories. For example, Piaget postulated that the cognitive maturation process proceeds in terms of an interaction between genetically based maturational forces and environmental experiences. Moral development is explained in very similar terms.

Cognitive-developmental theory has had an immense impact on our understanding of perceptual and cognitive processes in children and adolescents, but its practical impact has been largely confined to innovations in early childhood education. With the exception of some applications of Piaget and Kohlberg's (1984) description of moral development, this theory has had relatively little direct impact on the development of adolescent intervention strategies or assessment tools.

*Ecological Perspectives.* Another set of theories emphasize sociocultural approaches to the analysis of human development. The major impetus behind these theories is a recognition that psychological theories of

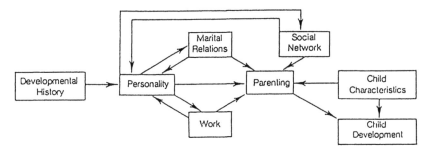

FIG. 2.2. Process model of the determinants of parenting. From J. Belsky (1984). The determinants of parenting: A process model. *Child Development,* *55*, 83–96. Reproduced with permission.

development have often focused too narrowly on the individual and have neglected the active role of the environment in shaping development and the reciprocal nature of the adolescent–environment relation.

One example of an ecological theory is that of Bronfenbrenner (1979, 1986), outlined earlier in Table 2.4. In this model, development proceeds in the context of forces operating at several levels, from the individual to the larger culture. Another example of an ecological model focusing on a specific aspect of development may be found in Belsky's (1981) analysis of the determinants of parenting. This model, outlined in Fig. 2.2, emphasizes that parental behavior is the product of multiple causes, including the actions of the child. The importance of considering development in a larger ecological contexts is one of the features of the newer theoretical and empirical approaches to the analysis of adolescent behavior, and I turn next to an overview of the most significant of these developments.

## Recent Theoretical and Empirical Developments

There is rather general agreement that in the past relatively less attention was paid to the analysis of adolescent behavior than to that of younger age groups. That relative neglect has, however, been corrected, and there has been a virtual explosion of interest in adolescent behavior. This work has resulted in some significant advances in methods for analyzing adolescent development and theoretical analyses of that development.

Compas et al. (1995) summarized these recent developments in terms of three overlapping themes in research and theory on adolescence: (a) emergence of broad ecological models; (b) discovery of developmental pathways linking childhood, adolescent, and adult behaviors; and (c) investigation of risk and protective factors associated with normal and maladjusted development. The following sections provide brief introductions to each of these important areas.

*Integrative Ecological Models.* .Most traditional models of development acknowledged that human behavior represents a product of complex
interactions among genetic, psychological, and environmental forces, but
individual theories generally provided for a relatively narrow focus on a
limited set of factors. Social learning theory, for example, searches for the
causes of behavior in the learning experiences of the individual, and cognitive-developmental theory, although acknowledging a role for environmental experiences, places primary emphasis on the impact of internal
maturational forces.

Contemporary theories of child and adolescent development now represent a more integrative and transactional view of development. This is
reflected, first, in efforts to incorporate a broader range of interacting
variables into the theoretical and empirical analyses.

One example of this type of development is represented in the efforts
of Brooks-Gunn and her colleagues (Brooks-Gunn, 1987; Brooks-Gunn &
Reiter, 1990; Brooks-Gunn & Warren, 1985; Paikoff & Brooks-Gunn, 1991)
to elucidate how interactions among biological, cognitive, emotional, and
social factors affect the behavior of the youth over the period of adolescence. To illustrate, the hypothesis has been advanced that the self-concept
and the social relations of young adolescent girls are directly affected by
interactions between breast development and hormonal changes. The
transactional nature of this theoretical formulation is illustrated by the
hypothesis of a reciprocal relation between mood and hormonal forces.

A second development within this approach involves an increasing
recognition in theoretical and empirical work of the need to focus more
closely on interactions between the developmental needs of adolescents
and the environmental forces they confront. In this context, adolescent
behavior is viewed in terms of a dynamic interaction between the youth
and the environment. Representative of this work are efforts to explain
some disturbances of adolescence as a mismatch between the needs of
adolescents at a particular point in their development and the kinds of
demands or expectations made by parents, the school, or other components
of their environments. For example, Eccles (Eccles, Lord, & Midgley, 1991;
Eccles et al., 1993) attempted to explain the decline in academic motivation
and self-esteem commonly observed in young adolescents as a mismatch
between their needs at that developmental stage and the demands and
expectations imposed by middle school environments.

*Developmental Pathways.* Traditional analyses of child development,
both theoretical and empirical, have long been concerned with tracking
the course of development over the life span. However, and as Compas
et al. (1995) pointed out, these efforts have generally involved a search
for a universal pattern that describes all individuals. More recent efforts,

though, are based on the assumption that different individuals may traverse different pathways in moving from childhood to adulthood.

A notable example of this work is efforts to track the development of conduct disorders from early childhood through adolescence to adulthood. This work has been represented in both empirical (e.g., Farrington, Loeber, & Van Kammen, 1990; Fergusson, Lynskey, & Horwood, 1996) and theoretical (e.g., Moffitt, 1993; Patterson, DeBaryshe, & Ramsey, 1989) efforts, and it is now beginning to yield important information about the way in which certain forms of antisocial behavior develop over the life span. The research has shown, for example, very different long-term prognoses for adolescents exhibiting antisocial behaviors depending on their histories; youths with a long history of conduct disorders present a much higher risk for future antisocial activity than adolescents exhibiting conduct disorders without such a history (Loeber & Hay, 1997).

*Risk and Resilience Factors.* This third theme, which overlaps in many respects with the previous two, involves a focus on risk and protective factors associated with adaptive and maladaptive development. Risk factors refer to variables that are associated with negative outcomes. Poor family functioning, inadequate parenting, emotional immaturity, and negative peer associations are all variables that have been clearly linked with disrupted development. Protective factors, on the other hand, are factors that negate or otherwise modify the effects of the risk factors. A positive temperament and availability of a supportive adult are two factors that have often been regarded as capable of buffering the individual from the effects of stresses or crises. Protective factors are associated with the concept of *resilience*; this is the phenomenon whereby some individuals show no negative effects from events producing these effects in others.

Significant theoretical advances with respect to resilience processes may be found in the work of Garmezy (1985), Jessor (1993), Luthar (1993), and Rutter and Rutter (1993). Representative of this work are Jessor's (1992, 1993) efforts to identify the range of risk and protective factors associated with adolescent functioning. This model, outlined in Fig. 2.3, shows that an understanding of adolescent development must take into account both protective and risk factors. The model is also important because it reflects the two other themes emerging in recent work: the effort to include in analyses of adolescent development a broad range of reciprocally interacting variables and a focus on individual differences in developmental pathways.

*Other Developments.* Three other developments reflected in recent theory and research on adolescent development are worth noting. First, there appears to be an increased willingness to incorporate interdiscipli-

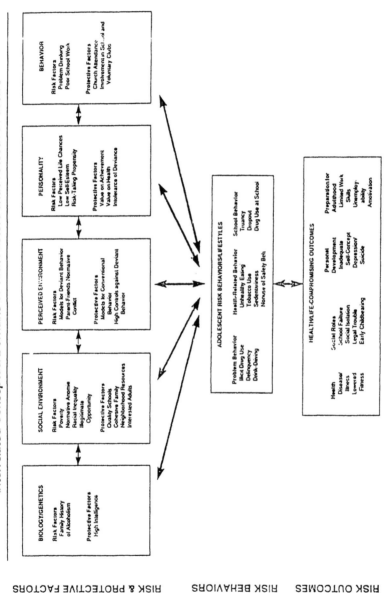

Interrelated Conceptual Domains of Risk Factors and Protective Factors

FIG. 2.3. A model of risk and protective factors operating during the adolescent period. From R. Jessor (1991). Risk behavior in adolescence: A psychosocial framework for understanding and action. In D. E. Rogers & E. Ginsberg (Eds.), *Adolescents at Risk: Medical and Social Perspectives* (pp. 19–34). Boulder, CO: Westview Press. Reproduced with permission.

RISK & PROTECTIVE FACTORS    RISK BEHAVIORS    RISK OUTCOMES nary approaches into the analyses. This is well represented in the Jessor (1992) model just described. A full implementation of that model would involve input from psychologists, sociologists, criminologists, physicians, and biologists.

Second, there is an increased sensitivity to gender, ethnic, and cultural differences in the analyses. This is reflected, for example, in Gilligan's (1982) demonstration of the importance of considering gender experiences in the analysis of moral development and Oliver's (1989) efforts to identify a distinctive role for racial identity in certain problems of adolescence.

Third, there is an increased willingness to involve adolescents in the scholarly process:

> A recurrent concern voiced by researchers is a tendency to bypass the step of collecting descriptive and qualitative data that reflect adolescents' organization of their own experiences. . . . The failure to take such a step may lead to a flawed understanding of normal development; it may also limit the effectiveness of interventions. (Zaslow & Takanishi, 1993, p. 190)

Any area of study that ignores its subject matter is, of course, placing itself at a serious disadvantage.

## IMPLICATIONS FOR ASSESSMENT AND TREATMENT STRATEGIES

These theoretical and empirical developments are important for understanding adolescent development. They also have important implications for the selection and refinement of our assessment and treatment tools.

There are two senses in which an understanding of the developmental process is important. First, the more valid and comprehensive our understanding of adolescent development, the more effective our tools and strategies will be. A strategy for treating depression in adolescents that is based on a misunderstanding of the condition will not be very effective. Similarly, an assessment of learning disability reflecting an erroneous analysis of learning processes is unlikely to demonstrate much validity.

Second, an understanding of the processes on which our procedures are based is important for justifying them to the recipients of our services. There is nothing wrong with using a battery of tests to identify an individual as developmentally delayed and recommending placement in a special program. However, we must be ready to defend that decision and show how the assessment reflects the actual competencies of the adolescent and links with the treatment recommendation. This can only be accomplished in the context of an understanding of the phenomena being assessed.

The search for an understanding of adolescent development is complicated by the existence of conflicting theories of development and an
acknowledgment that we do not yet have a universally accepted theory.
Nevertheless, there are some broad guidelines that can be drawn from
the accumulated body of theory and research.

One clear principle is that adolescent behavior is determined by a
complex network of factors, including biological mechanisms and influences from the individual's social environment. Further, a variety of
processes are at work in this network, ranging from direct genetic influences (on, e.g., the timing of hormonal changes) to direct environmental
influences. More often, though, the processes reflect complex interactions
between the two.

A second principle is that both risk and protective factors must be
considered in explaining and predicting behavior, particularly maladaptive behaviors. A consideration of the two sets of factors helps us to
understand why some adolescents succumb to certain risk factors and
others do not. This understanding is also important in identifying youths
in need of intervention and in designing effective intervention strategies.
It also has very important implications for assessment activities.

A third principle is that the forces affecting the adolescents' behavior
vary with developmental level. The importance of recognizing the timing
of development has, as we have seen, been long recognized. However,
some of the newer theoretical and empirical advances have even further
emphasized that different forces and different processes affect development at different periods in adolescence.

A fourth principle is that there are wide individual differences in the
timing of the developmental process and, perhaps, in the mechanisms of
development. Older theoretical efforts involved a search for universals of
development, but we now know that, although there may be some very
basic laws governing development, there is still considerable variability
in the actual experiences of adolescents.

A fifth principle is that many aspects of development are affected by
gender and ethnic or cultural group. Again, there are probably fundamental laws governing development, but it is clear from recent theory
and research that the course of development and the experience of development vary to some degree across these groups.

These principles have clear implications for assessment and treatment
strategies. Speaking very generally, they mean that our strategies must
acknowledge that behaviors are multiply determined, are affected by
developmental level, and reflect wide individual differences, some of
which are related to gender and ethnic group membership. These implications are considered further in chapter 3, which provides a more specific
focus on abnormal or maladaptive development.

# Identifying and Treating Problem Behavior in Adolescents

Chapter 2 focused on descriptions and explanations of the course of normal adolescent development. However, most assessment and intervention activities focus on aspects of abnormal or dysfunctional development, and an introduction to this topic is also appropriate. Dryfoos (1990), Hersen and Ammerman (1995), Millstein, Petersen, and Nightingale (1993), and Tolan and Cohler (1993) presented extended discussions of problematic development in adolescents, but this chapter provides an overview of major issues in defining and treating problem behaviors.

## DEFINING DYSFUNCTIONAL BEHAVIOR

The first step in any treatment or intervention process involves identifying that a problem exists, and the second entails describing the problem. The success of interventions depends to a great extent on the adequacy of these conceptualizations. The definition of what constitutes abnormal or problematic behavior is something that has preoccupied philosophers, theologians, and mental health professionals for a very long time. The issue is particularly thorny in the case of adolescents because there is a fundamental conflict here between two views of normal adolescent behavior.

One view is that social conflicts and emotional turmoil are normal in the case of adolescents. This position can be traced back to the writings of psychoanalytically oriented theorists such as A. Freud (1958) and Erikson (1963, 1982), but it is a view widely accepted by clinicians and educators and also by parents and the general public (Elmen & Offer,

1993). This view has important implications for interventions with adolescents: By normalizing problematic behaviors, we reduce the likelihood that they will be treated as problems.

The second view is that social conflicts and emotional turmoil are not characteristic of adolescence and that the majority of adolescents, although they will inevitably experience social and emotional problems, manage to traverse the teen years without serious disruption in their lives or the lives of those around them. As Elmen and Offer (1993) showed, empirical research continues to support this view. It is also a view that suggests a more serious attitude toward adolescent problems than the previous type of position.

It should be understood that both of these positions require a definition of abnormal or problematic behavior. One approach to developing such a definition was discussed in chapter 2. That definition was based on a statistical or normative criterion. Positive mental health is defined as behavior that adheres to some statistical average of behavior and abnormal or problematic behavior departs to some specified (although usually arbitrary) degree from that average. However, this represents an unsatisfactory approach because of the problem of identifying truly representative normative groups and because it confuses atypical and problematic behavior.

Kazdin (1993) proposed a more useful definition of mental health, one that recognizes two somewhat independent domains of functioning. The first domain of mental health "encompasses the *absence of dysfunction in psychological, emotional, behavioral, and social spheres*. Dysfunction refers to impairment in everyday life" (Kazdin, 1993, p. 128). Specific forms of dysfunction refer, then, to forms of emotional or behavioral disorder (e.g., depression, hyperactivity, substance abuse). These are defined as dysfunctions or abnormal behaviors to the extent that they interfere with or impair the functioning of the individual.

The second domain identified by Kazdin (1993) provides more of an emphasis on general adjustment:

> Mental health also refers to *optimal functioning or well-being* in psychological and social domains. Well-being is not merely the absence of impairment; rather it refers to the presence of personal and interpersonal strengths that promote optimal functioning. . . . In the case of adolescents, social competence reflects the ability to negotiate developmentally relevant social tasks and to utilize personal and interpersonal resources to achieve positive outcomes. (p. 128)

The key concepts in this approach do not relate to categories or dimensions of pathology but to attributes such as social competencies, emotional intelligence, maturity, and coping aptitudes.

These two conceptions of mental health represent useful ways of viewing adjustment and they have important implications for the development of intervention and assessment strategies. Still, as they stand, the conceptions beg the question of actually defining dysfunctional or problematic states. How do we establish these categories of dysfunction or dimensions of competence? I turn next to an overview of the major approaches to this issue.


## DEVELOPING DIAGNOSTIC CATEGORIES
## AND DIMENSIONS

A wide variety of diagnostic systems have been developed. These range from rather simple categorizations of personality—contrasting, for example, introverts with extroverts—to complex diagnostic systems. An example of the latter may be found in the Minnesota Multiphasic Personality Inventory–Adolescent (MMPI–A) with its large number of personality dimensions. The constructs underlying these systems have generally been derived through theory, clinical judgment, empirical procedures, or some combination of these strategies. The procedures actually parallel those for developing personality constructs reviewed in chapter 2.

### Theoretically Derived Diagnostic Constructs

The theoretical strategy involves, as the name implies, deriving descriptions of personality or pathology from theory. An example may be found in A. Freud's (1958) efforts to evolve a system for describing abnormal child and adolescent development from her psychoanalytic theory. Ego strength, drive regression, and aggressive drive are among the constructs represented in this system. A more recent example may be found in the dimensions of pathology represented in the Millon Adolescent Clinical Inventory, described in a later chapter. The dimensions included in this instrument (e.g., impulsivity propensity, anxious feelings) were derived from a formal theory of personality.

### Clinically Derived Constructs

A second strategy entails deriving the constructs from the accumulated experience of clinicians. The three most prominent examples of this approach are represented in the *DSM–IV* (American Psychiatric Association, 1994), the World Health Organization (WHO) system, and the GAP system (Group for the Advancement of Psychiatry, 1966).

The most prominent of these systems currently is *DSM–IV*. The core of this system is a set of diagnostic categories that define a wide range of pathological behaviors. Categories representing forms of developmental delay and academic difficulties are also included. Although recent versions of the manual have utilized empirical data to a greater extent than earlier ones, the system is still based largely on the clinical judgments of psychiatrists. Many of the assessment instruments examined in this volume relate either directly or indirectly to this system. In addition, the constructs of pathology represented in the system play important roles in many educational, clinical, and forensic contexts. The *DSM–IV* system is examined in more detail later.

**Empirically Based Systems**

This approach entails the derivation of personality and pathological constructs through empirical procedures. Instead of deducing constructs from a theoretical framework, constructs are induced from empirical data.

Two general strategies may be identified within this approach. The first strategy is termed the *criterion-group* or *contrasted-group method*. The procedure in this case is to uncover through statistical procedures, usually multiple discriminant functions analysis, characteristics that distinguish between known groups. This might involve, for example, contrasting alcoholics with nonalcoholics, schizophrenics with nonschizophrenics, or delinquents with nondelinquents. Pathological constructs are then induced from the discriminating characteristics. The dimensions represented in the MMPI–A were developed through this procedure.

The second strategy involves the use of multivariate statistical techniques, usually factor or cluster analysis, to derive constructs. This approach has, of course, been extensively used in the development of cognitive constructs. The definitions of cognitive functioning underlying our standard intelligence tests were derived through factor analyses of performance data.

The use of this methodology has also been very useful in the derivation of constructs of behavioral and emotional pathology, generally involving the use of factor analysis with data on observable behaviors provided by parents, teachers, and others familiar with the child. Hyperactivity, conduct disorder, and social withdrawal are among the behavioral constructs emerging from these analyses. Positive aspects of functioning relating to competencies and coping skills have also resulted from this type of analysis. Many of the interview and rating techniques examined in subsequent chapters are based on constructs derived through these empirical procedures.

## Forms of Problematic Behavior

Because the majority of assessment tools and procedures are designed to address relatively specific problematic behaviors, it would also be useful to identify the specific categories and dimensions employed in these analyses, although this is a difficult task. As just shown, a variety of approaches have been employed to develop diagnostic categories and dimensions. The different approaches have often yielded very different constructs and even within approaches there are often inconsistencies in the way constructs are defined.

Nevertheless, it seems important to attempt to identify the major categories of problematic behavior, and, although there are many criticisms of the system, I use the *DSM–IV* system as a starting point. Problems in applying this system are discussed in later chapters.

The *DSM–IV* system is composed of the five axes outlined in Table 3.1. Axis I is the most important for our purposes because it contains the major diagnostic categories. Table 3.2 lists the clinical disorders relevant to adolescents identified in *DSM–IV*, including disorders specific to childhood and adolescence as well as disorders primarily associated with adulthood that may sometimes be diagnosed in adolescents.

This represents only one effort to develop a system for categorizing problematic behaviors. Other constructs and dimensions have emerged through theoretical and empirical strategies. In some cases those efforts have yielded constructs consistent with those of *DSM–IV*. For example, most systems derived through the empirical analysis of behavioral data have yielded a construct similar to attention deficit hyperactivity disorder

TABLE 3.1
Five Major Axes of the *Diagnostic and Statistical Manual of Mental Disorders–Fourth Edition*

Axis I
  Clinical disorders
  Other conditions that may be the focus of clinical attention
Axis II
  Personality disorders
  Mental retardation
Axis III
  General medical condition
Axis IV
  Psychosocial and environmental problems
Axis V
  Global assessment of functioning

*Note.* Based on American Psychiatric Association (1994). *Diagnostic and statistical manual of mental disorders* (4th ed.). Washington, DC: Author.

TABLE 3.2
Disorders Identified in the *Diagnostic and*
*Statistical Manual of Mental Disorders–Fourth Edition*

| | |
|---|---|
| **Childhood and adolescent disorders** | |
| Mental retardation | Pervasive developmental disorders |
| Learning disorders | Attention-deficit and disruptive behavior |
| Motor skills disorders | disorders |
| Communication disorders | Other disorders of childhood and adolescence |
| **Adult disorders that may be diagnosed in adolescence** | |
| Substance-related disorders | Sexual and gender identity disorders |
| Schizophrenia and other psychotic disorders | Eating disorders |
| Mood disorders | Sleep disorders |
| Anxiety disorders | Impulse-control disorders not elsewhere |
| Somatoform disorders | classified |
| | Adjustment disorders |

*Note.* Based on American Psychiatric Association (1994). *Diagnostic and statistical manual of mental disorders* (4th ed.). Washington, DC: Author.

(ADHD) seen in *DSM–IV*. On the other hand, when we examine individual assessment instruments we see that a wide variety of other constructs have been developed for describing problematic behavior in adolescents.

## Some Additional Considerations

Problems associated with the actual assessment of dysfunctional behaviors are discussed in some detail in a later chapter. It is worth noting here, however, some general problems associated with these efforts.

One key issue concerns *construct validity*; that is, the extent to which the dimensions and categories represent meaningful constructs. What, for example, does it mean to categorize an adolescent as conduct disordered or to assign the adolescent a high score on a dimension of hyperactivity? Do these scores have real meaning so far as the functioning of the individual or the outcome of therapeutic intervention are concerned? As Anastasi (1986) and Messick (1989a, 1989b, 1995) showed, addressing the validity of psychological constructs is a difficult matter. However, it is an important one, and I have occasion to return to the issue in later chapters.

A fundamental issue observed in these efforts to define problematic behaviors concerns the relative advantages of categorical and dimensional constructs. Most of the clinically derived constructs such as those represented in *DSM–IV* reflect a qualitative or categorical approach to diagnosis; that is, the youth is diagnosed as conduct disordered or as exhibiting ADHD. The dimensional approach, on the other hand, involves locating the individual at some point on a continuum. Thus, instead of hyperactive, the individual might be characterized as at the 90th percentile (relative to some normative group) on a continuum of hyperactivity.

Another important issue concerns the degree of correspondence among similarly labeled constructs. For example, several definitions of global self-esteem are available in the literature, but there is reason to question the degree of correspondence among them (Byrne, 1996a). Similarly, Hoge and Andrews (1992) and Loeber, Keenan, Lahey, Green, and Thomas (1993) raised questions about the correspondence among a number of clinically and empirically derived definitions of the conduct disorder construct (also see Kagan, 1988).

Another thorny issue concerns comorbidity. Many taxonomic schemes, including *DSM–IV*, encourage a focus on single-syndrome diagnoses. In other words, where two pathological conditions appear to be associated, diagnostic rules are used to select one as the predominant diagnosis. On the other hand, there is considerable evidence that true comorbidity exists; that is, that individuals can demonstrate clinical levels of more than one pathological condition (see, e.g., Achenbach, 1995; Lilienfield, Waldman, & Israel, 1994). It is important to incorporate this possibility into our assessment systems.

Finally, it should be recognized that most of the constructs that have been developed reflect the first of Kazdin's (1993) definitions of mental health: they focus primarily on forms of dysfunction. Fewer efforts have been made to develop conceptualizations of positive mental health or competence, although the importance of this effort has been recognized:

> Treatment targets are typically specified in terms of disorders or problems to be ameliorated. However, in specifying targets for treatment, it is equally important to assess children's competencies. On the one hand, children may have important competencies that can facilitate treatment and can improve their chances for favorable outcomes. On the other hand, a lack of particular competencies may be an important target for treatment in its own right. (Achenbach, 1995, p. 52)

In this light, it is encouraging that increasing efforts are being made to develop tools for the assessment of competencies.

Two other issues relating to the analysis of problematic behaviors concern the prevalence of pathological conditions and the issue of stress.

## PREVALENCE OF PATHOLOGY IN ADOLESCENTS

Epidemiological studies have presented information about prevalence rates for specific pathological conditions. However, the question I raise here is a general one concerning the extent to which problematic behavior is normal in adolescents. There are two competing positions with respect to this issue. The first position is that conflicts, particularly with parents and other authority figures, and emotional turmoil are common among adolescents. These are considered normal features of adolescent growth. This position is seen in Erikson's (1963, 1982) theory, which represents adolescent development in terms of a series of conflicts relating to the evolution of a self-concept.

This type of position has an important implication for our attitudes toward problematic behaviors in adolescents, encouraging the view that problematic behaviors are normal and that intervention is generally not required. Thus, the adolescent exhibiting signs of depression or serious conflicts with parents is "just going through a phase" and will "grow out of the problem." In fact, some theorists, including A. Freud (1958) and Hall (1904), felt that efforts to intervene with these problems would disrupt the normal course of development.

The second position is that serious social conflicts and psychological problems are not characteristic of adolescents. In this view, the majority of adolescents, although they will inevitably experience stresses and conflicts, develop without serious disruption to their lives or those sharing their environment. This position recognizes that there are a small number of adolescents who will exhibit serious problem behaviors, but instead of the ubiquitous assumption that the behaviors are normal and inevitable, these are treated as problems and consideration is given to dealing with them as serious problems.

Elmen and Offer's (1993) review of the research literature strongly supports the second position. Their general conclusion follows:

> Persistent low self-esteem, depression, and other disturbances are unusual in adolescence. Most teenagers are well-adjusted and cope effectively with the biological, psychological, and social changes that are a part of adolescence. They relate well to their families and peers, and they learn to live within the parameters of their communities. (p. 16)

Although there is considerable variability across studies in the way in which problematic behavior is defined and measured, the majority of the reviewed studies indicate that approximately 20% to 25% of adolescents sampled exhibit problems serious enough to require intervention (Dryfoos, 1990; Elmen & Offer, 1993; Offord et al., 1987). Unfortunately, epidemiological studies generally also indicate that the majority of adolescents requiring treatment for problematic behavior do not, in fact, receive appropriate help.

## THE ISSUE OF STRESS

Hypotheses regarding the etiology of dysfunctions such as attention deficit disorder, social withdrawal, and conduct disorder have been derived from theories based on genetic, neurophysiological, psychological, and sociological foundations. Many can be traced back to theories reviewed in chapter

2. However, there is also agreement that the experience of stress underlies many problems of adolescence, and many of the interventions that have been developed are designed to address this (see Compas, 1987; Jessor, 1992, 1993; J. H. Johnson, 1986).

There is a considerable theoretical and empirical literature relating to stress, and there are serious difficulties in analyzing the construct. The most direct definition, though, states that stress represents a response to potentially threatening events, with the latter identified as *stressors*. The stress response may be represented in physiological, medical, or psychological terms. Psychological responses are generally represented in terms of psychological states such as anxiety, fearfulness, depression, or burnout.

The individual's responses to potentially stressful events depend on a variety of factors, but coping abilities are of paramount importance. *Coping responses* are defined as cognitive or behavioral activities designed to help manage potentially threatening events (Lazarus & Folkman, 1984). The two general approaches to coping involve (a) attempting to alter the event to remove its threatening properties (e.g., reconciling with a friend), or (b) altering the impact of the stressor (e.g., convincing oneself that the poor grade is not that important).

The concept of risk is also relevant here. Risk factors are those associated with later adjustment problems, and there is considerable overlap between risk factors and things commonly identified as stressors. For example, an adolescent's exposure to conflict between his or her parents generally represents a stressful event. That experience has also been identified as a risk factor because it is associated under some circumstances with behavioral, emotional, and academic problems.

Surveys reported by Armacost (1989), Adwere-Boamah and Curtis (1993), Kohn and Milrose (1993), Maguire, Pastore, and Flanagan (1992), Siddique and D'Arcy (1984), and Violato and Holden (1988) reveal a wide range of potential concerns and stressors that may impact adolescents. Table 3.3 identifies one set of stresses and hassles represented in a popular measure of adolescent stress. Table 3.4 lists a more serious set of problems experienced by a group of disturbed youths. The extent to which these circumstances and events operate as stressors varies widely, as does the extent to which they may represent risk factors for future adjustment.

## INTERVENTION MODELS

Psychological assessments are employed for a variety of purposes, but in the majority of cases they are designed to provide information relevant to intervention efforts. I consider the links between assessments and interventions in chapter 4, but it is useful at this point to provide an introduction to different approaches to treating problematic behaviors in adolescents.

## Levels of Intervention

Caplan's (1964) identification of three levels of intervention remains useful. The first level includes primary prevention efforts. These are programs, generally directed to an unselected population, designed to prevent the appearance of problems. The programs generally exhibit one of two foci. The first focus is altering environmental conditions that represent risks for the later problems. Programs designed to improve recreational programs for young people in a community would represent an example of this type of effort. The second focus is on providing the individual with the resources to avoid the risk factor. Educational programs designed to teach young people about the risks of smoking and to discourage them from beginning smoking is an example. Millstein et al. (1993) discussed the importance of primary prevention efforts with adolescents, and various chapters in that edited volume provide directions for these efforts.

Secondary prevention involves the identification of individuals at risk for a particular negative outcome and attempts to address the condition of risk before the problem actually develops. Unmarried adolescent mothers constitute a group at high risk for child neglect. Educational programs designed to teach parenting and life skills to these women during the period of pregnancy could be considered a secondary prevention effort. Ideally, these secondary prevention efforts are implemented before the risk condition actually manifests itself (Coie et al., 1993).

*Tertiary prevention* is something of a misnomer, because it refers to interventions introduced after the problem behavior has appeared. The goal in this case is to "cure" or eliminate the condition or to at least alleviate the symptoms of the condition. Traditional approaches to therapy and counseling generally represent cases of tertiary intervention.

Because primary prevention efforts are directed toward a general population (e.g., the entire population of the school or the community), assessments are generally not involved, although evaluations of the programs would necessarily involve some measurement activities. On the other hand, psychological assessments are widely employed in secondary and tertiary interventions, and a brief introduction to the various therapeutic strategies used in these approaches is provided.

## Categorizing Treatments

Attempts to categorize treatments are very frustrating. First, there is immense variety among different types of therapy and counseling programs available for use in secondary and tertiary interventions. Second, there is often little consistency in the definitions of treatments with the

TABLE 3.3

Sources of Stress and Hassles Relevant to Adolescents

| Factor | Sample Items |
|---|---|
| Social alienation | Disagreement with family—money |
| | Disliking fellow student(s) |
| | Disagreements with teachers |
| Excessive demands | Too many things to do at once |
| | Finding school subjects too demanding |
| | Not enough time for sleep |
| Romantic concerns | Dissatisfaction with romantic relationship |
| | Decisions about romantic relationship |
| Loneliness and unpopularity | Being without company |
| | Being ignored |
| | Dissatisfaction with looks |
| Assorted annoyances and concerns | Social disagreements over smoking |
| | Poor health of a friend |
| Social mistreatment | Friend betrays trust |
| | Being taken for granted |
| Academic challenge | Dissatisfaction with mathematics ability |
| | Lower grades than hoped |

*Note.* Adapted from "The Inventory of High-School Student's Recent Life Experiences: A Decontaminated Measure of Adolescent's Hassles," by P. M. Kohn & J. A. Milrose, 1993, *Journal of Youth and Adolescence, 22.*

TABLE 3.4

Sources of Stress Reported by a Sample of Disturbed
Adolescents (Ranked in Order of Frequency)

| Family Problems | Individual Problems |
|---|---|
| Emotional conflict at home | Poor self-image |
| Parent too strict | Depressed |
| Parental physical abuse | School attendance |
| Parental neglect | Bad grades |
| Parent drug or alcohol problems | In trouble with justice system |
| Family mental health problems | Drug abuse |
| Parental domestic violence | Alcohol abuse |
| Parental unemployment | Possibly suicidal |
| Wants to live with other parent | Conflicts with teacher |
| Parental sexual abuse | Learning disability |
| Physical or sexual abuse/other family | Custody change |
| Physical or sexual abuse/nonfamily member | Pregnancy |
| No parent figure | Other health problems/handicap |
| Parent is homosexual | Sexual identity issue |
| | Prostitution |
| | Venereal disease |

*Note.* Adapted from *Bureau of Justice Statistics Sourcebook of Justice Statistics*, by K. Maguire, A. L. Pastore, & T. J. Flanagan (Eds.). (1992). Washington, DC: United States Department of Justice.

same name. For example, child psychotherapy can mean very different things to different people. Third, and related to this, many treatments are poorly defined and thus difficult to categorize.

Cohen (1995), however, presented a useful framework for describing interventions. There are six dimensions in the framework. The first dimension refers to the theoretical emphasis of the treatment. Identifying this characteristic is easy in many cases. Psychoanalytic play therapy, for example, derives directly from A. Freud's (1958) theory of child psychopathology, whereas cognitive-behavioral therapy is based on social learning theory (Kendall, 1991). In other cases, however, the theoretical origins of a treatment are more obscure. Still, all interventions reflect some underlying assumptions about development and behavior.

The second dimension refers to the degree of structure represented in the treatment. Some treatments are highly structured, allowing little flexibility in application (e.g., some token-economy behavior modification programs). Other treatments are much more flexible and open. C. Rogers' (1951) client-centered therapy is an example of a therapeutic approach permitting the counselor considerable latitude in application.

The third dimension in Cohen's system relates to the scope of the intervention. Some interventions are very specific in their focus; that is, they are directed toward a narrowly defined target. An educational intervention designed to address problems in processing verbal instructions or a behavior modification program designed to improve on-task behavior would be examples of narrowly focused interventions. At the other extreme are the newer multisystemic treatment programs that represent broad and intensive interventions into the adolescent's life and are designed to provide general improvements in the adolescent's social and emotional competencies.

The recipient of treatment constitutes a fourth dimension. Most interventions with adolescents are delivered directly to the youth, but there are other interventions that involve the parents and the child or, under some circumstances, only the parents. Some interventions in the school setting might also involve the teacher directly. Related to this dimension is the setting in which the intervention is delivered. Traditional psychotherapy is generally delivered in an institutional setting, whether it is the clinician's office, a hospital, or another such setting. Certain forms of milieu therapy are specifically designed for delivery in residential situations. Other types of treatment are more flexible: Behavior modification, for example, is adaptable to almost any setting in which the adolescent is functioning.

Duration of treatment constitutes the fifth dimension. There is, of course, considerable variability of treatment length within therapies depending on the need of the client and other factors. Nevertheless, some types of treatment are designed for shorter and some for longer periods. Most forms of psychotherapy, for example, are designed for lengthy periods of treatment, whereas some forms of solution-oriented family therapy are designed for delivery in two or three sessions.

The sixth and final dimension involves the frequency of contacts between clinician and client. Some types of interventions (e.g., token economies) require almost continual monitoring of the client, whereas other forms of therapy might involve weekly or monthly meetings.

Cohen (1995) acknowledged an additional complication in attempting to characterize intervention efforts: Many interventions involve combinations of individual approaches. Thus, the child may be receiving psychotherapy from a psychologist, experiencing some sort of psychoeducational intervention in the school setting, and participating in family therapy sessions.

This analysis thus highlights the difficulty in attempting to characterize the nature of interventions appropriate for use with adolescents (also see Kazdin, 1988; Kratochwill & Morris, 1993). It is useful now to present an overview of the most commonly employed types of intervention.

## Alternative Interventions

Alternative types of intervention are discussed in terms of four categories: psychoeducational interventions, insight-oriented therapies, behavioral-cognitive therapies, and family therapies. Where feasible, the interventions are characterized in terms of the dimensions within Cohen's (1995) framework, and comments are made regarding the role of assessments in the different approaches.

*Psychoeducational Interventions.* This group includes a very wide range of treatment programs and interventions designed to specifically address academic deficits. At a very specific level there are tutorial programs targeting specific reading or mathematics performance deficits. There are also innumerable programs developed for addressing the various learning disabilities.

Broader educational interventions have also been developed. These include curricula designed to promote basic cognitive and academic skills. Hallahan, Kauffman, and Lloyd's (1985) metacognitive strategy training program represents an example of a broad-based program designed to address a range of deficits underlying poor academic performance. Another example may be found in the School Transitional Environmental Program developed by Felner and Aden (1988), designed to address specific performance deficits but also to address some of the emotional and social problems arising from the transition from the elementary to junior grades.

Psychoeducational interventions are too diverse to be easily summarized in terms of Cohen's (1995) model, but the implementation of psychoeducational programs generally depends very heavily on assessment activities. The careful identification of the nature of the deficit in question is usually critical for the success of the intervention. I show in a later chapter that significant advances are being made in the development of aptitude and achievement tests relevant to these assessments.

*Insight-Oriented Strategies.* A wide variety of therapies have been included in this category with the common assumption that resolving emotional problems rests with a therapist bringing the individual to a fuller understanding of his or her emotions and behavior. The goal, in other words, is to help clients gain insight into themselves.

Three forms of insight-oriented therapy are identified in Table 3.5. Traditional psychoanalysis derives, of course, from the theoretical and clinical work of Freud. This form of treatment was not originally designed for use with children and adolescents, but is has seen some applications at this level.

More important, though, are the many alternative therapies, identified as contemporary psychoanalytic therapies in Table 3.5, that have been derived from the original theory for application with adolescents. The most prominent of these applications are psychoanalytic play therapy (A. Freud, 1958), milieu therapy (Bettelheim, 1966), ego psychology (Erikson, 1963, 1982), and reality therapy (Glasser, 1965, 1969). These treatment strategies, although they all have their origins in psychoanalytic theory, represent very different approaches to the treatment of adolescent disorders. Other recent efforts to adapt psychoanalysis to the adolescent level may be found in Kohut and Elson (1987) and Masterson (1985).

The other group of therapies identified in this category are those reflecting a humanistic approach. The most prominent of these therapies

TABLE 3.5
Forms of Insight-Oriented Therapy

| *Type* | *Examples* |
|---|---|
| Traditional psychoanalysis | Psychoanalysis |
| Contemporary psychoanalytic therapies | Psychoanalytic play therapy |
| | Milieu therapy |
| | Psychodrama |
| | Adlerian psychotherapy |
| Humanistic therapies | Reality therapy |
| | Transactional analysis |
| | Client-centered therapy |

is represented in the original development of C. Rogers (1951), but other applications have been made for the treatment of adolescents.

In locating these therapies on the Cohen (1995) dimensions, we observe, first, that they all derive from the original psychoanalytic theory, although in some cases the assumptions of that model have been significantly altered. The therapies tend to be highly structured in that they follow relatively rigid guidelines, but they also have a broad focus in that they are designed to fundamentally alter the personality of the client. The therapies are usually delivered directly to the individual, but some are designed for application in group settings. These therapies are usually of a long duration and require a high level of contact between therapist and client.

Traditionally, structured psychological assessments have not played a major role in the application of insight-oriented therapies. Therapists using these methods have generally depended most heavily on unstructured clinical assessments. However, there has been criticism of this heavy dependence on informal assessments, and there are signs of an increasing willingness to utilize standardized psychological tests and interview schedules. This is reflected in part in efforts being expended in refining the *DSM–IV* diagnostic system and in developing instruments reflective of that system.

*Behavioral-Cognitive Therapies.* Therapies within this large category represent some of the most popular strategies for dealing with adolescent problems. The behavioral approach derived initially from theoretical and empirical efforts within the radical behaviorist and social learning theory orientations discussed in chapter 2. These initial efforts were characterized by a focus on overt, observable behaviors and a corresponding neglect of underlying personality or emotional states. They represented an effort to apply basic learning theory principles to the development of adaptive behaviors and elimination of maladaptive behaviors.

The first subgroup, behavior modification strategies, generally reflects the assumptions and procedures of the original behaviorist strategies, although there is a considerable variety of specific strategies within the approach. Some of this variety is illustrated in Table 3.6, which identifies a sampling of these strategies.

TABLE 3.6
Examples of Behavior Modification Strategies

| | |
|---|---|
| Assertion training | Aversive conditioning |
| Social skills training | Systematic desensitization |
| Contingency management | Shaping |
| Modeling | Contingency contracting |

The second subgroup within this category includes the cognitive-behavior therapies. These strategies combine the focus on observable behaviors with a concern for the cognitions or thoughts underlying that behavior. The term *cognitive restructuring* is also sometimes used to describe these therapies, reflecting a basic assumption of the approach that altering behavioral or emotional responses is best accomplished by modifying the cognitions underlying the actions. Problem-solving skills training (Shure & Spivack, 1978) and rational-emotive therapy (Ellis, 1962, 1971) represent two examples of this approach that have had considerable application to adolescents.

Because there is a wide variety of approaches within this category, it is difficult to locate the approach on the dimensions defined by Cohen (1995). Nevertheless, some observations may be made. First, the theoretical basis for these strategies rests, as we have seen, primarily on the various learning theory models. However, and particularly in the case of the cognitive strategies, the influence of cognitive-developmental theory and research may be detected, especially as that work has been applied to social cognitions. Regarding the structure dimension, most of these strategies are at the highly structured end of the continuum. The strategies also tend to be rather narrow in focus, with very specific target behaviors constituting the object of concern. Treatments within these approaches are usually delivered to the individual, although there are applications of behavior modification for families and parents. The treatments can be delivered in any setting, and in fact many applications for school, neighborhood, or residential settings have been devised. The applications are generally limited in duration; that is, they are designed to accomplish specific goals, and once the goal has been achieved the therapy terminates. Finally, these strategies generally involve a higher level of contact with the client than some other approaches. They are often based on a careful monitoring of behaviors, and this may require frequent intervention on the part of the therapist.

This particular approach has had a significant impact on the development of assessment tools. Many observational procedures, rating scales, behavioral checklists, and physiological measures were developed in association with the behavioral therapies. They were developed, in other words, in response to the need within the therapies for means of tracking overt behaviors. Many of these are examined in chapter 9. The development of the cognitive-behavioral therapies also created a need for measures of cognitions, beliefs, and attitudes, examples of which are presented in chapter 10.

*Family Therapies.* This category includes a large set of interventions designed for altering family dynamics or parental behavior. The goal is usually to change the family situation to effect improvements in the situ-

TABLE 3.7
Examples of Family and Parenting Therapies

| | |
|---|---|
| Conjoint family therapy | Behavioral marital therapy |
| Brief family therapy | Solutions-oriented family therapy |
| Multiple-family therapy | Functional family therapy |
| Family crisis therapy | Family play therapy |

ation and behavior of the adolescent. Various forms of family therapy are represented in Table 3.7, each reflecting a fundamentally different approach to intervention.

Insight-oriented family therapies have the same sources as insight-oriented individual therapies, as discussed earlier. These represent efforts to apply psychodynamic principles to the family setting. The therapies may be delivered to the family as a unit, to individual members of the family, or, typically, to some combination of those units. Conjoint family therapy (Goldenberg & Goldenberg, 1980) and psychodynamic family therapy (Nichols, 1984) represent two examples of this approach.

The second large class of family therapies identified in Table 3.7 includes those deriving from behaviorist principles. These therapies, based on behavior modification or cognitive-behavior modification strategies, are generally designed to replace maladaptive behaviors and cognitions of family members with more positive ways of relating to one another.

The third category is termed multisystemic therapy. These therapies are both child- and family-focused. They are designed to address the underlying problems of the adolescent and are directed toward all environments within which the youth is functioning: the family, school, and community. A wide variety of specific therapeutic techniques may be used in multisystemic therapy, but cognitive-behavioral strategies usually predominate. These therapies have generally been highly influenced by the integrative ecological models described in chapter 2. Henggeler's family preservation program represents an example of this approach (Henggeler, Melton, & Smith, 1992; Henggeler, Melton, Smith, Schoenwald, & Hanley, 1993).

Because there is such a diverse set of therapies represented within this category of family therapies, locating them on Cohen's dimensions is not particularly meaningful. These therapies do, however, place special demands on assessment activities. The implementation and evaluation of the family therapies requires instruments for assessing aspects of parenting and family dynamics. Although the development of instruments and procedures for assessing these dimensions has lagged somewhat behind the development of tools for assessing individuals, later chapters provide examples of interview, rating, and other types of measures appropriate for assessment in this area.

### Evaluating the Therapies

In an ideal world the selection of a therapy would be based on objective information about the effectiveness of the intervention. Unfortunately, the situation regarding therapies for adolescents is not that simple. There are, on the one hand, many examples of careful evaluations of therapeutic interventions. Illustrative is Klein, Alexander, and Parson's (1977) comparison of the effectiveness of three family therapy intervention modes: behavioral family therapy, client-centered family therapy, and psychodynamic family therapy. A no-treatment control group was also included. A more recent example may be found in Henggeler et al.'s (1992; Henggeler et al., 1993) effort to evaluate the effectiveness of a multisystemic therapy intervention program. On the other hand, there is general agreement that our ability to form generalizations from this program evaluation literature is very limited.

Recent reviews and meta-analyses of research on the efficacy of psychological interventions with children and adolescents have been reported by Diamond, Serrano, Dickey, and Sonis (1996), Jensen, Hoagwood, and Petti (1996), Lipsey and Wilson (1993), and Kazdin (1988, 1993). The most extensive work in this respect, though, has been carried out by Weisz and his associates (Weisz, Donenberg, Hans, & Kauneckis, 1995; Weisz & Weiss, 1993; Weisz, Weiss, Alicke, & Klotz, 1987; Weisz, Weiss, Han, Granger, & Morton, 1995). Two broad conclusions may be derived from their work. First, psychotherapeutic interventions with adolescents do produce statistically and clinically significant positive outcomes. Second, where behavioral methods of treatment are contrasted with alternative forms of therapy, the behavioral methods generally prove superior.

On the other hand, a number of qualifications and reservations regarding these conclusions have emerged from the various reviews and meta-analyses. It must be acknowledged, first, that the conclusions rest on a relatively small number of studies. Second, most attention has been paid in the evaluations to behavioral modes of therapy and considerably less attention has been afforded other strategies such as psychodynamic therapy or the family therapies. Third, much of the research has been conducted on therapeutic interventions developed especially for research purposes, and there are fewer efforts to evaluate the therapies as actually delivered in clinical settings. Fourth, although the situation is improving, many of the evaluation studies have exhibited serious design and measurement problems (see Kazdin, 1988; Kovacs & Lohr, 1995). Fifth, and perhaps most important, this body of evaluation research has not adequately represented the complexity of the subject matter. This is a significant point worth pursuing in a little more detail.

Much research and theory on the effectiveness of psychotherapies for children and adolescents has been guided by the overly simplistic question

"Is therapy effective?" The impact of therapy on the individual depends on a large number of interacting factors. Figure 3.1 represents one effort to conceptualize the therapeutic process (Hoge & Andrews, 1986).

The first set of factors includes values, attitudes, and beliefs of the larger environment in which the individual is functioning. This encompasses what Bronfenbrenner (1979, 1986) referred to as the meso-, exo-, and macrosystems. The influence of this type of variable is usually indirect, but there are circumstances in which they may exercise a more direct influence. For example, a rigid, militaristic boot camp may be an acceptable and effective treatment for youthful offenders in one community but may be rejected as a harsh and unacceptable treatment in another. Bernal,

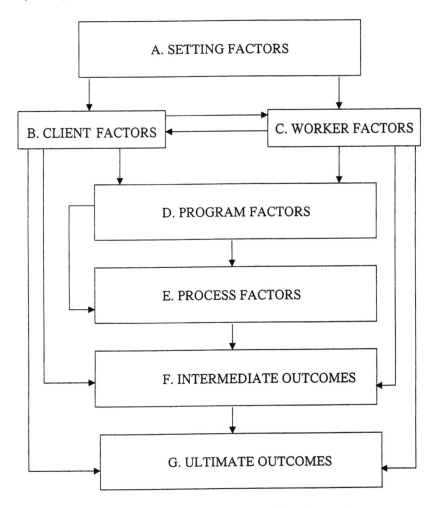

FIG. 3.1.  A model of interventions in social service agencies.

Bonilla, and Bellido (1995) discussed ways in which cultural factors may impact various facets of the therapeutic process.

The second set of factors is made up of client variables. Three classes of these variables may be identified: (a) demographic characteristics such as socioeconomic status (SES), race, gender, and developmental level; (b) cognitive, personality, and social characteristics; and (c) presenting problems. The general hypothesis of the model is that these variables have both direct and indirect impacts on the effects of intervention efforts.

Some of these client variables have been explored in research. For example, meta-analyses have identified gender as a potential moderating factor in the therapy–outcome link, with some support for the hypothesis that girls respond better to treatment than boys. Developmental level, the nature of the presenting problem, intelligence, reading ability, cognitive style, temperament, and motivation for treatment are some of the other client variables likely to impact the effects of therapy. The importance of these client variables is also emphasized in the integrative ecological and risk and resilience models discussed in chapter 2. They are also highly relevant to the various intervention models that stress the importance of matching therapy with relevant characteristics of the client (Arkowitz, 1992; Beutler, 1979; Beutler & Clarkin, 1990; Hoge & Andrews, 1986). In light of these considerations, it is unfortunate that so little attention has been paid to client variables in evaluations of the interventions.

A third set of factors includes therapist variables. The general hypothesis is that characteristics of the individual delivering the treatment may affect the impact of the treatment independent of the actual program being delivered. Four types of therapist variables have been identified. The first involve demographic factors such as age, gender, or ethnic group membership. Education, training, and professional experience represent a second group of factors. The third includes dimensions of relationship style. Considerable research with adults has demonstrated that the manner in which the therapist relates to the client (e.g., warm vs. distant, supportive vs. critical) has an impact on outcome. Finally, the clinician's beliefs about the intervention he or she is delivering and his or her practice preferences are likely involved. Some research on these issues has been conducted at the adult level (Beutler, Wakefield, & Williams, 1994) but very little work has been done in the context of child and adolescent therapy research (see Kazdin, 1988).

A fourth set of factors is program factors. Included here are factors that operate at the level of the agency or institution in which the counseling is provided. The general hypothesis is that the formal policies of the organization, program options, agency resources, and staff morale are capable of affecting the impact of programs:

> To some extent, the context within which counseling is offered will influence the operation of change factors. The length of client contact, types of psychological problems dealt with, and agency philosophy and resources will all affect to varying degrees the change elements occurring in therapy. Methodological problems inherent in isolating specific effects of situational parameters have made the task of examining their moderating role rather difficult. However, empirical scrutiny of potentially important factors needs to be undertaken. (Highlin & Hill, 1984, p. 364)

In fact, issues of this sort have not been addressed in connection with the treatment of adolescents.

The fifth set of factors, process factors, reflects the actual therapy delivered to the client. Therapeutic goals, message content, client–therapist relationship, and duration and density of contacts represent only some of the dimensions of therapy relevant to outcomes. It is extremely important in program evaluations to directly assess the actual processes involved in the interventions. This relates to the problem that in many cases there is a discrepancy between the formal description of a program and what is actually delivered. A cognitively based anger management program often means very different things when delivered by different therapists. This problem is widely recognized, but the problems of operationalizing treatments still represent barriers to effective evaluation research (Kazdin, 1988, 1993; Kovacs & Lohr, 1995).

Two levels of outcomes are identified in the model. The first are designated as *intermediate outcomes,* and they reflect changes in presenting problems, collateral changes in the client, and client satisfaction with service. The assessment of these variables is usually conducted at the end of the intervention or shortly afterward. They reflect the more immediate effects of the therapeutic intervention.

The *ultimate outcomes* reflect the longer term effectiveness of the therapeutic intervention. Many interventions have very specific goals such as the elimination of maladaptive behaviors or corrections of academic problems. However, there is usually a broader and longer term goal of improving the general functioning of the individual and enabling him or her to confront future problems and stresses. Only long-term evaluations of therapies can address this issue. Unfortunately, little research on this has been conducted in connection with children and adolescents (Kazdin, 1988, 1993).

This discussion has considered the elements of the model as individual contributors to intervention outcome. As indicated in Fig. 3.1, however, these elements interact with one another in complex ways. This point is also emphasized by the integrative ecological and developmental pathway models discussed in chapter 2. This complexity presents serious design and analysis problems for evaluation researchers and creates special demands on psychological assessments. The development of valid and reliable measures for the elements of the model present real challenges.

The representation of the therapeutic process shown in Fig. 3.1 highlights the complexity of the phenomenon and the difficulty of conducting meaningful evaluation research. However, the importance of this research should not be underestimated. First the collection of valid and objective information about the effectiveness of interventions is critical for the improvement of those programs. Perhaps the best illustration of the utility of program evaluation research may be found with compensatory education programs such as Head Start. Twenty-five years of evaluation research has proven invaluable in understanding the operation of these programs and in pointing to ways in which their effectiveness may be enhanced.

Second, the program evaluation research is important for demonstrating to funders of programs and other policymakers the effectiveness of the programs. Funds for primary, secondary, and tertiary programs are limited, and there seems to be an increased demand in both the public and private spheres for evidence of program effectiveness (see Frank, Sullivan, & DeLeon, 1994; Hoagwood, Jensen, Petti, & Burns, 1996).

# II

## AN INTRODUCTION TO PSYCHOLOGICAL ASSESSMENT

# Basic Concepts in Assessment

This chapter provides an introduction to some basic terms and concepts relevant to psychological assessments and chapter 5 discusses issues relevant to the actual use of assessments in applied settings. The reader is referred to texts by Aiken (1997), Ghiselli, Campbell, and Zedek (1981), and T. B. Rogers (1995) for extended treatments of topics relevant to psychological measurement and assessment.

## INTRODUCTION TO THE ASSESSMENT PROCESS

I have used the term psychological assessment to refer to the process whereby information is collected about characteristics of the individual and used to form an inference or judgment. These inferences may then be used as a basis for a decision about the individual. For example, a school psychologist might interview a classroom teacher about the performance of a student, observe that student in the classroom, examine the student's IQ and achievement test scores, and, on the basis of the information collected, infer that the youth suffers from an attention disorder. This in turn might lead to a recommendation that the student be referred for remedial treatment.

This book is primarily concerned with two components of this assessment process. The first component entails the collection of information about the individual through measurement tools and procedures. There is an important distinction in this respect between informal and unstandardized assessment procedures and standardized procedures. The former generally involve collecting information through unstructured interviews and observations. This is probably the predominant mode of data collection in most counseling, therapeutic, and guidance settings.

Standardized psychological assessments constitute the alternative method of collecting information about the individual's characteristics and circumstances. I defined these assessments in chapter 1 as instruments or procedures (a) with fixed stimulus, response, and scoring formats; (b) that yield quantitative scores; and (c) for which normative and psychometric data are provided. The Weschler Intelligence Scale for Children–III (WISC–III; Wechsler, 1991) represents an example of a standardized instrument; stimulus, response, administration, and scoring procedures are standardized, and normative and psychometric data are provided. This type of measure forms the primary focus of this book.

The second component of the assessment process of concern here involves use of the information to form an inference or judgment about the individual being assessed. This is sometimes referred to as the *diagnostic process*, and the outcome of this phase is referred to as an *assessment* or *diagnosis*. In some cases there is a close link between the score from the assessment instrument and the judgment. An example would be a case in which the examiner administers an IQ test to an adolescent, calculates a score of 135, and infers that the young person is intellectually gifted. In other cases a much higher level of judgment is called for. This is particularly true with diagnostic assessments involving various sources of information. To illustrate, a psychologist might conduct interviews with a youthful offender and his or her parents, collect behavior checklist scores from teachers, administer aptitude and personality tests to the youth, and examine his or her prior criminal record. On the basis of that information the examiner might infer that the youth suffers from a serious personality disorder and is at a high risk for committing further criminal offenses. These judgments required a higher level of information processing than was seen in the first example.

Level of structure also may vary in this phase of the process. The integration of information and the formation of an inference generally depend on what is termed *clinical judgment*: The clinician processes the information, and, on the basis of his or her training and experience, formulates a diagnosis. For example, the school psychologist might consider an adolescent's scores from IQ and personality tests, and from that information infer that the youth demonstrates exceptional academic abilities and aptitudes and predict that he or she will do well in an advanced academic program. The information about the adolescent is collected through standardized measures in this case, but the ultimate assessment or diagnosis is largely dependent on the clinician's cognitive processing.

However, it is possible to introduce structured procedures into the inferential phase of the assessment process through the use of statistical or actuarial formulas (see Cronbach, 1990; Lanyon & Goodstein, 1997; Meehl, 1965, 1986). These formulas represent empirically derived decision rules that link assessment information with a diagnosis or assessment. For example, there are formulas that allow one to translate scores from a standardized IQ test such as the WISC–III into predictions of performance in specific academic programs. Similarly, a behavioral rating scale described in chapter 8, the Personality Inventory for Children, provides actuarial formulas enabling a wide variety of predictions, including school failure, criminal activity, and substance abuse, from scale scores. I also show examples of composite measures designed to integrate information from multiple sources and provide predictions about specific outcomes.

An important goal of this book is to demonstrate that the introduction of increasing structure into the information collection and inference formation phases of the assessment process will lead to more valid assessments and more effective decisions. This involves increasing our reliance on standardized psychological assessments and structured inferential procedures.

Some arguments in favor of this position were reviewed in chapter 1. One key argument relates to the increasing availability of standardized psychological measures with demonstrated reliability and validity, many examples of which are reviewed in this book. This is in contrast with clinical assessment procedures, for which there is generally no information available about their psychometric properties. Some specific problems with clinical assessments are also discussed in connection with clinical interviews in chapter 9. Other arguments in favor of standardized assessments include their ability to enhance consistency and reduce bias in the assessment process and the fact that they provide explicit operational definitions for the basis for assessment. The latter is important for justifying the assessments to the client and others.

There is also some direct empirical support for the superiority of standardized assessments. This is based on meta-analyses contrasting the validity of clinical and statistical or actuarial predictions. These analyses have involved comparing cases in which the same information was utilized clinically or statistically to produce a diagnosis, usually in the form of a prediction. These reviews have been reported by Dawes, Faust, and Meehl (1989), Meehl (1954, 1957, 1986), and Sawyer (1966), who all concluded that, in the vast majority of cases, the structured psychological assessments were equal or superior to the clinical assessments.

## SOME CHARACTERISTICS OF ASSESSMENT INSTRUMENTS

A number of the characteristics of assessment instruments and some of the important terminology of the field are introduced in the following discussion.

### Types of Assessment Instruments

Table 4.1 provides an outline of the major types of assessment instruments encountered in this book, including some of the major subcategories of instruments.

It should be clear that the definitions of the categories are sometimes ambiguous and locating individual instruments in the categories is problematic. For example, the line between structured personality tests and self-report behavior checklists is sometimes a fine one. Similarly, there are some instruments that sometimes may be administered as interviews and other times as self-report measures.

Another observation is worth making at this point: Psychological tests constitute a major category of assessment instruments. In fact, most textbooks dealing with assessment issues feature the word *test* prominently in their title and, in fact, devote most attention to this category of assessment instrument. This, however, represents something of a paradox. As indicated in Table 4.1, tests constitute only one category of assessment instruments. Further, although clinicians do, in fact, depend heavily on tests, anyone with experience in applied assessment situations can attest that there is also a wide use of rating, checklist, observational, and interview tools in applied settings.

### Normative Versus Criterion-Reference Assessments

Most of the instruments encountered in this book represent normative assessments. That is, the individual's score on the measure is interpreted with reference to the scores of a sample of individuals (the *normative* or *standardization sample*). For example, a youth's score on the WISC–III is always interpreted with reference to the average score of a large sample of individuals at the same age level. An IQ score of 100 indicates that the individual's score equaled that of the mean score for the normative sample, whereas a score of 130 indicates that his or her performance fell 2 standard deviations above the mean for the normative sample. Raw scores on these measures acquire meaning only with reference to the performance of other individuals. Some issues associated with evaluating normative data are considered later in this chapter.

TABLE 4.1
Types of Assessment Instruments

| |
|---|
| Standardized tests |
| Projective tests |
| Judgmental measures |
|   Rating scales |
|   Checklists |
|   Ranking systems |
| Interview schedules |
| Observation schedules |
| Physiological measures |

*Criterion-referenced measurement* applies largely to achievement tests, although there are some types of observational measures of behavior that might be considered in this category. In the case of criterion-referenced achievement tests, raw scores are interpreted not with reference to the performance of a large group, but, rather, with reference to some established criteria of performance. For example, performance on a test of historical principles might be assessed with reference to the percentage of dates correctly recalled or the number of historical concepts correctly identified. Although this type of test is sometimes important in assessing performance in educational and organizational settings, it will not be dealt with in this book (see Gronlund, 1973; Linn, 1980).

## Scoring Formats

The description of the characteristics of individuals forms the basis for psychological assessments. In some cases these descriptions are qualitative in nature; that is, we describe the individual as gifted or extroverted or autistic. In most cases, though, our descriptions are quantitative; thus we want to describe the relative amount of intelligence displayed by the individual or the degree of hyperactivity exhibited. *Psychological measurement* is the term used to describe the processes involved in forming these quantitative indexes. Measurement "essentially is concerned with the methods used to provide quantitative descriptions of the extent to which individuals manifest or possess specified characteristics" (Ghiselli et al., 1981, p. 2).

A variety of types of measures are encountered in the instruments and procedures to reviewed in subsequent chapters, and an overview of the major forms may be useful.

Most of the instruments encountered represent normative-based measures. There are a variety of ways of expressing these scores, with *percentile ranks* constituting the simplest type of norm score. These express the proportion of individuals in the standardization sample scoring below a particular score. For example, if 30% of the individuals in the normative sample obtained a score below 62, then that score represents the 30th percentile. We would say that an individual who obtained a score of 62 was at the 30th percentile, and this means that they did better than 30% of those in the normative sample (or, conversely, approximately 70% of individuals in the normative sample did better than that individual).

An alternative type of normative measure is based on *standard scores*. These are expressed in terms of deviations from the mean of the normative sample. The most commonly used of the standard scores are $z$ scores, calculated according to the formula $z = X - M/SD$, where $X$ represents the raw score, $M$ the mean of the normative distribution, and $SD$ the standard deviation of that distribution. The mean of a $z$ score distribution is 0 and the $SD$ equals 1. There are also transformations of $z$ scores that enable elimination of 0s from the metric. One example is McCall's $T$ in which the mean is set at 50 and the standard deviation at 10. Another familiar example is the Scholastic Aptitude Test with a mean score of 500 and standard deviation of 100. The advantage of these standard scores is that they provide a uniform scale so that we can make comparisons across instruments with different metrics.

Another type of standard score is referred to as the *normalized standard score*. These are standard scores that have been transformed to fit a normal distribution. The advantage of normalized scores is that they enable us to make comparisons across measures with differently shaped distributions. The IQ scores derived from the WISC–III represent example results of an instrument employing normalized standard scores. The scores are based, first, on normative data collected for large groups of children at different age levels. These raw scores were transformed into $z$ scores, and those $z$ scores were transformed again into normalized $z$ scores. A final transformation involves setting the mean of the distribution at 100 and the standard deviation at 15. We know, then, that a child with a full-scale IQ score of 85 on the WISC–III fell 1 standard deviation below the normalized mean for his or her age group.

These quantitative types of indexes are widely used in expressing scores from psychological measures. However, there is another way of expressing assessments: This involves the use of qualitative indexes, usually expressed in terms of diagnostic categories. Thus, instead of expressing adolescents' cognitive aptitudes in terms of their relative position on a continuum (e.g., at the 65th percentile), they are described in terms of a discreet category (e.g., intellectually gifted, borderline retarded). Similarly, instead of describing a personality attribute in quantitative terms (e.g., a $T$-score of 70 on a scale of hyperactivity), qualitative indexes assign the individual to a diagnostic category (e.g., diagnosed as hyperactive).

These categorical systems are sometimes referred to as *taxonomic systems* and the diagnostic categories as *taxons*.

As we saw in chapter 3, many of the personality and pathology constructs derived from theoretical and clinical sources are expressed as diagnostic categories, with the most prominent example being the *DSM–IV*. However, there are also diagnostic systems that have been derived through empirical procedures. Thus, the concepts of hyperactivity, conduct disorder, and attention deficit disorder are sometimes treated as diagnostic categories.

These diagnostic categories are often very useful summarizing and conveying information about individuals, but their use is sometimes problematic (see Achenbach, 1995; McReynolds, 1989; Quay, Routh, & Shapiro, 1987; Scotti, Morris, McNeil, & Hawkins, 1996). First, these problems arise from questions about the validity of the constructs. In other words, there are often questions about the etiology and the behavioral and treatment implications of the diagnostic categories. Second, there are sometimes problems associated with the reliability of the diagnoses made in connection with the category. Third, there is often an issue of comorbidity; that is, the way to deal with cases in which the individual exhibits symptoms that match two or more categories. Some of these, of course, are problems that also arise in connection with the quantitative indexes.

## Scale Construction

Many complex technical issues arise in connection with the construction of tests, rating scales, interview schedules, and other assessment methodologies. For example, a wide range of choices exist in selecting formats for rating scales, including numerical, semantic differential, forced-choice, behaviorally anchored, Q-Sort, and graphic systems. There are then technical issues arising within those formats. Continual advances are being made in assessment methodology, particularly in the area of test construction (see, e.g., Steinberg & Thissen, 1995), and consideration of these technical issues is beyond the scope of this book. The reader is referred to Aiken (1996a, 1996b, 1997) and Saklofske and Zeidner (1995) for detailed treatment of these issues.

## COMPUTERS AND ASSESSMENT

Special mention should be made of the use of computers in the assessment process. They have already had a significant impact on all phases of the process, and it is likely that the impact will be even greater in the future.

Computers have long played a role in data analyses used to construct, refine, and evaluate psychological tests. It is unlikely, for example, that a test such as the Millon Clinical Multiaxial Inventory–II, although theoretical in origin, could have been developed without the capacities of a modern computer. Similarly, the sophisticated item analysis procedures currently being used in test construction are highly dependent on computers.

Computers have also been widely used in collecting and recording responses. Most students are familiar with scannable answer sheets on which responses are recorded with a pencil and read by the computer with the aid of optical scanning devices. New technologies relating to the use of special computer keyboards, touch screens, and light pens are also beginning to have an impact in this area. The major advantages of using computer technology to collect and record responses are accuracy and savings in clerical time.

The presentation of stimulus material is also being influenced by computer technology. Some of these developments represent only minor modifications to the stimulus material, so that instead of having the examinee read test or questionnaire items from a booklet, the material is presented on a computer screen. A related development is the presentation of interview items through a computer, with questions presented on the screen or through a speaker, and examinees recording their responses on the keyboard.

A somewhat more radical extension of the use of computers involves *computerized adaptive testing*. This essentially involves adjusting the items on a test as a function of answers to previous questions, meaning that the test can be instantly modified to suit the needs of the particular examinee. This type of procedure can increase the reliability of test administration and it also represents a considerable saving in time and money. The technology may be applied to other types of assessment tools, including the presentation of interview, rating, or questionnaire items (see Nurius, 1990).

The major drawback of adaptive testing relates to the difficulty of forming normative scores and establishing validity. Traditional methods for forming norms and evaluating validity are based on the assumption that stimulus material is presented in a standardized manner to all participants, and that assumption is clearly violated in the case of computerized adaptive testing.

The calculation of raw and standardized scores is another process efficiently performed by the computer. There are computer programs now available for scoring a wide range of standardized tests, rating scales, and checklists. There are, for example, several programs available for calculating standardized norm scores for the WISC–III, yielding the Full-Scale, Verbal, and Performance IQ scores, various subtest scores, and a variety of profile and other specialized scores. Many computerized scoring programs offer a choice of normative groups and also present the possibility of continually updating normative samples. These programs eliminate the tedious clerical work often involved in the scoring of instruments and they improve scoring accuracy.

There is, however, another controversial type of computer development, *computer-based test interpretation*. In this case a computer program yields not only the scores from the measuring instrument, but also an interpretation of the scores. The program is thus producing a psychological assessment or diagnosis.

The first efforts to develop a computer-based test interpretation were in connection with the Minnesota Multiphasic Personality Inventory (MMPI) in the early 1960s. That led to similar efforts with other standardized tests of personality and psychopathology, and this, in turn, has led to computer-based test interpretations of intelligence and other aptitude tests, neuropsychological batteries, and structured interview schedules (see Butcher, 1987).

The clinical and actuarial strategies discussed earlier represent the two basic approaches to the construction of computer-based interpretations. In the case of clinically derived interpretations, the judgments of experienced clinicians are translated into decision rules for processing by the computer. For example, the inference might be made that a particular profile across the Verbal subscales of the WISC–III represents difficulty in processing verbal information, and this inference would then be expressed as a decision rule. In the case of actuarial interpretations, the decision rules are formed from formulas constructed on the basis of analyses of empirical data. For example, scores above a certain level on a suicide prediction scale might have been associated with a 60% incidence of suicide attempts in a sample of adolescents and the interpretation would then express this level of risk.

Although computer-based interpretations, particularly clinically derived, have become widely available and very popular, their use has aroused considerable controversy (see Lanyon, 1984; Matarazzo, 1983, 1986; Moreland, 1985). The major criticism of this approach relates to lack of validity information for the computer-based interpretations. Although psychometric information may be available for the assessment tools underlying the interpretations, this is usually not the case for the interpretations themselves. This problem is compounded because the interpretations are often made available to individuals without the training and knowledge to utilize them effectively. The ethical issues raised by computer-based interpretations have received considerable attention from professional groups (see American Psychological Association, 1985, 1986, 1993), but they have by no means been resolved. I return to this topic in chapter 5.

# EVALUATING PSYCHOLOGICAL ASSESSMENTS

T. B. Rogers (1995) provided a useful historical review of developments relating to the evaluation of psychological assessments. He noted that a number of alternatives have been developed to the traditional psychometric model with its emphasis on the concepts of reliability and validity. Generalizability theory and various concepts that have emerged in behavioral assessment are two examples. On the other hand, the traditional or classical psychometric model continues to demonstrate its utility in the evaluation of assessments and it is the primary model used in the various ethical guidelines developed for psychological assessments.

The following sections contain discussions of some concepts relevant to the traditional psychometric model and Table 4.2 provides definitions of some of the key terms. The relation between these psychometric concepts and ethical issues is dealt with in chapter 5.

## Reliability

This concept is defined in terms of the consistency or stability of a measure. More formally, it refers to the relative proportion of true and error variance within a measure. It is important to recognize that reliability constitutes an essential condition of a psychological measure: Lack of stability or consistency in a measure seriously limits its utility.

TABLE 4.2
Definitions of Terms From the Psychometric Model

| Term | Definition |
| --- | --- |
| Reliability | The stability or consistency of a measure; formally defined as the relative proportion of true and error variance within a measure. |
| Content validity | Adequacy with which a measure represents the conceptual domain it is expected to encompass. |
| Construct validity | Theoretical meaning of scores from a measure; the accuracy with which the measure represents the construct in question; convergent and discriminant validity are two forms of construct validity. |
| Criterion-related validity | Extent to which scores from a measure relate to a criterion of performance; the two forms of criterion-related validity are concurrent validity and predictive validity. |
| Treatment validity | The sensitivity of a measure to changes in the dimension being assessed; sensitivity to treatment effects. |
| Incremental predictive validity | Extent to which a measure exhibits improvements in predictions relative to other procedures. |

The three major procedures for assessing reliability are outlined in Table 4.3. Each of those procedures yields indexes of the relative proportion of true and error variance within a measure, although each taps a somewhat different source of error.

The actual reliability coefficients yielded by the procedures are generally expressed in terms of correlation coefficients. A related concept, and one that should be familiar to anyone conducting psychological assessments, is that of the standard error of measurement. This is calculated according to the following formula:

$$S_m = S\sqrt{1 - r}$$

where $S_m$ = standard error of measurement; $S$ = standard deviation of scores; and $r$ = reliability coefficient. This index provides us with information about the range within which we would expect scores to fall given a certain reliability level. The concept can be illustrated with the following example:

Full-scale IQ = 115 ± 7 at the 95% confidence interval

In this case the individual obtained a score of 115, and, given the reliability level of this particular test, we would expect this individual to obtain scores between 108 and 122 on repeated testing 95 times out of 100. The range of scores is often referred to as the *percentile band* or *precision range*. The higher the reliability of a measure, the lower the range of scores, and the more confidence we can have in an individual score.

TABLE 4.3
Procedures for Evaluating Reliability

| Procedure | Definition |
|---|---|
| Test–retest | Instrument is administered twice under the same conditions with an interval between the two administrations; provides information about coefficient of stability. |
| Parallel forms | Two separate but parallel forms of the instrument are administered and compared; termed method of *interrater agreement* when used with rating measure and *interobserver* agreement with observational measure; provides information about coefficient of agreement. |
| Internal consistency | Extent of agreement among items within the measure or subsection of the measure evaluated; provides information about coefficient of internal consistency. |

## Validity

This is a somewhat more difficult concept for two reasons. First, and unlike reliability, there is no single definition of validity. Second, there is often ambiguity in the literature about the meaning of validity terms (see Messick, 1980). Nevertheless, validity is an extremely important concept in considering psychological assessments, and I provide a brief introduction to its most important forms.

*Content Validity.* This may be defined as the extent to which items within a measure reflect the domain of interest. We might ask, for example, how well the items on a mathematics achievement test represent the actual range of topics we wish to assess. Similarly, a question could be raised about how well the items on an intelligence test sample what we consider the domain of intelligence. Finally, in the case of an observational measure of aggressive behavior, we would ask how well the items in the observation schedule represent our conception of that particular behavioral domain. Content validity is often evaluated through subjective procedures, although as T. B. Rogers (1995) indicated, there are more structured means available.

*Face validity* is a term closely related to content validity. It refers to the examinees' evaluation of the content and relevance of the assessment. A common complaint among students is that an examination was "unfair" because test items did not represent a fair sampling of the material covered in the course. Similarly, respondents often react negatively to checklists or questionnaires because they do not seem to be relevant to the purposes of the assessment situation. This is a form of validity that is also difficult to assess systematically, but it often represents an important consideration in applied assessment situations.

*Construct Validity.* This constitutes the key concept in the traditional psychometric model (Anastasi, 1986; Messick, 1989a, 1989b, 1995), and it refers to the theoretical meaning of a measure. It is also sometimes defined as referring to the accuracy of a measure or, very commonly, as the extent to which a measure is measuring what it says it is measuring. Implicit within all of these definitions is the issue of the meaningfulness of scores from the assessment instruments or procedures.

Some illustrations may be useful. In raising a question about the construct validity of scores from an intelligence test, we would be asking about the actual meaning of scores from that instrument. What does a full-scale IQ score of 86 represent? What does it tell us about the cognitive functioning of the individual? We might also ask how accurately that score reflects the intellectual functioning of the individual. Consider another example: A child might be diagnosed with attention deficit disorder on the basis of an extensive neuropsychological and psychological battery of assessment instruments. It is legitimate, though, to raise a question about the construct validity of that diagnostic category. Just what does that diagnosis mean for the cognitive and behavioral functioning of that individual? To put it another way, how accurately does that diagnosis represent the underlying construct of attention deficit disorder?

Construct validity is obviously a key concept in the conduct of assessments because it raises questions about the meaningfulness of our constructs. Our measures of intelligence, achievement, learning disability, personality, emotional pathology, and behavioral adjustment often have important consequences when applied to individuals, and it is important to be able to articulate the actual meaning of those measures.

We encounter two general problems in attempting to assess the construct validity of psychological measures. The first relates to the fact that we often have difficulty defining our constructs. This difficulty is clearly evident in the case of the various aptitude measures of intelligence, giftedness, and learning disability. The controversies and ambiguities associated with the definitions of those constructs are well known (see Hoge, 1988, 1989; T. B. Rogers, 1995; Rourke & Del Dotto, 1994; Rourke & Fuerst, 1991). However, there are also problems associated with many of our personality, behavioral, and attitudinal constructs. For example, there has long been a vigorous debate about the meaning of the various taxonomic categories of emotional pathology such as psychosis, attention deficit disorder, depression, and conduct disorder (Achenbach, 1995; Blashfield, 1984; McReynolds, 1989; Quay et al., 1987; Scotti et al., 1996).

The second problem encountered in assessing construct validity relates to limitations on our construct validation procedures. The available procedures parallel the methods for deriving constructs discussed in chapter 4. Thus, it is possible to assess the construct validity of a measure by evaluating the measure against a theoretical definition of the construct or against the judgment of experienced clinicians. To illustrate the former, the construct validity of intelligence tests is often evaluated with reference to the traditional theory of intelligence. Similarly, diagnostic categories of emotional or behavioral pathology are sometimes evaluated with reference to clinical judgments. There are two problems with these strategies. First, they are dependent on very subjective and unsystematic procedures. Second, they are often contaminated by circular reasoning. For example, evaluating the validity of clinically derived constructs through clinical judgments provides little objective information about the constructs.

Empirical procedures constitute the preferred methods for evaluating construct validity. There are a variety of empirical procedures available for this purpose, but they all represent in one way or another an effort to locate scores from the measure within a nomological network (Cronbach & Meehl, 1955). The concern, in other words, is with explicating the way in which the measure relates to variables with which it should theoretically bear some relation. This has also been represented as a hypothesis-testing exercise (Landy, 1986; Messick, 1995; T. B. Rogers, 1995).

The terms *convergent* and *discriminant validity* are also relevant at this point. These are two aspects of construct validity, with convergent validity representing the extent to which scores from a measure relate to measures with which they should theoretically be related and discriminant validity representing the extent to which they do not relate to measures with which they should theoretically not be related. Therefore, a demonstration that scores from a rating measure of physical aggression correlated significantly with scores from an observational measure of physical aggression would provide support for the convergent validity of the rating measure. Similarly, a demonstration that scores from that rating measure of physical aggression show a nonsignificant relation with a behavioral rating of withdrawal would provide support for the discriminant validity of the measure. This also illustrates the point that construct validity research is best represented as a hypothesis-generation exercise.

The construct validity hypotheses are generally evaluated by means of correlation coefficients. Thus, in the preceding example of convergent validity we would simply correlate the rating and observational measures. Campbell and Fiske (1959), however, provided a more elaborate framework for evaluating construct validity. This is based on the multitrait-multimethod procedure. This procedure enables one to systematically assess both convergent and discriminant validity and also provides a determination of what is termed *method variance*, or variability in a measure determined by the measuring operation rather than the variable being assessed.

Messick's (1980, 1989b) efforts to expand the definition of construct validity include the actual consequences of the use of the assessment. Messick used the term *evidential basis* for test interpretation to emphasize the importance of incorporating the social consequences of use of the measure into the evaluation of a test or other type of assessment tool. To illustrate, a particular intelligence test might demonstrate high levels of reliability and validity and might even predict academic performance with some accuracy. However, using scores from that test as a basis for placing an adolescent in a remedial program in which he or she would receive no meaningful interventions would represent an inappropriate use of the test. Consider another example involving an assessment battery designed to diagnose conduct disorder. Using that battery to identify and label a youth as conduct disordered but taking no action from the diagnosis might be considered an invalid use of the assessment procedure.

*Criterion-Related Validity.* This constitutes another form of validity of particular concern in applied assessment situations and it is the extent to which scores on a measure relate to some criterion of performance. The two forms of criterion-related validity are *concurrent validity* (in which predictor and criterion scores are collected at the same time) and *predictive validity* (in which predictor scores are collected at one point and criterion scores at a later point). To illustrate, correlating scores from a personality test with academic grades collected at about the same time would reflect on the concurrent validity of the personality test scores. Correlating personality test scores collected when an individual is in the seventh grade with achievement test scores collected 2 years later would represent an evaluation of predictive validity.

There are several bases for expressing criterion-related validity. They are most commonly expressed in terms of correlation coefficients and their accompanying confidence indexes. For example, the criterion-related validity of an intelligence test (evaluated against teacher grades) might be expressed as follows: $r(60) = .33, p < .01$. The correlation of .66 provides us with information about the degree of association between the predictor (the intelligence test score) and the criterion (teacher grades), and the confidence index tells us that there is less than 1 chance in 100 of obtaining a correlation of that magnitude due to the operation of chance factors (given 60 degrees of freedom).

There are other ways of expressing criterion-related validity that are sometimes useful in applied situations, including contingency tables. These provide direct information about links between dichotomous predictor and criterion variables. To use signal detection theory terminology, they provide us with information about the relative proportion of "hits" and "misses" provided by a predictor.

Table 4.4 provides an example of a contingency table based on hypothetical data. The prediction in this case is based on an assessment battery designed to provide information about students' potential performance in a gifted program. The scores from that measure are expressed dichotomously: (a) predict success, or (b) predict failure. The criterion is also expressed dichotomously: (a) succeeded in program, or (b) failed in program. The latter measure is based on an assessment of performance after the students had been in the program for 1 year.

The first part of Table 4.4 describes the basic structure of the contingency program. Two types of correct decisions are recognized: true positives (positive prediction and positive outcome) and true negatives (negative prediction and negative outcome). The two types of incorrect decisions (misses) are false positives (positive prediction and negative outcome) and false negatives (negative prediction and positive outcome).

The second part of the table illustrates the contingency table with some hypothetical data. Criterion-related validity in this case may be expressed

TABLE 4.4
Illustrations of Prediction Accuracy Contingency Tables

*Illustration of Terminology*

| | Actual Outcome | |
|---|---|---|
| | Succeeded | Failed |
| Predict success | True positive | False positive |
| Predict failure | False negative | True negative |

*Hypothetical Illustration of a Prediction Accuracy Contingency Table*

| | Actual Outcome | | |
|---|---|---|---|
| | Succeeded | Failed | N |
| Predict success | 106 | 52 | 158 |
| Predict failure | 64 | 121 | 185 |
| N | 170 | 173 | 343 |

in a variety of ways. For example, we can express the proportion of correct predictions by adding the number of true positives and true negatives and dividing by the total number of predictions. In the example, 61% of the predictions are correct predictions. Other types of indexes that may be derived from contingency tables and procedures for assessing the statistical significance of the indexes were described by Loeber and Dishion (1983). Still other procedures for assessing decision accuracy were presented by Ghiselli et al. (1981) and T. B. Rogers (1995); included are procedures for incorporating cost–benefit indexes into the formulations.

*Treatment Validity.* This can be considered a special form of criterion-related validity. It is of particular concern when one is concerned with using an assessment instrument to track changes in a client or to evaluate the impact of a treatment over time. It refers more specifically to the sensitivity of a measure to changes in the dimension being assessed. We may ask, for example, whether or not the Beck Depression Inventory is capable of measuring changes in depression levels produced by a particular intervention. Lambert (1994) discussed the importance of considering this form of validity in selecting outcome measures but also noted that information about treatment validity is rarely available.

*Incremental Predictive Validity.* This is the extent to which a psychological measure improves the accuracy of predictions above the level achieved with either no assessments or alternative assessments: To what extent, for example, does the inclusion of a standardized intelligence test in a selection battery improve the ability of that battery to predict success or failure in job performance?

This is often an important consideration in applied assessment situations because there are often significant monetary costs associated with the conduct of assessments.

There are likely many situations where the costs of the assessment are not really justified in terms of the gains in accuracy of prediction being provided. The problem is that we often have great difficulty conducting such cost–benefit analyses because of problems in attaching monetary values to our outcomes, but there is more than a monetary consideration involved here. Our goal in any assessment situation should be to intrude as little as possible in the life of the client. We should avoid, then, any assessment that is not fully justified by the goals of the intervention.

### Normative Data

Most standardized instruments are scored in terms of normative or standardized scores; that is, scores are expressed relative to the scores of a sample of individuals. The adequacy of those normative or standardization samples depends on their relevance for the groups or individuals being evaluated, which in turn depends on the extent to which the samples reflect demographic characteristics of the groups or individuals, with these characteristics including age, gender, ethnic, cultural and other variables that might be related to performance on the measure. The adequacy of these samples is a critical point in considering the relevance of a measure for a particular individual.

Two other considerations are relevant to the evaluation of normative data. First, it is critical that the formation of the normative samples reflects developmental considerations. Norms for a personality test based on scores from samples of 11-year-olds may not be relevant to the 16-year-old adolescent. Second, because diagnoses of pathological or maladaptive functioning are often based on comparing scores with clinical samples, great care must be taken in evaluating the way in which those clinical samples were formed.

Norms are usually collected by test developers and reported in manuals accompanying the instrument. Ideally, these are presented in a form so that raw scores can be easily transformed into some type of standard score. In an increasing number of cases, however, scoring and conversion procedures have become so complex that they must be performed through computer processing.

**Quality of Materials**

There is one other basis for evaluating a standardized psychological measure, and this relates to the quality of material presented with the measure. Manuals accompanying tests or other measurement tools should clearly present the procedures for administration, scoring, and interpretation of the measure and those procedures should be comprehensible to those expected to administer and interpret the measure. Further, manuals should fully present all psychometric information relevant to the instrument or procedure. Specific standards regarding assessment material are presented in various ethical guidelines (see chap. 5).

# Practical and Ethical
# Issues in Assessment

A number of issues relating to the use of psychological assessments in applied and research settings are raised in this chapter, beginning with a review of the different uses made of psychological assessments and the contexts in which they are applied. This is followed by an introduction to professional and ethical issues relevant to assessments, and this in turn by a discussion of some practical issues that arise in the use of assessments.

## USES OF PSYCHOLOGICAL ASSESSMENTS

There are a variety of ways of characterizing the purposes of psychological assessments, but this discussion is organized around four categories of use: screening, placement and referral, instructional and treatment planning, and outcome evaluation.

### Screening

Psychological assessments are widely used for the initial identification of individuals satisfying a particular criterion. In some cases the screening activities are employed as a first step in identifying individuals with exceptional competencies. For example, some school boards have screening procedures for the initial identification of candidates for gifted or enriched educational programs. More often, though, screening procedures are used for an initial identification of pathological or maladaptive conditions:

> The screening process represents a relatively unrefined sieve that is de-signed to segregate the cohort under assessment into "positives" who pre-sumptively have the condition, and "negatives" who are ostensibly free of the disorder. Screening is not a diagnostic procedure per se. Rather, it rep-resents a preliminary filtering operation that identifies those individuals with the highest probability of having the disorder in question for subsequent specific diagnostic evaluation. (Derogatis & DellaPietra, 1994; p. 23)

As is clear from this definition, the only legitimate decision that may follow from a screening procedure relates to whether or not to proceed with further assessment.

Screening procedures are employed in connection with both tertiary and secondary interventions. They are used in tertiary interventions to provide a preliminary identification of individuals already exhibiting a pathological or maladaptive condition. Those identified as positive by the screening are then further assessed as a basis for an intervention decision. An example is a large-scale intervention study conducted with university students by Szulecka, Springett, and De Pauw (1986). Entering students were administered the General Health Questionnaire, a self-report meas-ure designed for preliminary identification of a range of pathological conditions. Those exhibiting signs of disorder were offered additional assessment and counseling services.

The use of screening procedures for identifying existing maladaptive conditions is particularly important in light of the research cited in chapter 3 indicating that significant percentages of individuals with a psychologi-cal disorder are never identified and receive no treatment. If we assume that early identification and treatment of pathological conditions is desir-able, then the value of screening procedures of this sort becomes obvious. Further, these procedures may play a role in assessing the urgency of treatment needs; an important consideration when dealing with suicide, violence, and other such risk areas.

Screening procedures are also relevant to what we have termed sec-ondary interventions. The assessment procedures are used in these cases to identify individuals who have not yet exhibited the pathological con-dition but are at risk for the condition. These are often referred to as *risk assessments*. An example is a multistage assessment procedure developed by Loeber, Dishion, and Patterson (1984). This procedure is designed for identifying adolescents at risk for later delinquency. The initial step in the procedure is the screening phase, and this is based on teacher ratings of social adjustment. Adolescents scoring above a criterion on that meas-ure are identified as at risk for delinquency and moved to the next as-sessment phase.

Brevity and ease of use are major criteria in the selection of screening instruments, with clinical interviews and rating and checklist instruments most commonly employed. Many of the instruments reviewed in subsequent chapters are capable of being used for screening purposes. One example of an instrument specifically designed for use as a screening measure is the Symptom Checklist–90–R, a self-report inventory designed for assessing pathological conditions in a variety of domains.

Both construct and criterion-related validity are relevant to the evaluation of screening measures. It is important to understand the meaning of the constructs being measured by the screening instrument and to establish the way in which the measure relates to current and future functioning. However, the issues that arise in this connection are similar to those observed with placement and referral decisions and they are discussed in connection with that topic in the next section.

There are advantages and disadvantages of screening assessments. Two related advantages may be identified. The first relates to the economy associated with the use of the relatively simple instruments generally employed in the procedures. The use of self-report measures and brief clinical interviews in clinical settings is considerably less expensive than intensive psychological assessments. Similarly, in educational settings the use of group testing for initial screening purposes is often more feasible than mass assessment with individual assessment instruments. The second advantage is that the use of the relatively inexpensive screening procedures enables us to assess larger numbers of individuals. This is particularly important in light of the frequent finding that large numbers of individuals with pathological conditions are never assessed or treated.

The major drawback associated with screening procedures relates to the limits on reliability and validity associated with their use. The psychometric properties of these measures are usually weaker than those associated with more intensive psychological assessments. The extent to which this represents a drawback depends partly on the actual reliability and validity of the screening devices but also on the uses being made of them. The real problem often arises in connection with the identification of false negatives; that is, with those individuals identified on the basis of the screening as not requiring further assessment but who do in fact exhibit the conditions in question. This issue is addressed further in the next section.

### Referral and Placement

Psychological assessments are also widely used in educational, organizational, community, and clinical settings as a basis for referral and placement decisions. As an illustration of the extent to which this type of decision is involved in educational institutions, Salvia and Ysseldyke (1991) identified 29 separate categories of exceptionality utilized in the

different states with examples including autism, mental retardation, behavioral impairment, and a range of physical handicaps. Most states have
also established guidelines for the diagnosis of the conditions and standardized psychological tests are nearly always involved in the decision
process.

Referral and placement decisions are also made in community contexts
and psychological assessments often play important roles in these cases.
These decisions have to do with the placement of children into institutional settings such as foster homes or hospitals and with decisions regarding youthful offenders. Hoge and Andrews (1996b), for example,
discussed the importance of psychological assessments in determining
appropriate dispositions for youths convicted of crimes.

The criteria for referral and placement decisions are sometimes explicit,
but in other cases there is considerable ambiguity associated with the
criteria. Some educational jurisdictions, for example, have very explicit
guidelines regarding the identification and placement of academically
exceptional students, whether gifted or developmentally delayed, whereas
in other jurisdictions there is considerable latitude regarding the definitions of these categories (see Hoge, 1988, 1989; Sattler, 1992). Further, in
some cases the assessment instruments to be employed are specified. More
often, however, the choice of assessments is left open. For example,
although the Education for All Handicapped Children Act of 1975 (Public
Law 944-142) specifies that eligibility decisions under that act must be
made by teams of professionals, it does not specify which assessment
tools are appropriate. Osborne (1996) discussed some of the legal issues
arising from applications of eligibility criteria.

A key argument of this book is that decision processes are improved
with the use of standardized psychological assessments, and this is true
of referral and placement decisions. Very often in the past these decisions
have been based on informal and unsystematic assessments, and many
cases of inequitable and unfair treatment of adolescents have been documented. This is probably less true today because we are somewhat more
sensitive to ethical and professional issues, but there are still cases in
which important decisions about young people are being made through
inadequate procedures.

In using psychological assessments for making these referral and placement decisions it is necessary to attend to the reliability and validity of
the measures. Both construct and criterion-related validity are of particular concern in these situations.

Construct validity is important in two senses. First, the better our
understanding of the measures, the more meaningful our referrals or
placements will be. For example, if we fail to understand just what is being
measured by the battery of instruments being used to assess learning

disability, the placements we make with that battery are not going to be very meaningful. If, on the other hand, we are able to identify the precise areas of disability being identified, then we will be able to provide a more meaningful referral.

Construct validity is also important for justifying our referral or placement decisions. This is particularly important because a labeling process is so often associated with these decisions. Thus, the children are being labeled developmentally delayed, seriously emotionally disturbed, attention deficit disordered, or at high risk for conduct disorder. We are dealing, in other words, with very powerful decisions and labels, and we must be able to show how our assessments are linked with them. If a child is going to be labeled developmentally delayed on the basis of a set of standardized tests, then we should be able to demonstrate how scores from those measures represent the retardation. Because referral and placement decisions involve actual consequences for the youth, Messick's (1980, 1989a) concept of the evidential basis of test interpretation is also relevant. This is, as we saw in chapter 4, the notion that we should be able to demonstrate the relevance of our assessment instruments for the actual use made of them.

Instruments used for referral and placement purposes must also be evaluated in terms of their criterion-related validity. Predictive validity is of particular concern because so often the placements are based on an assumption that a condition exists that, unless intervention is introduced, will be associated with later problems. Two examples of this type of reasoning are presented.

Young people in trouble with the law are sometimes assessed for risk for future conduct problems. Those identified at high risk are then placed in special intervention programs designed to address their needs and prevent the appearance of the problem. The assumption is that, in the absence of intervention, high risk scores are associated with future problems. Consider a second example. Young people are sometimes assessed to identify those with high academic potential. Those so identified are then placed in special enriched or gifted programs. The assumption underlying the assessment is that those so identified will do well in the special programs and, in fact, will perform better there than had they remained in the regular program. Conversely, it is assumed that those identified on the basis of the assessment as of lower potential would not do well if placed in the special program.

The assumptions in both of these examples would be assessed through predictive validity procedures. We saw in chapter 4 that there are a variety of ways of evaluating criterion-related validity, but those procedures based on decision accuracy analyses are most relevant to referral, placement, and screening decisions.

The goal, of course, is to employ assessment tools that maximize the number of correct decisions (true positives and true negatives) relative to the number of incorrect decisions (false positives and false negatives). Both types of incorrect decisions are undesirable, although the relative costs of the two will vary with the situation. False positives are costly because they may lead to the delivery of services to individuals who do not require the intervention. The false negatives are costly because services may be denied to those who truly need the intervention.

A particular problem encountered in the case of referral, placement, and screening decisions is that we are often dealing with phenomena with low base rates, and this sometimes distorts the validity evaluations. For example, the rate of serious violent crimes on the part of young people is actually quite low, meaning that any assessment designed to identify youth at high risk for violent crime is going to exhibit a high rate of false positives (i.e., youths identified at risk but not exhibiting the criminal activity).

There are, as we saw in chapter 4, other problems associated with establishing the construct and criterion-related validity of psychological assessments. Still, a basic premise of this book is that standardized psychological assessments provide a better basis for these decisions than the informal and unsystematic procedures sometimes encountered in these situations. Further, the benefits associated with the improved decisions will in most cases compensate for the added costs associated with the assessments.

## Treatment and Instructional Planning

Referral and placement decisions often have implications for the services to be supplied the client. However, it is also useful to consider the role of assessments in creating specific guides for treatment in clinical and educational settings. The issue is discussed in connection with treatment planning in clinical and counseling contexts, but many of the points also apply to the planning of instructional strategies in educational settings.

There are two basic questions in treatment planning: (a) Should services be provided, and (b) what type of intervention is appropriate? Answers to these questions depend in part on the types of interventions available to the agency or service dealing with the client. They also depend, though, on characteristics of the client and his or her circumstances and on the assumptions made about the best way of addressing the problems identified. The latter issue is beyond the scope of this book (see Arkowitz, 1992; Beutler & Clarkin, 1990; Beutler et al., 1994), but the assessment of client characteristics is of direct concern.

The discussion in chapter 2 concluded with the statement that the personality and behavior of the individual is affected by a complex set of interacting factors. A similar point was reflected in the model of intervention effects presented in chapter 3. It was argued in the latter case that the impact of any treatment program depends on interacting factors represented in situational, client, therapist, program, and process factors. It follows from these considerations that decisions about treatment should take into account a broad range of client characteristics and circumstances. This notion is related to the concepts of differential therapeutics and systematic treatment selection (Beutler & Clarkin, 1990; Beutler et al., 1994; Frances, Clarkin, & Perry, 1984).

Andrews, Bonta, and Hoge (1990) conceptualized these assessment requirements in terms of the concepts of risk, need, and responsivity. The risk factor refers to the severity of the problem identified. Decisions about whether or not to offer services and about the intensity of services offered will depend on the level of risk identified. For example, cases of mild, situational depression generally call for minimal or no intervention, whereas an assessment of an immanent risk for suicide would, of course, call for immediate and intensive services.

The need factor refers to the actual service requirements of the client. This would include the personality, behavioral, or other disorders being brought to the clinical setting. It also includes, to use Beutler et al.'s (1994) terminology, problem complexity and the stage of change exhibited by the client. There are also cases where the external circumstances of the client may be recognized as need factors. If, for example, conflicts with parents are part of the presenting disorder, then parenting may be included as a need factor.

Responsivity factors refer to characteristics of the client relevant to his or her responsiveness to different types of treatment. Resistance potential and coping style are two such factors identified by Beutler et al. (1994). Other features of the client that may be relevant include intelligence, literacy, cognitive style, or cultural attitudes. These are all factors that may have a bearing on the way in which the client responds to a particular treatment.

The assessment of what I am calling risk, need, and responsivity factors has often depended on clinical judgments. This is certainly the case in clinical settings where intake assessments have traditionally depended on unstructured interviews and informal observations conducted by the clinician. We know, however, that the reliability and validity of these informal procedures is questionable, and the argument presented here is that both treatment and instructional planning decisions would be improved through the use of standardized psychological instruments and, where available, structured diagnostic procedures.

The entire range of instruments and procedures to be reviewed in subsequent chapters is relevant to these assessments, but there are some cases where instruments have been specifically adapted to yield treatment guidelines (see Beutler et al., 1994). An example is the MMPI–A, which links identified pathological conditions with specific treatments. Similarly, some of the behavioral and cognitive-behavioral measures provide more or less explicit guidelines for intervention.

Reliability, construct validity, and criterion-related validity are all relevant to the evaluation of instruments employed in planning treatment and instructional interventions. Treatment validity is also important to evaluating the relevance of these instruments because we will often employ them to evaluate the progress of therapy.

There remains, of course, the issue of the means for incorporating the standardized psychological assessments into the therapeutic process. There is sometimes resistance on the part of professionals to utilize tests or other standardized instruments, part of which likely arises from a common tendency of professionals to overestimate their clinical skills. Partly, though, the resistance relates to more justified fears that these instruments may interfere with the therapist–client relationship or may undercut the decision-making authority of the therapist or counselor. However, neither of these are necessary consequences of using standardized assessments, and, as I show in greater detail later, there are ways of incorporating the assessments into the clinical process that benefit both therapist and client.

### Outcome Evaluation

We saw in chapter 4 that psychological assessments play an important role in program evaluation research. These are studies in which an effort is made to evaluate the actual impact of instructional, therapeutic, or counseling interventions. These program evaluation studies are important for (a) effecting improvements in the programs, (b) ensuring that organizational resources are used effectively, and (c) justifying the programs to funders.

The model of program impact presented in chapter 3 identified two sets of outcomes, immediate and ultimate, with the former collected soon after delivery of the service and the latter evaluating longer term effects of the program. However, assessment needs are similar in the two cases.

One concern is with the extent to which the intervention effected improvements in the presenting problem. Did the tutoring correct the reading processing problem? Did the therapy reduce the adolescent's level of depression? This evaluation is often accomplished by readministering the assessment instruments utilized at intake. For example, the Beck Depression Inventory might be administered at intake and again following therapy, and changes in scores might be used as a basis for evaluating the effectiveness of the intervention. Many of the instruments we explore in the following chapters are appropriate for evaluating client change variables.

We are often also concerned with the clients' reactions to the intervention. Were they satisfied with the services offered? Do they feel that they benefited from the intervention? Some efforts have been made to develop standardized measures of satisfaction (e.g., Attkinson, Roberts, & Pascoe, 1983), but relatively few efforts have been made to develop such instruments specifically for use with adolescents.

The impact of programs on clients' satisfaction with service and the specific problem bringing them for service are important, but we are generally also interested in the effects of the intervention on the broader functioning of the individual. To illustrate, the immediate goal of an educational intervention designed to address a deficiency in processing written information is to improve the youth's processing capacities in that area; the broader goal, though, is to improve the student's overall academic performance. Similarly, the immediate goal of a cognitive-behavior modification program might be to replace an adolescent's antisocial attitudes with more prosocial attitudes. The broader goal, though, is to ensure a better social adjustment for that individual, and to steer him or her away from antisocial behaviors.

We have a variety of means available for evaluating the broader impacts of the interventions. In the case of academic performance we can access truancy and dropout rates, teacher ratings of adjustment and performance, academic achievement test scores, and so on. Success in finding a job and indexes of performance on the job may also be relevant. The impact on social adjustment might be assessed through parent ratings of adjustment, observations of parent–adolescent interactions, or indexes of criminal activity. All of these would represent efforts to assess the broader impact of the intervention on the individual's functioning.

Three other types of measures are relevant to the broader impact of the interventions. These include measures of social competence, self-esteem, and well-being. Instruments within these groups are all designed to assess very broad aspects of the individual's social functioning and feelings of self-worth, and, as such, represent important elements of a program evaluation effort. Examples of these instruments relevant to assessment in these categories are presented in later chapters.

Reliability and construct validity represent important considerations in selecting instruments for outcome assessments. Also of particular importance are specialized forms of criterion-related validity, particularly treatment validity. This would be demonstrated, for example, through evidence that the Beck Depression Inventory is capable of detecting changes in depression levels resulting from an intervention.

## CONTEXTS OF ASSESSMENTS

The basic nature of assessment activities is relatively constant, but some variations may be observed as they are applied in different contexts. I consider five in this section: educational, medical, clinical and counseling, organizational, and forensic. Professional and ethical issues arising in these contexts are discussed later.

### Educational Contexts

Discussions by Salvia and Ysseldyke (1991) reveal the wide range of assessment and decision activities involved in educational settings. There are, first, decisions relating to special educational placements: opportunity classes for the developmentally delayed, enrichment classes for the intellectually exceptional, programs for emotionally disturbed students, and classes for the learning disabled are some examples of the many types of special settings available in the schools. Second, and where the youth has been judged as requiring some sort of intervention, there are decisions to be made about the nature of the intervention to be provided. These treatment or instructional interventions may focus on emotional or behavioral disorders, problems of academic performance, career guidance, or any of the other myriad types of services provided to young people in the school setting.

Some of these referral, placement, and treatment decisions are institutionalized either through school policy or external regulations, and these generally involve formalized assessment procedures. There are, on the other hand, a number of decisions made at the level of the classroom or school that depend on informal and unstructured assessment procedures conducted by the classroom teacher or educational administrator. Our argument, again, is that the quality of these decisions would nearly always be improved through the use of more systematic assessments.

Psychologists are not the only professionals involved in conducting psychological assessments in the schools, but they are the primary deliverers of such services. Three general points should be kept in mind in considering their activities. First, the conduct of assessments usually forms only one part of the school psychologist's responsibilities, and the assessments must be integrated into his or her larger role. Second, the conduct of assessments will often be guided by policies or guidelines specific to the school or board within which the psychologist is working. Third, the school psychologist must be continually aware of the impact of his or her activities on the students they are serving, the youths' parents, teachers, principals, and other professionals working within the school. This often presents real challenges for the school psychologists.

## Medical Settings

Psychologists have come to play an expanding role in hospital and other medical settings (see McManus & Richards, 1992; Roberts, Koocher, Routh, & Willis, 1993; Rozensky, Sweet, & Tovian, 1997), and this has involved an expanded role in the conduct of psychological assessments as adjuncts to medical treatment. Assessments of pain, stress, health attitudes, and personality factors associated with illness are some areas of current interest. In addition, neuropsychological assessments performed by psychologists have come to assume an increasingly important role in the diagnosis and treatment of head injuries. As Rozensky et al. (1997) showed, special demands are often made on the psychologist conducting assessments in medical settings. In many cases the psychologist is working as a consultant to a physician or psychiatrist. Communicating assessment results to these professionals and developing a workable professional relationship often require special skills. Although not primarily concerned with medically relevant assessments, many of the tools and procedures to be reviewed in succeeding chapters do have relevance in this context.

## Clinical and Counseling Contexts

Psychological assessments have, of course, always played an important role in the provision of psychological treatments, whether provided in institutions, community clinics, or psychologists' offices. Decisions about whether or not to offer services, and, if so, what type of service to offer depend on assessments of the client and his or her circumstances. Treatment planning assessments are the most important ones, but screening and outcome assessments also have roles to play. Unfortunately, these assessments have generally been based on informal and unstructured procedures, and it is hoped that this volume will encourage the introduction of standardized assessments into these contexts.

## Organizational Settings

The reference in this case is to the use of psychological assessments for selection and placement decisions in organizational settings. Decisions about whether or not to hire an individual for a job, where to place him or her in the organization, and, under some circumstances, whether to retain him or her, depend on assessments of the characteristics and performance levels of the individual. There is an extensive literature on issues in personnel selection and placement (see, e.g., Murphy & Davidshofer, 1994; Riggio & Porter, 1996), but the assessment principles that apply there are no different than those represented in any other decision area.

**Forensic Contexts**

There are a wide range of legal decisions affecting adolescents that involve assessment activities in one form or another. One involves the treatment of criminal activity on the part of young people. Hoge and Andrews (1996b) discussed the various types of assessment and decision activities that may occur with the processing of adolescents in juvenile justice and correctional systems. Competency to stand trial, risk of reoffending, and need for treatment are just three examples of the types of assessments common in these settings.

There are other forms of legal processing affecting young people that may also involve psychological assessments. Removal of the youth from home for protection purposes, commitments to mental health facilities, or designations of mental incapacity are three examples of decisions requiring assessments of the youth and his or her situation. These assessments are also sometimes important in custody conflicts involving adolescents. Melton, Petrila, Poythress, and Slobogin (1987), R. Rogers and Mitchell (1991), and Swenson (1993) provided useful discussions of assessment issues as they arise in this context.

## PROFESSIONAL AND ETHICAL ISSUES

We have seen that assessment activities are often associated with important decisions about individuals. The establishment and monitoring of these activities assumes, then, considerable importance. Relevant issues are discussed here under three headings: standards for the conduct of assessments, regulating the profession, and ethical issues relating to assessments.

**Standards for Assessment**

Considerable efforts have been made to develop standards for the development and application of assessment tools. Many of these standards have been developed with specific reference to psychological tests, but generally they apply to all types of assessment tools and procedures.

Table 5.1 presents an outline of the major sources of guidelines and standards relevant to the conduct of psychological assessments. The most important of these from the point of view of professional influence and comprehensiveness of content are the *Standards of Educational and Psychological Testing* (American Psychological Association, 1985) and the *Ethical Principles of Psychologists and Code of Conduct* (American Psychological Association, 1992). These documents provide rigorous guidelines regard-

TABLE 5.1
Major U.S. and Canadian Sources of Guidelines and Standards
Relevant to the Conduct of Psychological Assessments

*Code of Fair Testing Practices in Education* (American Psychological Association, 1988)
*Standards for Educational and Psychological Testing* (American Psychological Association, 1985)
*A Canadian Code of Ethics for Psychologists* (Canadian Psychological Association, 1991)
*Ethical Guidelines for Forensic Psychology* (American Psychological Association, 1991)
*Guidelines for Educational and Psychological Testing* (Canadian Psychological Association, 1987)
*Guidelines for Child Custody Evaluations in Divorce Proceedings* (American Psychological Association, 1994)
*Ethical Principles of Psychologists and Code of Conduct* (American Psychological Association, 1992)
*Record Keeping Guidelines* (American Psychological Association, 1993)
*Guidelines for Computer-Based Tests and Interpretations* (American Psychological Association, 1986)

ing the construction, application, and interpretation of psychological assessments. The major sections of the *Standards of Educational and Psychological Testing* are outlined in Table 5.2. However, the *Standards* do not reflect the most recent developments in psychometrics or assessment ethics and are now undergoing a revision.

Efforts have also been made to develop standards for the distribution of tests and other assessment tools (American Psychological Association, 1954). Three classes of instruments are identified (Levels A, B, and C), varying in level of expertise required for administration and interpretation. These are outlined in Table 5.3. Test publishers and other distributors

TABLE 5.2
Outline of the Standards for Educational and Psychological Testing

Part I: Technical standards for test construction and evaluation
Standards relating to validity, reliability, test construction, scaling, and normative data are presented. The section also includes guidelines regarding information to be included in manuals and user guides.
Part II: Professional standards for test use
This section includes very detailed standards regarding the actual application of assessments. It includes statements about the qualifications of assessors and specific guidelines for the administration and interpretation of assessments. Recommendations regarding the use of assessments within specific settings (e.g., schools, organizations) are also presented.
Part III: Standards for particular applications
Guidelines regarding the use of assessment tools with linguistic minorities and handicapped individuals are presented in this section.
Part IV: Standards for administrative practice
Ethical issues relating to informed consent, confidentiality, labeling, and the sharing of assessment information are considered in this final section of the Standards.

*Note.* Based on American Psychological Association (1985). *Standards for educational and psychological testing.* Washington, DC: Author.

TABLE 5.3
Levels of Test Complexity

---

Level A

  This includes tests and other assessment instruments that require no special training or expertise beyond reading a manual. Many paper-and-pencil tests of interests, attitudes, and achievement fall within this category. These instruments may be administered and scored by teachers, educational administrators, human resource personnel, or other such professionals.

Level B

  Instruments within this category require a background in psychology or related discipline and training in statistics and psychological assessment. A minimum of a master's-level degree in psychology or education with relevant training in assessment is usually required, although other professionals may utilize the instruments with special training. Many aptitude, achievement, and personality tests fall within this category.

Level C

  This category includes measures requiring an intensive grounding in assessment technology and special training in administering the instrument in question. A minimum of a master's-level degree in psychology or education is generally required, although a PhD and licensure or certification by a relevant professional body might also be required. A PhD or equivalent is generally required. Individual intelligence tests, projective tests, and neuropsychological batteries fall within this group.

---

of assessment material are asked to consider this in making instruments available. There is, however, some question about the effectiveness of these regulations (Fremer, Diamond, & Camara, 1989; Oles & Davis, 1977). I return to this issue in chapter 12.

Finally, standards and guidelines relating to psychological assessments are in the process of emerging from legislative activities relating to assessments and from the considerable litigation that has been associated with these tools, particularly in the United States (see Bersoff, 1995; Osborne, 1996). These actions eventually become incorporated into assessment standards, although there is sometimes a considerable lag before that happens. In any case, practitioners in educational, clinical, and counseling settings are advised to remain current regarding legal developments within their areas of practice.

## Professional Regulation

The establishment of standards and guidelines for assessment is one issue; the other side of the coin is the enforcement of those standards. The application of legal remedies constitutes, of course, one way in which these activities are regulated. Beyond this level, however, regulation becomes problematic because different professional groups are involved in the conduct of assessments.

Psychiatrists, social workers, human resource personnel, nurses, child-care workers and other professional groups may, under some circumstances, conduct psychological assessments. The psychology profession has no direct control over their activities, but we do have the means for regulating our own activities, and the acceptance of the psychological profession depends very directly on our capacity to do this.

There are two levels of regulation that apply to the psychology profession. The first is through nonregulatory, voluntary bodies. The most important of these are the national groups such as the American, Canadian, and British Psychological Associations. Smaller groups include the various state associations and specialized groups such as the National Association of School Psychologists and the American Board of Clinical Neuropsychology. All of these organizations have adopted codes of conduct, including standards regarding psychological assessments. Membership in the organizations is voluntary, but members are obligated to observe their ethical standards.

The second level of regulation occurs through regulatory bodies of professional psychologists. These exist on a state level in the United States and provincial level in Canada (Association of State and Provincial Psychology Boards, 1993). These are created by acts of the state or provincial legislatures and serve to regulate the profession of psychology in the respective jurisdictions. Table 5.4 contains a summary of the typical functions of these regulatory bodies. These constitute the major means for ensuring the ethical conduct of assessments by psychologists.

TABLE 5.4
Functions of Professional Regulatory Bodies

1. Protection of the public served by psychologists from incompetent or unethical practitioners;
2. Determination of entry requirements for registration or licensure of individual psychologists;
3. Development, adoption, monitoring and enforcement of ethics and professional conduct standards to be observed by registered or licensed psychologists;
4. Periodic review of registrants' or licensees' competence to continue to practice as psychologists;
5. Complaint and discipline procedures and enforcement, both with reference to the professional work of registered or licensed psychologists, and to the work of nonpsychologists presenting themselves to their clients as psychologists;
6. Informing the public about the regulation of psychology; and
7. Periodic review and updating of the standards and procedures according to which the profession is regulated by the board.

*Note.* Adapted from "Regulation and Accreditation in Professional Psychology: Facilitators? Safeguards? Threats?," by H. P. Edwards (1994), *Canadian Psychology, 35.*

**Major Ethical Concerns**

The various guidelines and standards outlined in Table 5.1 present detailed information concerning ethical issues arising in connection with the conduct of psychological assessments. The volumes by Bersoff (1995) and Eyde (1993) also provide useful discussions of these issues. Here, I provide a brief introduction to some of the major ethical concerns.

One issue concerns the appropriateness and fairness of the assessments employed in a particular situation. It is important to ensure that instruments and procedures have demonstrable reliability and validity for the individual being assessed and for the purposes for which they are being used. Further, if scores are to be interpreted with reference to normative samples, the samples must be relevant to the individual being assessed. The issue of test bias is a complicated one (see T. B. Rogers, 1995), but it must be considered in any application of an assessment instrument.

Informed consent constitutes another important ethical consideration. Assessment always constitutes some invasion of the individual's privacy. Under most circumstances that invasion is justified only when the individual has freely consented to the action. The capacity to understand the terms of the assessment becomes somewhat complicated in the case of children and adolescents, but in most cases adolescents are considered capable of this understanding, and obtaining their consent (rather than approaching the parent) is generally considered appropriate.

The informed consent procedures must take care to communicate the uses that are to be made of the assessments, and then efforts must be made to ensure that no other uses are made of the information. It would be unethical, for example, for a school to perform an assessment on a youth for purposes of assignment to a special class and then later release the assessment information to a juvenile court for use in a predisposition hearing.

Ownership of the assessment data and the conditions under which information can be released are another issue. This problem often takes the form of conflicts over the release of raw data on which the final assessment report is based. Parents, for example, often request access to such data. In some jurisdictions there are laws governing this type of issue, but the issue is best dealt with by establishing clear rules regarding the release of data and by ensuring that those rules are communicated before the assessment commences.

Another type of ethical issue concerns the use of assessment tools by individuals unqualified to administer and interpret the instruments. Unfortunately, there is considerable anecdotal support for the view that tests and other assessment devices are being employed by unqualified individuals. There is little that psychologists can do to control the use of these tools by nonpsychologists, but it is important that we make continuing efforts to ensure competent use of assessments by psychologists.

A more general ethical (and moral) issue that confronts psychologists carrying out assessments concerns the focus of their responsibility. Is the school psychologist primarily responsible to the youth being assessed or to his or her school employer? Is the forensic psychologist conducting an assessment of a youthful offender primarily responsible for protecting the interests of the youth or does he or she have primary responsibility to the court? In many cases there is no real conflict, but in other cases serious ethical dilemmas arise and must be addressed in a responsible manner.

These important ethical issues are discussed in greater detail in the references cited earlier. A useful summary of the issues has also been presented by T. B. Rogers (1995), who expressed them as a Bill of Rights for Test Takers, outlined in Table 5.5.

## PRACTICAL CONSIDERATIONS

The quality of decisions made about adolescents depends greatly on the reliability and validity of the assessments on which they are based. The

TABLE 5.5
Bill of Rights for Test Takers

---

1. *Respect and Dignity.* Test takers must be treated with dignity and respect.

2. *Fairness.* All tests and uses of test data related to individual test takers must be demonstrably fair to the test taker.

3. *Informed Consent.* Test takers must have the explicit opportunity to accede to testing with a clear knowledge of what will happen. They must also have the right to refuse participation.

4. *Explanation of Test Results.* Test takers must receive an appropriate explanation of the outcome of the testing event.

5. *Confidentiality.* Test takers must be guaranteed that their testing results will not be made available, intentionally or otherwise, to other parties, unless they give their explicit permission.

6. *Professional Competence.* Test takers have the right to expect optimal competence on the part of test users with whom they come into contact.

7. *Least Stigmatizing Labels.* When reporting test results includes assignment of the test taker to categories, the category label with the least negative connotations, consistent with accurate reporting, must be used.

8. *Members of Linguistic Minority Communities.* Test takers from linguistic minority communities, whose proficiency in a majority language is weak, must be tested with instruments whose reliability, validity, or utility are not compromised by majority language performance.

9. *Disabled Persons.* Persons with disabilities must be tested with instruments that have been properly designed and validated on the disabled population to which the test taker belongs.

---

*Note.* Adapted from *The Psychological Testing Enterprise: An Introduction* by T. B. Rogers (1995), Pacific Grove, CA: Brooks/Cole. Reproduced with permission.

quality of the assessments depends, in turn, on the care with which they are conducted and interpreted. A number of practical issues relating to the conduct of assessments are considered in this section.

### Professional Competence

The importance of training and experience in the conduct of assessments cannot be overemphasized:

> Tests and other assessment procedures are powerful tools, but their effectiveness will depend on your skill and knowledge. When wisely and cautiously used, assessment procedures can assist you in helping children, parents, teachers, and other professionals obtain valuable insights. When used inappropriately, they can mislead those who must make important life decisions, thus causing harm and grief. (Sattler, 1992, p. 5)

Unfortunately, there are cases in which children and adolescents have been harmed because of assessments conducted by unqualified individuals.

The level of knowledge and expertise required for conducting assessments varies widely. Some instruments are relatively simple to administer and interpret, including some of the behavioral rating scales, checklists, and some group achievement tests that are designed for use by classroom teachers. Even in these cases, however, some elementary knowledge about psychological measurement is important.

Many other assessment tools require higher levels of expertise. The administration, scoring, and interpretation of instruments such as the WISC, the MMPI, and the Vineland Adaptive Behavior Scales call for specialized training. As described earlier in the chapter, efforts have been made to categorize instruments according to the degree of expertise required for their administration (see Table 5.3) and it is extremely important that those guidelines be followed in assessment situations.

Competence in administering individual assessment instruments is, however, only one aspect of the issue. The conduct of assessments and diagnoses with adolescents requires knowledge and expertise in a number of other areas as well.

A thorough grounding in measurement theory is essential. This should include a knowledge of basic principles of measurement, psychometric theory, behavioral assessment, and test construction. Significant methodological advances are taking place in these areas, and professionals involved in the conduct of assessments should be capable of following those developments. Unfortunately, as Aiken, West, Sechrest, and Reno (1990), Byrne (1996b), and Meier (1993) pointed out, graduate training in psychology often does not offer a firm grounding in these areas. This represents a serious handicap for many of those involved in the conduct of assessments.

A background in the literature on both normal and pathological adolescent development is also essential for the conduct of adolescent assessments. Valid judgments about the characteristics of an adolescent must be grounded in an understanding of the dynamics of development. Also required is an understanding of the dynamics of the particular situation in which the assessment is to be conducted. Thus, the conduct of assessments in school, clinical, community, medical, or forensic settings requires a thorough understanding of the functioning of adolescents in those environments. Working with special groups such as those with physical handicaps, the developmentally delayed, or culturally unassimilated may also require special training.

Both nonregulatory bodies such as the American Psychological Association and the legally mandated regulatory bodies existing in the various states and provinces play an important role in ensuring that psychologists demonstrate the qualifications and expertise to engage in assessment activities. The move toward the establishment of specialty designations is also an important development in this respect and should bolster the effort to enforce high standards in the provision of psychological services.

### Selecting Assessment Tools

There are a number of criteria to be observed in selecting instruments. First, the instruments must be relevant to the purposes of the assessment. For example, the MMPI is of little utility when the primary concern is establishing the cognitive competence of the youth, and an intelligence scale would be of little value in attempts to assess anger management skills. Unfortunately, we often encounter situations in which inappropriate instruments are used, sometimes because of ignorance and sometimes laziness.

Many assessment situations will call for more than one assessment tool. For example, efforts to assess aptitudes for gifted programs might involve individual intelligence and achievement tests, a personality test, and teacher ratings of attitudes and motivation. In some cases a decision will be made to include multiple measures of the same construct. For example, in assessing emotional pathology, measures are sometimes collected from the adolescent, parents, and teachers. The complex issues involved in combining data from multiple sources have been discussed by Achenbach (1995), Bird, Gould, and Staghezza (1992), and Lanyon and Goodstein (1997) and are considered again later in this book.

The second criterion is whether the instrument is appropriate for the individual being assessed. This is established by determining the adequacy of normative, reliability, and validity data. This depends in part on the age of the youth. If the instrument is being administered to a 15-year-old, then we must establish that adequate normative data for that age group are available and that reliability and validity have been established for that level. However, age is not the only consideration. Adolescents with physical or mental handicaps or from special circumstances often require special assessment tools. Normative data for the standard individual intelligence tests may, for example, be inappropriate for children with disabled motor functioning. Similarly, reliability and validity information for a delinquency risk instrument collected from a sample of adolescent boys may not generalize to a sample of girls. The issues of generalizing normative, reliability, and validity data are serious ones, and those involved in applied assessment must be continually sensitive to them (see Hunter & Schmidt, 1990).

There are two other criteria to consider in evaluating the suitability of measures. The first concerns the costs of the material and their administration. Psychological services are sometimes expensive and must be weighed against potential benefits. The concept of incremental validity introduced in chapter 4 is relevant. It is important in many cases to establish that new instruments or procedures actually represent improvements over existing practices. The second criteria concerns the consistency of the instruments with the values and objectives of the organization and their acceptability to the adolescents and their parents are also important considerations.

There are a number of sources of information regarding assessment tools and practitioners should be familiar with these. Catalogs provided by commercial test publishers constitute one source of information. However, these do not always represent the most objective source of information, and they should be used with some caution.

Table 5.6 identifies some of the more objective sources of information about psychological measures. One category includes journals such as *Psychological Assessment*, which provide the most current data regarding instruments. The various handbooks and reference tools such as *The Mental Measurement Yearbook* and *Test Critiques* series also represent invaluable sources of information. There are also an increasing number of Internet sites providing information about assessment issues and tools. The American Psychological Association's testing site is one example (http://www.apa.org/science/test.html).

*Conducting the Assessment.* There are three important practical issues to be raised with respect to the actual conduct of the assessment. The first concerns preparation. It is extremely important that the examiner enter the situation with all of the materials necessary to conduct the assessment

TABLE 5.6

Major Sources of Information About Psychological Assessments

Texts and Handbooks

  *A Consumers' Guide to Tests in Print* (2nd ed.; Hammill, Brown, & Bryant, 1992)

  *Assessment of Children* (3rd ed.; Sattler, 1992)

  *Computer Use in Psychology: A Directory of Software* (Stoloff & Couch, 1992)

  *Psychological Testing* (9th ed.; Anastasi & Urbina, 1997)

  *Tests and Measurement in Child Development* (O. Johnson, 1976)

  *Test Critiques* (Keyser & Sweetland, 1994)

  *Tests* (3rd ed., Sweetland & Keyser, 1991)

  *12th Mental Measurements Yearbook* (Conoley & Impara, 1995)

Journals

  *Adolescence*

  *Applied Psychological Measurement*

  *Assessment*

  *Educational and Psychological Measurement*

  *Journal of Abnormal Child Psychology*

  *Journal of Clinical Psychology*

  *Journal of Consulting and Clinical Psychology*

  *Journal of Educational Measurement*

  *Journal of Personality Assessment*

  *Journal of Psychoeducational Assessment*

  *Journal of Research on Adolescence*

  *Journal of Youth and Adolescence*

  *Psychological Assessment*

and with the capacity to administer the instruments in an efficient manner. This is important because the utility of standardized psychological assessments depends very directly on a consistent administration of the instruments. Departures from standard procedure may render the results meaningless. It is also important because inefficient administration of the materials may interfere with the relationship established with the examinee and somehow distort the information collected from him or her.

The second practical issue concerns the type of rapport established with the examinee, and this is, by general agreement, a critical consideration in the conduct of assessments. There may be therapeutic or counseling situations in which the goal is to observe the examinee under conditions of anger or stress. Generally, however, the intention is to put the examinee at ease and to collect information under the most natural conditions possible.

Anyone with experience working with adolescents knows that establishing a positive relationship is often problematic. Many adolescents will enter an assessment situation with a friendly and cooperative attitude, but there are cases in which the youth's approach is hostile, suspicious, resistant, or withdrawn. These attitudes are often particularly pronounced in young people with serious emotional or behavioral problems. The description of these negative attitudes may, of course, be an important element of the assessment process. On the other hand, the failure to establish at least a working relationship with the youth may interfere with the assessment of other dimensions. For example, it may be very difficult to establish the cognitive capacities of an extremely hostile and uncooperative examinee.

Establishing a working relationship may be very difficult under these circumstances, but there are some rules of conduct to be noted. First, it is important to provide the youth at the beginning of the session with an open and frank review of the goals of the assessment and the procedures to be followed. Second, the examiner should never lose control of the assessment situation, but the youth should be as involved as possible in the process. It should be made clear that the assessment is being conducted for the youth's benefit, and that his or her opinions are important. Third, it is critical that the examiner maintain a calm and, to the extent possible, supportive manner throughout the session. This is not always easy, particularly when faced with attitudes of hostility or indifference or even verbal abuse. Still, the psychologist is a professional and must be expected to behave professionally.

A third practical issue concerns the importance of the careful observation of the young person in the assessment situation. This is important for the conduct of the assessment; signs of frustration, distraction, or fatigue may call for some change in the procedure. The observations may also be important in the formation of the final assessment or diagnosis. Primary dependence should be placed on the standardized assessments, but the informal observations are often important for filling in gaps or suggesting the need for additional assessments.

### Preparation of the Final Report

It is often the case in clinical and counseling situations that the assessment is used only by the individual conducting it. In most applied situations, however, the assessment is conducted for a third party or agency and there is a necessity to prepare a written report of the assessment.

The real challenge in preparing these reports is this: The assessor must provide an accurate summary of the findings and conclusions of the assessment in a language comprehensible to the recipient. This is a challenge because the interpretation of assessment instruments is not always an easy matter, and there are many cautions associated with the interpretations. Communicating the complexities involved in these interpretations to teachers, educational administrators, physicians, juvenile court judges, and other professionals expected to make use of the reports is often very difficult.

The structure of the assessment report, of course, depends on the purpose and nature of the assessment. Some reports will be very brief and straightforward. The school psychologist, for example, will communicate to the teacher the youth's relative standing on a standardized achievement test. Many assessments, however, are complex, requiring the integration of information from a variety of sources. Detailed discussions of the preparation of these reports have been provided by Kellerman and Burry (1997), Sattler (1992), and Tallent (1993), and I do not deal with the issue at length. Some significant issues in report writing, however, are noted.

Comprehensive psychological assessments typically involve a variety of sources of information about the youth: data from official records; impressions gained from the clinical interview and informal observations; information obtained from parents, teachers, and others; and data from standardized psychological instruments. The integration of this information and its translation into conclusions about the examinee generally involves a clinical or judgmental process. As we saw earlier, however, the extent to which clinical judgment is involved may vary, and a basic premise of this book is that the reliability and validity of assessments are enhanced where increased structure is introduced into the process. This may be accomplished in part by utilizing standardized tools as much as possible and placing greater weight on those instruments than on more informal sources of information. There are also ongoing efforts to develop standardized diagnostic procedures for integrating information.

A related issue that arises in connection with the preparation of reports concerns the utilization of computerized scoring and interpretation summaries. I have already addressed this issue and noted some of the serious problems with the uncritical use of these in communicating the results of psychological assessments. A total reliance on these is rarely if ever justified.

The issue of communicating cautions is also very important. As we have seen, there are always limits to interpretations associated with our psychological measures, and these must be acknowledged in the report. It is often necessary, for example, to provide precision ranges for test scores. These are based on reliability values and provide information on the range of scores to be expected with repeated testings. If diagnostic categories or labels are employed in the report, then warnings should be provided about the limits associated with them. Similarly, limits associated with statements involving long-range predictions should be noted. The real challenge, of course, is to communicate these cautions without undermining the credibility of the report. It may also be necessary to stress one of the central points made earlier: Although there are limits associated with the conclusions drawn from standardized psychological assessments, the conclusions are generally more sound than those based on informal and unsystematic assessment efforts.

Communicating assessment results to adolescents or their parents, whether through a written report or otherwise, often presents special challenges. Not only must the psychologist consider the clarity of his or her language, but the psychologist also must consider the potential impact of the revelations on the youth and his or her family. There are no rules to be followed in this respect, but the professional psychologist may be expected to remain sensitive to the issues involved. The necessity for revealing assessment information and the form it might take is a subject of legal or policy guidelines in some jurisdictions.

# III

## ASSESSMENT INSTRUMENTS

# 6

## Measures of Aptitudes
## and Achievement

This chapter focuses on measures of cognitive aptitudes and achievement levels. The term *aptitude* is used broadly in this case to refer to underlying cognitive abilities or capacities, and *achievement* refers to acquired knowledge or skills. It should be understood, though, that the distinction between aptitude and achievement measures is sometimes a fine one, and that all of the measures described are based on acquired competencies. It is also worth noting at the beginning that many of the general and specific aptitude tests refer to themselves as intelligence tests. However, and because of ambiguities associated with the term *intelligence*, there seems to be a move away from that terminology. These are generally referred to in this chapter, then, as aptitude tests.

The instruments reviewed range from individually administered tests of general cognitive aptitudes through more specialized aptitude measures to group tests of academic achievement. These tests perform important roles in educational, clinical, and organizational contexts. Individual tests of general cognitive aptitudes are, for example, widely used in schools for screening, placement, and diagnostic purposes. Similarly, tests of specialized aptitudes and achievement levels are important tools in vocational guidance and personnel selection settings.

The level of expertise required for administering, scoring, and interpreting these measures varies, but most of the tests reviewed in this chapter require a background in psychological assessment and special training in administration. The importance of using these tests with care is emphasized by the fact that they are often used for making diagnoses that may have important implications for the individual being assessed.

Learning disabled, mild developmental delay, gifted, and underachieving are some examples of diagnostic categories or dimensions used in connection with these measures. These diagnoses may in turn be associated with significant decisions for the individual, including referrals to special classes or schools, placement in treatment programs, and recommendations that the youth pursue a particular type of vocation.

The basic premise of this book is that these diagnostic and decision-making processes will be facilitated through the use of standardized psychological assessment tools. On the other hand, there are important cautions to be observed where using these measures. These are discussed further in the final section of this chapter.

The measures of aptitudes and achievement are discussed under the following headings:

- Individual Tests of General Cognitive Aptitudes.
- Group Tests of General Cognitive Aptitudes.
- Specialized Aptitude Measures.
- Vocational Aptitude Tests.
- Measures of Achievement.

The review of measures within those categories is selective, but an effort has been made to include the most widely employed instruments and those that are the object of continuing research and evaluation activity. Aiken (1997), Reynolds and Kamphaus (1990), Sattler (1992), and Sternberg (1994) described additional measures within this category. Tools for assessing neuropsychological functioning are considered in a later chapter.

## INDIVIDUAL TESTS OF GENERAL COGNITIVE APTITUDES

This category includes individually administered tests designed for assessing a broad range of cognitive and academic aptitudes. It includes the instruments traditionally referred to as tests of general intelligence. The five tests to be reviewed are identified in Table 6.1, representing the most widely used of all psychological assessment instruments, and one or the other generally forms a key tool for psychologists engaged in assessment activities, particularly in school settings.

There are some important differences among the five measures, but some commonalities may be noted. These are all individually administered measures that require advanced training in psychological assessment and a period of supervised experience with the instrument. Further,

TABLE 6.1
Individual Tests of General Cognitive Aptitudes

| Measure | Source/Reference |
|---|---|
| Detroit Tests of Learning Aptitude–3 | PRO-ED |
| Kaufman Adolescent and Adult Intelligence Test | American Guidance Service |
| Kaufman Brief Intelligence Test | American Guidance Service |
| Stanford–Binet Intelligence Scale–4 | Riverside Publishing Company |
| Wechsler Intelligence Scale for Children–III | Psychological Corporation |
| Wechsler Adult Intelligence Scale–Revised | |

with the exception of the Kaufman Brief Intelligence Test, administration is time consuming (1–2 hours). The scoring of the instruments is also rather complicated, although this has been considerably simplified with the aid of computer-based scoring procedures.

All of these tests yield scores reflecting overall levels of cognitive ability and scores reflecting aptitudes in specific cognitive areas. These scores, in turn, have been linked through research with a wide range of outcomes. We have data, for example, on the way in which the overall score from the Stanford–Binet Intelligence Scale (4th ed.) is linked with future academic achievement or the way in which patterns of scores on the verbal subscales of the WISC–III are linked with responses to certain treatments for reading disabilities. The psychologist can use the scores, then, for making specific diagnoses and treatment recommendations.

Performance on these measures may also be employed in the wider sense of enabling the tester to assess certain noncognitive dimensions. These include attentional abilities, motivational characteristics, interpersonal skills, and other personality and academic attributes.

## Detroit Tests of Learning Aptitude–Third Edition (DTLA–3)

This represents the third edition of a test first published in 1935; it is a significant revision of the second (1985) version. This individually administered test is appropriate for children and adolescents (6–17 years old).

The DTLA–3 is composed of 11 subtests: Word Opposites, Design Sequences, Sentence Imitation, Reversed Letters, Story Construction, Design Reproduction, Basic Information, Symbolic Relations, Word Sequences, Story Sequences, and Picture Fragments. The subtests are composed of a mixture of verbal and nonverbal items. Unlike most individually administered cognitive ability tests, items are presented sequentially rather than as subscales.

The conversion of raw to standardized scores is based on a sample of 2,587 students considered representative of the U.S. population. A variety of scores may be derived, including 11 scores based on the subscales just described and an overall composite score formed from responses to all of the subscales. The latter represents a measure of general cognitive ability. A variety of other composite scores are also described in the manual, including an optimal level composite. The latter is based on the four highest subtest scores and presumably reflects the individual's cognitive potential.

Even though the manual indicates that the DTLA–3 is appropriate for use by any professional with a background in assessment, administration and scoring are actually quite complicated and high levels of expertise and experience are required for efficient use of the measure. The administration of the measure is also more time consuming than most of the other individually administered instruments (1–2 hours).

Evaluations of the DTLA–3 by Mehrens (1995) and Poteat (1995) note a number of positive and negative points. The instrument is the product of a long period of development and the test and its supporting materials are attractively designed and presented. Although the administration and scoring of the instrument are complicated, guidelines presented in the manual are clear.

The reviewers also noted the wide range of reliability and validity studies reported in the manual. That research provides support for the internal consistency of scores from the measure and also shows that DTLA–3 scores are related to a variety of criteria of academic performance. Some support for the construct validity of the instrument is provided through its correlation with alternative measures of cognitive ability. On the other hand, the reviewers noted that support for test–retest reliability is limited. Further, and although the construct validity of the overall composite score is well supported, factor analytic studies have provided only limited support for the construct validity of the other composite scores. Some other criticisms developed by Mehrens (1995) and Poteat (1995) relate to the adequacy of the standardization sample and inadequate warnings in the manual regarding the level of training required for administering the instrument.

### Kaufman Adolescent and Adult Intelligence Test (KAIT)

This is a relatively recent test with a more thoroughly developed theoretical base than others in this category. The structure and scoring of the test are said to be consistent with theoretical conceptions developed by Piaget, Luria, and Horn and Cattell. In fact, the scoring of the instrument directly reflects Horn and Cattell's (1966) distinction between fluid and crystallized intelligences.

The KAIT is designed for individuals 11 years and older. Administration time ranges from 60 to 90 minutes. The manual provides clear administration and scoring guidelines, but some specialized training is required. The measure is scored in terms of three basic intelligence scales and a set of subscales. The first of the basic scales is labeled Fluid Intelligence, which measures the ability to solve abstract and novel problems. The second scale is labeled Crystallized Intelligence and it assesses the ability to solve problems involving acquired knowledge. These two scales are each composed of three subscales. The third basic score is based on all subscales and is labeled Composite Intelligence. A variety of optional supplementary scales are also available; these provide for the assessment of various dimensions of memory and of mental status.

Recent reviews of the KAIT by Flanagan (1995) and Keith (1995) note a number of positive points. First, the instrument is clearly linked with a theoretical framework and this may be an aid to interpretation. Second, the instrument displays excellent technical properties. Administration and scoring procedures are clearly presented and the standardization sample has been carefully selected. The reliability of the basic scales and the subscales are excellent. One other positive point is that most adolescents and adults find the test interesting and challenging, which is not always the case with the individual IQ tests.

On the other hand, the reviewers did note some cautions respecting the validity of the KAIT scores. Although considerable evidence is presented regarding the content, construct, and criterion-related validities of the measure, questions still remain about the construct validity of the fluid and crystallized intelligence scores and the various subtest scores. The suggestion is that the actual meaning of those scores has not yet been established. Keith (1995) wrote, "The test seems to provide a good measure of general intelligence. It is unclear, however, the extent to which the test measures crystallized, and especially fluid, intelligence" (p. 532). The test is the object of continuing research attention, and it is likely that additional clarification of these issues will emerge.

### Kaufman Brief Intelligence Test (K–BIT)

This individually administered test of general intelligence is appropriate for use with children, adolescents, or adults. Its major features relate to brevity (administration time of 15–30 minutes) and ease of administration and scoring. The manual indicates that the instrument can be used by non-professionals, but some specialized training would be required in this case.

The K–BIT was developed by A. S. Kaufman and N. L. Kaufman (1990) in conjunction with the previously described KAIT, although it is not an actual adaptation of that measure. The K–BIT is primarily designed as a screening instrument. That is, it yields an index of general cognitive functioning that can be used to identify individuals requiring more intensive assessments. For example, it would be useful in the initial identification of adolescents who might benefit from an enriched educational program and to screen individuals who would not benefit from an intervention requiring a high level of abstract problem solving. Because this is a screening instrument, it should not be used as the sole basis for a decision.

The scoring of the K–BIT parallels that of the KAIT in that it yields a composite IQ score and a Vocabulary (crystallized intelligence) and a Matrices (fluid intelligence) score. The scales are composed of a total of 93 items. These scores are also designed to parallel the basic scores yielded by the WISC–III: Full Scale IQ, Verbal IQ, and Performance IQ.

Reviews of the K–BIT by Jirsa (1994), Miller (1995), and J. W. Young (1995) praise the high technical standards observed in developing the test and the accompanying materials. The normative sample is carefully selected, and the reliability of the scales is well established. The reviewers did, however, note some limits with respect to validity. The construct validity of the measure appears adequate when evaluated against alternative measures of general intelligence, but there are few independent evaluations of the meaningfulness of the three basic scales. Further, criterion-related validity information has not been presented for all of the recommended uses of the instrument. To illustrate, there is only limited information on the ability of scores on the measure to predict success in different educational programs (see Prewett, 1992). In sum, the K–BIT can be recommended for situations in which a brief and easily administered intelligence test is required, but the instrument should be used with caution and in association with other sources of information about the client.

**Stanford–Binet Intelligence Scale: Fourth Edition (SBIS:4)**

This represents the most recent version of the original 1916 Stanford–Binet Intelligence Scale. It follows the 1937 and 1960 revisions, but it is presented as an extensively updated version of the earlier editions. The instrument is based on a theory of cognitive functioning that recognizes four levels. The first is a general reasoning factor ($g$), representing a composite of all the areas of cognitive activity assessed. The second level is divided into three factors. The first is labeled *crystallized abilities*, relating to the ability to reason with acquired knowledge and skills. The second factor, labeled *fluid-analytic abilities*, refers to cognitive skills employed to solve novel problems involving abstract or nonverbal material. The third factor is labeled short-term memory. The third level is formed from two scales within the crystallized abilities factor (Verbal Reasoning and Quantitative Reasoning), the Abstract/Visual Reasoning scale under fluid-analytic abilities, and a Short-Term Memory scale. The fourth level is formed from the 15 subscales subsumed under those four scales. The instrument is designed for individual 2 to 23 years old.

Thirteen of the 15 scales are administered to the adolescent age group. Sixty to 90 minutes are usually required to deliver the full test battery. Administration and scoring of the instrument is complicated and requires rather extensive training and experience. Use of the measure is facilitated by the availability of a wide variety of interpretive guides and computer-based scoring protocols.

The scoring of the SBIS:4 is based on a large normative sample newly formed for this edition. The manual describes a variety of types of scores that may be derived from the measure (also see Delaney & Hopkins, 1987; Sattler, 1992). These include a composite score corresponding to the $g$ factor and four factor scores corresponding to third level as just described: verbal reasoning, quantitative reasoning, abstract/visual reasoning, and short-term memory. The pattern of scores (scatter) across the four factor scores is then examined, as is the pattern of subscale scores within each of the factors. A final level of interpretation involves the qualitative analysis of specific responses to items and general observations of the testee's behavior.

Evaluations of the SBIS:4 by Sattler (1992) and Spruill (1987) highlight a number of strengths and weaknesses. Strengths include the fact that this is a highly refined instrument based on a long history and an explicit theoretical foundation. Further, the reliability and criterion-related validity of the instrument are well established. Scores from the measure have, for example, been related to a wide range of educational and occupational performance indexes. Support for construct validity has been obtained by relating scores from the measure to a variety of other measures of cognitive functioning.

The reviewers noted some weaknesses as well. The SBIS:4 is sometimes difficult to administer and score. Further, the tester is given the option of omitting some subtests, and this introduces an arbitrary element that may be undesirable in a standardized test. The normative sample, although adequate in size, apparently overrepresents higher SES cases. An adjustment was made for this in forming the norms, but the adjustment has been questioned (Spruill, 1987). Another problem concerns a lack of comparability of score ranges across the age range. Because of this lack, it is not possible to compare, for example, an individual's SBIS:4 score collected at age 8 with his or her score at age 16. Finally, both Sattler (1992) and Spruill (1987) noted factor analytic studies are not fully supportive of the system of scoring.

The various versions of the Stanford–Binet have proven useful tools in the psychologist's repertoire for many years, and this version has also proven itself a valuable instrument for assessing cognitive functioning in children, adolescents, and adults. As with all measures, however, it must be used with a full awareness of its strengths and weaknesses.

## WISC–III and the Wechsler Adult Intelligence Scale–Revised (WAIS–R)

Two of the tests developed by Wechsler are relevant to the assessment of general cognitive ability in adolescents. The WISC–III was designed for use with youths between 6 and 16 years old and the WAIS–R may be used with those 16 and older. These instruments are similar in format and scoring procedures, and only the WISC–III is described here.

WISC–III represents the 1991 revision of this popular instrument. The measure is composed of six verbal and seven performance subtests. The basic scores yielded by the subtests and the total scale are outlined in Table 6.2. Interpretation of scores usually begins with the Full Scale IQ, Verbal IQ, and Performance IQ scores. Individual subscale scores are then examined. Considerable weight is also placed on discrepancies between Verbal and Performance scores and on the profiles exhibited across those two sets of subscores. A four-factor scoring format is also available. This is based on scores reflecting verbal comprehension, perceptual organization, freedom from distractibility, and processing speed. Discussions of these and other scoring formats are presented in the WISC–III manual and by A. S. Kaufman (1979, 1994) and Sattler (1992). Scoring and interpretation of the test are now considerably simplified with the availability of computer-based scoring and interpretive protocols.

The scoring of the WISC–III is based on a large and representative standardization sample. Gender, age, parental education level, ethnicity, and region were the factors considered in selecting the sample. It is generally recognized that the standardization sample within this revision represents a considerable improvement over the earlier version. Canadian standardization data are also available, as are foreign-language versions

TABLE 6.2
Basic Scale Scores for the Wechsler Intelligence Scale for Children–III

| | |
|---|---|
| Composite scores | |
| Full Scale IQ | |
| Verbal IQ | |
| Performance IQ | |
| Subscales | |
| Verbal Scales | Performance Scales |
| Information | Digit Symbol |
| Similarities | Picture Completion |
| Arithmetic | Block Design |
| Vocabulary | Picture Arrangement |
| Comprehension | Object Assembly |
| Digit Span | |

Note. Based on D. Wechsler (1991). *Wechsler Intelligence Scale for Children–III.* San Antonio, TX: The Psychological Corporation.

of the instrument. Adolescents 17 years and older should be tested with the WAIS–R; that instrument may also be considered for high-functioning younger adolescents.

Braden (1995) and Sandoval (1995) presented reviews of the WISC–III. They noted, first, that the instrument is built on a predecessor, the Wechsler Intelligence Scale for Children–Revised (WISC–R), that demonstrated sound psychometric properties. The various WISC–III scores demonstrate high levels of internal consistency and test–retest stability. This new version also provides data on interrater agreement values for scoring of the subtests. They also noted the considerable body of validity data available for both the current and older versions of the measure. Construct validity is supported through factor analytic studies and data on relations between WISC–III scores and scores from parallel cognitive measures. Criterion-related validity has been established through numerous studies linking WISC–III scores both concurrently and predictively with academic performance indexes and by showing that scores from the test are capable of discriminating among clinical groupings (e.g., learning disabled, gifted, developmentally delayed).

It is generally recognized that the WISC–III represents an improvement of an already strong instrument, but some limitations are noted. Braden (1995) and Little (1992), for example, noted that support for the four-factor structure remains inconsistent and that only limited information exists regarding the treatment validity of the WISC–III scores. There are, in other words, very few data bearing on the ability of the test scores to predict different types of intervention outcomes.

## GROUP TESTS OF GENERAL COGNITIVE APTITUDES

This section contains reviews of four measures of general aptitudes suitable for group and individual administration (see Table 6.3). These tests exhibit two distinguishing features: (a) they require only minimal involvement on the part of the examiner, and (b) scoring is purely objective. The instruments present two general advantages over the individual tests just reviewed. First, they may represent a savings in time and money because they can be administered to more than one individual a time. Most are actually designed for administration to an entire class of students. Second, these measures generally require less expertise to administer and score than the individual tests. In fact, most are suitable for use by classroom teachers, personnel officers, or other such groups without formal training in psychological assessment. They are widely used in educational, counseling, and organizational settings as screening instruments in educational

TABLE 6.3
Group Tests of General Cognitive Aptitudes

| Measure | Source/Reference |
| --- | --- |
| The Cognitive Abilities Test | Riverside Publishing Company |
| Henmon–Nelson Tests of Mental Ability | Riverside Publishing Company |
| Multidimensional Aptitude Battery | Research Psychologist Press/Sigma |
| Shipley Institute of Living Scale–Revised | Western Psychological Services |

planning, career counseling, and personnel selection and they are also widely used in research studies.

These group aptitude tests do have roles to play in these applied assessment contexts, but there are some important cautions to be noted. First, the group testing situation with minimal examiner involvement may represent a handicap for students with motivational or attitudinal problems. Second, the ease with which these tests can be administered and scored sometimes contributes to abuses. Although the tests may be easy to administer, the interpretation and utilization of scores from these measures requires a thorough understanding of the limits associated with standardized assessment tools. Third, the group tests provide only limited information about cognitive functioning. None of these tests provides the breadth of diagnostic information yielded by individual aptitude tests.

These limitations do have implications for the role played by the group tests in assessment situations. Their most important role is as screening devices for the initial identification of individuals meriting more intensive assessments. They are, for example, often used for a preliminary identification of children with exceptional cognitive abilities. Those identified on the basis of the group testing would be subjected to further assessments. Similarly, the group tests are sometimes used for an initial screening of individuals who may not have the capacity to perform certain types of jobs. However, and because of the dangers associated with the use of screening instruments discussed in chapter 5, the group tests should not be used as the sole basis for even these screening decisions.

## The Cognitive Abilities Test (CAT)

The current version of this test represents the fifth revision of an instrument that evolved from the Lorge–Thorndike Intelligence Tests. The CAT represents a multilevel battery that is suitable for students in Grades 3 through 12. It is based in part on the SBIS:4. An important feature of this test is that it has been conormed with two achievement batteries, the Iowa Tests of Basic Skills and the Tests of Achievement and Proficiency. This procedure facilitates explorations of aptitude–achievement correspondence in educational diagnoses.

TABLE 6.4
Subtests of the Cognitive Abilities Test

| Verbal Battery | Quantitative Battery | Nonverbal Battery |
|---|---|---|
| Verbal Classification | Quantitative Relations | Figure Classification |
| Sentence Completion | Number Series | Figure Analogies |
| Verbal Analogies | Equation Building | Figure Analysis |

Note. Based on R. L. Thorndike & E. P. Hagen (1997), *Manual for the Cognitive Abilities Test*. Chicago, IL: Riverside Publishing Company.

Items within the CAT are organized into three batteries and nine subscales. These are identified in Table 6.4. Administration of the subtests is timed, with each of the three batteries requiring about 30 minutes. The manual recommends that testing be spread over 2 days. The test yields verbal, quantitative, and nonverbal scores plus nine subscores. Scores can be expressed as normalized standard scores with a mean of 100 and standard deviation of 16 or as grade percentile ranks. Scoring is based on a large and carefully selected normative sample.

Ansorge (1985) provided a review of an earlier version of the CAT and concluded that reported reliability and validity data indicate satisfactory psychometric properties for the instrument. That conclusion would also apply to the current version. The substantial correlations between CAT and Stanford–Binet scores are particularly noted. The reviewer also called attention to the care taken in eliminating items reflecting any form of cultural bias. Ansorge did, however, note the high correlation among the three battery scores and raised a question about the necessity for administering the full set of subscales.

## Henmon–Nelson Tests of Mental Ability (HNTMA)

This is a carefully constructed and well-standardized test of general academic aptitudes appropriate for either group or individual administration. It is suitable for adolescents between 12 and 18 years old. Administration is highly standardized and requires approximately 30 minutes to complete. The 90 multiple-choice items of the test are divided into three groups: word problems, number problems, and graphical representation. The test yields a single score produced by summing the number of correct responses. This score presumably reflects the individual's overall level of cognitive ability. Standard scores may be expressed in either grade- or age-equivalent terms.

Reviews of the HNTMA by Clark and Gardner (1988) and E. F. Gardner and Slocum (1978) note some significant strengths. The test is carefully constructed and administration and scoring procedures are clearly described in the manual. Satisfactory levels of validity have been established by correlating scores from the measure with scores from individual tests of general aptitudes and with various indexes of academic achievement. On the other hand, some questions have been raised about the adequacy of the reliability assessments as reported in the manual. The major criticism of the instrument relates to the fact that it yields only a single score reflecting general cognitive abilities. This may have some utility in screening and research contexts, but in most cases we are looking for more information about the individual's functioning in a broad range of areas.

## Multidimensional Aptitude Battery (MAB)

This general aptitude test is appropriate for adolescents 16 years and older. It was developed as a parallel measure to the WAIS. Unlike that measure, however, the MAB is appropriate for group administration and is based on an objective scoring format. The MAP items parallel those of the WAIS and the test yields the same set of scores. These include (a) a full-scale IQ score, (b) verbal and performance subscores, and (c) scores for the 10 subscales of the WAIS (e.g., Information, Similarities, Picture Arrangement).

Adequate reliability levels for the various scales are presented in the manual. Support for construct validity is based in part on significant correlations between parallel scores from the MAB and WAIS. This is important because this group instrument is often used in place of an individual aptitude test. A review of the measure by Krieshok and Harrington (1985) stresses the care with which the test has been constructed and the strong evidence of a link with the individual aptitude tests. On the other hand, some questions have been raised regarding the level of language skill required by the measure and the construct validity of the Verbal and Performance subscales (also see Kranzler, 1991; Lee, Wallbrown, & Blaha, 1990).

## Shipley Institute of Living Scale–Revised (SILS–R)

The SILS was originally developed as a measure of cognitive impairment. It has, however, evolved into a group-administered measure of general cognitive aptitudes. It is one of the most easily administered of all of the general cognition measures and requires only about 20 minutes for completion of the full battery. It can be administered in a paper-and-pencil or computer format. The advantages of the latter are that it provides for precise timing of subtests and quick scoring. The test may be used with adolescents 14 years of age and older.

The 60 multiple-choice items of the test are divided into two subtests: Vocabulary and Abstractions. The test yields a total score and subscores for the Vocabulary and Abstractions subtests. The manual provides for the expression of these as age-adjusted *T*-scores. It is also possible to translate the total SILS–R score into a WAIS–R full-scale IQ score.

Evaluations of this measure have been provided by John and Rattan (1992) and R. G. Johnson (1986), who noted that the major strengths of the instrument relate to ease of use and brevity. Also positive is the fact that scores from the SILS–R correlate significantly with WAIS–R scores. This is important because the SILS–R is sometimes used in place of the individual instrument. On the other hand, there is only limited information linking the SILS–R with the WISC–III, the instrument that would normally be used with individuals younger than 16 years old. Other cautions are also stated by the reviewers. SILS–R has a limited floor and ceiling and thus is not appropriate for extremely low- or high-functioning individuals. Further, the instrument is not appropriate for use with examinees with limited or impaired language skills. Finally, although the instrument is easily administered and scored, the interpretation of scores requires a high level of knowledge and expertise in assessment, which is carefully stressed in the manual.

## SPECIALIZED APTITUDE MEASURES

Perusal of the catalogs of test publishers reveals a wide variety of aptitude tests with more specialized application. Some of these are designed for assessing specific cognitive activities such as memory, whereas others are designed for application to special populations. Five specialized tests with particular application to adolescents are described in this section (see Table 6.5). Some of these tests require individual administration, but others are suitable for use with groups.

### Culture Fair Intelligence Test (CFIT)

This is a nonverbal measure of fluid intelligence, or the ability to engage in analytic and reasoning activities with abstract and novel materials. This is a widely used test, particularly for examinees with language or cultural

TABLE 6.5
Specialized Aptitude Measures

| Measure | Source/Reference |
| --- | --- |
| Culture Fair Intelligence Test | Institute for Personality and Ability Testing |
| Peabody Picture Vocabulary Test–Revised | American Guidance Service |
| Raven's Progressive Matrices | The Psychological Corporation |
| Test of Nonverbal Intelligence–3 | PRO-ED |
| Wide Range Assessment of Memory and Learning | Jastak Associates |

deficits. The test was originally designed by Cattell (1940) as a culture-free measure of cognitive aptitudes and is composed of items without any verbal content. However, questions were raised about the extent to which the test was completely free of cultural content, and the name was later changed to Culture Fair Intelligence Test.

Several versions of test are available, but it is Scale 3 that is most appropriate for adolescents (although Scale 2 might be more appropriate for low-functioning adolescents). The scale is composed of four subtests, with each subtest comprising 12 or 13 items. The subtests are labeled Series, Classification, Matrices, and Conditions. All items are free of verbal content. There are actually two forms of the scale, and the examinee can be given either one or both of the forms (administering both probably enhances reliability). Each form requires about 30 minutes for completion, and CFIT may be treated as a timed or untimed test.

Evaluations of the CFIT by Koch (1984) and Stoddard (1994) have stressed the care with which the test has been developed. Reliability values for the measure are adequate and satisfactory levels of validity have been demonstrated in relation to scores from individual aptitude tests and indexes of achievement. On the other hand, the reviewers raised some questions about the adequacy of the normative sample on which scoring is based and the extent to which the instrument is actually free of cultural bias.

### Peabody Picture Vocabulary Test–Revised (PPVT–R)

This is a widely used nonverbal test of receptive vocabulary knowledge designed for assessing the ability to comprehend spoken words. This is a revised version of the original instrument, which was published in 1959. The instrument is used primarily as a screening measure in educational and organizational contexts. The PPVT–R is often used, for example, in screening foreign language speakers for placement in educational programs. It is suitable for the entire age range.

The PPVT–R is extremely simple to administer and score, but it does require individual administration. Examiner instructions are clearly presented in the manual. Scoring is based on a large and representative normative sample, with scores expressed as age or grade equivalent scores. These replace the "mental age" and "intelligence quotient" terms of the earlier edition. Administration of the instrument involves the examiner reading words aloud and the examinee responding by pointing to the picture that best represents the meaning of the word. Administration generally requires from 10 to 20 minutes.

Evaluations of the PPVT–R by Sattler (1992) and Umberger (1985) stress a number of positive features of the instrument. It is very easy to administer and score, and, although it requires individual administration, administration time is very short. Adequate reliability levels have been established for the measure and construct and criterion-related validity have been demonstrated through correlations of PPVT–R scores with Verbal subtests of the WISC–R and achievement indexes. On the other hand, the PPVT–R does not represent a substitute for the general measures of verbal performance. Although the information about receptive vocabulary provided by this measure may be of value for screening and diagnostic purposes, this represents only one aspect of cognitive aptitudes.

### Raven's Progressive Matrices (RPM)

The RPM represents a nonverbal test of reasoning ability suitable for either group or individual administration, used for assessing one component of general intellectual ability, Spearman's $g$ or general factor. The test has been used for many years in assessing general reasoning abilities in individuals with language, auditory, or physical handicaps.

Two forms of the instrument are appropriate for use with adolescents, the Standard Progressive Matrices and Advanced Progressive Matrices. The latter is used with high-functioning individuals. Items within both forms involve solving problems comprised of figural material. Raw scores are expressed in terms of percentile ranks based on updated normative samples.

Adequate levels of reliability have been reported for the various forms of RPM. Significant correlations have also been established between RPM scores and scores from individual tests of intelligence and indexes of academic achievement. Recent reviews of the instrument have been provided by C. J. Mills, Ablard, and Brody (1993) and Sattler (1992). The reviewers noted the care with which the instrument has been conducted and acknowledged that the instrument is of value as a nonverbal measure of reasoning abilities. They also raised some questions, however, about the construct validity of the instrument; it is not entirely clear what aspects of cognitive aptitude are being assessed. It is clear, however, that RPM scores are not equivalent to the abstract reasoning scores yielded by an instrument such as the WISC–III. Gudjonsson (1995) also raised some questions about the comparability of scores yielded by group and individual administrations of the measure.

### Test of Nonverbal Intelligence–3 (TONI–3)

This represents the most recent revision of an established nonverbal and nonmotor measure of general cognitive functioning. The test requires no reading, writing, or speaking on the part of the examinee. Further, instructions are nonverbal; administration is through gesture and panto-mime. The test is therefore appropriate for assessing individuals with impaired auditory, language, or motor functioning or those not fluent in English. For example, it has been widely used in assessing developmen-tally delayed, autistic, and learning-disabled children.

The administration and scoring of the TONI–3 are relatively straight-forward and do not require an extensive background in assessment. The test is presented as suitable for group administration, although this might not be feasible where dealing with individuals with handicaps. Adminis-tration requires about 15 to 20 minutes. Standardized scores are based on a new normative sample formed for the current edition. Scores are ex-pressed as percentiles or as deviation scores with a mean of 100 and standard deviation of 15.

A considerable amount of psychometric information has accumulated for this test. Internal consistency indexes and short-term test–retest coef-ficients are generally in the adequate range. The manual also describes an impressive array of construct and criterion-related validation studies. Reviews of the earlier version of this instrument by Murphy (1992) and Watson (1992) conclude that the instrument is appropriate for use in assessing cognitive functioning in disabled individuals. They cautioned, however, that only a very narrow range of cognitive functioning is being assessed by the instrument and that it is not a substitute for measures providing a broader and more intensive assessment of functioning.

## Wide Range Assessment of Memory and Learning (WRAML)

This instrument was first published in 1990 and remains one of the few standardized tools for assessing memory capacities in children and ado-lescents. Although the test was not based on a particular theory of mem-ory, it is constructed to yield scores reflecting a range of memory functioning, including memory for verbal and visual material, short- and long-term memory, recognition and recall, and the ability to use memory in learning tasks.

The WRAML is composed of nine subtests assessing verbal and visual memory and learning efficiency. Additional scales are available for as-sessing delayed recall of verbal and visual material, sound symbols, and stories. The test must be administered individually. The nine basic subtests can be administered alone as a screening instrument, which requires 10 to 15 minutes. Administration of the entire battery takes about 1 hour.

Administration and scoring procedures are clearly described in the manual. Calculation of standardized scores is straightforward and is based on representative samples of youths between 5 and 17 years old. The instrument yields four basic scores: Verbal Memory, Visual Memory, Learning, and General Memory. The latter is a composite score based on the nine subscales. Separate scores may also be calculated for immediate and delayed recall.

Franzen (1992) reviewed the WRAML and concluded that it represents a useful tool in assessing memory capacities. He noted that the instrument is carefully constructed and that the various scores do reflect meaningful dimensions of memory functioning. Further, reported reliability values for the instrument are encouraging, including analyses of interscorer reliability, an important consideration in an instrument requiring some judgment in scoring procedures. On the other hand, this is a recently developed instrument and validity information is rather limited at present. Franzen also pointed out that the test does not include a developmental perspective. There is reason to believe that the nature of memory processes may change over the childhood and adolescent years, and these qualitative changes are not reflected in the construction of this test.

## VOCATIONAL APTITUDE TESTS

Guidance regarding vocational choices is often required in counseling adolescents. This guidance is often institutionalized in the high school with special guidance departments, but there are other settings where such guidance is required. For example, counselors and youth care workers dealing with young offenders are often in a position to assess vocationally relevant strengths and weaknesses in the youth.

Vocational counseling is, of course, a specialized type of service, and both Lowman (1991) and L. Seligman (1994) provided useful texts in the area. As those references indicate, there is a wide range of standardized vocational aptitude assessment tools available. Many are designed for assessing specific aptitude areas, including the Accounting Orientation Test and the Bennett Mechanical Comprehension Test. There are also a set of more general batteries designed for assessing a broader range of aptitudes. These are often useful to counselors and personnel officers dealing with adolescents. Three of these are discussed (see Table 6.6).

### Differential Aptitude Tests–Fifth Edition (DAT–5)

The initial version of this test appeared in 1947, with the fifth edition released in 1990. The measure is specifically designed for assessing academic and occupational aptitudes in high school students. Two versions of DAT–5 are available, one for students in Grades 7 to 9 and the other for students in Grades 10 to 12. The instrument is composed of eight

TABLE 6.6
Vocational Aptitude Tests

| Measure | Source/Reference |
| --- | --- |
| Differential Aptitude Tests–5 | Psychological Corporation |
| General Aptitude Test Battery | United States Employment Service |
| Occupational Aptitude Survey and Interest Schedule | PRO-ED |

subtests: Verbal Reasoning, Numerical Ability, Abstract Reasoning, Clerical Speed and Accuracy, Mechanical Reasoning, Space Relations, Spelling, and Language Usage. Scores in those areas are expressed as percentiles and stanines, and these, in turn, are based on large representative normative samples. Scores are calculated separately for boys and girls. A wide range of supporting materials are available for the DAT–5, including computer-generated interpretations of the scores for the examinee. A short version and a computerized adaptive version of the measure are also available.

Both Hattrup (1995) and Schmitt (1995) observed that this version of the DAT represents a considerable improvement over earlier editions. The positive changes relate largely to improvements in the normative sample and a revision of item content to reduce the possibility of gender or ethnic bias. Internal consistency values for the subscales are generally satisfactory, although other forms of reliability have not been assessed. There is also substantial support for the construct validity of the measure as assessed against other paper-and-pencil measures of academic and occupational aptitudes. Criterion-related validity has been established by relating scores, both concurrently and predictively, to indexes of academic achievement.

The reviewers did, however, note weaknesses of the DAT–5. First, evidence linking scores from the measure with indexes of occupational performance is sparse. This is a serious omission because the instrument is widely used in career planning. Second, analyses do not support the independence of the eight subscales. This suggests a caution in using those as guides for specific academic or career guidance.

**General Aptitude Test Battery (GATB)**

This is one of the oldest and best established of the general aptitude batteries. The instrument was developed by the United States Employment Service and it is used primarily by state employment offices. It is, however, available to high school counselors under some circumstances.

The test has undergone numerous revisions since its introduction and has been the object of considerable research.

The GATB can be administered individually or to small groups. Very clear guidelines for administration are presented in the manual, but administration is complicated and experience is required. About 2.5 hours are needed to deliver the entire battery, which is composed of eight paper-and-pencil and four apparatus tests. The test is most appropriate for adults and adolescents 17 years of age and older.

The test is designed to measure a wide range of academic and occupational aptitudes. This is reflected in the nine factor scores yielded by the measure: Intelligence, Verbal Aptitude, Numerical Aptitude, Spatial Aptitude, Form Perception, Clerical Perception, Motor Coordination, Finger Dexterity, and Manual Dexterity. An alternative scoring format based on three composite scores has been proposed by Hunter (1994); these composites are labeled cognitive, perceptual, and psychomotor. Raw scores may be converted to standard scores. There is another type of scoring system that is based on extensive research, which involves comparing an individual's profile of scores with profiles associated with successful performance in a variety of occupations. The actual comparisons may be done through the use of multiple cutoffs or multiple regression equations (see Hunter, 1994).

The GATB is one of the most extensively researched of all aptitude tests and it is undergoing continual refinement. Adequate reliability levels have been established for scores from the measure and both concurrent and predictive validity have been established for the measure with a wide variety of occupations. Kirnan and Geisinger (1986), however, developed some criticisms of the profile analysis scoring procedures and suggested that they be used with some caution. On the whole, though, this has proven a valuable component of vocational assessment procedures for many years.

## Occupational Aptitude Survey and Interest Schedule–2 (OASIS–2)

The two parts to OASIS–2 include an aptitude test and an interest schedule. The aptitude test contained within this battery is based on the GATB. It is, however, shorter and easier to administer than that instrument and it is suitable for either individual or group administration. Administration and scoring are straightforward, but some level of professional competence is required for interpreting the scores.

OASIS–2 is designed to assist counselors in guiding adolescents into career paths consistent with their aptitudes. The manual stresses that career decisions should not be based solely on scores from the test, but, rather, that the test form part of a comprehensive battery of instruments assessing career interests and aptitudes.

OASIS–2 yields six scores: General Ability, Vocabulary, Computation, Spatial Relations, Word Comprehension, and Making Marks. The latter is an index of dexterity. Scoring is based on a standardization sample of 1,505 students drawn from Grades 8 through 12. Scores are expressed as percentiles or stanines.

Barnes (1995) and Dinero (1995) provided recent reviews of this instrument and both stressed that it is a carefully constructed measure with adequate reliability. Construct validity has been established by relating scores from the measure to alternative vocational aptitude tests, including the GATB. The major criticism of the instrument concerns the lack of criterion-related validity information. It has not been shown that scores from OASIS–2 predict performance in different occupations. Continued research to correct this shortcoming is required.

## MEASURES OF ACHIEVEMENT

Another set of tests are designed to measure acquired knowledge or skills. As indicated earlier, the line between achievement tests and aptitude tests is sometimes a fine one. In fact, all of these tests assess acquired knowledge or skills. However, the achievement tests generally focus more closely on information that is explicitly taught to the individual, whereas the intelligence and other aptitude tests center on more basic competencies.

All of the achievement tests to be reviewed are designed as normative assessment devices; that is, they may be used to evaluate a student's achievement level relative to his or her age or grade level. Some tests may also be employed as diagnostic instruments as they are capable of yielding information about specific areas of academic deficiency. The instruments have wide-ranging uses for screening, referral, placement, and treatment planning purposes in educational settings. It may also be noted that aptitude and achievement tests are frequently used together. For example, many definitions of learning disability are based on specific discrepancy levels between general cognitive aptitude test and achievement test scores.

Group-administered achievement tests constitute one type of achievement measure widely used in school settings. The Iowa Tests of Basic Skills, the Stanford Test of Academic Skills, and the California Achievement Tests constitute three examples of these measures. Tests of this type are primarily used for institutional purposes, and this review focuses on

TABLE 6.7
Achievement Tests

| Measure | Source/Reference |
|---|---|
| Diagnostic Achievement Test for Adolescents–2 | PRO-ED |
| Kaufman Test of Educational Achievement | American Guidance Service |
| Peabody Individual Achievement Test–Revised | American Guidance Service |
| Woodcock–Johnson Psycho-Educational Battery–Revised | Riverside Publishing Company |

four individually administered instruments suitable for screening, placement, and treatment decision purposes (see Table 6.7).

## Diagnostic Achievement Test for Adolescents–2 (DATA–2)

This test was developed from the Diagnostic Achievement Battery, an instrument designed for assessing achievement levels in the elementary and middle grades. The DATA–2 is appropriate for students in Grades 7 through 12 and it is designed for assessing achievement in a variety of academic areas. The test may be used to assess the individual's progress through the academic areas relative to a normative group and to identify specific academic weaknesses.

Table 6.8 identifies the 10 core subtests and 3 supplemental subtests of the instrument. It is recommended that the entire battery of subtests be administered, although the manual indicates that individual subtests can be utilized. Administration of the entire battery requires from 1 to 2 hours. Administration and scoring are relatively simple, but interpretation depends, of course, on a background in assessment. Scores are expressed

TABLE 6.8
Subtests of the Diagnostic Achievement Test for Adolescents–2

| Core Subtests | Supplemental Subtests |
|---|---|
| Word Identification | Science |
| Reading Comprehension | Social Studies |
| Spelling | Reference Skills |
| Writing Comprehension | |
| Mathematics Calculations | |
| Mathematics Problem Solving | |
| Receptive Vocabulary | |
| Receptive Grammar | |
| Expressive Vocabulary | |
| Expressive Grammar | |

Note. Based on P. L. Newcomer & B. R. Bryant (1993), *Manual for the Diagnostic Achievement Test for Adolescents* (2nd ed.). Austin, TX: PRO-ED.

as percentiles or standard scores and are based on a large and representative normative sample.

Stuempfig's (1988) review of the earlier version of DATA–2 stresses the care taken in constructing the instrument and its ease of use. He also concluded that the available reliability and validity data indicate adequate support for the measure. He concluded, however, that the test is mainly of value as a general index of achievement. In spite of the term *diagnostic* in the title of the instrument, it provides only limited information about specific achievement deficits. The DATA–2 is, then, of primary value as a screening instrument to identify broad areas of academic strengths and weaknesses.

## Kaufman Test of Educational Achievement (KTEA)

This is one of the more recently developed of the individual achievement tests, and its developers were able to incorporate the latest advances in test construction. Two separate forms of the instrument are available, each with its own manual. The Brief Form is primarily designed as a screening measure and the Comprehensive Form permits a more intensive exploration of the student's achievement level. The advantage of this arrangement is that the Brief Form can be used for the initial screening and then the Comprehensive Form can be administered to individuals identified as requiring more detailed assessment. The short form requires about 30 minutes for administration and the longer form requires about 60 minutes. The test is appropriate for students in Grades 1 through 12.

The Comprehensive Form of the KTEA contains five subtests: Reading Decoding, Reading Comprehension, Mathematics Applications, Mathematics Computation, and Spelling. The Brief Form is composed of three subtests: Reading, Mathematics, and Spelling. Both forms yield standardized scores expressed as percentiles or age- and grade-equivalent normative scores. The manual provides guides for calculating and interpreting discrepancies between KTEA and individual intelligence test scores. Instruction is also provided for interpreting errors made in connection with items from the Comprehensive Form. The latter feature enables use of the test for the diagnosis of specific performance weaknesses.

Reviews of the KTEA by Doll (1989), Henson and Bennett (1985), and Sattler (1992) stress the care taken in constructing the instrument, the quality of the normative samples, and the ease with which the measure is administered and scored. The authors also indicated that satisfactory reliability levels have been established through internal consistency and test–retest procedures. The validity of the measure has been established by relating scores concurrently to alternative standardized achievement tests and other indexes of academic performance. However, this is a fairly new instrument and additional research on construct and predictive validity is required.

## Peabody Individual Achievement Test–Revised (PIAT–R)

This test was previously identified as one of the most widely used devices for the assessment of adolescents. It is a parallel test to the PPVT discussed earlier. The PIAT–R is primarily designed as a screening device for use with children between 6 and 18 years old. It is an individually administered instrument requiring about 60 minutes for delivery. This version represents a considerable revision of the original 1970 instrument.

The PIAT–R is composed of six subtests: General Information, Reading Recognition, Reading Comprehension, Mathematics, Spelling, and Written Expression. The latter is a new addition to the revised version. The instrument may be scored in terms of these six subtests or for three composites: total test (based on all subtests), total reading (Reading Recognition and Reading Comprehension), and written language (Written Expression and Spelling). Scoring is based on a large and representative normative sample, and scores may be expressed as age or grade equivalents, percentile ranks, stanines, or standard scores with a mean of 100 and standard deviation of 15.

Evaluations of the PIAT–R were provided by Benes (1992) and B. G. Rogers (1992). Both observed that this revised version of the measure represents a considerable improvement over its predecessor. Improvements in item content and the standardization sample are regarded as positive developments. Reliability levels for the subtests are adequate, although they appear to be somewhat lower for the Written Expression subtest. Construct validity has been established by relating scores from the measure to other standardized achievement tests and through factor analyses. However, the latter demonstrate a very heavy verbal component to test performance. Only limited support exists for the predictive validity of the subtest scores. This instrument is recommended largely as a screening device.

## Woodcock–Johnson Psycho-Educational Battery–Revised (WJR)

This test represents something of a hybrid in that it incorporates both a measure of general cognitive aptitudes (tests of cognitive ability) and a measure of achievement (tests of achievement). The current version represents a revision of the original 1977 test. The revision responds largely to criticisms that were advanced against the cognitive ability component of the original version (see Sattler, 1992). This revised version of the Tests of Cognitive Ability is based on Horn and Cattell's (1966) theory of fluid and crystallized intelligence.

The WJR is designed to assess a broad range of cognitive and scholastic aptitudes and achievement levels. It is composed of a total of 39 tests, although not all are administered to an examinee. The administration of the measure is complicated and requires a thorough background in assessment and specific training in the instrument. Delivery of the entire battery requires from 2 to 3 days of testing. The scoring procedures are also quite complicated and computer-based scoring is highly recommended.

The tests of cognitive ability component of WJR is based on seven factors: Long-Term Retrieval, Short-Term Memory, Processing Speed, Auditory Processing, Visual Processing, Comprehension-Knowledge, and Fluid Reasoning. The achievement component is based on five achievement clusters: Broad Reading, Broad Mathematics, Broad Written Language, Broad Knowledge, and Skills. Each of the basic factors and clusters is divided into numerous subareas.

The WJR is designed to serve a variety of purposes, and, hence, a number of alternative scoring formats are available. For example, the manual includes tables for directly calculating aptitude and achievement discrepancies. These indexes are sometimes required, as we have seen, for determining learning disability diagnoses. It is also possible to use normative standard scores from the achievement subtests to identify specific areas of scholastic strengths and weaknesses. The calculation of standard scores is based on a large and representative normative sample.

Cummings (1995) and Lee and Stefany (1995) reviewed the technical and psychometric adequacy of the current revision and reported a generally positive evaluation. They noted that the revision rests on a firmer theoretical foundation than the earlier version, that the normative sample has been improved, and that the item revisions further strengthen the measure. They also indicated that reported reliability and concurrent validity support is generally adequate. On the other hand, R. E. Webster (1994) noted weaknesses with respect to predictive and construct validity. Relatively little evidence is available as yet regarding the ability of scores from the measure to predict future academic success or failure. Further, very little evidence exists regarding the meaningfulness of specific scores from the measure. The WJR will likely continue as a part of psychologists' assessment battery, but these cautions should be kept in mind.

## GENERAL CONSIDERATIONS

Anyone with experience in applied assessment situations is aware of the prominence of these standardized aptitude and achievement measures. Their importance is also emphasized in the frequency of use data presented earlier. The WISC, SBIS, PPVT, WRAT, and WJR are identified as among the most widely used of all instruments in assessing adolescents.

These standardized tests serve important roles as screening instruments in educational, clinical, and organizational settings. School psychologists, for example, often depend heavily on group aptitude tests for the preliminary identification of students with potential learning problems. Similarly, these group tests are often used in schools for an initial screening of students who might benefit from enriched educational programs. The group aptitude and achievement tests are also useful as screening devices in vocational guidance and personnel selection situations, in which they can provide initial information about cognitive, academic, and occupational assets and liabilities.

The measures also represent important tools in referral, placement, and treatment planning decisions. We saw in chapter 4 that these decisions often involve inferences about risk, need, and responsivity factors, and aptitude and achievement instruments are well suited for supporting those inferences. For example, a decision to refer an adolescent to a special educational placement will often depend in part on estimates of the severity of the learning problem exhibited. Assessments utilizing a combination of general aptitude and achievement tests are often of value in making that estimate. Similarly, in making decisions about the nature of the treatment or intervention, a precise evaluation of the actual needs of the individual is important. A general aptitude measure such as WISC–III is capable of providing information about the specific cognitive and academic needs of the client. The instruments are also of great value in assessing responsivity to treatment. For example, cognitive ability is often a determinant of how well individuals will respond to certain types of treatment. Thus, a student with limited abstract conceptual abilities will probably not respond well to a program requiring complex problem solving. Here, too, the individual and group aptitude tests may play an important role.

These aptitude and achievement measures are of value in these different contexts, but certain limitations must be emphasized. First, lacunae exist with respect to evaluations of the reliability and validity of the tests, in spite of the fact that most of the instruments are the product of long periods of development. This point is particularly true with respect to criterion-related validity. Most of the tests reviewed in this chapter present some information about the way in which the test scores relate concurrently and predictively to indexes of academic and occupational performance, but in no case are data presented for the entire range of uses made of the instruments. To illustrate, individual aptitude tests such as the WISC–III and SBIS:4 are widely used in selecting candidates for enriched programs. However, only very limited support exists for their ability to predict success in those programs. Similarly, scores from batteries composed of aptitude and achievement tests are used to stream students into special remedial programs. Here, too, however, only limited support exists for the ability of the batteries to predict success or failure in those programs. This relates to the issue of treatment validity raised in chapter 4. The *Standards for Educational and Psychological Testing* (American Psychological Association, 1985) clearly state that psychometric support must be provided for specific uses of a measure. Practitioners are advised to keep this point in mind in selecting instruments.

Problems also exist with the construct validity of these measures, and these problems take a number of forms. There is, first of all, the issue of the meaning of the constructs being measured. These instruments are presented as measures of intelligence, cognitive aptitudes, verbal intelligence, technical aptitudes, math achievement, and so forth. These constructs are defined empirically and operationally by the items represented in the tests. However, we often encounter difficulty in explicating these constructs and independently establishing their validity. The best example of the point may be found in the concept of intelligence. The meaning of that construct has been endlessly debated without any real resolution (see Anastasi & Urbina, 1997; Sternberg, 1994).

As we saw in chapter 4, construct validity becomes a particularly important issue when measures are used for a labeling process. This occurs, for example, whenever an aptitude test is used to describe a youth as gifted, low cognitive functioning, learning disabled, or average intelligence. These are powerful labels, and it is important for assessors to keep in mind that ambiguities often exist and these labels should be used with great caution.

One other dimension of the construct validity issue should be noted at this point. H. Gardner (1993), Sternberg (1997), and others have objected that the construct of intelligence or general cognitive aptitudes represented in the aptitude tests reviewed in this chapter represent too narrow a definition. The primary focus in all cases, and this includes the so-called nonverbal tests, is on aptitudes relating to academic performance. The argument is that the range of aptitudes required for effective functioning in life is considerably broader than that. It is worth noting in this connection that efforts are being made to develop alternatives to these standard measures (see Daniel, 1997; Sternberg, 1997). These have not yet evolved into practical measuring devices, but practitioners are advised to remain current regarding these developments.

One set of cautions, then, relates to limits on the psychometric properties of these tests, and a second set concerns the actual use of the measures. The need for care in the utilization of psychological assessments has been emphasized in this and preceding chapters, but it may be useful to again stress certain points. The administration, scoring, and interpretation of most of the tests reviewed in this chapter require an extensive background in psychological assessment and special training in use of the instrument in question. Most are Level B or C tests (see chap. 5). Administration of the individual tests also requires some measure of clinical skills because they involve the establishment of a professional relationship with the examinee. A. S. Kaufman (1979, 1990) and Sattler (1992) provided excellent guides for the conduct of aptitude and achievement assessments.

Some of the instruments, particularly the group tests, do not require such a high level of expertise for administration or scoring. However, the interpretation of the scores from these measures still requires knowledge and experience, and misuses often arise where the measures are used by unqualified personnel. A similar problem, which I address in a later chapter, arises in using the computer-based interpretations that are becoming more widely available.

There are limits to the reliability and validity of these measures, and their application makes special demands on the examiner. However, these limitations should not be overemphasized. Decisions about adolescents are based on assessments of their cognitive functioning and achievement levels, and grounding those assessments in standardized instruments of the sort reviewed in this chapter is preferable to a dependence on informal and unstructured assessments.

# 7

## *Personality Tests*

This chapter provides a review of personality tests appropriate for use with adolescents. These instruments are variously referred to as structured personality tests, structured personality inventories, or objective personality tests. They are regarded as structured or objective because they contain a fixed number of items, they are presented in a standardized fashion, and they are scored according to structured formulas. These features distinguish these tests from the projective tests with their unstructured, ambiguous items and high degree of interpretation in scoring. Because the focus of this book is on standardized psychological assessments, the projective techniques are not reviewed. Readers are referred to discussions of these measures provided by Aiken (1996a) and Kratochwill and Morris (1993).

As indicated earlier, classifying assessment instruments is sometimes problematic, and this point is well illustrated in the case of personality tests. Many self-report behavioral checklist and rating measures and some measures of attitudes and beliefs yield scores resembling the constructs represented in personality tests. For example, the self-report version of the Child Behavior Checklist (Achenbach, 1994) yields a score labeled Somatic Complaints that also appears on several of the structured personality tests. However, these behaviorally oriented measures are discussed in later chapters.

Some of the personality tests reviewed in this chapter are designed to yield information about dysfunctional personality traits or syndromes. As such, they play important roles as screening, referral, and treatment planning instruments in therapeutic and counseling contexts. For example, the adolescent version of the MMPI has been shown to be useful in guiding treatment decisions in clinical settings.

Other measures are designed for assessing personality traits or dimensions of normal individuals. These instruments have important uses for guiding decision making in school, organizational, and community contexts. For example, personality tests such as the California Psychological Inventory and the NEO Personality Inventory–Revised have long been used as aids in educational and career counseling.

Aiken (1996a) and T. B. Rogers (1995) discussed the historical development of modern personality tests. It is clear from their reviews that significant progress has been made in the development of these instruments. This progress derives, in part, from advances in personality theory, but it is also due to the increasing availability of sophisticated statistical procedures and computer technologies.

In spite of this progress, some questions remain about the utility of the approach to assessment represented in these standardized personality tests. The questions arise partly from controversies discussed earlier regarding assumptions about the existence of stable personality traits. Most of the tests assume that these traits exist and that they can be meaningfully assessed. On the other hand, many experts, particularly those with a more behaviorist orientation, question the utility of these trait constructs. A related issue is the operation of response sets or biases in self-report measures. Responses to the measures may be affected by faking and other types of response distortions. I return to these issues later in this chapter.

All of the tests to be described are self-report measures. Most are in paper-and-pencil formats, although there are an increasing number of computer-based stimulus presentation and response modes. Computer scoring and interpretation programs are also increasingly available for the personality tests. The instruments are discussed under three headings: general measures of personality, measures of self-concept and personal constructs, and measures of specific personality states.

## GENERAL MEASURES OF PERSONALITY

The tests in this category are all designed to yield a general or broad assessment of the individual's personality. Some provide for a focus on the normal personality whereas others are designed for the identification of pathological states or conditions. The nine instruments reviewed in this section are identified in Table 7.1. The source or reference for the test is also indicated in the table.

### Basic Personality Inventory (BPI)

This instrument was developed by Jackson (1996) from a theoretical base and through the application of multivariate procedures. The instrument parallels the MMPI in some respects, but it is designed to yield descrip-

TABLE 7.1
General Measures of Personality

| Measure | Source/Reference |
| --- | --- |
| Basic Personality Inventory | Research Psychologist Press/Sigma |
| California Psychological Inventory | Consulting Psychologist Press |
| The High School Personality Questionnaire | Institute for Personality and Ability Testing |
| The Jesness Inventory | Multi-Health Systems |
| Millon Adolescent Personality Inventory and Millon Adolescent Clinical Inventory | National Computer Systems |
| Minnesota Multiphasic Personality Inventory–Adolescent | National Computer Systems |
| NEO Personality Inventory–Revised | Psychological Assessment Resources |
| Personality Inventory for Youth | Western Psychological Services |
| Psychological Screening Inventory | Research Psychologist Press/Sigma |
| Symptom Checklist–90–Revised | National Computer Systems |

tions of both normal and abnormal dimensions of personality. Unlike the MMPI, it also yields scores reflecting strengths as well as weaknesses of personality.

The test is composed of 240 items and is suitable for children with at least a fifth-grade reading ability. Scoring is based on 12 scales: Hypochondriasis, Depression, Denial, Interpersonal Problems, Alienation, Persecutory Ideas, Anxiety, Thinking Disorder, Impulse Expression, Social Introversion, and Self-Depreciation. High scores on the scale may be used to infer levels of dysfunction, whereas lower scores denote areas of strength and normal functioning. The scale does not contain separate validity scales. However, the Denial and Self-Depreciation scores are sometimes used as validity indexes. Standardized scores for the BPI are based on a large and representative sample of adolescents between 12 and 18 years old. The instrument may be hand-scored, although computer scoring and interpretation are available.

Some evidence with respect to reliability (internal consistency and test–retest) and construct validity are presented in the manual and some additional psychometric evaluations with adolescents have appeared in the research literature (e.g., Austin, Leschied, Jaffe, & Sas, 1986). On the other hand, it must be acknowledged that there is a relative dearth of empirical information regarding the criterion-related validity of the instrument as used with adolescents (Butcher & Rouse, 1996).

On a positive side, the BPI is a carefully developed instrument with a solid theoretical foundation. It is relatively easy to administer and score, and, in this sense, is a more practical instrument than the MMPI–A. Further, the measure has been widely used for many years for assessing adolescents in a variety of school, community, and organizational contexts, and a considerable body of case evidence supports its utility in those settings. LaVoie's (1989) earlier review supported these conclusions, as does more recent research on the instrument.

### California Psychological Inventory (CPI)

This is a widely used instrument appropriate for assessing adolescent personality. It was developed from the MMPI, and some of the items in the inventory were directly borrowed from that instrument. However, the CPI is primarily designed for assessing personality states in normal individuals. The scales of the instrument were originally developed by Gough (1957, 1968) to represent "folk" concepts of personality; that is, they were designed to measure dimensions of personality meaningful to laypersons as well as psychologists.

The measure is composed of 462 items and it requires about 45 min to 1 hour for administration and a Grade 7 reading level. The CPI is scored in terms of the 20 scales identified in Table 7.2. Gough (1987) also described an alternative scoring system based on three personality themes or vectors: (a) interpersonal orientation (externality vs. internality), (b) normative perspective (norm favoring vs. norm questioning), and (c) realization (poor vs. superior integration). Three validity scales are also included. Scoring of the instrument is relatively straightforward. However, and even though the scales represent "common sense" concepts, interpretation of the scores requires considerable expertise and training.

The psychometric soundness of the CPI was reviewed by Wegner (1988). The reliability of the measure is generally judged to be satisfactory, although internal consistency values for some of the subscales are relatively weak. Substantial evidence supporting the criterion-related validity of the instrument is reported in the manual. On the other hand, questions have been raised about the construct validity of the scales (Wegner, 1988).

This is a very popular instrument that has seen practical application for a variety of screening, referral, and educational planning purposes in educational and organizational settings. Lowman (1991), for example,

TABLE 7.2
California Personality Inventory Scales

| | | |
|---|---|---|
| Dominance | Capacity for Status | Sociability |
| Social Presence | Self-Acceptance | Independence |
| Sense of Well-Being | Empathy | Responsibility |
| Socialization | Self-Control | Tolerance |
| Good Impression | Communality | Achievement-Conformance |
| Achievement-Independence | Intellectual Efficiency | Psychological Mindedness |
| Flexibility | Femininity | |

*Note.* Based on H. G. Gough (1987), *California Personality Inventory Administrator's Guide.* Palo Alto, CA: Consulting Psychologist Press.

showed that the instrument has particular utility in vocational guidance settings. The strengths of the instrument relate to ease of administration and scoring, and the considerable empirical and clinical support for its practical utility. Complexity of interpretation and problems of construct validity constitute the major bases for caution.

## The High School Personality Questionnaire

This instrument was originally developed by Cattell to reflect his trait-view theory of personality assessment (Cattell, 1968; Cattell & Cattell, 1975). It is designed as a broad measure of personality in adolescents aged 12 to 18 and has for many years seen wide use in counseling, therapeutic, and personnel selection situations. The High School Personality Questionnaire is a parallel instrument to the Sixteen Personality Factor Questionnaire (16 PF).

This 142-item paper-and-pencil questionnaire requires a Grade 6 reading level. It is scored in terms of 14 dimensions of normal personality: Outgoing, Abstract Thinking, Ego Strength, Excitability, Dominance, Enthusiasm, Conscientiousness, Boldness, Tender-Mindedness, Withdrawn, Guilt Prone, Self-Sufficient, Controlled, and Tense. Scores are also available for four secondary dimensions: Extroversion, Anxiety, Tough Poise, and Independence.

Some basic psychometric information is presented in the manual for this instrument. It must be acknowledged, however, that this instrument is not as well researched as the adult version, the 16 PF, and that only limited support exists for its reliability or validity.

## The Jesness Inventory (JI)

This self-report inventory was originally developed for assessing characteristics of delinquents and is associated with a classification scheme referred to as the Interpersonal Maturity Level Classification System (I-Level; Jesness, 1996; Jesness & Wedge, 1984, 1985). The latter categorizes individuals in terms of increasing levels of perceptual, cognitive, and interpersonal maturity; it has been widely used in juvenile justice settings to aid in placement and treatment decisions. The measure has, however, been increasingly utilized for the assessment of children and adolescents exhibiting the entire range of psychological disturbances.

The measure is composed of 155 true–false items requiring at least Grade 8 reading ability. Scoring of the instrument is in terms of 11 trait and attitude scales: Social Maladjustment, Immaturity, Alienation, Withdrawal-Depression, Repression, Asocial Index, Value Orientation, Autism,

Manifest Aggression, Social Anxiety, and Denial. Two response set scales are also available: Random Responding and Lie Scale.

The administration and scoring of the JI is quite straightforward; it is probably the most easily administered of the personality inventories being reviewed. LaVoie's (1994) review also indicates that the scale yields satisfactory levels of reliability and concurrent validity. The latter has been demonstrated by showing that scores from the measure can distinguish delinquent from nondelinquent adolescents and can also discriminate among types of conduct disorder. On the other hand, LaVoie (1994) cited a relative lack of construct validity evidence for the JI and difficulties in interpreting scores as drawbacks. However, a new manual has recently been made available (Jesness, 1996), containing new reliability and validity information and providing more explicit guidance regarding score interpretation. Also on the positive side is the fact that considerable research has now been reported for the JI.

## Millon Adolescent Personality Inventory (MAPI) and Millon Adolescent Clinical Inventory (MACI)

The original measure, the MAPI, has been widely used for some time in the personality assessment of normal adolescents. The MACI is a more recent adaptation of that instrument, specifically designed for assessing maladaptive personality development. Both are based on a theory of personality developed by Millon (1987, 1990).

The MAPI yields scores reflecting (a) personality style, (b) areas of concern, and (c) aspects of behavioral adjustment (Millon, Green, & Meagher, 1982). These scores are defined in Table 7.3. Interpretation of the scores is designed to provide a comprehensive picture of the personality and behavioral functioning of the youth. The MACI assesses the same dimensions, but it defines them in terms of pathological dimensions rather than dimensions of normal personality (Millon, Millon, & Davis, 1993). It also provides for the identification of some of the personality disorders defined in *DSM–IV*. Further, the behavioral correlates scores have been changed to clinical syndromes. Academic Noncompliance, Drug Proneness, and Suicidal Ideation are examples of the clinical scales. This instrument includes a set of validity scales, although the MAPI does not. The MAPI is a 150-item true–false, self-report inventory, whereas the MACI contains 160 items. Both require at least a sixth-grade reading ability.

Scoring of the two instruments is quite complex, and the use of computerized scoring procedures is recommended. Interpretation, on the other hand, is relatively straightforward, although cases in which individuals present elevated scores on multiple scales may present more difficulty.

TABLE 7.3
Millon Adolescent Personality Inventory Scales

| Personality Styles | Expressed Concerns |
|---|---|
| Introversive | Self-Concept |
| Inhibited | Personal Esteem |
| Cooperative | Sexual Acceptance |
| Sociable | Peer Security |
| Confident | Social Tolerance |
| Forceful | Family Rapport |
| Respectful | Academic Comptence |
| Sensitive | |
| | |
| Behavioral Correlates | |
| Impulse Control | |
| Societal Conformity | |
| Scholastic Achievement | |
| Attendance Consistency | |

*Note.* Based on Millon, T., Green, C. J., & Meagher, R. B. (1982), *Millon Adolescent Personality Inventory Manual*. Minneapolis, MN: National Computer Systems.

The MAPI is a well-established instrument, and information regarding its psychometric properties is presented in the manual and elsewhere (see Woodward, Goncalves, & Millon, 1994). Generally satisfactory levels of reliability are reported and there is some evidence in support of content and construct validity. However, and as noted in reviews by Retzlaff (1995) and Stuart (1995), there appear to be relatively few efforts to assess the criterion-related validity of the measure against meaningful educational or other applied criteria. The instrument continues to be the object of research, and it is likely that these analyses will appear in the future. Some psychometric analyses are also now being reported for the MACI (see Millon et al., 1993; Woodward et al., 1994).

## Minnesota Multiphasic Personality Inventory–Adolescent (MMPI–A)

This test represents an adaptation for adolescents of the original MMPI. The latter instrument has been used for many years in the assessment of pathological states in adolescents. However, at the same time a revision of MMPI was undertaken (resulting in the MMPI–2), a decision was made to develop a form specifically for adolescents. The MMPI–A retains much of the content and scoring format of the MMPI–2, but items and scoring have been modified to make the instrument more suitable for adolescents. For example, three new scales particularly relevant to adolescents have been added: *ACK* (Alcohol/Drug Problem Acknowledgment), *PRO* (Alcohol/Drug Problem Proneness), and *IMM* (Immaturity). Standardization, reliability, and validity research has also been undertaken with new samples of adolescents.

The MMPI–A is composed of 478 true–false items. Scoring of responses may be done through hand-scoring templates or computer programs (computer-based interpretations are also available from a variety of commercial publishers). Normative data reported in the manual derive from a group of 1,620 adolescents (805 boys and 15 girls) between 14 and 18 years of age (Butcher et al., 1992). Separate norms have also been reported for a sample of 13-year-olds (Archer, 1992, 1997).

The scoring scheme for the MMPI–A retains some elements of the original MMPI, but some of the basic scales have been modified, and a number of new content and supplementary scales have been created. Scoring is based on 17 Basic Profile scales and 21 Content and Supplementary scales. The former include two groups of scales. Seven Validity scales are designed to assess various types of response biases (e.g., faking good, faking bad, random responding). The remaining 10 Basic Profile scales reflect the various dimensions of pathology defined in the original MMPI instrument (e.g., Depression, Paranoia, Social Introversion). The 21 Content and Supplementary scales then reflect various aspects of personality dysfunction. They include scales such as Anger, Anxiety, Family Problems, Alcohol/Drug Problem Potential, and Anxiety. Many of these scales were adapted from the original MMPI, but additional ones have been developed from research with clinical samples of adolescents.

Interpretation of the MMPI–A is discussed in the test manual and by Archer (1992, 1994, 1997). The first step involves examination of the validity scales. These establish the framework within which the remaining scales may be interpreted. The profile across the 10 Basic Profile scales is then examined and used to provide inferences regarding basic personality disorders. Examination of the Content and Supplementary scales then permits a refinement of the personality diagnosis.

Psychometric evidence relating to the MMPI–A derives in part from the large body of research conducted with the original instrument (see Archer, 1992, 1994, 1997). To the extent that the MMPI–A is based on the earlier measure, the reliability and validity information collected in the earlier research may be considered relevant to the new measure. There are limits, however, to the extent to which those data can be generalized, and it is encouraging to note that psychometric support for the new instrument is beginning to appear (see Archer, 1992, 1994; Butcher et al., 1992; Williams, Butcher, Ben-Porath, & Graham, 1992). It is also worth noting that efforts are being made to develop a scoring format for the MMPI–A based on the Five-Factor Model of Personality (McNulty, Harkness, Ben-Porath, & Williams, 1997) and a format specifically applicable to adolescent delinquents (Pena, Megargee, & Brody, 1996).

There are several strengths to be noted in connection with the MMPI–A. First, although psychometric support for this version of the instrument is only beginning to appear, it is based on an instrument supported by a wealth of psychometric information. Second, we have now had nearly 50 years of experience in using the MMPI with adolescents in a wide variety of clinical and counseling contexts. Third, the measure has excellent validity scales; an important aid in interpretation. Finally, the interpretive guidelines included in the manual represent useful aids to interpretation.

There are also several cautions to be noted. The first concerns the relative lack of supporting psychometric data for this new version of the instrument. There are also two practical considerations. First, the MMPI–A is a lengthy instrument requiring at least a seventh-grade reading ability, so it may not be suitable for all adolescents. Second, even with the aid of the interpretive guidelines, the scoring and interpretation of the instrument is complicated and requires special training. Computer-based scoring and interpretive programs are also available for the MMPI–A, although, as is often the case with these programs, validation information is not always available.

## The NEO Personality Inventory–Revised (NEO PI–R)

This personality test is appropriate only for adolescents 17 years of age and older. It is included here because it has emerged as one of the most important inventories for assessing personality in normal individuals.

The NEO PI–R was developed by Costa and McCrae (1992) to measure the personality domains represented in the Five-Factor model of personality. The latter model identifies the following as the major domains of adult personality: Neuroticism, Extroversion, Openness, Agreeableness, and Conscientiousness. Those domains have also been shown relevant to the description of personalities of older adolescents.

The NEO PI–R is composed of 243 items (including three validity items). A shorter version of the scale is available, as is a parallel version designed for completion by an outside observer (Costa & McCrae, 1988, 1992). The scale is easily administered, and may, in fact, be administered in a group setting by a layperson with some basic training in test administration. The scoring of the instrument is based on 30 scales; these are composed of six facets for each of the five personality domains, identified in Table 7.4.

The NEO PI–R has been widely used in a variety of counseling, guidance, and personnel selection and placement settings, and is usually identified in surveys as one of the most widely used of the personality tests. Lowman (1991), for example, discussed the utility of the instrument for career and vocational assessments.

TABLE 7.4
Domain and Facet Scores for the NEO Personality Inventory–Revised

| Domains | Facets | |
| --- | --- | --- |
| Neuroticism | Anxiety | Self-Consciousness |
| | Angry Hostility | Impulsiveness |
| | Depression | Vulnerability |
| Extroversion | Warmth | Activity |
| | Gregariousness | Excitement Seeking |
| | Assertiveness | Positive Emotions |
| Openness | Fantasy | Actions |
| | Aesthetics | Ideas |
| | Feelings | Values |
| Agreeableness | Trust | Compliance |
| | Straightforwardness | Modesty |
| | Altruism | Tender-Mindedness |
| Conscientiousness | Competence | Achievement Striving |
| | Order | Self-Discipline |
| | Dutifulness | Deliberation |

*Note.* Based on Costa, P. T., Jr., & McCrae, R. R. (1992). *Manual for the Revised NEO Personality Inventory (NEO–PI–R) and NEO Five-Factor Inventory (NEO-FFI).* Odessa, FL: Psychological Assessment Resources.

Reviews by Leong and Dollinger (1990) and Tinsley (1994) reveal considerable support for the reliability and construct validity of the NEO PI–R. Reviews also indicate a growing body of evidence supporting the criterion-related validity of the instrument in a variety of applied contexts. On the other hand, there remain gaps in the validity evidence, particularly where used with adolescents. The absence of validity scales is also the subject of some concern, as are more fundamental questions about the validity of the Five-Factor Model on which the instrument is based (Block, 1995).

**Psychological Screening Inventory (PSI)**

This is an interesting instrument in that it was specifically designed as a screening tool. The 130-item true–false, self-report measure provides a means for identifying individuals with signs of emotional disturbance who might profit from a more intensive assessment. The author of the instrument explicitly states that use of the PSI as a diagnostic tool is not appropriate. The instrument's greatest value is as a screening tool in community clinics, counseling centers, therapeutic residences, and correctional settings, where an easily administered instrument is required for the initial assessment of clients.

The items on the PSI are clearly written and easily understood, and the scale can be completed in 15 to 20 minutes. Scoring is relatively simple, although, as with all such tools, the interpretation of the scores requires some background in personality assessment. The instrument is scored in terms of five scales: Alienation, Defensiveness, Discomfort, Expression, and Nonconformity. Although they are not represented in the most recent version of the manual, Lanyon (1993) reported some efforts to develop validity scales from PSI items.

Considerable reliability and validity information for the PSI is presented in the manual, and reviews of the available psychometric information by Vieweg and Hedlund (1984) and Steiner (1985) indicate adequate support for reliability and concurrent validity. On the other hand, there appears to be only limited support for the ability of PSI scores to predict the outcome of more intensive assessments or the effects of therapeutic interventions (Steiner, 1985). This is a rather serious lacunae because this is the purpose for which the measure was developed. More recent psychometric evaluations of the measure by Boswell, Tarver, and Simoneaux (1994) and Feazell, Quay, and Murray (1991) have also yielded mixed results.

**Symptom Checklist–90–Revised (SCL–90–R)**

This self-report inventory is designed for assessing levels of psychological distress currently experienced by the client within a variety of areas of functioning. The test is easily administered and scored and requires only about 15 minutes for completion. A shorter version of the inventory, the Brief Symptom Inventory, is also available.

The instrument is scored in terms of nine symptom dimensions and three global indexes. The nine symptom dimensions are as follows: Somatization, Obsessive-Compulsive, Interpersonal Sensitivity, Depression, Anxiety, Hostility, Phobic Anxiety, Paranoid Ideation, and Psychoticism. The three global indexes are the Global Severity Index, the Positive Symptom Distress Index (intensity of distress) and Positive Symptom Total (number of symptoms). The first index combines both the intensity and number variables and provides a measure of the overall level of distress being experienced by the client. Norms are available for a nonclinical sample of adolescents. However, data for clinical samples appear to be available only for adults. It is recommended that interpretation of the scores should take account of the global indexes, the symptom dimensions, and responses to individual items (see Derogatis & Lazarus, 1994).

The SCL–90–R is an extensively researched instrument with considerable information available regarding reliability and validity. Those data are summarized in the manual and by Derogatis and Lazarus (1994). These psychometric analyses have included efforts to assess the treatment validity of the instrument, an important consideration for instruments used in evaluating the outcomes of therapy. Two cautions should be noted. First, most of the reliability and validity research has been conducted with adults, and less information is available for adolescents. Second, not all psychometric analyses have yielded support for the measure (e.g., Hafkenscheid, 1993; McGough & Curry, 1992).

## MEASURES OF THE SELF-CONCEPT

I earlier noted that identity development forms an important aspect of adolescent personality. The adolescent's view of himself or herself and of his or her relation to the social and academic world forms a critical force in adaptation to the world. I also identified two components of identity development: self-concept, or the image individuals hold of themselves and their relation to the world, and self-esteem, or individuals' evaluations of their self-concept, the extent to which they view themselves in positive and negative terms.

Measures of self-concept and self-esteem form important components of many assessment efforts. For example, self-concept measures often provide useful information in guiding decisions in counseling and therapeutic efforts with depressed or anxious teens. They are also useful in academic and vocational guidance situations: Difficulties in academic areas often can be traced to the adolescent's lack of confidence in his or her abilities in those areas.

We saw in chapter 2 that some controversy exists about the definition of the self-concept and self-esteem constructs. There appears to remain some attachment to the notion of a concept of global self-concept or self-worth, but most researchers seem to have embraced a multidimensional construct in which the self-concept is represented in terms of a set of relatively independent facets. The Shavelson et al. (1976) model that distinguishes among a variety of academic, social, and personal areas of self-concept was presented as an example of such a formulation.

Bracken (1996) and Byrne (1996a) provided detailed information on a large number of self-concept measures. Five measures of particular relevance for the assessment of adolescents are briefly described in this section (see Table 7.5).

### Multidimensional Self-Concept Scale (MSCS)

This instrument is based on the hierarchical model of Shavelson et al. (1976) discussed in chapter 2. The instrument, reflecting the model, is based on six dimensions of self-concept: Social, Competence, Affect, Academic, Family, and Physical. Those dimensions are assumed to be mod-

TABLE 7.5
Measures of Self-Concept

| Measure | Source/Reference |
| --- | --- |
| Multidimensional Self-Concept Scale | PRO-ED |
| Piers–Harris Children's Self-Concept Scale | Western Psychological Services |
| Self-Description Questionnaire II | SDQ Institute |
| Self-Perception Profile for Adolescents | Harter (1988) |
| Tennessee Self-Concept Scale | Western Psychological Services |

erately related to one another, and the existence of a general factor corresponding to global self-worth is postulated.

This 150-item scale is easy to administer and score. Standardization data are based on large and representative samples of to 19-year-olds. The instrument yields the six dimension scores just identified and a total self-concept score. The various subscales can also be administered individually. The manual provides very explicit guidance regarding both research and clinical uses of the measure (Bracken, 1992).

Although this is a relatively new instrument, considerable information supporting its psychometric properties has already accumulated (Archambault, 1995; Byrne, 1996a). It would seem to have utility as both a research and clinical instrument.

### Piers–Harris Children's Self-Concept Scale (PHCSCS)

This is a well-established measure appropriate for use with individuals between 10 and 18 years old. It is an 80-item paper-and-pencil test requiring only a third-grade reading ability. It has been widely used as a research instrument and has also proven useful as a screening and diagnostic device in clinical and counseling settings. The measure was particularly developed for use with youth exhibiting academic or social problems.

The PHCSCS yields a total score reflecting global self-esteem and six subscores reflecting specific areas of the self-concept: Behavior, Academic Status, Physical Appearance, Anxiety, Popularity, and Happiness and Satisfaction. It is also possible to obtain validity scores reflecting the operation of response biases, an unusual feature in a self-concept measure. The manual provides clear guidelines for administration and scoring and adequate standardization data. Reliability and validity data for the instrument are also reported and a considerable body of other psychometric studies of the instrument have accumulated. On the other hand, Byrne's (1996a) recent evaluation raises some questions about the construct validity of subscale scores from the instrument, and she concluded that some of the newer self-concept measures such as the MSCS and the Self Description Questionnaire II might be more effective measures.

## Self-Description Questionnaire II

This instrument was developed from the Shavelson et al. (1976) model of self-concept described earlier and from the considerable empirical and theoretical work on the self-concept by Marsh and his colleagues (e.g., Marsh, 1990; Marsh, Byrne, & Shavelson, 1988). The instrument has the most solid theoretical grounding of all the self-concept measures.

This 102-item instrument is appropriate for use with adolescents between 13 and 17 years old. It is easily administered and scored and the manual provides standardization data for large and representative samples of youths. The instrument may be individually or group administered and can be utilized by nonprofessionals with minimal training. The structure of the scale reflects the components of the Shavelson model and includes a global self-concept scale and 10 subscales.

The manual contains clear directions for administering, scoring, and interpreting the instrument. In addition, considerable evidence relating to the reliability and validity of the measure is presented. Reviews of the available psychometric data by Boyle (1994) and Byrne (1996a) support the view that this is one of the most carefully developed of the self-concept measures and it is supported by a very strong body of psychometric data.

Two related measures designed for a finer assessment of self-concept in specific areas are also available. These include the Academic Self-Description Questionnaire (Marsh, 1993a) for assessing self-perceptions in specific academic areas and the Physical Self-Description Questionnaire (Marsh, 1993b) for evaluating facets of physical self-concept.

## The Self-Perception Profile for Adolescents (SPPA)

This self-concept measure represents an adaptation for adolescents of the Self-Perception Profile for Children (Harter, 1985). The adolescent version contains a revision of item content and the addition of subscales particularly relevant to this age level. The structure of the instrument reflects the Shavelson et al. (1976) multidimensional model of the self-concept described earlier.

The SPPA is composed of 45 items and is appropriate for adolescents between 15 and 18 years old (the Self-Perception Profile for Children may be used with younger adolescents). It yields a total score reflecting global self-esteem and eight subscales: Scholastic Competence, Athletic Competence, Social Acceptance, Physical Appearance, Job Competence, Close

Friendship, Romantic Appeal, and Behavior. The manual contains clear instructions for administration and scoring, and standardization data based on representative samples of adolescents are included. Considerable psychometric support for the original Self-Perception Profile for Children have been reported, but, as Byrne (1996a) noted, less information is available regarding the reliability and validity of this more recent measure.

## Tennessee Self-Concept Scale (TSCS)

This has been a very popular instrument for use in assessing self-concept in adolescents. It is appropriate for use with individuals 12 years old and older and is appropriate for use with both well-adjusted and disturbed adolescents.

The scale is composed of 100 items and is available in two forms. The Counseling Form, simpler to administer and interpret, is designed for providing direct feedback to the client. It yields a total self-concept score as well as subscores reflecting self-concept in eight areas: Identity, Self Satisfaction, Behavior, Physical Self, Moral-Ethical Self, Personal Self, Family Self, and Social Self. A validity scale reflecting defensive responding is also calculated. The second form of the instrument, the Clinical and Research Form, yields more information but is more complicated to score and interpret. In addition to the scores yielded by the Counseling Form, this version provides scores reflecting response distortion and indexes of personality integration, self-actualization, and consistency within perceptions of the self.

Extensive reliability and validity information is reported in the most recent manual, as are satisfactory standardization data. Byrne's (1996a) review indicates that criticisms of the construct validity of the measure have been common in the past, but that recent psychometric research has considerably strengthened support for the instrument.

## SPECIALIZED PERSONALITY TESTS

There are a wide variety of personality tests and inventories designed to assess more specific personality traits or dimensions. Many of these are also treated as behavioral constructs, and alternative measures of such constructs as depression, withdrawal, and aggressiveness are addressed in subsequent chapters dealing with rating scales and checklists (chaps. 9 and 10) and interview schedules (chap. 8).

Among the most useful of the specialized personality tests are those designed for assessing depression and anxiety. These have wide use as

TABLE 7.6
Specialized Personality Tests

| Measure | Source/Reference |
| --- | --- |
| Beck Depression Inventory | Psychological Corporation |
| Children's Depression Inventory | Western Psychiatric Institute and Clinic |
| Revised Children's Manifest Anxiety Scale | Western Psychological Services |
| Reynolds Adolescent Depression Scale | Psychological Assessment Resources |
| State–Trait Anger Expression Inventory | Psychological Assessment Resources |
| State–Trait Anxiety Inventory | Psychological Assessment Resources |

screening, therapeutic, and research instruments. Several of these measures are described, along with one measure of anger management (Table 7.6).

## Beck Depression Inventory (BDI)

This is one of a number of instruments derived from Beck's (1967, 1976) Cognitive Model of Psychopathology. Two related instruments, the Beck Hopelessness Scale and the Dysfunctional Attitudes Scale, are discussed in chapter 10, dealing with behavioral and cognitive measures.

The BDI is appropriate for use with adolescents older than 17, whereas the instrument to be described next, the Children's Depression Inventory (CDI), is suitable for younger individuals. The 21 items of the BDI were derived theoretically, and the diagnosis yielded by the scale is designed to reflect *DSM–III* criteria for Major Depressive Disorder. It is scored in terms of an overall depression score as well as scores reflecting cognitive-affective and somatic-performance components. Scores for these scales are expressed in terms of three categories: normal, mild-moderate depression, and moderate-severe depression. This is a widely used clinical instrument for which considerable research data are available. A review by Sundberg (1992) concludes that reliability and validity support for the inventory are sufficient to justify its use as a screening instrument. As with the CDI, however, the measure should be used with caution for deriving diagnoses. Kendall, Hollon, Beck, Hammen, and Ingram (1987) advised that the instrument must be used in conjunction with clinical and structured interviews to derive a definitive diagnosis.

## The Children's Depression Inventory (CDI)

This widely used measure represents an adaptation of the BDI for use with children and adolescents. It is appropriate for use with youths between 8 and 17 years old; the BDI is then used with older adolescents. The scale is composed of 27 items and yields a total score reflecting the severity of depression being experienced by the individual. The instrument is very easy to administer and score. Reviews (e.g., Siegel, 1986) generally indicate favorable evaluations of the reliability and validity of the measure, although all experts agree that the diagnosis of depression in young people should be made with great caution. Fristad, Emery, and Beck (1997) noted particularly dangers of using this instrument for determining diagnostic status. The instrument is primarily useful as a screening device to detect children with potentially problematic levels of depression.

### Revised Children's Manifest Anxiety Scale (RCMAS)

This represents an adaptation of the adult version of the Manifest Anxiety Scale. It is appropriate for use with youths between 6 and 19 years old. This self-report measure contains 37 items, and it yields a Total Anxiety Score as well as three subscores: Physiological Anxiety, Worry/Oversensitivity, and Social Concerns/Concentration. A validity scale, labeled the Lie Scale, is also provided. The manual for the measure provides clear guidelines regarding administration and scoring and also extensive normative data. Considerable reliability and validity information have accumulated for this measure. Rabian (1994) recently reviewed those data and concluded that they do support the reliability and validity of the total score, but that more work needs to be done with respect to the validity of the subscales. Reynolds and Richmond (1997) recently presented a revised version of the instrument, but only limited information is available for the measure.

### Reynolds Adolescent Depression Scale (RADS)

This appears to be the only standardized measure of depression specifically developed for use with adolescents. This 30-item self-report measure yields a total score that presumably reflects severity of depression. The instrument is easily administered and scored, and separate norms are available for Grades 7 through 9 and 10 through 12. The manual for the instrument contains considerable psychometric information on the instrument and a detailed discussion of interpretive guidelines. Evaluations of the measure generally indicate that it has utility in screening, therapeutic, and research contexts (Evans, 1988).

### State–Trait Anger Expression Inventory (STAXI)

There are occasions in counseling adolescents where an assessment of their experience of anger and of their management of anger would be desirable. The STAXI is one of a number of standardized measures avail-

TABLE 7.7
Scores for the State–Trait Anger Expression Inventory

| Scale | Description |
|---|---|
| State Anger | Intensity of angry feelings |
| Trait Anger | Disposition to experience anger |
| a. Angry temperament | Propensity to experience anger without provocation |
| b. Angry reaction | Propensity to experience anger in response to provocation |
| Anger-in | Tendency to repress or suppress anger |
| Anger-out | Mode of expressing anger |
| Anger Control | Frequency with which anger is controlled |
| Anger Expression | General index of frequency of anger expression |

Note. Based on Spielberger, C. D. (1988), *Manual for the State–Trait Anger Expression Inventory, Research Edition.* Odessa, FL: Psychological Assessment Resources.

able for this purpose. The instrument is based on a well-developed theory of anger expression (Spielberger, Krasner, & Solomon, 1988).

This self-report instrument is easily administered and scored and useful guides for interpretation are presented in the manual. It is suitable for use with individuals 13 years old and older. Separate norms are provided for boys and girls. Table 7.7 summarizes the various scores yielded by the measure, which reflect both the experience of anger and the youth's mode of coping with anger.

As noted, the STAXI was developed from a comprehensive theory of anger. Sophisticated empirical procedures have also been used for item development and refinement. A number of reliability and validity studies are reported in the manual. The latter have generally involved relating scores from the instrument to scores from alternative anger measures or to health-related outcomes (e.g., blood pressure). Extensive factor analytic investigations are also reported. Moses (1992) concluded in his review that the available psychometric data for the instrument are impressive, but that there remain a number of gaps in evaluations of construct and criterion-related validity. He suggested that the instrument would have utility in clinical settings when used with these cautions in mind.

## State–Trait Anxiety Inventory (STAI)

This instrument is designed for assessing the extent of both state (transitory) and trait anxiety in adolescents and adults. The 40-item scale is easily scored and interpreted. A valuable feature of the manual is the provision of norms for both clinical and nonclinical populations. Considerable data supporting the reliability and validity of the instrument are reported in the manual, although some recent research has raised questions about the construct validity of scores yielded by the measure (Carey, Faulstick, & Carey, 1994).

## GENERAL CONSIDERATIONS

All of the personality tests reviewed in this chapter represent highly developed measuring instruments, and all are based on firm theoretical foundations, empirical foundations, or both. They are capable of yielding information about strengths and competencies that may be important for a wide range of screening, placement, and treatment and instructional planning purposes. As we have seen, some of the tests are designed to assess pathological conditions, whereas others, such as the High School Personality Inventory and the NEO PI–R, are designed for normally functioning individuals.

Most of the tests have been developed with the aid of sophisticated item analysis procedures. Standardization data for representative samples of adolescents are available in all cases and some instruments also present norms for special groups (e.g., learning disabled, delinquents). All of the manuals present clear directions for administration and scoring of the instruments. It should be noted, however, that the interpretation of the test scores sometimes places special demands on the examiner. For example, a test such as the MMPI–A requires a high level of expertise and experience in scoring and interpretation. The task of interpreting these tests is being made easier through the increasing availability of computerized interpretive guides, but those must be used in light of the cautions discussed elsewhere in this volume.

The utility of these instruments also depends on their psychometric properties, and it must be acknowledged that the situation is somewhat mixed in this respect. Extensive research has been conducted with all of the instruments reviewed. However, as we have seen, information to support specific uses of the measures is often missing. Many of these gaps are in the process of being filled, but in the meantime the use of any of the measures must be carried out with a full understanding of any limits that may exist with respect to their psychometric supports.

Some general comments can be made regarding psychometric evaluations of the tests. The item structures of the various instruments have generally been well researched and refined. In most cases, subscales demonstrate satisfactory levels of internal reliability and factor integrity. Test–retest reliability values are also satisfactory in most cases, although the level of stability tends to decline with increasing intervals between testings.

Although the construct validity of most of these personality tests has been explored, it must be acknowledged that there often remains controversy over the meaningfulness of the scores yielded by the measures. Some of that controversy relates to conflicts over the definition of personality traits and pathological conditions, discussed in chapters 2 and 3.

For example, considerable debate has revolved around the best way of defining depression in adolescence. Similarly, differences exist in definitions of the self-concept construct. Even where there is an agreed definition of a construct, there are often questions about the validity of the personality test's measure of the construct. This is reflected, for example, in controversies over the correspondence between the MMPI–A Psychopathic Deviate score and the traditional definition of psychopathy.

Limitations with respect to construct validity do not, of course, render these tests useless. They are still capable of providing meaningful information about individuals and may well demonstrate adequate levels of concurrent and predictive validity. The limitations do mean, however, that the tests should be used with caution in labeling and categorizing individuals. For example, an MMPI–A profile with significant elevations on the Psychopathic Deviate and Mania scales may signify an individual with a particular set of characteristics who is likely to respond in a certain way to a particular treatment. However, labeling that individual as a manic psychopathic deviate may not be particularly useful.

The instruments also display varying levels of criterion-related validity support. As shown, there are a number of forms of this type of validity of interest in applied settings. In some cases we are concerned with the ability of the test scores to predict future adjustment or performance. We are interested, for example, in the ability of scores from the BPI to predict future academic performance or antisocial activities. Our ability to use those scores in making intervention and counseling decisions depends on their predictive validity. Treatment validity, another form of criterion-related validity, is also relevant to the utility of the instruments. This refers to the ability of tests scores to track treatment effects.

Strictly speaking, criterion-related and treatment validity evidence should be presented for any use made of the personality test. This point was developed in chapters 4 and 5. For example, if a test is being used to assess the probability that a 12-year-old boy will commit a serious crime in the next 2 years, data should be presented to support the prediction for that particular group. Criterion-related validity evidence is accumulating for all of the instruments reviewed in this chapter, but the information is currently incomplete. Again, this does not render the measures meaningless, but it does mean that the instruments should be used with these limitations in mind.

Two other issues regarding the use of these personality tests bear mention. The first issue concerns the question of response distortions. It is quite clear that responses to personality tests reflect variables other than the personality characteristics of the individual. Researchers such as Jackson and Messick (1958) and Paulhus (1984, 1994) have generally distinguished two kinds of response distortion. *Response style* refers to a tendency to distort responses in the same manner across all situations. Acquiescence or yea-saying is an example of response style; this is a tendency to provide positive responses regardless of the content. *Response sets*, on the other hand, represent distortions arising from a conscious or unconscious desire to present oneself in a particular way. Efforts to portray oneself in extremely favorable or extremely unfavorable ways represent one type of this response set. This is also referred to as *socially desirable* (or undesirable) *responding* or *faking good* (or bad).

Two general procedures are available for dealing with these response biases. The first involves constructing the tests in such a way that biases are rendered less likely. For example, phrasing half the questions in a positive manner and half in a negative manner may reduce the likelihood of acquiescence responding. The second procedure involves the incorporation of validity scales into the personality test. The MMPI–A, for example, includes subscales designed to directly assess acquiescent and socially desirable responding and a number of other forms of distortion. Some of the tests reviewed in this chapter have included such validity scales.

There is general agreement in the literature that these response distortions are capable of affecting personality test scores (or, for that matter, scores on any self-report measure), but there is considerable debate over the role of these in interpreting test scores (see, e.g., Hogan & Nicholson, 1988; Paulhus, 1984, 1994). It is not necessary to explore that debate here, but users of personality tests are advised to consider the possibility of these sources of bias.

The second issue concerns comorbidity, the situation where the individual exhibits two or more pathological conditions. As we saw earlier, comorbidity creates a problem with diagnostic systems such as *DSM–IV* that encourage a focus on a single syndrome. This is generally not a problem with the standardized personality tests reviewed in this chapter because most are scored in terms of dimensions of personality, and it is possible to locate the individual in a multidimensional space. There is a related problem, however, that sometimes arises with the specialized personality tests. In using, for example, one of the tests of depression, it is important to keep in mind that the youth may be exhibiting problems in other areas. Thus, a diagnosis of severe depression may be associated with other problems not being tapped by the depression measure.

Users of personality tests should have a full understanding of these limitations. They should also be aware of the properties of the particular instruments they are using and interpret the instruments in light of the available psychometric evidence. These limitations aside, it should also be recognized that these standardized personality tests are capable of yielding valid information about individuals that can contribute to more effective decisions.

# 8

## *The Interview*

The face-to-face interview in which the professional directly collects information from the client or an individual familiar with the client constitutes the most widely used of all assessment tools. Interview-based assessments have always played a critical role in therapeutic, counseling, personnel selection, and research situations. They are particularly important, for example, in clinical settings where they are used to generate information about biographical factors, presenting problems, and responsivity considerations. That information may then be used to make decisions about the type of treatment to provide. Interviews may also be used in these settings for evaluating the progress and outcomes of therapy.

The purpose of the clinical interview varies, of course, with the context in which it is employed. In clinical settings with a psychodynamic focus the concern will generally be with use of the interview for diagnosing underlying psychological disturbances, whereas more behaviorally oriented clinicians would be concerned with using the interview to identify dysfunctional overt behaviors that might serve as targets for change. The interview is also widely used in efforts to evaluate levels of risk for antisocial or dangerous behaviors. Workers in youth justice systems, for example, are often called on to provide assessments of a youth's risk for violent criminal acts and these assessments are more often than not based on interview information. Finally, professionals in vocational guidance and human resource settings will employ the interview to evaluate an individual's interests and aptitudes relevant to career paths or particular jobs.

Conducting interviews with adolescents often presents special challenges for the mental health professional. Young people sometimes approach these sessions with suspicious, hostile, or indifferent attitudes, and this often complicates the collection of accurate information. On the other hand, the interview may present an opportunity to deal with these negative attitudes and establish a working relationship with the youth.

Discussing the interview is complicated by the considerable variability in the way in which the method is applied in different settings. One way of characterizing this variability is in terms of the degree of structure represented in the interview. At one extreme is the completely unstructured interview, which simply involves a conversation between the professional and client. This type of interview is actually quite common in applied situations where the concern in the initial contact with the client is to put them at ease and collect some preliminary information.

The typical clinical interview, however, usually demonstrates somewhat more structure in the sense that the mental health professional would generally use more or less formal guidelines to guide the questioning. Still further along the structure dimension is the semistructured interview, in which there is a standard set of questions, but where the professional still has some measure of flexibility in conducting the session. This is in contrast to the structured interview, in which the questions to be asked and the response categories are specified and the professional has no flexibility. The most extreme form of the structured interview is the computer-based interview, in which the questions are presented through the computer and the client responds to them through the computer. It should be recognized that the line between a highly structured interview schedule and a rating or checklist measure might be a fine one.

A wide variety of interview schedules are now available for collecting information from adolescents and parents (see Edelbrock & Costello, 1988; Sattler, 1992, 1997). Some of these are relatively unstructured instruments designed to assist the professional in conducting a clinical interview, whereas others represent more structured instruments. Some of the latter may also be considered standardized measures. That is, they are structured instruments for which normative and psychometric information are available. It is this type of measure that forms the primary focus of this volume, and these instruments are examined in more detail later in this chapter. However, because the clinical interview continues to play an important role in psychological assessments, even those involving standardized assessments, it is appropriate to provide some attention to this method.

## THE CLINICAL INTERVIEW

The interview may be represented as a conversation between the mental health professional and the client. Its purpose is the same as any psychological assessment, to collect information from the client for purposes of forming inferences about his or her status or characteristics. The latter are then used to assist in a decision about the individual. The clinical interview may be guided by more or less structure, but it generally involves a fairly high level of flexibility and depends heavily on the clinical skills of the interviewer.

The clinical interview is capable of yielding two types of information. First, the content of the interview may provide the professional with information about aptitude, personality, motivational, behavioral, and circumstantial factors. Second, the behaviors observed in the client during the course of the interview may yield valuable cues regarding client characteristics. Skilled clinicians, for example, are often capable of making judgments about the accuracy of information being provided by the client by observing his or her emotional and behavioral reactions to questioning. Similarly, inferences about anxiety levels, depression, and other such emotional states are often based on observations collected in the interview.

Several other advantages are often cited in connection with the clinical interview. First, the flexibility of the procedure is seen as an advantage in that it allows the professional to explore directions that might not be followed in a more structured kind of assessment procedure. Second, the format provides an opportunity for the professional to establish a relationship with the client. This may be important for motivating the client to participate in the process. Also, in some cases the interview is used as part of the therapeutic or counseling process. A third and related point applies in those cases where the interviewer is to be directly involved in the delivery of the service, whether a therapeutic intervention of some sort or a decision about the client. By having the professional directly involved in the total process we avoid the sometimes undesirable consequences of separating the assessment and service delivery processes. Finally, providing a direct, face-to-face contact between the client and the professional may be important in humanizing the process.

There are, on the other hand, a number of cautions to be observed in connection with the clinical interview (see Gresham, 1984; Hersen & Van Hasselt, 1998; Lanyon & Goodstein, 1997; Sattler, 1992, 1997). Difficulty exists in evaluating the reliability and validity of the approach. In this case flexibility may become a handicap. We generally have no real basis for evaluating the psychometric quality of the information collected in the average interview.

Some systematic research on this issue has been conducted, particularly in connection with employment selection interviews. Reviews of this research by M. M. Harris (1989), Huffcutt and Arthur (1994), McDaniel, Whetzel, Schmidt, and Maurer (1994), and Wiesner and Cronshaw (1988) have generally concluded that levels of reliability and validity for the clinical interview are relatively low, although they do increase as increasing structure is introduced into the interview. Those reviews also make clear that there are substantial individual differences in interviewing skills.

Research has also identified a number of sources of error that may affect the quality of information collected in the interview, some of which are summarized in Table 8.1. As the table indicates, the error may arise from the way in which the interview is conducted, from characteristics of the respondent, or from the interviewer.

Interviewer's biases and preferences constitute one of the most important potential sources of error within the interview: "The interview is extremely susceptible to interviewer bias. Interviewer bias refers to the interviewer's unintentionally encouraging or discouraging the expression

TABLE 8.1
An Overview of Sources of Error in the Interview

Structure of the interview
  Lack of specificity in the question
  Concepts of question are complex and multidimensional
  Sequence of questions
  Number of questions
  Question structure
  Unwarranted assumptions in the question
  More than one question embedded in a single question
  Sensitive or threatening element in the questions
  Wording of the question
    Inexact terms
    Ambiguous or vague terms
    Complex terms and sentences
    Biased words
Respondent
  Need to give socially desirable answers
  Lack of understanding of the questions
  Memory lapses
  Experience of questioning as stressful
  No true opinion
  Differing emotional intensity among respondents
  Variable perceptions of the situation and purpose
  Timing of interview
Interviewer
  Interviewer characteristics
  Preferences and biases
  Variable emotional intensity
  Variable verbal facility
  Variable understanding of the questions
  Recording errors

*Note.* Adapted from "Research on the Clinical Interview," by J. G. Young, J. D. O'Brien, E. M. Gutterman, & P. Cohen, 1987, *Journal of the American Academy of Child and Adolescent Psychiatry, 26,* 613–620. Reproduced with permission.

of certain facts or opinions, causing interviewees to distort their communications to please the interviewer" (Sattler, 1992, p. 464). The biases may also operate by affecting the questions asked or the manner in which the interviewer relates to the client. The key problem, as Sattler indicated, is that these biases operate very subtly and sometimes unconsciously.

A question often arises about the ways in which interviewer training and experience might impact on the quality of the information collected and the validity of the inferences made from that information. Garb (1989) and Lanyon and Goodstein's (1997) review of the literature suggests that focused training programs can improve the accuracy of judgments formed within clinical assessments. On the other hand, they found no evidence that increased clinical experience was associated with enhanced validity.

The current evidence suggests, then, that the validity of the clinical interview is highly variable, but that it can be improved through training in interviewing and the introduction of increasing structure into the interview. Edelbrock and Costello (1988), Hersen and Van Hasselt (1998), and Sattler (1992, 1997) presented numerous examples of structured and semistructured schedules that may be useful in collecting information from adolescents and their parents. Table 8.2 presents examples of items from a semistructured interview schedule designed for collecting information from parents.

## STANDARDIZED INTERVIEW SCHEDULES

The clinical interview involving a face-to-face relationship between professional and client and in which the professional is able to adapt his or her approach to the circumstances will always play a role in counseling and therapeutic settings. It follows from the basic premises of this volume, however, that the quality of information collected in the interview could be improved through the use of standardized interview schedules. These are structured or semistructured schedules with fixed formats for which psychometric data are available. I begin with some general comments on these measures and refer the reader to Gutterman, O'Brien, and Young (1987), Hodges (1993; Hodges & Zeman, 1993), and Young, O'Brien, Gutterman, and Cohen (1987) for further discussions.

All of the schedules to be reviewed are designed for assessing the presence and severity of emotional pathologies. Most were originally developed in connection with the DSM–III and DSM–III–R schedules, although some have now been adapted to reflect DSM–IV categories. Most of the instruments were originally developed as research tools for use in

TABLE 8.2
Sample Items From a Semistructured Clinical
Interview Schedule for Use With Parents

Parental relations
44. How does _____ get along with (each of) you?
45. What does _____ do with (each of) you regularly?
46. What are the good times like with (each of) you?
47. What are the bad times like with (each of) you?
48. Are there other adults present in the home?
49. (If yes to Question 48) How does _____ get along with them?
50. (If yes to Question 48) What are the good times like with each adult?
51. (If yes to Question 48) What are the bad times like with each adult?
52. Does _____ listen to what he (she) is told (that is, is _____ compliant)?
53. How do you discipline _____?
54. Which parent is responsible for discipline?
55. Which techniques are effective?
56. Ineffective?
57. What have you found to be the most satisfactory ways of helping your child?

*Note.* Based on J. Sattler (1992). *Assessment of children* (3rd ed., rev.). San Diego, CA: Jerome M. Sattler, Publisher. Reproduced with permission.

epidemiological research or studies exploring the dynamics of emotional pathologies. They are, however, seeing increasing use as clinical assessment instruments.

All of the schedules are structured measures in that they include a fixed set of stimulus and response items. They vary, however, in the flexibility provided the interviewer in the order of questioning and the opportunity to introduce probes. Some of the schedules are highly structured in that the interviewer must follow exactly the content of the schedule, whereas in other cases the examiner may be permitted a certain amount of freedom to probe for responses.

As indicated, most of the instruments yield scores reflecting the diagnostic categories of one or the other versions of the *DSM*. The scores are generally expressed as diagnostic categories (e.g., affective disorder, attention deficit disorder, oppositional disorder) or in terms of the severity of the disorder (symptom severity), with the latter based on the number of symptoms checked within a diagnostic category. Some also provide additional scales for recording the youth's overall level of functioning (corresponding generally to the Global Assessment Scale of *DSM–IV*) and some make provision for recording informal observations collected in the context of the interview.

The instruments also vary somewhat in the degree of structure represented in the scoring procedures. The most standardized schedules provide algorithms that are designed to yield pathology diagnoses without any clinical judgment, whereas other instruments require some measure of clinical inference in the formation of diagnoses. One departure from the definition of a standardized psychological measure is the fact that none of these instruments provides for normative scoring. Scoring is based in all cases with reference to the *DSM* schedule.

The degree of structure represented in the administration and scoring of the interview has important implications for the qualifications of those administering the schedule. The highly structured schedules are designed for administration by lay interviewers with some training in use of the instrument. Some of the structured schedules are, in fact, being adapted for computer-based administration and scoring. Other schedules with somewhat less structured formats requiring some measure of clinical expertise in scoring are designed for use by mental health professionals.

As previously indicated, a major advantage of structured or unstructured interview schedules over the clinical interview is the opportunity presented for evaluating psychometric properties. It is encouraging to note that considerable psychometric research is now being conducted with these measures. Most of the reliability evaluations have focused on interrater agreement procedures. This is important because one of the goals of introducing increasing structure into the interview is to improve the reliability of the diagnoses.

Validity research with these schedules has generally focused on construct validity. The concern, in other words, has been with the meaningfulness of the diagnoses yielded by the schedule. This is a difficult matter to deal with because, as we saw in chapter 3, there is often considerable uncertainty about the meaning of diagnostic categories reflecting emotional pathology. This is a particular problem in dealing with children and adolescents because these constructs have generally not been thoroughly explored.

The construct validity evaluations that have been reported have generally involved relating diagnoses yielded by the interview schedules to scores from alternative measures of pathology or to alternatively derived diagnoses. The latter are usually based on comparisons of youths who have been referred for psychiatric treatment with those who have not or on diagnoses formed through clinical procedures. The validity analyses in this case are often based on sensitivity and specificity indexes. The former refers to the rate of true positives and the latter to the rate of true negatives. The issues of reliability and validity are addressed again at the end of the chapter.

The following sections contain reviews of five structured or semistructured interview schedules that are the object of current research (see Table 8.3). Note that several other schedules involving an interview format but

TABLE 8.3
Standardized Structured and Semistructured Interview Schedules

| Measure | Source/Reference |
| --- | --- |
| Adolescent Diagnostic Interview | Western Psychological Services |
| Child Assessment Schedule | Hodges (1997) |
| Diagnostic Interview for Children and Adolescents | Reich & Welner (1988) |
| Diagnostic Interview Schedule for Children | Shaffer et al. (1996) |
| Schedule for Affective Disorders and Schizophrenia | J. Kaufman et al. (1997) |

incorporating a broader range of information sources are presented in chapter 11.

**Adolescent Diagnostic Interview (ADI)**

Most of the interview schedules to be reviewed in this section provide for a broad survey of emotional and behavioral disorders. The ADI is an exception because it focuses primarily on substance abuse. The instrument was developed as part of the Minnesota Chemical Dependence Adolescent Assessment Package, which also includes the Personal Experience Inventory (see chap. 9). It is designed as an intake and diagnostic tool and may be administered by mental health professionals with some background in assessment. It requires a minimal level of clinical judgment.

The interview schedule consists of 306 structured items, although the actual number administered varies with the extent of substance use in the respondent. Items relate to alcohol and cannabis use and to a variety of other drugs (e.g., amphetamines, cocaine, hallucinogens). Assessments of substance abuse are based on *DSM–III–R* and *DSM–IV* diagnoses of psychoactive substance use disorder. The interview also collects information about a variety of other psychological conditions. Administration of the interview requires about 45 minutes, although the actual time will depend on the extent of substance use.

The ADI yields a number of different types of scores. These include, first, the *DSM* diagnoses of substance use disorder. These may be obtained for each of the abused substances and for multiple substance abuse. Second, the instrument yields a global index that reflects the youth's functioning in various areas, often affected by substance abuse, including peer relations, school performance, and adjustment at home. Third, a global index of Severity of Psychosocial Stressors may be calculated. This reflects the numbers of stressful life events experienced by the youth during the previous 12-month period. Finally, Psychiatric Status Screen scores provide information about the presence of emotional and behavioral disorders that often accompany substance abuse. These include diagnostic categories such as depression, attention deficit disorder, eating disorder, and conduct disorder.

Wright, Ford, and Kiser (1992) concluded in their review that the ADI represents a promising tool for assessing psychoactive substance abuse in adolescents, but that psychometric support for the measure is very limited at the present time. Generally adequate levels of reliability are reported in the manual; these are based on both test–retest and interrater agreement procedures. However, only limited support for the validity of the measure has been presented to date. Toneatto (1992) was somewhat more critical in his review. Noting the relatively weak psychometric support for the measure, he also questioned the construct validity of the substance abuse and psychological screening diagnoses. It is worth noting, however, that research with the instrument is continuing (see, e.g., Winters, Stinchfield, Fulkerson, & Henly, 1993), and it is likely that refinements will appear in the future.

## Child Assessment Schedule (CAS)

This semistructured interview has a relatively long history, with four versions having appeared since 1978. The schedule is designed as a clinical instrument appropriate for yielding diagnoses of general and specific emotional and behavioral pathologies. The interview was originally developed for use with children between 7 and 12 years old, but it has been used successfully with adolescents. Separate versions of the instrument are available for administration to children and parents. It is important to note that the schedule requires some level of clinical expertise and should only be administered by a mental health professional with some background in child and adolescent pathologies. A companion instrument, the Child and Adolescent Functional Assessment Scale, is available for assessing the level of impairment exhibited by the youth. That instrument is discussed in chapter 11.

The CAS is divided into three parts. The first is a series of questions relating to a variety of content areas, examples of which are identified in Table 8.4. Questions relevant to diagnoses are interspersed among more general queries about the content areas. For example, the items within the School content area include five items relevant to attention deficit disorder, one to oppositional disorder, one to separation anxiety, and four to depression. A second set of questions elicit information about the onset and duration of symptoms identified in the first part. The third part of the instrument is then used to record behavioral observations collected during the interview. This includes impressions of cognitive abilities, emotional expression, quality of interpersonal interactions, and physical features.

TABLE 8.4
Examples of Content Areas for the Child Assessment Schedule

| Scale Name | Scale Content |
|---|---|
| School | Relationship with teachers, grades, homework, concentration, attendance |
| Friends | Friendships, enjoyment of activities with peers, quality of friendships, degree of conflict, trustfulness |
| Activities | Hobbies, current interest in activies, loneliness, ability to be by himself or herself |
| Family | Constellation of family, current relationship with biological parents or parental figures, qualitative description of relationship with parental figures, desired changes for the family |
| Self-Image | General inquiry to elicit description of self, specific inquiry about self-perception in various domains |
| Expression of Anger | Precipitating situations and coping skills, impulsivity, difficulty with anger and temper, trouble following rules, variety of questions relevant to conduct disorder and oppositionality, use of alcohol or drugs |

*Note.* Based on Hodges (1997). *Manual for the Child Assessment Schedule.* Ypsilanti: Eastern Michigan University, Department of Psychology.

All items are scored with "yes," "no," "ambiguous response," or "not scored." Items are structured so that those relevant to a diagnosis are keyed and lead to further questions probing for information about onset and duration. Manuals for the child and parent versions of the CAS present explicit guidelines regarding the administration of questions and recording responses.

The CAS may be scored, first, in terms of 11 content areas. These scores reflect the levels of pathology represented in each of those areas. A total pathology score may also be derived as an index of overall psychopathological symptomatology. Diagnoses corresponding to *DSM* classifications may also be derived; these include the following areas: conduct disorder, oppositional disorder, attention deficit disorder, major depressive disorder, dysthymia, separation anxiety, and overanxious disorder. Information about a variety of other disorders can also be obtained (e.g., substance abuse, sleep problems, eating disorders), although formal diagnoses of those conditions are not provided. Responses may be scored in terms of the qualitative diagnostic categories, and quantitative scores may also be calculated for the categories from the number of items checked within each grouping. Thus, the interview may yield a diagnosis of conduct disorder and also an index of the severity of that condition based on the number of items checked in the conduct disorder category.

The scoring of the CAS is standardized and scores may, in fact, be calculated with computer algorithms. Hodges (1997) also suggested that the CAS may be used simply as a clinical interview guide. In this case the structured scoring procedures are bypassed, and the information collected in the interview is used by the clinician to derive a diagnosis.

Clark (1987) and Gutterman et al. (1987) provided critical reviews of earlier psychometric analyses of the CAS. Both reviewers concluded that, although preliminary, reliability and validity support for the instrument were impressive. Since those reviews, a number of other psychometric analyses have been reported, primarily by Hodges and her colleagues (see Hodges, 1987, 1993; Hodges & Zeman, 1993, for reviews of that research). Those analyses continue to provide support for the psychometric soundness of the measure. There are, however, several cautions: First, levels of reliability and validity are not consistent across all symptom areas. Second, most of the research has been conducted with children, and relatively little information is available regarding use of the scale with adolescents. Third, the diagnosis and symptom scores are based directly on *DSM* categories, and there remain unanswered questions about their construct validity.

## Diagnostic Interview for Children and Adolescents (DICA)

The most notable characteristic of this highly structured interview schedule is that it is suitable for administration by lay interviewers. The schedule was originally developed to assess diagnostic categories represented in the International Classification of Psychiatric Disorders, but a 1981 revision was patterned on the National Institute of Mental Health Diagnostic Interview Schedule, which was in turn based on the *DSM* system. The most recent version of the schedule, DICA–R, reflects the *DSM–III–R* diagnostic system.

A version of DICA–R for use with adolescents (13–17 years old) is available, as is a parallel version suitable for use with parents. The administration of the schedule is highly structured and is designed for use by clinicians or paraprofessionals with specific training in the instrument. The instrument can be hand or computer scored using an algorithm developed for the schedule.

DICA–R is scored in terms of all diagnostic categories relevant to children and adolescents represented in the *DSM–III–R*. It yields information regarding the onset, duration, and severity of symptoms within those categories. The schedule also provides summary scores in six areas: Relationship Problems, School Behavior, School Learning, Neurotic Symptoms, Somatic Symptoms, and Psychotic Symptoms.

Hodges (1993; Hodges & Zeman, 1993) concluded in her reviews that only limited support exists for the psychometric properties of the DICA–R. Further, a study by M. H. Boyle et al. (1993) reported considerable variability in reliability levels across diagnostic categories. They also reported relatively low levels of parent–adolescent agreement, although levels of agreement between trained lay interviewers and child psychiatrists were generally satisfactory. In sum, this represents a promising instrument for the collection of diagnostic information by paraprofessionals, but considerably more psychometric research is needed before it can be recommended for clinical application.

## Diagnostic Interview Schedule for Children (DISC)

This is the second of two interview schedules suitable for administration by lay interviewers. Scoring of the instrument is also simplified because it is based on algorithms requiring no clinical judgment. In fact, versions of the schedule that permit computer-based administration and scoring and involve no human involvement are now available.

The initial version of this instrument was developed as a research tool for use in large-scale epidemiological studies (see Shaffer et al., 1993). It was designed for collecting information about the prevalence of mental disorders in samples of children and adolescents. The instrument has undergone several revisions, with the current version identified as DISC–2.3.

DISC–2.3 is appropriate for use with children and adolescents between 9 and 17 years old. Two parallel versions of the schedule are available, one for administration to the youth and the other for parents. The latter version may also be administered to a professional familiar with the youth. A preliminary version of the schedule suitable for administration to teachers has also been reported (Lahey et al., 1994).

The current version of the schedule is designed to reflect *DSM–III–R* diagnostic categories, although it is likely that revisions to reflect changes in *DSM–IV* will become available soon. The schedule is composed of 249 stem questions relating to the various *DSM* categories applicable to children and adolescents. Each of the stem questions requires a yes or no response. Yes responses lead to a set of additional questions designed to elicit information about the intensity, frequency, duration, context, and age of onset of the symptom. The schedule is designed to reflect current levels of emotional function and most questions refer to states existing within the previous 6 months.

Table 8.5 identifies the major diagnostic categories assessed within DISC–2.3. These are further broken down into six diagnostic modules: Anxiety, Mood, Disruptive, Substance Abuse, Psychotic, and Miscellaneous Disorders. Several different formats for deriving diagnoses have been described by Costello, Edelbrock, Dulcan, Kalas, and Klaric (1984) and Shaffer et al. (1996). These represent various ways of determining whether or not the criteria for the *DSM* diagnostic categories have been satisfied.

TABLE 8.5
Major Diagnostic Categories Included in the
Diagnostic Interview Schedule for Children

| | |
|---|---|
| Simple phobia | Social phobia |
| Agogaphobia | Separation anxiety |
| Overanxious | Any anxiety |
| Nocturnal enuresis | Major depression |
| Any depression | Attention deficit/hyperactivity |
| Oppositional defiant | Conduct disorder |
| Any disruptive | |

*Note.* Based on Shaffer et al. (1993). The Diagnostic Interview Schedule for Children–Revised Versions (DISC–R): Preparation, field testing, inter-rater reliability and acceptability. *Journal of the American Academy of Child and Adolescent Psychiatry, 32.*

One of the formats also provides for incorporating both parent and adolescent data into the scoring.

The standard scoring procedures for DISC–2.3 depend on the diagnostic categories of the *DSM* classification system, although as noted there is provision in some scoring formats for providing severity ratings in connection with the diagnosis. Thus, the youth may be diagnosed as exhibiting mild to moderate conduct disorder, severe conduct disorder, or no conduct disorder. An alternative scoring format based on quantitative pathology scales was described by Rubio-Stipec et al. (1996). They were able to empirically derive four dimensions of pathology from data collected with DISC–2.3: Depressive, Attention Deficit, Oppositional Defiant, and Conduct Disorder.

The DISC–2.3 was specifically developed for use by lay interviewers or paraprofessionals. A structured training program is available, and this generally requires 3 or 4 days. Total administration time for the instrument ranges from 40 to 60 minutes. As noted, a fully computerized version of the schedule is now available (Fisher, Blouin, & Shaffer, 1993).

Reviews of earlier versions of DISC by Gutterman et al. (1987) and Hodges (1993; Hodges & Zeman, 1993) were generally negative regarding its psychometric properties. Reviewers noted weaknesses in the reliability indexes for the various diagnostic categories and uneven support for construct and criterion-related validity. Hodges and Zeman (1993) did, however, conclude that the schedule shows greater strength for the adolescent than younger age groups.

The instrument has, however, been revised since those reviews (see Shaffer et al., 1996) and several new psychometric analyses have appeared (see, e.g., C. A. King, Katz, Ghaziuddin, & Brand, 1997; R. Roberts, Solovitz, Chen, & Casat, 1996; Schwab-Stone et al., 1996; Shaffer et al., 1996). This research seems to demonstrate improved levels of reliability and validity for the measure. It is important to keep in mind, however, that the DISC was originally developed as a research tool, and its use in clinical settings presents some dangers. Although its ease and economy of administration and scoring are appealing, there is potential for misuse on the part of individuals without the training and expertise to understand the limits associated with information from such a measure.

## Schedule for Affective Disorders and Schizophrenia (K–SADS)

This semistructured interview schedule is designed for use with children and adolescents, and it derives from the Schedule for Affective Disorders and Schizophrenia (Endicott & Spitzer, 1978), an instrument developed for assessing mental disorders in adults. K–SADS has gone through a number of revisions, with the most recent version labeled the Schedule for Affective Disorders and Schizophrenia for School-Age Children–Present and Lifetime version (K–SADS–PL; J. Kaufman et al., 1997). This revision represents an integration of two earlier versions, one of which assessed current and past episodes of disorder (K–SADS–E) and the other only current episodes (K–SADS–P). This revision also incorporates a number of other changes from earlier editions, including an expanded range of diagnostic categories, the incorporation of changes represented in *DSM–IV*, and some alterations in scoring formats. The schedule is appropriate for use with children between 6 and 17 years old.

There are several features that set K–SADS–PL apart from most of the other schedules considered in this section. First, and although the instrument can be administered solely to the youth, it is typically administered to both the youth and a parent, interviewed separately. Additionally, the interviewer is encouraged to examine other information about the youth (e.g., file information, test scores) and record that information as well. Second, the instrument departs from most others in this category by basing the actual diagnosis on a clinical judgment. Thus, after collecting the information through the structured set of questions, the interviewer is then required to determine whether a diagnosis is appropriate or not. Administration and scoring of the K–SADS–PL thus requires a high degree of clinical expertise and judgment.

As indicated, the K–SADS–PL is generally administered separately to the youth and a parent, with each interview taking from 45 to 90 minutes. The interview is divided into three parts. The first, the introductory interview, is designed to establish rapport with the client and collect some background information. This is followed by the screening interview. This is composed of a set of structured questions that elicit information about 20 diagnostic areas, encompassing all of the Axis I diagnoses relevant to children and adolescents included in *DSM–IV*. Scores from the screening interview provide initial information about the existence of symptoms within a diagnostic category. The third part of the interview, the diagnostic supplements, provides for a further exploration of diagnoses meeting the threshold score in the screening interview. For example, if the youth is judged to meet the criteria for conduct disorder during the screening, a supplementary set of questions are administered within that category as a means of refining the diagnosis and providing information about the severity, chronicity, and age of onset of the disorder. Items in the diagnostic supplements are divided into five categories: Affective Disorders; Psychotic Disorders; Anxiety Disorders; Behavioral Disorders; and Substance Abuse, Eating, and Tic Disorders. Scores from the instrument reflect the presence or absence of the 20 diagnostic categories.

There are two reasons why evaluating the psychometric properties of the K–SADS–PL is problematic. First, a number of different versions have appeared over the years, and psychometric analyses conducted with one may not apply to others. Second, some analyses are based on information collected from parents alone, some from the youth alone, and some from both parent and youth. Some assessments have also included collateral information whereas others have not. This, too, has created some confusion regarding the generality of the psychometric analyses. However, Gutterman et al. (1987) and Hodges (1993; Hodges & Zeman, 1993) reported generally favorable evaluations of K–SADS based on the limited psychometric information available to that point, and J. Kaufman et al. (1997) reported some preliminary analyses for the latest version of the instrument.

## GENERAL CONSIDERATIONS

A major theme of this volume is that psychological assessments should as far as possible be based on standardized tools and procedures. It is in this sense that advances in the development of these standardized interview schedules is so encouraging. Problems remain with these schedules, but they do promise to lead to more valid assessments of emotional and behavioral pathologies than the more clinical procedures.

There are several senses in which the structured and semistructured schedules represent advances over clinical interviews. First, they present an opportunity to evaluate the reliability and validity of information collected through the procedures, an opportunity rarely available with clinical interviews. Second, there seems clear evidence that reliability levels exhibited with the structured schedules are higher than those yielded by clinical interviews, and that the reliability levels are continuing to improve as the structured schedules are refined.

One reason the structured interviews produce higher levels of reliability, particularly interrater reliability, is that they discourage the operation of bias in the conduct of the interview. The same information is collected from all clients no matter what the beliefs or assumptions of the clinician. A related advantage is that use of these schedules encourages a broad and detailed assessment of the client's functioning and situation (Hoge, Andrews, Robinson, & Hollett, 1988). This is important in light of the theoretical models reviewed in chapters 1 and 2 showing that human behavior is multiply determined and that decisions about interventions should be based on comprehensive surveys of client characteristics and circumstances.

Standardized structured and semistructured interview schedules are also seen as superior to the type of self-report questionnaires and checklists to be described in chapter 8. Hodges (1993) expressed the point as follows:

> It appears that self-report questionnaires are not sufficient for subject selection or for outcome measurement when the presence of a clinical level of symptomatology is of interest. . . . These measures cannot be used to determine diagnosis because the items do not parallel diagnostic criteria, and onset and duration information is not requested. Additionally, there is evidence that the sensitivity of questionnaires is too low for diagnostic purposes when recommended cut-off points are used. (p. 51)

To illustrate, a structured interview schedule such as DISC and a behavioral checklist such as the Revised Behavior Problem Checklist will likely not yield parallel diagnoses of conduct disorder. Further, the latter will probably produce a lower sensitivity value—or fewer true positives—than the former. This issue was explored by Hoge and Andrews (1992).

There are significant strengths associated with the development of these structured and semistructured interview schedules, but there are also some weaknesses to be noted. First, there are limitations inherent within the structured format. It has been suggested, for example, that following a structured set of questions may interfere with establishing rapport with the client. The interviewer does not have the opportunity to vary questioning with the feedback being provided by the client. Further, the structured format constrains the interviewer from pursuing lines of inquiry that emerge during the course of the interview. The problems of establishing rapport and of collecting information not provided by the interview can, of course, be dealt with either before or after administration of the formal interview.

It should also be recognized that the use of a standardized interview schedule does not entirely eliminate the operation of interviewer bias. There is still considerable room for variability in the way questions are asked and in the nonverbal cues of the interviewer. Further, in the case of instruments such as the K–SADS where the interviewer is required to exercise clinical judgments in forming the diagnoses, there is still considerable latitude for individual beliefs, assumptions, and biases to operate. Related to this is Hodges' (1993) point that training in the use of the structured and semistructured interviews is critical: "There is a general consensus that training to reliability is necessary for using any of the diagnostic interviews, even when the interviewers are experienced professionals" (p. 52).

An issue that seems to preoccupy the developers of these schedules concerns disagreements among respondents (see Bird et al., 1992). Information provided by children and parents sometimes yields conflicting diagnoses. Some schedules, such as the K–SADS, employ rather complicated scoring procedures to resolve these conflicts. However, as discussed in chapter 4, these conflicts should not be viewed as problematic. Rather, it should be recognized that different respondents bring different perspectives to the assessment and each should be viewed as useful.

Another problem area concerns the time frame represented in the interview. There are actually two problems here. First, there is sometimes ambiguity within schedules about the time frame to be employed (Gutterman et al., 1987). For example, some schedules require that the assessment of symptoms be based on "present" conditions, but this latter is not always clearly defined. The other problem in this respect is that there are variations across schedules in time frame, and this means that direct comparisons of diagnoses from different schedules are not always possible. Some schedules, for example, will base the assessment on the previous 2 weeks, others on a 6-week interval, and still others on a 1-year range. This variability exists in spite of the specific time intervals represented in the *DSM*.

Still another issue is the lack of normative data for the interview schedules, and this represents a serious departure from the criteria used to define standardized psychological assessments. All of these schedules can be represented better as criterion-referenced rather than norm-referenced instruments. That is, diagnostic and symptom severity scores are based on theoretically derived operational criteria, usually deriving from a version of the *DSM*. In some cases prevalence data are presented for the various diagnostic categories, but these have generally not been translated into normative scores. This seems a serious omission, but one that will likely be corrected in the future.

Another issue is the absence of information about impairment and strengths. Information about the presence of a diagnosis is generally not a sufficient basis for a decision about intervention. We also need to know the extent of the impairment and its effects on the functioning of the individual. Some of the schedules do provide severity scores, with the latter based on the number of symptoms present within the diagnosis. However, this information, although useful, still does not tell us very much about the functioning of the individual. Two of the instruments do provide for collecting this information. The K–SADS schedule includes a global impairment index corresponding to the Global Assessment Scale of the *DSM–III–R*, and a parallel instrument for assessing levels of impairment accompanies the CAS. This measure, the Child and Adolescent Functional Assessment Scale, is discussed in chapter 11. This instrument is also unique in that it provides for the assessment of strengths or protective factors along with the diagnoses of pathology. The lack of attention to these factors in the other schedules should be seen as an important omission in light of the research reviewed in chapter 2 supporting the importance of considering protective factors and risk factors in diagnostic assessments.

There are also some issues associated with evaluations of the validity of these schedules. On the positive side, all are the object of current research activity. This in itself, however, has created something of a problem. Each of the instruments has undergone several revisions, and it is sometimes difficult to know to what extent psychometric information can be generalized from one version to another.

There are several other more fundamental problems associated with evaluations of the validity of these schedules. The first relates to construct validity, which concerns the meaningfulness or accuracy of the diagnostic and symptom severity scores yielded by the interview schedules. That issue is, however, complicated by controversies over the meaningfulness of the diagnostic categories on which those scores are based. The latter derive largely from versions of the *DSM*, and, as we have seen, considerable debate revolves around those definitions.

The usual procedures in these validation efforts have involved comparing the interview-based diagnoses with those derived from other expert opinion, with the latter generally based on assessments of experienced mental health professionals. There is, however, an inherent circularity in this type of procedure. The need in this case is for systematic investigations of the convergent and discriminant validities of the schedules, with those investigations conducted in the context of theoretical frameworks incorporating the psychiatric diagnoses. This research would illuminate not only the construct validity of the interview schedules but would also contribute to a refinement of the diagnostic system on which they are based.

The second fundamental problem is the need for further investigations of predictive validity. Diagnoses yielded by these instruments are used to make intervention decisions; that is, decisions about whether or not to provide intervention, and, if so, the type of intervention to provide. It is important, then, to provide information regarding what we earlier referred to as treatment validity. This would reflect the ability of the interview-based scores to predict the outcomes of treatment. As these instruments are also used to assess the progress and outcomes of interventions, there is also a need for dynamic predictive validity studies. That is, research in which it is demonstrated that scores from the measures can reliably track changes in the client.

It is appropriate to conclude this discussion with Sattler's (1997) observation that there is a role for both unstructured clinical interviews and structured standardized interviews in assessment activities. Both are capable of providing important information about clients, but both must be used with a full awareness of the strengths and limitations associated with them.

# 9

Behavioral Ratings
and Checklists

This chapter contains a review of standardized rating and checklist measures focusing on observable behaviors. The emphasis in nearly all of the instruments is on pathological behaviors or states, but there are a few instruments providing for measures of positive competencies and adjustment.

All of the instruments reviewed involve a checklist or rating scale format. Some are self-report measures; that is, the rating is provided by the individual being assessed. The line between self-report instruments of this sort and personality tests is sometimes a fine one. Most of the measures, however, are designed for completion by an independent observer familiar with the individual. This typically involves a parent or teacher, although child-care workers, counselors, and others in contact with the youth might also serve as respondents.

The instruments reviewed in the chapter exhibit a variety of formats. Some are in the form of checklists or cumulated point scales. In this case the respondent simply indicates whether a behavior is present or not. Subscores and total scores are then formed by adding the number of items checked. Other instruments are in the form of rating scales. These usually involve what are referred to as *graphic scales* employing 3, 4, or 5-point Likert scales; that is, the respondent is provided with a set of response points (e.g., 1 = *very true*, 2 = *somewhat true*, 3 = *somewhat false*, 4 = *very false*).

These behavioral rating and checklist instruments are widely used for screening, diagnostic, and research purposes. Teacher checklist measures of behavioral pathology have proven, for example, very useful in the initial identification of problem students. Similarly, standardized teacher, parent, and self-report ratings have proven invaluable to clinicians and counselors in the formation of diagnoses and treatment recommendations. They have also been used in these contexts for tracking the effectiveness of interventions over time. Research and epidemiological studies have also depended very heavily on this type of assessment instrument.

Several strengths of rating and checklist instruments can be identified. First, and perhaps most obvious, they generally represent very economical ways of collecting information about behavior. This is particularly true where compared with personality tests and structured observation procedures that usually involve more time and more expertise in administration, scoring, and interpretation. Second, these instruments are of value in the sense that they permit the collection of information about the social, behavioral, and emotional status of the individual under naturalistic conditions. The parent or teacher is providing information about the youth's behavior within the home, school, or other normal setting. Further, most of the measures provide information about specific behaviors (e.g., starts fights, disobeys instructions) and broader dimensions (e.g., anxious, withdrawn). To this extent they are particularly useful in behavior modification interventions.

There is another important sense in which these standardized judgmental instruments represent valuable assessment tools. If we accept that parents, teachers, and the client himself or herself represent important sources of information about the client, then the collection of that information through structured procedures with established reliability and validity represents a better approach than a dependence on informal and unstructured procedures. Too often in the past counselors and clinicians have relied on subjective impressions communicated through informal means. This has often yielded poor information and led to invalid decisions. Further, and where normative data are available, the clinician is able to interpret the behavioral information with reference to other youths at a particular age level. This can be especially useful when one is attempting to assess the degree of deviance represented in a child's behavior.

Many of these rating and checklist instruments were originally developed as adjuncts to behavior therapies where they were considered important in identifying target behaviors and tracking behavior change. Initially there was little effort to treat these as standardized assessment instruments. That situation has, however, changed. These instruments have typically not received the intensive psychometric attention accorded personality tests, but there is clearly much more of a concern today for developing structured administration procedures, assessing reliability and validity, and developing normative data. In fact, some of the broad-based behavioral checklist measures have now achieved as sophisticated a level of development as some of the established personality tests. The issue of the strengths and weaknesses of rating and checklist measures is addressed again at the end of the chapter.

There are probably hundreds of checklist and rating scale instruments reported in the literature (see Aiken, 1996b; Hersen & Bellack, 1988). The following review is, therefore, necessarily selective. I have, however, made an effort to include instruments that are widely available and that are the subject of continuing research and evaluation activity. They are discussed under two headings: broadband measures and narrow-band measures. Some related instruments are discussed in the chapters dealing with measures of attitudes, values, and cognitions (chap. 10) and composite measures (chap. 11). The latter includes a discussion of measures of adaptive functioning.

## BROAD-BAND MEASURES

All of the rating and checklist measures discussed in this section represent efforts to assess a broad range of behavioral dimensions. The 10 instruments discussed are identified in Table 9.1.

### Behavior Assessment System for Children (BASC)

This system includes five parallel measures. The two basic measures, teacher and parent rating scales, are considered in this section. The other measures include a self-report rating form, an observation schedule, and a developmental history inventory.

Sophisticated item analysis procedures were used to develop the teacher and parent rating measures. They are scored in terms of three dimensions of pathology: Externalizing Problems, Internalizing Problems, and School Problems. The scales also yield information about adaptive

TABLE 9.1
Broad-Based Rating and Checklist Measures

| Measure | Source/Reference |
|---|---|
| Behavior Assessment System for Children | American Guidance Service |
| Behavior Disorders Identification Scale | Hawthorne Educational Services |
| Child and Adolescent Adjustment Profile | Consulting Psychologist Press |
| Child Behavior Checklist Instruments | University Associates in Psychiatry |
| Conners Rating Scales | Multi-Health Systems |
| Devereux Adolescent Rating Scale | Psychological Corporation |
| Jesness Behavior Checklist | Consulting Psychologist Press |
| Personality Inventory for Children | Western Psychological Services |
| Personality Inventory for Youth | Western Psychological Services |
| Revised Behavior Problem Checklist | Psychological Assessment Resources |

behaviors or strengths; an important feature in light of the previous discussion of resilience. Normative scores are based on clinical or non-clinical samples, with the latter coded by gender and age group. The measures are appropriate for ages 4 to 18 years.

Recent reviews by Sandoval (1998) and Witt (1998) commend the care taken in constructing this set of instruments and the high quality of the manual and supporting materials. They note as well the wide range of reliability and validity data that have been presented in support of the measures, particularly the teacher and parent rating forms. Limitations are noted regarding the representativeness of the normative samples and the ease of integrating scores across the different measures. On the other hand, the instruments within the system are the objects of continuing research attention, and these weaknesses will undoubtedly be addressed.

### Behavior Disorders Identification Scale (BDIS)

Two versions of this rating scale exist, one designed for completion by teachers and the other by a parent. The scale is somewhat unique in that it was developed specifically to assess emotional and behavior disorders contained in Public Law 94-142. It is designed, then, as an aid for identifying children eligible for the provisions of that act. In addition, the manual describes procedures for developing individual educational plans appropriate for different BDIS profiles.

The instrument is appropriate for use with the age group between 4.5 and 21 years old. It yields five scores corresponding to the problem areas identified in Public Law 94-142: Learning, Interpersonal Relations, Inappropriate Behavior, Unhappiness/Depression, and Physical Symptoms/ Fears. Scoring is based on a large and representative sample of youths. Administration and scoring guidelines are clearly presented in the manual, along with practical advice on using the instrument for formulating intervention strategies from the BDIS profiles.

Some information regarding the reliability and construct validity of the instrument is presented in the manual but there appear to be relatively few independent evaluations of the instrument. Fairbank (1995) presented a generally favorable review of the instrument, but Stientjes (1995) addressed some criticisms toward the psychometric evaluations and the interpretive guidelines presented in the manual.

### Child and Adolescent Adjustment Profile (CAAP)

This is a brief, easily administered rating scale suitable for completion by parents, teachers, counselors, or other professionals familiar with the youth. It was developed through both theoretical and empirical procedures.

The 20 items of the CAAP refer to specific aspects of behavior (e.g., unresponsive to discipline), and the respondent is asked to indicate the frequency with which the behaviors were observed during the preceding month. A 4-point scale ranging from 4 (*often*) to 1 (*never*) is provided. The scale yields a total score reflecting overall level of adjustment and five factor scores labeled Peer Relations, Dependency, Hostility, Productivity, and Withdrawal. Separate norms are provided for boys and girls ages 12 to 18.

Paludi's (1987) review of the instrument indicates satisfactory levels of internal consistency and test–retest reliability. She also noted that validation studies based on comparing CAAP scores of various clinical groupings of subjects are generally supportive of the measure. Also, and unlike many studies in this category, evidence for treatment validity is presented in the manual. However, it must be acknowledged that construct and criterion-related validity evaluations of the measure are somewhat limited at the present time, and additional research with the measure is desirable.

### Child Behavior Checklist Instruments (CBCL)

We are dealing in this case with a family of instruments designed for assessing competencies and behavioral pathologies in children and adolescents. Three of these are based on a checklist format and are considered in this section: the Child Behavior Checklist (CBCL) designed for completion by a parent, the Child Behavior Checklist–Teacher Report Form (CBCL–T) for completion by teachers, and a self-report inventory termed the Youth Self-Report Inventory (YSRI).

This group of instruments is unique in a number of respects. First, there are some variations in the scoring of the instruments, but they all reflect a common model of behavioral competence and pathology in children and adolescents. Second, the instruments form part of a coherent assessment system. Achenbach (1994; Achenbach & McConaughy, 1987) described this as a multiaxial empirically based assessment system. The assessment is based on information provided by multiple sources, with the interpretation of the information supported by empirical research. Third, the set of instruments is unique because it includes efforts to assess positive competencies as well as dimensions of pathology. This is important in light of the previous discussion of an increasing concern for identifying protective factors in analyzing development.

Each of the three checklist instruments contains two sets of items, one reflecting competencies and the other behavioral pathologies. The items differ somewhat across instruments depending on the respondent. To illustrate, the CBCL includes 15 items reflecting three areas of competence: Activities, Social, and School. The pathology checklist is composed of 118 items reflecting specific behaviors or behavioral states (e.g., "gets in many fights"; "unhappy, sad, or depressed"). The respondent, in this case the parent, indicates whether the item is "not true," "sometimes true," or "very true" of the child.

The most recent scoring format for the instruments is based on an effort to achieve some consistency across the parent, teacher, and self-report instruments. Each instrument is scored in terms of eight factor scores common across multiple age ranges (ages 4–18), both genders, and the three instruments. Additional scores are then provided that are unique to gender, age, and informant groupings. In addition to the eight narrow-band scores, the checklists yield a total behavior problem score and two broadband scores termed Internalizing and Externalizing. It should be noted that, although some factor scores are common across groupings, norms for the scores are specific for boys and girls and for the age and informant groupings. For example, there are separate norms for the CBCL–T for boys and girls and for different age groups.

Table 9.2 identifies the eight cross-informant syndrome constructs for the three checklist instruments (CBCL, CBCL–T, and YSRI). Profile scores for the instruments are based on norms specific to the instrument, gender, and age group and are expressed as *T*-scores or percentiles. Figure 9.1 presents an example of a CBCL profile for a 15-year-old girl. Note that a clinical cut-off has been established at a *T*-score of 70. The normative scores in this case are based on a nonclinical sample of youths. Achenbach (1991) also presented a procedure for directly comparing profiles yieded by the CBCL, CBCL–T, and YSRI.

There is rather limited information available for the competence scales of the instruments and for the recently developed YSRI, but a wealth of psychometric information has accumulated for the parent and teacher versions of the CBCL. This is presented in the manuals and elsewhere (Achenbach, 1994). As with all instruments of this type, there remain some questions about the construct validity of the syndrome or factor scores, an issue discussed further in the final section of this chapter. That issue aside, there is considerable support for the reliability and criterion-related validity of the CBCL and CBCL–T instruments, and their continued use in research and clinical settings would appear to be justified (Kelley, 1985; Martin, 1988). In addition, there is now available a considerable range of sophisticated supporting materials for the instruments, including computer-scoring procedures and interpretative guides.

## The Conners Rating Scales–Revised (CRS–R)

The Conners scales were originally developed at Johns Hopkins Hospital for use in assessing drug effects in treatment evaluation studies (Conners, 1969). The focus of the original work was on hyperactivity and attentional

## TABLE 9.2
### Cross-Informant Syndrome Constructs for the Child Behavior Checklist Instruments

| Internalizing | Neither Internalizing nor Externalizing | Externalizing |
|---|---|---|
| Withdrawn | Social problems | Delinquent behavior |
| Somatic complaints | Thought problems | Aggressive behavior |
| Anxious/depressed | Attention problems | |

*Note.* Based on T. M. Achenbach (1994). Child Behavior Checklist and related instruments. In M. E. Maruish (Ed.), *The use of psychological testing for treatment planning and outcome assessment.* Hillsdale, NJ: Lawrence Erlbaum Associates, Inc.

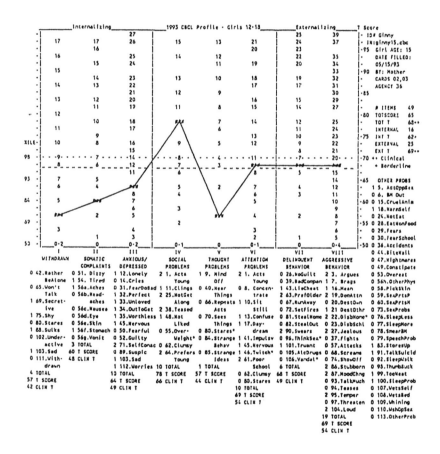

FIG. 9.1. Example of a Child Behavior Checklist profile. Source: T. M. Achenbach (1993). *Empirically based taxonomy: How to use syndromes and profile types derived from the CBCL/4-18, TRF, and YSR.* Burlington: University of Vermont, Department of Psychiatry. Reproduced with permission.

problems, but, in fact, the scales provide assessment of a broad range of behavioral disorders. The scales in their various forms have been widely used for screening behavioral problems, as diagnostic instruments—particularly in evaluating the effectiveness of interventions—and as research tools.

Revised versions of the original scales have recently appeared, including a new self-report version (Conners, 1995). These include: (a) a long form of the parent rating scale (CPRS:L) with 80 items, (b) a short form of the parent rating scale (CPRS:S) with 48 items, (c) a long form of the teacher rating scale (CTRS–R:L) with 59 items, (d) a short form of the teacher rating scale (CTRS:S) with 28 items, (e) a long form of the self-report version titled the Conners–Wells' Adolescent Self-Report Scale Long (CASS:L) with 87 items, and (f) a short form of the CASS (CASS:S) with 27 items. The parent versions may also be used by professionals familiar with the child (e.g., probation officers, child-care workers)

Items on all versions of the CRS represent expressions of behavioral dysfunction. The respondent—whether parent, teacher, or youth—indicates the extent to which a behavior has been a problem in the preceding month; a 4-point Likert response scale is used to indicate the extent of the problem. Items in the revised versions of the instruments have been modified in some cases.

Scoring of the CRS is based on both factor analysis derived scores and rationally formed scores. It should be noted that the scores differ somewhat from those of previous versions. Table 9.3 lists the subscales for the CPRS:L version. Subscales for the CTRS:L are similar but do not include the Psychosomatic scale. Subscales for the short forms of both parent and teacher instruments are as follows: Oppositional, Cognitive Problems, Hyperactivity, and ADHD Index.

Several observations regarding the scales are appropriate. First, the availability of parallel forms of parent, teacher, and youth scales is very useful for the clinician seeking to compare alternative sources of information about behavior problems. Second, an effort has been made in these revised versions to incorporate *DSM–IV* diagnostic categories. The *DSM–IV* Symptom Subscales represent a separate set of subscores. Finally,

TABLE 9.3
Subscales for the Conners Parent Rating Scale: Long

| | |
|---|---|
| Conduct Disorder | Anxious-Shy |
| Restless-Disorganized | Learning Problem |
| Psychosomatic | Obsessive-Compulsive |
| Antisocial | Hyperactive-Immature |

*Note.* Based on Conners, C. K. (1989), *Manual for the Conners Parent Rating Scales*. Toronto: Multi-Health Systems.

the Hyperactivity and Attention Deficit Disorder scales represented in all versions of the CRS derive from earlier versions of the scales, and they have proven very useful over the years.

The revised versions of the CRS are accompanied by updated and expanded normative groups. These include representative samples of youths from the United States and Canada. Scoring of the parent and teacher versions is based on children aged 3 to 17 and 12- to 17-year-old adolescents for the self-report version.

The current versions of the CRS are the product of a long history of development and they are now accompanied by a wide range of sophisticated supporting material. The manuals are informative and clearly written and computerized scoring programs are available. Feedback forms for communicating the outcomes of the assessments to parents and teachers are also available. On the other hand, the ease with which the instruments can be administered and scored can create problems in the hands of inexperienced or untrained individuals: Interpretation and application of the information yielded by the scales still requires a knowledge of the limitations of such information.

The previous versions of the parent and teacher checklists have been available for some years and a considerable body of psychometric data accumulated. A review of that research by Hutton (1994) concluded that the parent and teacher forms of the scales demonstrate levels of reliability and validity sufficient to justify their use as screening, diagnostic, and research instruments. The strongest evidence exists for the long version of the CTRS, with rather less attention having been paid to the parent version or either of the two short versions, although their psychometric properties are also judged satisfactory. The construct validity of this type of measure is addressed in the final section of the chapter. Some data have been reported in the manual for the revised versions of the teacher and parent scales, but there is still a dependence on data reported for the earlier versions. The generality of those data for the new versions may, however, be viewed as problematic. Only limited information is available as yet for the self-report instruments (CASS:L and CASS:S).

### The Devereux Adolescent Rating Scale

The original version of this scale appeared about 30 years ago (Spivack, Haimes, & Spotts, 1967). It was originally designed for use in assessing behavioral pathology in youths confined to residential facilities, where the scale would be completed by residential counselors, child-care workers, nurses, or other professionals with extensive contact with the child. Interestingly, the scale has also come to be used widely by school psychologists and teachers, although a parallel measure, the Hahnemann High School Behavior Rating Scale (Spivack & Swift, 1972), is considered more appropriate for use by respondents whose contact with the child is confined to the school setting.

The 84 items of the scale reflect specific behaviors and are phrased in terms comprehensible to nonpsychologists. The respondent indicates on a 5-point Likert scale the relative frequency with which the child has exhibited the behavior over the previous 2 weeks. Raw scores from the measure are translated into behavioral profiles, with the latter based on 12 factor scores (e.g., Defiant-Resistive, Poor Emotional Control), three cluster scores (e.g., Paranoid Thought, Anxious Self-Blame), and 11 item scores (e.g., compulsive acts, withdrawn). The formation of the profiles is rather complicated, but the profiles do present good graphic pictures of behavioral adjustment and may be interpreted with reference to clinical and nonclinical standardization groups.

The Devereux Adolescent Rating Scale has several strengths. First, the initial development of the scale was based on a careful review of theoretical and clinical information regarding dysfunctional behaviors of adolescents in residential settings. Second, this is one of the few instruments specifically developed for assessing the behavior of children in residential treatment settings (most measures are primarily designed for use by parents or teachers). Third, the measure has been developed to encompass the entire adolescent range, including 17- and 18-year-olds.

There are, on the other hand, some cautions to be observed. An earlier review by Hufano (1985) indicated rather sketchy support for the psychometric properties of the instrument, and although research continues on the instrument, there remain some gaps in this respect. The manual and the standardization data are also rather dated. In some senses this should be regarded as an instrument in a state of development. For example, new factor scores are continuing to be identified for particular groups such as substance abusers and delinquents (see, e.g., Williams, Ben-Porath, & Weed, 1990). Nevertheless, the measure has proven useful as a screening tool for use in residential settings and, where used with the appropriate cautions, continues to have utility in those settings.

### Jesness Behavior Checklist (JBC)

Two parallel versions of this instrument are available, one for completion by an observer (teacher, parent, counselor, etc.) and a self-report version. The scale was originally developed for use with delinquent adolescents, but it has been modified for use with all adolescents.

The JBC is composed of 80 items and is scored is terms of 14 bipolar subscales, some of which were derived through factor analytic procedures and others through rational procedures. Because these are bipolar scales, the instrument is capable of yielding information about positive and negative competencies. Examples of subscales include Friendliness versus

Hostility, Rapport versus Alienation, and Effective Communication versus Inarticulateness. Scores are based on a large sample of delinquent youths, ages 13 to 20. Another feature of the measure is that it provides for direct comparisons of profiles yielded by observers and the youth.

Drummond (1986) reviewed the JBC and concluded that the instrument could be of value to clinicians for the collection of information about behaviors from the client or an independent observer. He noted, however, some bases for caution that are still relevant. First, only limited information exists for the construct or criterion-related validity of the measure. Second, the instrument was developed and normed with samples of delinquent adolescents and its relevance for other groups has yet to be established. Third, both the observer and self-report versions are reported as somewhat difficult to complete. Therefore, the instrument may be of value to clinicians and counselors, particularly those dealing with offenders, but it should be used with these cautions in mind.

### Personality Inventory for Children–Revised (PIC–R)

This is a well-established and widely used screening and diagnostic device appropriate for use with children between 3 and 16 years of age. The scale is designed for completion by a parent or other individual well acquainted with the youth. It is particularly designed for use as a screening tool or for diagnostic assessments in which systematic information from parents is considered important.

The PIC–R is composed of true–false items that refer to specific behaviors or events relating to the child or the family environment (e.g., "My child has threatened to kill himself (herself)"; "Our marriage is full of turmoil"). The full scale includes a total of 420 items, which yields the most detailed information. However, standard administration involves use of the first 280 items and a short version is formed from the initial 131 items.

Table 9.4 identifies the scales yielded by the 280- and 420-item versions of the PIC–R. The scales are divided into three groupings: clinical scales, broadband factor scales, and validity and screening scales. The inclusion of the validity and screening scales is unusual in a scale of this type. The Lie and Defensiveness scales are designed to reflect conscious or unconscious distortions of responses on the part of the parent and the Frequency scale detects the deliberate exaggeration of responses. Adjustment provides an overall index of poor psychological adjustment.

The conversion of raw scores to the scaled scores is based on large and representative samples of children from 6 to 16 years old. The deviation scores are expressed as T-scores, with higher scores indicating higher levels of psychopathology or behavioral deficit. Administration and scoring procedures are clearly explained in the manual. Although interpretation of the scale scores is rather complicated, a wide range of supporting

TABLE 9.4
Scales for the Personality Inventory for Children–Revised

| Clinical Scales | Validity and Screening Scales | Broadband Factor Scales |
|---|---|---|
| Intellectual Screening | Lie | Undisciplined/Poor Self-Control |
| Social Skills | Frequency | Social Incompetence |
| Delinquency | Defensiveness | Internalization/Somatic Symptoms |
| Family Relations | Adjustment | Cognitive Development |
| Achievement | | |
| Withdrawal | | |
| Hyperactivity | | |
| Development | | |
| Psychosis | | |
| Somatic Concern | | |
| Depression | | |
| Anxiety | | |

Note. Based on Lachar, D. (1982), *Personality Inventory for Children–Revised (PIC–R)*. Los Angeles: Western Psychological Services.

materials are now available to aid interpretation including a variety of hand-scored and computerized scoring formats and computer-based interpretation services. The latter yield narrative reports that include specific treatment and placement recommendations, predictions regarding academic performance, and *DSM–IV* diagnoses.

It is important to note that the PIC–R is one of the few instruments available for use with adolescents for which computer-based actuarial test interpretations have been developed (Lachar & Gdowski, 1979; LaCombe, Kline, & Lachar, 1991). These analyses enable the clinician to translate PIC–R profiles into specific predictions. For example, PIC–R Delinquency scores in the range $T = 80$ to $T = 89$ are associated with a 10% probability that the individual will be involved with the police and a 42% probability that he or she will drop out of school. The links between $T$-scores and the probability statements are provided in a set of actuarial tables. The actuarial interpretations also provide specific treatment and placement recommendations.

However, only limited support exists for the psychometric properties of the actuarial formula. On the other hand, a large body of research has accumulated for the instrument itself (Lachar & Kline, 1994; Wirt, Lachar, Klinedinst, Seat, & Broen, 1990). Reviews of that research by Dreger (1982), Reynolds (1985), and Tuma (1985) have been somewhat mixed, but generally satisfactory levels of reliability and criterion-related validity have been reported. As usual with an instrument of this sort, some questions remain regarding the construct validity of the scoring dimensions. The instrument remains the subject of active research attention.

## The Personality Inventory for Youth (PIY)

This is a self-report measure designed to parallel the parent-completed PIC–R. It is appropriate for administration to individuals between 9 and 18 years old. It may be used to supplement the information collected from parents or simply as a structured source of information from the youth.

The PIY is composed of 270 items and requires a third-grade reading level. Paralleling the PIC–R, the items in this scale reflect specific behaviors or behavioral states (e.g., "I never clean my room," "Little things upset me"). Scoring of the instrument is based on nine clinical scales, with 24 subscales subsumed within the clinical scales (see Table 9.5). These scales were derived through factor analytic procedures. Four validity scales are also included: Defensiveness, Dissimulation, Inconsistency, and Carelessness. The calculation of T-scores is based on a large and representative sample of youths.

This is a newer instrument than the PIC–R and, hence, less information is available regarding its properties. On the other hand, the authors have reported preliminary reliability and validity data supportive of the instrument (Lachar & Gruber, 1993; Lachar & Kline, 1994) and the instrument continues to be the attention of research activity.

TABLE 9.5
Clinical Scales for the Personality Inventory for Youth

| | |
|---|---|
| Cognitive Impairment | Somatic Concern |
| Poor Achievement and Memory | Psychosomatic Syndrome |
| Inadequate Abilities | Muscular Tension and Anxiety |
| Learning Problems | Preoccupation With Disease |
| Impulsivity/Distractibility | Psychological Discomfort |
| Brashness | Fear and Worry |
| Distractibility and Overactivity | Depression |
| Impulsivity | Sleep Disturbance |
| Delinquency | Social Withdrawal |
| Antisocial Behavior | Social Introversion |
| Dyscontrol | Isolation |
| Noncompliance | Social Skills Deficit |
| Family Dysfunction | Limited Peer Status |
| Parent–Child Conflict | Conflict With Peers |
| Parent Maladjustment | |
| Marital Discord | |
| Reality Distortion | |
| Feelings of Alienation | |
| Hallucinations and Delusions | |

*Note.* Based on Lachar, D., & Gruber, C. P. (1994). A Manual for the Personality Inventory for Youth (PIY). A Self-Report Companion to the Personality Inventory for Children (PIC). Los Angeles: Western Psychological Services.

### Revised Behavior Problem Checklist (RBPC)

This instrument derives from the Behavior Problem Checklist (BPC; Quay & Peterson, 1979), one of the earliest standardized rating scales for assessing pathological behaviors in children and adolescents. That instrument was widely used in clinical and research settings, and this revision was developed from this body of work. The RBPC is primarily designed as an instrument for screening behavior disorders and as an aid in clinical diagnosis. It has also been adapted for use in classifying youthful offenders (Quay, 1987; Quay & Peterson, 1987).

The RBPC is generally completed by a parent or teacher, although any observer familiar with the youth's behavior could serve as a respondent. The 85 items in the scale refer to relatively specific overt behaviors (e.g., "disruptive," "tendency to annoy and bother others," "temper tantrums"). Three response categories are provided: "not at all a problem," "mild problem," and "severe problem." The scale yields a total score reflecting the youth's overall level of behavioral maladjustment as well as six factor scores: Conduct Disorder, Socialized Aggression, Attention Problems, Anxiety-Withdrawal, Psychotic Behavior, and Motor Tension Excess. The manual presents norm scores based on teacher ratings for Grades K–12 and schedules for converting raw scores to T-scores. However, the BPC and RBPC have been criticized for weaknesses in the normative sample (e.g., T. Roberts, 1986), and this would appear to remain a problem with the current version of the instrument.

A wealth of clinical and empirical information had been collected for the earlier version of the instrument, the BPC. Because the RBPC retains the factor structure of that measure and many of its items, Quay and Peterson (1987) argued that the supporting reliability and validity data from the earlier work is relevant to the newer version of the instrument. In addition, some evaluations of the revision are reported in the manual. In any case, reviews of the RBPC by Lahey and Piacentini (1985) and T. Roberts (1986) have concluded that relatively strong support exists for the reliability and validity of the scale. Both noted, however, weaknesses associated with the normative sample on which the scoring is based.

## NARROW-BAND MEASURES

Measures focusing on more specific behavioral domains are discussed in this section (see Table 9.6). These measures are designed for assessing substance abuse, delinquent behaviors, eating disorders, and other specific behavioral disorders.

TABLE 9.6
Narrow-Band Rating and Checklist Measures

| Measure | Source/Reference |
| --- | --- |
| Adolescent Drinking Index | Psychological Assessment Resources |
| Attention Deficit Disorders Evaluation Scale (ADDES) | Hawthorne Educational Services |
| Carlson Psychological Survey (CPS) | Research Psychologist Press/Sigma |
| Eating Disorder Inventory 2 (EDI–2) | Psychological Assessment Resources |
| Personal Experience Inventory (PEI) | Western Psychological Services |

### Adolescent Drinking Index

This 24-item self-report inventory is designed for assessing severity of alcohol abuse in adolescents. The items reflect four dimensions of dysfunctional drinking: (a) loss of control over drinking, (b) disturbances of interpersonal relationships, (c) mood-altering functions, and (d) physical consequences. The instrument yields an overall score reflecting the severity of the adolescent's drinking problem and two subscales labeled Self-Medicated Drinking and Rebelliousness. The latter are, however, treated as research scales and have limited clinical utility. The instrument is primarily designed as a tool for use by clinicians in evaluating substance abuse in adolescent clients. The authors indicate that it is not appropriate for use as a screening instrument.

Normative data for the Adolescent Drinking Index have been carefully developed based on three groups of 12- to 17-year-olds: (a) unselected adolescents, (b) adolescents under evaluation for psychological problems, and (c) adolescents in substance abuse treatment programs. Reviews of the instrument by Donlon (1995) and McCarthy and Dralle (1995) indicate satisfactory levels of internal consistency and test–retest reliability for the scale, but they conclude that validity support is rather weak. The scale has no provision for assessing for response sets such as faking or socially desirable responding, a particular problem in attempting to assess substance abuse because conscious and unconscious denial are often evident in these clients. On the whole, though, this index can form an important standardized tool in the clinical or counseling process.

### Attention Deficit Disorders Evaluation Scale (ADDES)

This measure was developed from the definition of attention deficit disorders presented in the *DSM–III*. It is designed to assess the three dimensions contained in that definition: inattention, impulsiveness, and hyperactivity. Two versions of the measure are available: a 60-item version for completion by teachers or other school personnel (ADDES–School) and a 46-item version for completion by a parent (ADDES–Home). These are parallel versions, but items have been adapted for the two settings.

Normative data are based on a large and representative sample of individuals between 4.5 and 21 years old. The norms are stratified by gender and age group and are used to convert raw scores into a total attention deficit score and three subscores: inattentive, impulsive, and hyperactive. We have seen before that questions are often raised about the construct validity of pathology scores derived from *DSM* definitions. Nevertheless, recent reviews of this instrument by Collins (1995) and Olejnik (1995) have concluded that the reliability and validity data for this instrument are sufficiently sound to recommend its use as a screening and diagnostic instrument in assessing attentional disorders.

### Carlson Psychological Survey (CPS)

This self-report measure is specifically designed for assessing behavioral and substance abuse problems of adolescents engaged with the criminal justice system. It was developed with samples of adolescent and young adult offenders and most of the psychometric data for the instrument are based on offender samples.

The CPS is composed of 50 items and may be administered to individuals with a minimum fourth-grade reading competence. It is scored in terms of four content scales: Antisocial Tendencies, Chemical Abuse, Self-Depreciation, and Thought Disturbance. A validity scale is also included for detecting response biases. The manual also presents a system for using scores to classify the respondent into one of 18 offender categories.

An earlier critique of the instrument by Holden (1985) concluded that the CPS has some utility as an instrument for screening and placing youths as they enter juvenile justice systems and as an instrument for tracking behavioral changes resulting from interventions. Holden concluded, however, that support for the construct and treatment validity of the instrument was relatively weak. The latest version of the manual indicates that psychometric research has continued and some additional validity support has appeared.

### Eating Disorder Inventory 2 (EDI–2)

This self-report measure assesses behaviors, cognitions, and feelings associated with bulimia and anorexia nervosa. It represents a revision of an earlier instrument that had been the object of considerable research attention. The current version contains additional items and some new scales.

TABLE 9.7
Behavioral Dimensions for the Eating Disorders Inventory 2

| | |
|---|---|
| Drive for thinness | Interpersonal distrust |
| Body dissatisfaction | Interoceptive awareness |
| Bulimia | Asceticism |
| Maturity fears | Impulse regulation |
| Ineffectiveness | Social insecurity |
| Perfectionism | |

*Note.* Based on Garner, D. M. (1991), *The Eating Disorders Inventory 2 Professional Manual.* Odessa, FL: Psychological Assessment Resources.

Some of the 91 items on the scale refer to specific eating behaviors, whereas others relate to aspects of general well-being or adjustment. The instrument is scored on the 11 behavioral dimensions identified in Table 9.7. The scores are designed to yield information about the severity and frequency of the client's eating problems. It should be noted that the final three dimensions (9, 10, and 11) are presented as "provisional" scales; they represent additions to this revised version. Scoring of the 11 dimensions is based on updated norms drawn from various clinical groupings (e.g., anorexia nervosa bulimics, bulimia nervosa) and nonclinical samples. Because the nature of eating disorders varies with developmental level, care should be taken in selecting the appropriate age norms (see Phelps & Wilczenski, 1993). An associated instrument, the EDI Symptom Checklist, is also available for collecting information regarding the client's eating and menstrual history.

The EDI–2 is recommended as a screening instrument for use with nonclinical populations and as a diagnostic tool. It may be used in the latter case to guide treatment decisions and to track treatment progress. Because it is composed of discrete dimensions of eating disorder, it is particularly useful in tracking the effectiveness of targeted interventions. Reviews of the instrument by Ash (1995) and Brookings (1994) indicate general support for the psychometric properties of the instrument, with some qualifications. Many of the reliability and validity data cited in support of EDI–2 were collected in connection with the earlier version and there is less information available regarding this version. Further, there is only limited support available for the treatment validity of the measure; that is, its ability to accurately track changes over time. Finally, the fact that this is a self-report measure raises the usual question regarding the operation of response sets. These are important cautions, but to the credit of the author (Garner, 1991, 1996), care is taken in the manual to stress that the instrument represents a useful tool in screening and diagnosing eating disorders, but that it should form part of a larger assessment package.

## Personal Experience Inventory (PEI)

This is designed as an instrument for assessing the nature and severity of drug and alcohol abuse in adolescents. It is a well-researched instrument developed from a coherent theory of adolescent substance abuse. It is a parallel instrument to the Adolescent Diagnostic Interview discussed in chapter 8.

The PEI yields a variety of scores reflecting substance abuse and psychological and circumstantial factors frequently related to such abuse. Table 9.8 provides examples of factors represented in the three subscales of the instrument. The scale also provides direct information about the nature and extent of various substances. The calculation of scores is based on large normative samples of 12- to 18-year-old male and female adolescents.

Reviews of the instrument by Dahmus, Bernardin, and Bernardin (1992) and Toneatto (1992) indicate generally positive support for the reliability and validity of the measure. A screening version of the instrument, the Personal Experience Screening Questionnaire, is also available.

## GENERAL CONSIDERATIONS

There has long been a dependence on ratings, checklists, and other types of judgmental measures in clinical, counseling, and research settings, and it is something of a paradox that they have been the objects of so little research attention. In the past they have generally been taken for granted.

TABLE 9.8
Sample Factors From the Three Subscales
of the Personal Experience Inventory

| |
|---|
| Problem Severity Scales |
|   Effects from drug use |
|   Polydrug use |
|   Psychological benefits of drug use |
|   Preoccupation with drugs |
| Psychosocial Scales |
|   Negative self-image |
|   Deviant behavior |
|   Absence of goals |
|   Family estrangement |
| Problem Screens |
|   Sexual abuse |
|   Eating disorder |
|   Suicide potential |
|   Psychiatric referral |

*Note.* Based on Winters, H. C., & Henly, G. A. (1991), *Manual for the Personal Experience Inventory.* Los Angeles: Western Psychological Services.

We have seen, however, that this situation is changing. There are increasing efforts to refine these measures, to evaluate their reliability and validity, and to develop meaningful norms.

The potential advantages of this type of instrument have already been reviewed. They relate to economy of administration and interpretation and to the opportunity they present for the collection of reliable and valid information about the individual's behavior under naturalistic conditions. There are also some problems associated with rating and checklist instruments that deserve some attention. I provide an overview of these issues, but the reader is referred to Aiken (1996b), Edelbrock (1988), Elliott, Busse, and Gresham (1993), and Lanyon and Goodstein (1997) for more detailed discussions.

The internal consistency values of most of the rating and checklist measures have been generally satisfactory, as are coefficient of stability values, at least over short and medium evaluation periods. Assessments of reliability through interrater agreement procedures have, on the other hand, generally yielded somewhat lower values. The interpretation of interrater agreement values in the case of these behavioral measures is, however, a tricky issue. As Achenbach, McConaughy, and Howell (1987) showed, one should not necessarily expect high levels of agreement across different informants. For example, teachers and parents may have different experiences with the same child and, hence, provide different information. In general, however, the instruments do exhibit adequate levels of interrater agreement across parallel informants. Some sources of error that may contribute to unreliability in these measures are reviewed later.

The content validity of the measures should also be judged as adequate. All of the measures reviewed have been carefully derived from theories of adolescent pathology or the statistical analyses of empirical data. Further, most of the instruments demonstrate face validity; that is, the items generally represent accepted aspects of behavioral pathology.

Criterion-related validity information for the rating and checklist instruments reviewed in the chapter is, however, somewhat variable. In some cases, such as the CBCL set of measures, extensive information has been generated regarding links with scholastic indexes and measures of social and emotional adjustment. In other cases only limited information is available regarding the way in which scores from the measures relate to important aspects of adolescent development. It should also be noted that very little information is presented in this literature regarding the ability of scores from the measures to predict future levels of performance or adjustment. Similarly, very few evaluations of what I have termed treatment validity are available; that is, evaluations of the sensitivity of the measures to treatment effects. This is a rather serious omission because these measures are often used to assess changes in the client as a result of treatment.

Construct validity should also be regarded as problematic in some senses. Some of the instruments are scored through rationally derived scales, but the scoring of most of the measures is based on indexes that have generally been derived through sophisticated factor analytic procedures, and in the majority of cases the factor analyses have been supported through replication. Further, evidence is presented for most of the measures indicating that they do distinguish between clinical and nonclinical groups and among diagnostic subgroups. The level of decision accuracy is, however, variable.

The problem arises in the interpretation of the scale scores. As we have seen, most of the instruments reviewed here provide for a focus on behavioral pathologies. They generally yield a total score reflecting overall level of pathology and a variety of narrow-band scores reflecting most specific behavioral maladjustments. The latter have labels such as conduct disorder, attention deficit disorder, withdrawn, and anxious. The problem arises in trying to assess the meaningfulness of those constructs, and that problem relates to inadequacies in definitions of the constructs. In some cases, the definitions derive from those presented in *DSM–IV*, but as we saw in chapters 3 and 4, controversies often exist over the meaning of the constructs represented in that diagnostic schedule.

An illustration of the problems that arise in assessing the construct validity of the behavioral pathology scores may be found in an analysis reported by Hoge and Andrews (1992) that involved contrasting the operational definitions of the conduct disorder construct represented in three standardized teacher rating measures. It was demonstrated that there were inconsistencies in definitions of that construct across the three measures as well as with the conduct disorder construct as defined in the *DSM–III–R*. Loeber et al. (1993) presented a similar type of analysis, and Edelbrock (1987), Quay et al. (1987), and Waldman, Lilienfield, and Lahey (1995) provided general discussions of the issue of the construct validity of pathological constructs.

A related problem concerns the use of total scores as indexes of overall level of behavioral pathology and the establishment of clinical cutoff scores. The latter usually involves arbitrarily identifying a particular point on a normative distribution as the criterion for pathology: Individuals with scores below that point are labeled normal and those above the point are labeled clinical or pathological. The problem is that there is generally very little empirical support for these global constructs. The issue relates to the difficulties in defining dysfunctional or pathological behavior as discussed in chapter 3 (also see Dwyer, 1996; Wakefield, 1992).

Limitations regarding the construct validity of these behavioral measures are particularly important when the instruments are used for labeling and categorization purposes. Identifying youths with conduct disorder or attention deficit disorder or withdrawal may have serious consequences for their treatment, and hence when we use these labels, we should be able to defend them. The point emphasized in chapter 3 regarding the role of cultural variables in defining pathological conditions should also be kept in mind. What is regarded as dysfunctional behavior in one setting may be regarded as functional in another situation.

It may also be useful to review some of the potential sources of error associated with these rating and checklist measures. These represent factors that may detract from the reliability and validity of the indexes.

A set of systematic errors exist that have been widely investigated, particularly in the personnel selection literature. The first type is *errors of leniency*, in which the rater is either very lenient in his or her ratings (positive leniency) or very severe (negative leniency). Some teachers, for example, may see a very large number of problematic behaviors in a student, whereas another teacher with a different set of standards will see relatively few problems. The *halo effect* constitutes another type of error. In this case the respondent allows his or her judgment on one dimension to affect judgments on all other dimensions. For example, the teacher may view the child as problematic regarding attentional skills and provide negative ratings on all of the other dimensions, even though those dimensions are independent of that rating. Another source of unreliability in these measures is the *central tendency error*. This is applicable to rating scales and involves a tendency to provide only neutral responses; the respondent is reluctant to provide extreme responses. Aiken (1996b) and Lanyon and Goodstein (1997) discussed some procedures for reducing these types of errors, but it is important for users of the instruments to be sensitive to them.

Several other aspects of these rating and checklist measures require additional research attention. First, increased efforts should be made to provide for the assessment of competencies or resilience factors. The CBCL and associated instruments represent one of the few cases in which competence dimensions are incorporated into the measure. The importance of identifying this type of factor was emphasized in chapters 3 and 4, where it was shown that decisions about interventions require valid information about the youth's strengths and risk factors.

Second, efforts should be made to incorporate into the measures means for assessing situational or contextual factors. The focus in most of these rating and checklist measures is on the behavior of the youth, although in a few cases some aspects of the family situation are also represented. On the other hand, the models of normal and abnormal adolescent development discussed in chapters 2 and 3 emphasize that the behavior of the individual is a product of complex interactions among personal and situational variables. It would seem desirable, therefore, to incorporate both behavioral and situational assessments into a single instrument. Some efforts in this direction are reviewed in a later chapter dealing with composite measures.

Third, increased attention should be paid to the development of instruments for collecting information from peers. Parents and teachers constitute very important sources of information about the adolescent, but there are circumstances in which the most useful information could be provided by the youth's peers. Gresham and Little (1993) reviewed some useful tools for collecting assessments from peers, but most of the instruments they reviewed must be regarded as experimental. There are, to be sure, some ethical and practical issues involved in soliciting information from peers, but efforts in this direction might be of value.

Fourth, enhanced efforts should be made to improve the standardization samples on which the scoring of the instruments is based. Considerable strides have been made in some cases toward ensuring that the samples are representative, but this is a feature that still requires work. Lanyon and Goodstein (1997), for example, questioned the relevance of the standardization data reported for some instruments for different gender, age, and ethnic groups. This is particularly important in the case of these behavioral measures because, as we have seen, they are often used as a basis for identifying behaviors as dysfunctional or pathological. Standardization data are important in providing a "standard" against which to assess behavior, but it is extremely important that those data be relevant to the adolescent being assessed.

There are a number of problems associated with these rating and checklist instruments, but it is appropriate to end on a positive note. One must be impressed with the significant advances that have been made in the development and refinement of these measures. In many cases, the formats of the instruments and accompanying material such as manuals and interpretive guides have been improved. Further, much more attention is being paid to the psychometric properties of the measures. These instruments have long played an important role in psychological assessments and their value will increase as these advances continue.

# Rating and Questionnaire Measure
# of Attitudes, Values, Interests,
# and Cognitions

This chapter presents a survey of a variety of instruments that share a focus on underlying cognitive structures or states. This includes, first, a set of instruments for assessing attitudes, values, and beliefs. These represent more or less stable cognitions and affective states that orient the individual to objects or events. Second, there are instruments designed for accessing specific cognitions. There is considerable overlap between this and the previous category, but the cognitive measures are somewhat unique in that they have emerged directly from cognitive-behavioral interventions. The third group of instruments include vocational interest inventories specifically designed for assessing attitudes and values relating to vocational choices.

Several general observations may be made about these measures. First, the distinctions among these three categories of measures is often a fine one. All are designed in one way or another to tap underlying cognitive states. Second, information about attitudes, values, and cognitions is also provided in many of the personality tests, interview schedules, and behavioral measures reviewed in previous chapters. Further, the lines among some of these categories are not always clear. For example, the Beck Depression Inventory fits as easily in the category of cognitive measures as it does personality tests where it is dealt with in this volume. Third, some of these attitudinal and cognitive measures are not as fully developed as standardized psychological measures as, for example, the personality tests. In some cases normative data are not available and in other cases only limited psychometric data are available. Nevertheless, these measures often have a role to play in assessing adolescents, and, when used with care, can make a useful contribution to those assessments.

A wide variety of techniques has been utilized to assess these attitudinal and cognitive measures, including interviews, direct observations, and projective techniques. This chapter focuses on self-report measures based on rating scale or questionnaire techniques. The reader is referred to Aiken (1996b) and Robinson, Shaver, and Wrightsman (1991) for useful discussions of technical issues associated with this type of measure.

## MEASURES OF ATTITUDES, VALUES, AND BELIEFS

Considerable ambiguity attaches to the definition of these three constructs and social psychologists continue to debate their utility and nature (J. M. Olson & Zanna, 1993). One of the most widely used systems for defining the constructs is that presented a number of years ago by Rokeach (1968, 1973). He viewed attitudes, values, and beliefs as constituting a hierarchy, with beliefs the basic unit of analysis. Beliefs are represented as cognitions about objects, events, or people that represent predispositions to action. Values are beliefs representing higher order evaluative standards; they are not tied to specific topics. Attitudes, in turn, are represented as clusters of beliefs that focus on relatively specific objects or circumstances. To illustrate the distinction, one may hold beliefs about the efficacy of early education programs, which in turn may be associated with broad values regarding the provision of services for young children. These values may, in turn, be associated with positive attitudes regarding early childhood education programs.

There remain controversies over the definition of these terms, but it has long been recognized that these cognitive states do play an important role in the direction of behavior. They have been particularly prominent in social psychology, where theorists such as Bandura (1986) have long stressed the importance of considering beliefs and attitudes in analyzing human behavior.

There also seems something of a revival in interest in using attitudinal measures in clinical assessment settings. This is illustrated, for example, in forensic assessments, where it is recognized that the individual's attitudes, values, and beliefs regarding antisocial behaviors constitute important predictors of criminal behavior (Hoge & Andrews, 1996b; Hoge et al., 1994). The point is also demonstrated in educational counseling situations in which the student's attitudes toward the school and academic work are often of concern (Elliott & Busse, 1993).

An examination of texts and handbooks such as those prepared by Aiken (1996b), Brodsky and Smitherman (1983), Robinson et al. (1991), and Shaw and Wright (1967) reveal that a vast number of attitudinal rating scales and inventories have appeared over the years. A small

TABLE 10.1
Measures of Attitudes, Values, and Beliefs

| Instrument | Source/Reference |
| --- | --- |
| Criminal Sentiments Scale–Modified | Simourd (1997) |
| Learning Style Inventory | Price Systems |
| Rokeach Value Survey | Consulting Psychologist Press |
| Sex-Role Egalitarianism Scale | Research Psychologist Press/Sigma |
| Survey of Interpersonal Values | Science Research Associates |

selection of those measures are reviewed in this section (Table 10.1). These instruments have been selected because they may be of value in counseling and therapy activities with adolescents and because they are the subject of continuing research activity. It should be noted, however, that some of these measures do not meet all of the criteria of standardized psychological assessments and they should be used with this in mind.

## Criminal Sentiments Scale–Modified (CSS–M)

This is an adaptation of an earlier scale developed by Gendreau, Grant, Leipciger, and Collins (1979) for assessing beliefs, attitudes, and cognitions relating to antisocial activities. The need for such a measure is highlighted by a recognition that an individual's attitudes toward these issues forms an important predictor of criminal and other antisocial behaviors.

The CSS–M was developed for use with adults, but it seems appropriate for use with adolescents and some preliminary psychometric data have been collected for this group. The CSS–M consists of 41 items grouped into five subscales. These relate to attitudes toward (a) the law (e.g., "pretty well all laws deserve our respect"), (b) courts (e.g., "almost any jury can be fixed"), (c) police (e.g., "the police are honest"), (d) tolerance for law violations (e.g., "a hungry man has right to steal"), and (e) identification with criminal others (e.g., "people who have broken the law have the same sorts of ideas as me"). Higher scores on the scale and subscales indicate higher antisocial attitudes. The scale is very simple to administer and score.

Some information in support of the reliability and validity of the current and previous versions of the CSS–M are available (Simourd, 1997; Wormith & Andrews, 1995), although not all validity analyses have yielded positive results (see J. F. Mills & Kroner, 1996). Some preliminary evaluations of the validity of the scale with adolescent samples were also reported by Shields and Simourd (1991) and Shields and Whitehall (1994), but the use of this instrument with adolescents must be regarded at the present time as experimental. However, it does fulfill a need in many applied assessment situations, and practitioners are advised to remain alert to future research with the measure.

### Learning Style Inventory (LSI)

This popular instrument is designed for assessing students' preferences for different types of educational environments. It is based on a coherent model of learning styles (Dunn & Dunn, 1978) and it has undergone numerous revisions since its introduction in 1975. The scale has been widely used to assist in placement and counseling decisions and seems to have particular value in counseling gifted and learning-disabled students (e.g., Dunn, 1989; Griggs, 1991).

The LSI version suitable for adolescents is composed of 104 items divided into 22 empirically derived scales that tap a variety of aspects of the learning environment. Examples include level of noise, the presence or absence of authority figures, and the degree of responsibility preferred. The scale is easily administered, but it must be computer scored either through a service provided by the publisher or through a software program. A variety of standard scores are available.

As indicated, the LSI has seen wide use in counseling and decision-making activities, particularly with special needs students. The scale has considerable face validity and for this reason it is appealing to educational practitioners. Drummond (1987) noted in his review of the measure that considerable psychometric data have been reported for the measure. Some of those data are supportive, but he also pointed to a lack of detail regarding the psychometric evaluations and the relative dearth of criterion-related validity data. However, research with the instrument is continuing (e.g., Hong, Perkins, & Milgram, 1993; Yong & McIntyre, 1992), and it is likely that these deficiencies will be corrected.

### Rokeach Value Survey (RVS)

This is an older instrument that continues to be the object of research. It has been used primarily as a research tool, but it may also have utility in individual counseling contexts in which it is desirable to gain some insight into a youth's value system.

Rokeach (1973) defined a value as an "enduring belief that a specific mode of conduct or end-state of existence is personally or socially preferable to an opposite or converse mode of conduct or end-state of existence" (p. 5). Each of the items of the RVS represents a particular value, with these divided into two categories: *Instrumental values* represent desirable modes of conduct and *terminal values* represent desirable end states. The 36 values in these categories are identified in Table 10.2.

TABLE 10.2
Categories of the Rokeach Value Survey

| | |
|---|---|
| Terminal values | |
| A comfortable life | An exciting life |
| Sense of accomplishment | World at peace |
| Equality | Family security |
| Freedom | Happiness |
| Inner harmony | Mature love |
| National security | Pleasure |
| A world of beauty | Salvation |
| Self-respect | Social recognition |
| True friendship | Wisdom |
| Instrumental values | |
| Ambitious | Broadminded |
| Capable | Cheerful |
| Clean | Courageous |
| Forgiving | Helpful |
| Honest | Imaginative |
| Independent | Intellectual |
| Logical | Loving |
| Obedient | Polite |
| Responsible | Self-controlled |

*Note.* Based on M. Rokeach (1973). *The nature of human values.* New York: The Free Press.

Each of the 36 values is represented as an item in the scale. The respondent's task is to rank instrumental values in the order that he or she perceives them as important and then to repeat the ranking for the terminal values. Normative data are presented in the manual, but scoring is usually based on an ipsative procedure, or the relative ranking of the values provided by the individual.

Adequate levels of test–retest reliability are presented in the manual. Some validity data supporting the instrument are also reported, with these based for the most part on contrasting value rankings of different educational, income, and ethnic groups. On the other hand, some recent construct validity studies have yielded rather mixed results (Gibbins & Walker, 1993; Johnston, 1995). Recent reviews of the instrument by Brookhart (1995) and Sanford (1995) indicate that the available reliability and validity support is promising although somewhat limited. A caution is also advanced regarding the use of the instrument with younger adolescents and those with limited reading and cognitive skills.

## Sex-Role Egalitarianism Scale (SRES)

This instrument is primarily designed as a research and teaching tool. However, where used with care, it may have utility in counseling situations where systematically collected information about the individual's attitudes toward male and female roles is desired.

The SRES was originally developed by Beere, King, Beere, and King (1984) as a measure of attitudes toward women and men functioning in a variety of traditional and nontraditional roles. The roles are divided into five domains: marital, parental, employment, social-heterosexual, and educational. Of particular interest are attitudes toward women and men in nontraditional roles such as men functioning as full-time parents or women as neurosurgeons.

The scale is composed of 95 attitudinal statements answered on a 5-point Likert scale ranging from 5 (*strongly agree*) to 1 (*strongly disagree*). Higher values are indicative of more egalitarian attitudes. It is possible to calculate a total score and scores for the five domain areas. Normative scores are reported in the manual for the adolescent age group. Administration and scoring of the scale is relatively simple. An abbreviated version of the scale is also available.

L. A. King and D. W. King (1997) recently summarized the psychometric data available for the SRES. Considerable support for the reliability of the measure has been reported, and a wide range of validity studies have also yielded generally strong support for the scale. The latter studies have focused both on criterion-related and construct validity. McHugh and Frieze (1997) also provided a positive evaluation of the instrument, although they noted that some questions remain regarding the definition of egalitarian attitudes.

### Survey of Interpersonal Values (SIV)

This instrument is specifically designed for the measurement of values regarding the way in which individuals relate to one another. It may have some utility in counseling situations in which information about the adolescent's attitudes and values regarding social relationships are of interest. The scale is based on Gordon's (1975) analysis of values that identifies six independent dimensions of interpersonal trust: support, conformity, recognition, independence, benevolence, and leadership. These dimensions were derived empirically through factor analytic procedures.

The SIV is composed of 90 items arranged in groups of three. The respondent is required to rank the three from most to least important. The scale can be administered individually or to groups, requires only about 15 minutes for completion, and is easily scored. Scores reflect the relative rankings of the six dimensions previously identified. For example, an individual with the highest ranking scores for support and conformity could be contrasted with an individual with high rankings of independence and leadership. Normative data for various age groups are presented in the manual, although scoring is generally based on the relative rankings provided by the respondent.

Reviews by Braithwaite and Scott (1991) and Mueller (1985) assert that reliability support for the SIV is adequate. Considerable validity data have also been reported, although the results of this research are somewhat mixed and the studies have not always been methdologically sound. Reviewers also acknowledged questions regarding the construct validity of the value scores because there remains some ambiguity regarding the extent to which the scale actually assesses values.

## COGNITIVE MEASURES

We saw in chapter 2 that cognitive behavioral interventions have assumed increased importance in the treatment of dysfunctional and pathological behaviors. The cognitive behavioral analyses on which these interventions are based incorporate affective, behavioral, and ecological factors, but the primary focus is on cognitive states. The goal of cognitive behavioral treatments is to provide the individual with "a cognitive structure for future events that includes the adaptive skills and appropriate cognition associated with adaptive functioning" (Kendall, 1993, p. 236).

Kendall (1985, 1993) showed that cognitive dysfunctions underlie many pathological states, and he identified two forms of dysfunction. *Cognitive deficiencies* relate to an absence of thinking or a failure to engage in information processing: The individual acts without thinking. *Cognitive distortions*, on the other hand, relate to dysfunctional or inappropriate thoughts.

The concepts can be illustrated with reference to the analysis of anti-social behavior in adolescents. As Kendall (1993) noted, recent research has made clear that many acts of violence can be traced to a failure to think through a situation, to consider alternative courses of action, or to adequately assess the consequences of an action. They involve, in other words, cognitive deficiencies. Research such as that reported by Dodge and Newman (1981), Dodge et al. (1990), and Slaby and Guerra (1988) shows that violent acts are often the product of distorted cognitions. The misattribution of hostile motives and underestimates of victim suffering are two examples of such distortions. Similar kinds of analyses of been developed for anxiety, depression, attention deficit disorder, and other maladaptive states (see Kendall, 1985, 1993).

K. R. Harris (1985) and Meichenbaum (1977) discussed the special assessment demands made within the cognitive-behavioral approach. There is, first, a wide range of constructs that need to be assessed, includ-

TABLE 10.3
Cognitive Measures

| Instrument | Source/Reference |
| --- | --- |
| Automatic Thoughts Questionnaire | Hollon & Kendall (1980) |
| Beck Hopelessness Scale | Psychological Corporation |
| Children's Attributional Style Questionnaire–Revised | Kaslow & Nolen-Hoeksema (1991) |
| Dysfunctional Attitude Scale | Weissman & Beck (1978) |
| Positive Automatic Thoughts Questionnaire | Ingram & Wisnicki (1988) |
| Suicidal Ideation Questionnaire | Psychological Assessment Resources |
| Suicide Probability Scale | Western Psychological Services |

ing expectancies, attributions, current concerns, beliefs, and social cognitions. A wide range of techniques have also been developed for assessing the constructs. These include interviews, thought sampling procedures, and rating scales and questionnaires. It is the latter type of measure that is the focus of this section.

Practitioners and researchers have developed a large number of self-report measures for accessing these cognitive structures and states. However, most have been used in very specific situations with little effort to develop them as standardized psychological assessments. Table 10.3 identifies a set of cognitive measures that are the object of current research and evaluation activities and that have relevance for the assessment of adolescents.

## Automatic Thoughts Questionnaire (ATQ)

This instrument was specifically developed for assessing negative "automatic thoughts" associated with depression. It derives from a theory of depression that hypothesizes that depressive symptoms derive in part from negative thoughts about the self, the larger society, and the future (see Kaslow, Brown, & Mee, 1994). The instrument is suitable for use with adolescents and a version for younger children was reported by Kazdin (1990). A parallel instrument, the Positive ATQ, is described later in this section.

The ATQ is a 30-item inventory of negative self-statements (e.g., "I can't get things together," "I'm worthless," "My life is a mess"). The respondent indicates on a 5-point Likert scale the frequency with which they experienced each thought during the preceding week. The scale yields a total score indicating the severity of negative automatic thoughts.

Some psychometric data supporting the ATQ have appeared (e.g., Burgess & Haaga, 1994; Joseph, 1994; Kendall, Howard, & Hays, 1989). However, the instrument should be considered experimental and used with some caution in applied assessments until further research is reported.

## Beck Hopelessness Scale (BHS)

This is one of a number of measuring instruments developed from Beck's (1967, 1976) cognitive model of psychopathology. Two of these instruments, the BDI and the CDI, were described in chapter 7, and two others, the BHS and the Dysfunctional Attitude Scale, are dealt with in this section.

The BHS is designed to assess negative attitudes about the future. These attitudes are thought to underlie some psychopathological states and are hypothesized as relevant to suicidal intent. The scale is recommended for use with individuals 17 years and older and should be used with caution for younger adolescents.

The scale is composed of 20 true–false statements describing thoughts experienced during the past week. These statements involve either endorsing a pessimistic statement or denying an optimistic cognition. The instrument is easily administered and scored, but the interpretation of the scores should only be done by a professional mental health practitioner. The scale yields a total score reflecting the level of hopelessness being experienced by the respondent. The manual also provides clinical cutoff scores that may be used to assess the level of symptomatogy exhibited by the client.

Evaluative reviews of the BHS by Auld (1994) and Glanz, Haas, and Sweeney (1995) cite the wide range of reliability and validity research reported in connection with the measure. The reliability data are based on internal consistency and test–retest procedures and are generally supportive. The results of content, criterion-related, and construct validity are also generally positive. However, the reviewers noted three reservations. First, although the criterion-related validity studies based on predictions of suicide yielded impressive levels of true positives, levels of false positives were also quite high. Second, there remain some questions about the actual meaning of the hopelessness scores yielded by the scale, particularly the links between the hopelessness and depression constructs. Third, the influence of response sets on BHS scores remains unresolved.

## Children's Attributional Style Questionnaire–Revised (CASQ–R)

The learned helplessness model developed by Abramson, Seligman, and Teasdale (1978) and Seligman (1975) links attributions or explanatory styles to depression. The latter constructs represent cognitive processes that the individual uses to explain success and failure in his or her life. One dimension of the constructs relates to attributions: These may be internal (attributing success or failure to one's own actions) or external (attributions to an external source). A second dimension relates to stability, or the tendency to perceive the situation, whether internal or external, as consistent over time. Poor emotional adjustment, including depression, is postulated as associated with (a) a tendency to blame negative events on stable internal causes (it was my fault, and there is nothing I can do about it), and (b) unstable external events (it was not my fault, it was just bad luck).

The CASQ–R is one of a number of self-report instruments developed for assessing attributional style in children and adolescents. It was developed from an earlier instrument, the Children's Attributional Style Questionnaire (Seligman et al., 1984). The CASQ–R consists of 24 forced-choice items consisting of hypothetical success and failure situations, with the respondent asked to select between two attributions for the cause of each event. Half of the situations represent good outcomes and half represent bad outcomes. A composite score reflecting a dysfunctional attributional style is derived, and that scores is presumably associated with greater risk for depression.

A limited amount of psychometric data for the CASQ–R and its predecessor instrument were reported by Nolen-Hoeksema, Girgus, and Seligman (1986, 1992), Panak and Garber (1992), Robinson, Garber, and Hilsman (1995), and Seligman et al. (1984). The scale displays moderate to strong levels of internal consistency and test–retest reliability. Validity studies have shown associations between scale scores and alternative measures of the construct, and the scale has also been shown to predict the later appearance of depressive symptoms.

## Dysfunctional Attitude Scale (DAS)

This is another instrument developed from Beck's (1967, 1976) cognitive theory of pathology. The specific purpose of the DAS is to detect dysfunctional cognitive schemas that interact with external stressors to produce pathological conditions. For example, a perception that taking risks at any level usually leads to negative consequences can produce problems for the individual when it interferes with reasonable decisions. The dysfunctional cognitions are, then, generally neutral, but they become problematic when they prevent the individual from dealing effectively with potential stressors. The DAS has seen particular use in diagnosing depressive symptoms.

It should be noted at the outset that the DAS is at present an experimental instrument and that most of the work with the instrument has been with adults (18 and older). Nevertheless, the instrument does have potential value for use with adolescents and practitioners should remain current with respect to new developments.

The current version of the DAS consists of 80 items addressing specific cognitions or beliefs (e.g., "Whenever I take a chance or risk I am only looking for trouble") to which the respondent indicates agreement or disagreement with 7-point Likert scale. Higher scores indicate more distorted thinking. Recent work by Beck, Brown, Steer, and Weissman (1991) has also yielded nine factor scores that may be utilized in scoring: Vulnerability, Need for Approval, Success-Perfectionism, Need to Please Others, Imperatives, Need to Impress, Avoidance of Appearing Weak, Control Over Emotions, and Disapproval-Dependence.

Research reported by Beck et al. (1991) and Cane, Olinger, Gotlib, and Kuiper (1986) with adults has generally supported the reliability and construct validity of the measure. Some limited research validity research with adolescents has begun to appear (Lewinsohn, Rohde, & Seeley, 1993; Moilanen, 1995), but, as already indicated, more work is needed before the instrument can be recommended for clinical use with adolescents.

### Positive Automatic Thoughts Questionnaire (PATQ)

This instrument was developed out of the ATQ described earlier, which focuses on negative cognitions. However, some cognitive theorists, including Ingram, Smith, and Brehm (1983), argue that deficits in positive cognitions may be as predictive of maladaptive adjustment disorders such as depression as negative cognitions. The argument follows that therapeutic interventions focusing on increasing positive cognitions may be as effective, or perhaps more effective, than efforts to reduce negative cognitions. The PATQ was developed as a tool for assessing these positive cognitions.

The PATQ is modeled closely on the source instrument but, instead, contains items reflecting positive rather than negative cognitions. Examples of the 30 items are as follows: "I have friends who support me," "My life is running smoothly," and "I'm fun to be with." A 5-point Likert scale is used to indicate the frequency with which these thoughts are experienced. Scores range from 30 to 150, with higher scores denoting higher levels of positive thoughts.

One criticism of many standardized psychological assessments developed earlier is that they tend to focus heavily on maladaptive states and conditions. The PATQ is an encouraging development in this respect because it provides an opportunity to focus directly on a positive dimension of functioning.

Ingram, Kendall, Siegle, Guarino, and McLaughlin (1995) reviewed the psychometric data that have accumulated for the PATQ. The review shows that, although this is a relatively new instrument, considerable evidence has been reported supporting both reliability and validity. Of particular interest are the demonstrations of treatment validity able to cite studies showing that PATQ scores are sensitive to changes produced by therapeutic interventions. Validity assessments with adolescent samples are also beginning to appear (Jolly & Wiesner, 1996). In sum, and although the PATQ must continue to be regarded as an experimental instrument, an impressive body of research in support of the measure is becoming available.

### Suicidal Ideation Questionnaire (SIQ)

Assessing risk for suicide constitutes one of the most difficult challenges for a professional working with adolescents. The consequences of such an act are, of course, devastating for all associated with the young person. There are no psychological assessment tools that permit perfect predictions of suicide risk, but two instruments designed to aid the professional in assessing the risk are discussed in this section. The first of these, the SIQ, was developed as a supplement to the RADS described in chapter 7. The SIQ is designed as a screening instrument for identifying cognitions associated with serious self-injurious behaviors including suicide. The manual is careful to present the instrument as a screening measure for identifying those potentially at risk for such behaviors; it is not capable of identifying with certainty those who will actually attempt suicide.

Two versions of the scale are available, one suitable for students in Grades 7 through 9 and the other for students in Grades 10 through 12. It is appropriate for group or individual administration and can be completed in about 10 minutes. The test is composed of a set of items, each of which reflects a thought associated with self-destructive behaviors. Respondents indicate with a 7-point Likert scale the frequency with which they have experienced the thought. Scoring of the instrument is quite simple; however, the interpretation and utilization of scores should only be done by a trained professional.

Several scoring procedures are suggested in the manual. One is based on the interpretation of the total raw score; scores above a specified cutoff denote elevated risk and alert the examiner to the need for further assessments. The cutoff was established empirically from data relating scale scores to a variety of outcomes including actual suicide attempts. Other scoring procedures are based on interpretations of responses to individual items. Scores may also be interpreted in terms of a large and representative normative sample.

Bascue (1991) concluded in his review that considerable evidence exists in support of the reliability and validity of the SIQ. The validity data include evidence of associations between SIQ scores and alternative measures of self-destructive and depressive cognitions and predictions of suicide attempts. Recent research by Keane, Eick, Bechtold, and Manson (1996) and Pinto, Whisman, and McCoy (1997) continues to support the utility of the measure as a screening instrument.

## Suicide Probability Scale (SPS)

This is a second cognitive measure suitable for use in efforts to assess the likelihood of self-injurious behaviors. Items for this self-report scale were originally developed from a theoretical and clinical base, but empirical analyses, including factor analysis, have been used to develop the final version.

Respondents are asked to indicate the frequency with which they experience 36 thoughts and feelings. Responses are recorded in terms of a 4-point Likert scale ranging from 1 (*none or little of the time*) to 4 (*most or all of the time*). The scale yields an overall suicide risk score and scores for four subscales: Hopelessness, Suicide Ideation, Negative Self-Evaluation, and Hostility. Separate norms are provided for nonclinical, psychiatric patient, and lethal suicide attemptor samples. The latter group included individuals who had made potentially lethal suicide attempts. The scale is simple to administer and score, although, as usual, interpretation of the scores should be made only by a trained professional.

Results for the internal consistency and test–retest reliability of the scales are reported in the manual and appear adequate. Some support for the content, criterion-related, and construct validity of the measure is also provided. More recent research has, however, yielded somewhat mixed results for the validity of the instrument (Larzelere, Smith, Batenhorst, & Kelly, 1996; Tatman, Greene, & Karr, 1993). Bardwell (1985) concluded in her review that the SPS does have some utility as a suicide prediction screening instrument, but that it should be supplemented with other information about risk levels in the client.

## VOCATIONAL INTEREST INVENTORIES

Career counseling often constitutes an important part of the services provided to adolescents in educational and other settings. Steering students into educational and career paths consistent with their aptitudes and interests has important implications for their future adjustment and satisfaction. The counseling is also important, however, in a more immediate sense. Observers of adolescent development such as Erikson (1963, 1982) note that career planning is often an integral part of the youth's development of a self-identity. It is also often a source of confusion and anxiety for the adolescent and therefore should receive attention in counseling efforts. L. Seligman (1994) presented an interesting discussion of the developmental aspects of career assessment and counseling and showed how youths are affected by career concerns at different phases of adolescent development.

Lowman (1991) identified three domains of assessment relevant to career guidance. The first domain includes aptitudes and abilities associated with success in different occupational groups. Chapter 6 provided a discussion of some of the major vocational aptitude tests in current use. The second domain includes personality attributes. The assumption is that, for any occupation, certain personality traits will be associated with job success and satisfaction and other traits with lower performance and satisfaction. There are no established personality tests specifically designed for use in career counseling, but many of the measures described in chapter 7 have been adapted for use in that context (see Lowman, 1991; L. Seligman, 1994). The third domain includes career and vocationally relevant interests, and measures of that domain form the subject of this section.

Interests reflect the preferences of the individual for activities or objects. When talking about vocational or career interests, focus is on the individual's likes or dislikes regarding the components of different occupations. One individual, for example, may be attracted to the high level of regimentation and order represented in a military occupation, whereas another might prefer a job in which there is more freedom afforded the individual and an opportunity to exercise personal creativity. A basic assumption is that the degree of match between an individual's interests and the demands and rewards associated with a particular occupation has important implications for the productivity and satisfaction of the individual (Lowman, 1991). Information about vocational interests is important, then, in making intelligent career choices. However, as Table 10.4 indicates, there are other benefits for the individual of this type of information.

Some of the general measures of personal values discussed later in this chapter are relevant to career choices, but there is also a set of interest inventories specifically designed for use in vocational counseling settings. Two general approaches have been used in developing these inventories. The most common is the actuarial approach, based on empirically establishing the types of interests represented by existing members of different occupational groups or, ideally, successful members of the groups. The interest scores of an individual are then assessed against those established for the different occupational groups.

The second approach, the trait-and-factor approach, uses a theoretical starting point. These measures derive originally from a model that attempts to analyze the components of different occupational groupings and to deduce interests from those components. Holland's (1985) six-factor theory of occupational choice is an example of this approach, and it is a model that underlies a number of the interest inventories discussed in this section.

TABLE 10.4
Potential Uses of Vocational Interest Inventories

- Promote awareness and clarification of interests.
- Introduce unfamiliar occupations.
- Increase knowledge of the world of work.
- Highlight discrepancies between interests and abilities and between interests and expressed occupational goals.
- Translate interests into occupational terms.
- Organize interests in meaningful and useful ways.
- Stimulate career thought and exploration.
- Provide insight into the nature of a person's academic and occupational dissatisfaction.
- Increase the realism of one's career goals.
- Reassure people who have already made appropriate tentative career plans.
- Facilitate conflict resolution and decision making.

Note. Adapted from *Developmental Career Counseling and Assessment* by L. Seligman, 1994, Thousand Oaks, CA: Sage. Reproduced with permission.

Holland's model represents an effort to theoretically define "types" of individuals distinguished on the basis of their occupational interests and values. The six types represented in the model are outlined in Table 10.5. The theory also assumes that occupational environments can be described in the same terms. In other words, there are work environments that emphasize artistic and investigative achievement just as their are individuals who prefer those activities. The goal in vocational counseling is to match an individual's preferred orientations with compatible work environments. Some of the most recent measurement efforts in this area have combined the actuarial and trait-and-factor approaches.

Five instruments appropriate for assessing vocational interests in high school students are surveyed in this section (Table 10.6). The reader is referred to Lowman (1991), L. Seligman (1994), and Spitzer and Levinson (1988) for discussions of other instruments of this type.

TABLE 10.5
Dimensions of Holland's Six-Factor Theory of Occupational Choice

| Factor | Description |
| --- | --- |
| Realistic | Preference for active, hands-on, independent, outdoor pursuits |
| Investigative | Preference for task-oriented, creative, independent activities |
| Artistic | Preference for individual, unconventional, creative activities |
| Social | Preference for working with people, assisting people, social problem solving |
| Enterprising | Preference for opportunities for achievement in sales, managerial, or political pursuits |
| Conventional | Preference for structured, predictable, dependent positions |

Note. Based on J. L. Holland (1985). *Making Vocational Choices: A Theory of Vocational Choices and Work Environments* (2nd ed.). Englewood Cliffs, NJ: Prentice-Hall.

TABLE 10.6
Vocational Interest Inventories

| Instrument | Source/Reference |
|---|---|
| Career Assessment Inventory | National Computer Systems |
| Jackson Vocational Interest Survey | Research Psychologist Press/Sigma |
| Kuder General Interest Survey | CTB Macmillan |
| Self-Directed Search | Psychological Assessment Resources |
| Strong Interest Inventory | Consulting Psychologist Press |

## Career Assessment Inventory (CAI)

The CAI is specifically developed for assessing career interests and goals for individuals without postsecondary education. It is especially appropriate for adolescents who do not intend to pursue education beyond high school and who are aiming for occupations that do not require postsecondary education. The CAI closely resembles the Strong Interest Inventory, described later in this section; the latter is designed for use with those pursuing careers requiring higher levels of education.

The CAI is written at the Grade 6 level and is appropriate for adolescents age 15 and older. The scale is easy to administer in either an individual or group setting, but it does require computer scoring. Efforts have been made in constructing the test to ensure equity for gender and ethnic groups.

Scoring is based on the Holland model discussed earlier. First, standard scores are provided for each of the six theme areas of that model: Realistic, Investigative, Artistic, Social, Enterprising, and Conventional. Second, scores are provided on 25 basic interest scales reflecting degree of interest in general activity areas (e.g., mechanical, clerical, scientific, physical). Third, the basic interests of the examinee are matched with 91 occupations, with an emphasis on skilled trade and service occupations.

Reviews of the CAI by Kehoe (1992) and Vacc (1992) indicate that the instrument does have utility for a group that is often neglected in vocational assessment contexts. Psychometric support for the instrument is judged as adequate, although note should be made of limited predictive validity evaluations.

## Jackson Vocational Interest Survey (JVIS)

This is a relatively new instrument originally developed through a theory-guided and rational approach. The measure has, however, undergone considerable empirical refinement to reach its present form.

The JVIS consists of 289 pairs of statements describing job-related activities. This forced-choice format is used as a means of reducing the operation of response sets, particularly socially desirable responding. The instrument is scored in terms of 34 basic interest scales, divided into two subscales: (a) work role scales that measure interests relevant to occupational themes such as life sciences, engineering, or business; and (b) work style scales that assess expressed needs and personality styles relevant to different working environments. Scores have also been developed for general occupational themes. These derive from Holland's six themes and are labeled Expressive, Logical, Inquiring, Practical, Assertive, Social, Helping, Conventional, Enterprising, and Communicative.

The instrument requires a minimum Grade 7 reading ability, and it is usually completed within 1 hour. It may be administered individually or in a group setting. Instructions for administering the instrument and for hand scoring are clearly presented in the manual. This procedure yields standard scores for each of the 34 basic interest and general occupational theme scales. Earlier versions of the measure were criticized for small and nonrepresentative normative samples, but the norms have recently been updated, and the standard scores may be used with considerable confidence. However, considerably more information can be obtained when the computerized scoring procedure is utilized. This procedure provides information on additional scales, including validity indexes, and comparisons of the interest profiles with the demands of various occupational and educational themes.

Reviews of the JVIS by Brown (1989) and Shepard (1989) praise the care taken in the development, refinement, and psychometric evaluation of the instrument. Because this is a relatively recent measure, the developers were able to utilize highly sophisticated procedures in item development and scaling. Considerable efforts have also been made to ensure gender equity in test construction and scoring. Reliability and validity support for the measure are adequate, and the instrument continues to be the object of research attention. The major criticism noted by the reviewers concerned inadequacies in the normative samples on which scoring is based. However, the latest version of the instrument is based on a considerably expanded normative sample of high school and college students.

### Kuder General Interest Survey (KGIS)

This is an instrument with a long history, deriving from the original Kuder Preference Record first published in 1948. This version is specifically designed for use with adolescents. It differs from a parallel instrument, the Kuder Occupational Interest Survey, in that it provides information about broad educational and vocational interests rather than interests corresponding to specific occupational groups. This broader approach is thought more suitable for adolescents who are generally in the early stages of vocational decision making.

The KGIS employs a forced-choice response format, with the examinee required to indicate the most liked and least liked activities from a set of three alternatives. It is scored in the following broad interest areas: Outdoor, Mechanical, Computational, Scientific, Persuasive, Artistic, Literary, Musical, Social Service, and Clerical. The test also yields a validity score indicating the presence of response biases. The instrument may be scored in a normative or ipsative fashion. In other words, it yields scores reflective of the performance of a normative sample or of the relative ranking of the interest areas within the examinee's scores.

The KGIS is suitable for use with students in Grades 6 through 12 and requires a Grade 6 reading level. The test is designed for individual or group administration and total testing time is between 45 minutes and 1 hour. The manual presents clear directions for administering and hand scoring the test. More complete information is available, however, with computer-based scoring procedures that are widely available. Separate norms are provided for boys and girls and for two grade levels (Grades 6–8 and Grades 9–12). The most recent version of the test also incorporates elements of Holland's six-factor theory into the scoring. This is an advantage because it makes it possible to access the broad range of vocational selection materials associated with that scoring scheme.

Pope (1995) and Thompson (1995) recently reviewed the KGIS, and both reported favorably on its construction and psychometric properties. They noted that the instrument builds on a long history of research into the assessment of vocational interests. Further, the manual and supporting materials reflect a high level of professionalism. Its ease of administration and scoring also recommend it. The available reliability and validity data are generally supportive of the utility of the measure, with the most significant weakness involving a relative lack of research on the ability of scores from the measure to predict future occupational choices.

## Self-Directed Search (SDS)

This instrument was directly developed from Holland's (1985) six-factor theory of occupational choice. The major feature of the measure is that it is specifically designed as a self-administered, self-scored, and self-interpreted vocational counseling instrument. It is appropriate for providing adolescents with quick feedback about their vocational interests and the way in which those interests match the demands of various occupational groups.

The SDS is appropriate for use with individuals 15 years old and older and is suitable for individual or group administration. It may be hand scored, although computerized scoring and interpretive services are also available from commercial publishers. The instrument can be completed in from 30 to 50 minutes. Reading level is estimated at Grade 7, although an alternate version suitable for those with reading problems is available.

Test items are divided into six scales: Occupational Daydreams, Activities, Competencies, Occupations, and Self-Estimates of Abilities and Skills (two scales). Scoring of the items is based on the Holland theory previously discussed above; this means that a score is calculated for each of the following six theme areas: realistic, investigative, artistic, social, enterprising, and conventional. Scores for the individual may be transformed into standard scores to reflect the person's standing relative to a normative sample. An ipsative scoring format is also possible. In this case, a three-level summary code is derived that reflects the three theme areas receiving the highest weights for the individual. This summary code is then used to match the individual with work environments and occupations consistent with that pattern of interests. For example, an individual with their highest scores in the artistic, investigative, and realistic areas might be directed toward occupations such as anthropology, investigative journalism, or medical researcher.

Reviews of an earlier edition of the SDS by Daniels (1989) and Manuele-Adkins (1989) were generally favorable. They praised the ease of use of the instrument, the care taken in its construction, and the professional quality of the manual and accompanying materials. Reliability levels are adequate and validity information, although somewhat limited, is generally supportive. The major weakness in this respect relates to the limited availability of predictive validity information. The reviewers noted weaknesses with respect to the normative samples, but those problems appear to have been addressed with the latest revision of the instrument. Two problem areas remain. First, there is the possibility that the examinee will make mistakes in calculating his or her scores, and this may distort the information generated. Second, there are always potential dangers when the individual is required to interpret a psychological test. The instructions and interpretive guides accompanying the SDS are quite clear, but there is always an opportunity for misinterpretation.

### Strong Interest Inventory (SII)

Surveys generally indicate that this is one of the most commonly used of all vocational interest inventories (Watkins, Campbell, & Nieberding, 1994). It is also an instrument with a long history and a very good record of revisions based on research results. The original instrument, the Strong Vocational Interest Blank, first appeared during the 1920s. That instrument was based on an empirical procedure, the *empirical keying technique,* in which interest items were associated with a particular occupation where the item distinguished successful members of the occupation from an unselected comparison group. Two criteria were observed in forming the first group: (a) the individuals had been in the occupation for at least 3 years, and (b) they expressed satisfaction with their jobs.

The original instrument has undergone numerous revisions over the years and the current test represents a significant advance over earlier editions in a number of respects. One important change involved the use of Holland's (1985) six-factor theory of occupational choice to introduce a theoretical framework to guide test interpretation. This version of the instrument reflects, then, both empirical and trait-and-factor approaches. A second significant refinement is creation of new norms for women and men for a wide range of occupational choices. The test developers have taken great care over the years to ensure equitable assessment of men and women, and the development of these norms is an important part of those efforts.

The SII consists of 317 items divided into seven parts that reflect different aspects of occupational and other activities: occupations, school subjects, activities, amusements, types of people, preference between activities, and personal characteristics. The test is suitable for group or individual administration and requires about 30 minutes. The manual and user guide present extremely clear instructions for scoring, interpretation, and the provision of feedback to clients. In addition, commercial publishers have made available a wide range of computer-based interpretive guides and other supporting material. The test is probably not suitable for those under the age of 16.

A variety of types of scores may be derived from responses to the SII. It is possible, first, to obtain six general occupational theme scores derived from Holland's (1985) six-factor theory: realistic, investigative, artistic, social, enterprising, and conventional. These reflect types of individuals with distinctive traits and interests. Second, it is possible to derive scores from 25 basic interest scales that reflect the individual's interest in a variety of areas such as mechanical activities, mathematics, athletics, and science. Finally, scores are reported for the occupational scales that involve comparing the individual's interest scores with interest scores of successful employees within 109 occupations. Separate norms for men and women are presented for most of the occupations. It is possible, for example, to determine the extent to which a female client's interests match those of a sample of women satisfied with their position as mechanical engineer.

The SII is one of the most extensively researched of all psychological tests, and a broad range of psychometric data have accumulated. Recent reviews by Busch (1995) and Worthen and Sailor (1995) indicate that those data are supportive of the reliability and validity of the instrument.

Test–retest reliability indexes are quite respectable, and considerable support has been presented for both construct and criterion-related validity. Evidence for predictive validity is particularly impressive, with a number of demonstrations that scores from the measure do predict later occupational choice. On the other hand, several cautions are stated by the reviewers. These relate to (a) the absence of information regarding subspecialties within occupational groups, (b) a lack of information about response rates in forming the normative groupings, and (c) dangers associated with nonstandardized administration in group settings.

## GENERAL CONSIDERATIONS

The instruments reviewed in this chapter display considerable variety, although all represent self-report measures of cognitive states. The value of these instruments derives from the considerable evidence accumulated over the years demonstrating the importance of considering attitudinal and cognitive variables in explaining and predicting human behavior. This evidence has emerged particularly through social psychological research and work done in connection with cognitive-behavioral interventions. It follows from this work that these measures should be assigned an important role in assessment activities.

The caution stated at the beginning of this chapter should be emphasized again. Although all of the instruments reviewed have been the subject of active research and evaluation interest, many of the measures have not been as fully developed as standardized psychological assessments as have personality tests and behavioral ratings. The absence of attention to social desirability and other response biases is a specific problem that should be emphasized. Most of these measures have not incorporated procedures for checking the operation of these biases. In spite of these limitations, this type of measure does have an important role to play in applied assessments, and practitioners are encouraged to familiarize themselves with this literature.

# Composite and Environmental Measures

This chapter presents reviews of a variety of psychological measures and batteries that do not easily fit within the categories used in the preceding chapters. The measures represent a variety of formats, but they generally provide for a broader assessment of the individual than the measures previously reviewed. They are grouped under the headings Neuropsychological Assessment Batteries, Measures of Adaptive Functioning, Parent and Family Environment Measures, and Broad-Based Risk Measures.

## NEUROPSYCHOLOGICAL ASSESSMENT BATTERIES

It should be clear that we are dealing in the case of neuropsychological evaluations with a highly specialized assessment activity that requires intensive training and experience. However, some introduction to this area of assessment and some of the more popular batteries are appropriate, as psychologists in applied assessment are often required to integrate the outcomes of these assessments into their cases.

Neuropsychological assessments are designed for evaluating observable behaviors and performances for the purpose of identifying generalized and specific cerebral impairments. Sattler (1992) expressed the goal in the following way: "The aim of neuropsychological evaluation is to draw inferences about the organic integrity of the cerebral hemispheres as well as to specify the adaptive strengths and weaknesses of the child" (p. 689). These assessments are sometimes employed in conjunction with neurological assessments, which employ medical procedures for evaluating the etiology and locus of brain impairments. However, in psychological assessments the actual causes and nature of the damage are often of less concern than the expression of the impairments and the impact of those impairments on the functioning of the individual.

The construction and interpretation of neurological and neuropsychological assessment tools depends on an understanding of the functioning of the central nervous system. Unfortunately, that understanding is incomplete at present. This complicates the assessment enterprise. The issue is further complicated in the case of children and adolescents because we do not fully understand the developmentalal processes involved in the evolution of cerebral structures. This means, for example, that it may be impossible to predict the longer term consequences of a head injury sustained at 12 years of age, even though the locus of the injury and its immediate consequences can be documented. Advanced texts in the neuropsychology of children by Reynolds and Fletcher-Janzen (1997) and Rourke, Bakker, Fisk, and Strang (1983) document the considerable progress being made in this area, but there remain many unanswered questions.

Neuropsyhological assessments generally focus on a broad range of perceptual, sensory, motor, and cognitive functioning. Linguistic and higher order abstracting abilities are often of particular concern, as are attentional capacities. Emotional and social competencies may also be evaluated. There are, however, some general issues that arise in connection with the conduct of these assessments. I provide a brief overview of those issues here, and the reader is referred to Hynd and Willis (1988), Lezak (1995), Rourke, Fisk, and Strang (1986), and Sattler (1992) for more detailed discussions of psychoneurological assessments.

One key conflict that arises in connection with neuropsychologial assessments is a choice between qualitative and quantitative assessments. Qualitative assessments are based on reviews of medical and social history information, interviews with parents and other observers, and behavioral observations of the patient. This information is interpreted by clinicians through their training and experience and it is used to yield a diagnosis. Quantitative assessments, on the other hand, depend on the use of standardized psychological measures with their structured administration, scoring, and interpretive formats and systematically collected reliability and validity data.

It must be recognized, however, that this distinction is somewhat artificial. Clinical diagnoses are often based on relatively structured procedures and standardized psychological assessments nearly always involve some level of judgment on the part of the psychologist. Further, even in the context of highly structured procedures the examiner may be expected to collect and utilize more informal observations. It is probably more useful in this case to talk about a continuum within the assessment process, with the dimension defined in terms of the level of judgment called for on the part of the examiner. The theme of this book, however, is that the validity of the assessment process will be improved to the extent that standardization procedures are introduced.

A second and related controversy concerns the strategy employed for collecting the information. The usual distinction is between the fixed battery and flexible battery approaches. The fixed battery approach involves the use of a fixed set of standardized psychological tests administered in all cases. Some examples of these batteries are described later. The advantages of using a fixed battery are those shown to be associated with standardized psychological assessments: They provide a uniform basis for evaluating the performance of the individual and their psychometric properties are known.

The flexible battery approach takes a number of different forms, but it is generally distinguished from the battery approach in that it depends more heavily on qualitative assessments and is less dependent on standardized psychological tests. Further, where tests are used they are selected to meet the requirements of a particular situation. This approach often employs a hypothesis generation strategy whereby hypotheses are formed on the basis of case history, interview, and informal observation data and the hypotheses are assessed through the administration of standardized tests specifically selected as relevant to the hypotheses. This approach is more flexible and, hence, more efficient than the battery approach, but it has the disadvantages of not providing a uniform database for forming assessments and of not being conducive to reliability and validity assessments.

Some comment on the contexts in which neuropsychological assessments are employed may also be appropriate. Traditionally, psychoneurological assessments have been performed in medical settings where the goal is to identify the presence and locus of cerebral damage and to assess its impact on functioning. They are also employed in those contexts for planning rehabilitation interventions and for evaluating the effects of those interventions (see Hynd & Willis, 1988; Lezak, 1995). As noted, these assessments are often performed in conjunction with neurological evaluations.

Psychoneurological assessments are employed in other contexts as well. Information about cerebral dysfunction is often required in forensic settings, including both criminal and civil proceedings. For example, the issue of potential brain damage is sometimes a consideration in juvenile court, where decisions must be made regarding fitness to stand trial or the appropriateness of various penalties. Similarly, evidence of cerebral damage and its impact on short- and long-term functioning is often required in civil cases in which compensatory damages must be assessed.

Sbordone (1991) provided a useful discussion of these applications. Finally, efforts are being made to apply psychoneurological assessments to other areas, particularly the assessment of learning disabilities (see Rourke & Del Dotto, 1994; Rourke et al., 1986; Taylor & Fletcher, 1990).

Hynd and Willis (1988), Lezak (1995), Rourke et al. (1986), and Sattler (1992) described a wide range of standardized psychological tests useful in assessing cerebral dysfunction. These range from general aptitude tests such as the WISC–III to measures of specific functioning such as the Bruininks–Oseretsky Test of Motor Proficiency and the Test of Right–Left Discrimination. There are also fixed batteries appropriate for use in the psychoneurological assessment of adolescents, and the two most important of these are discussed in this section (see Table 11.1). It should be stressed again, however, that the administration and interpretation of these batteries requires intensive training and experience. Further, their use requires registration with the American Board of Clinical Neuropsychology.

### Luria–Nebraska Neuropsychological Battery (LNNB)

This neuropsychological test battery is based on Luria's (1973) theory of brain functioning and the procedures he developed for assessing cerebral functioning. The battery was originally developed by Golden (1981) as a standardized version of the ad hoc battery employed by Luria. The LNNB is designed to provide a global index of neurological functioning and a basis for diagnosing specific deficits, including lateralization and localization of specific brain damage. This instrument is designed for use with adolescents 13 years old and older. Younger adolescents may be administered the Luria–Nebraska Neuropsychological Battery–Children's Revision (Golden, 1987), a downward extension of the LNNB.

The battery is composed of 269 items and requires 2 to 3 hours for administration. Items are grouped into the 12 clinical scales identified in Table 11.2. Scoring is based on those scales and a set of summary scores. The latter are designed to assess the overall level of cerebral dysfunction and the extent of damage in the right and left hemispheres. Finally, a set of scales may be calculated for more specific localization of cerebral damage. This involves locating the damage in either the right or left frontal, sensorimotor, parietal-occipital, or temporal areas.

TABLE 11.1
Neuropsychological Assessment Batteries

| Measure | Source/Reference |
| --- | --- |
| Luria–Nebraska Neuropsychological Battery | Western Psychological Services |
| Halstead–Reitan Neuropsychological Test Battery–Older Children | Reitan Neuropsychological Laboratory |

TABLE 11.2
Clinical Scales of the Luria–Nebraska Neuropsychological Battery

| | |
|---|---|
| Motor Functions | Rhythm |
| Tactile | Visual |
| Receptive Speech | Expressive Speech |
| Writing | Reading |
| Arithmetic Skills | Memory |
| Intellectual Processes | |

*Note.* Based on Golden, C. J., Purich, A. D., & Hammeke, T. A. (1980), *Manual for the Luria–Nebraska Neuropsychological Battery.* Los Angeles: Western Psychological Services.

The LNNB has been the object of considerable research attention since its first appearance. The internal consistency of subscales and test–retest reliability has been well established for the instrument. Validity has been established by relating scores from the battery to alternative measures of cerebral functioning and evaluating the ability of LNNB scores to discriminate between brain-damaged and nondamaged samples, with the latter established through neurological assessment procedures. However, and in spite of these positive results, most reviewers of the LNNB express caution about using the battery for identifying specific areas of dysfunction (see Delis & Kaplan, 1983; Lezak, 1995; Snow, 1992; Van Gorp, 1992). The major criticism is that the validity of the subscales identifying specific loci of dysfunction has not been well established. Another criticism relates to the LNNB's emphasis on language functioning and relative neglect of processing in other modalities. Research with this instrument is, however, continuing, and it is possible that these weaknesses will be dealt with in later revisions. (Evaluations of the children's version have been provided by Ayers and Burns [1991] and Sattler [1992]).

## Halstead–Reitan Neuropsychological Test Battery–Older Children

This version of the Halstead–Reitan family of neuropsychological instruments is appropriate for use with adolescents through 14 years of age, whereas those 15 and older should be administered the adult version (Halstead–Reitan Neuropsychological Test Battery). The two forms are similar in format and content.

The instrument is composed of the nine tests identified in Table 11.3. The battery is nearly always supplemented with the WISC–III, but other standardized achievement and memory tests may also be employed. Administration of the instrument requires a high level of training and experience.

Considerable psychometric research has been carried out with the adult version of this instrument and its reliability and validity have been es-

TABLE 11.3
Tests Included in the Halstead–Reitan Neuropsychological Batteries

| | |
|---|---|
| Category Test | Tactual Performance Test |
| Speech-Sounds Perception | Rhythm Test |
| Trail Making | Finger Oscillation Test |
| Aphasia Screening Test | Sensory Imperception |
| Strength of Grip | |

*Note.* Based on Reitan, R. M., & Wolfson, D. (1985), *Manual for the Halstead–Reitan Neuropsychological Test Battery for Older Children.* Tucson, AZ: Neuropsychology Press.

tablished (see Dean, 1985), but rather less evidence has been presented for the adolescent version. Reviews by Dean and Gray (1990) and Sattler (1992) stress that a high level of clinical judgment is called for in scoring and interpreting the battery and that only limited support is as yet available for the construct validity of the measure. In addition, some questions have been raised about the adequacy of the standardization sample on which scoring is based (Leckliter & Forster, 1994). Interpretations of the instrument should be made with these cautions in mind.

## MEASURES OF ADAPTIVE FUNCTIONING

A variety of measures designed for assesssing adaptive behaviors in developmentally delayed individuals are described in this section. The identification and assessment of developmentally delayed or mentally retarded adolescents is frequently required where decisions are to be made about educational or institutional placements, and they are also sometimes necessary in determining eligibility for program supports.

There is a long history of controversy over the diagnosis of mental retardation and that controversy continues today. Part of the problem, of course, is that we are dealing with a complex construct: "One point that cannot be made too forcefully is that mental retardation does not consti-tute a disorder or a single condition but is instead a common set of symptoms that applies to a myriad of clinical conditions" (Aman, Ham-mer, & Rojahn, 1993, p. 321). The failure to recognize this complexity has often led to inadequate assessments of young people and, in some cases, to unfortunate decisions.

The most influential definition of mental retardation is that presented by the American Association on Mental Retardation (AAMR), although it should be acknowledged that the AAMR's efforts to develop a definition have always been the subject of great controversy. The most recent AAMR definition is as follows:

Mental retardation refers to substantial limitations in present functioning. It is characterized by significantly subaverage intellectual functioning, existing concurrently with related limitations in two or more of the following applicable adaptive skill areas: communication, self care, home living, social skills, community use, self-direction, health and safety, functional academics, leisure and work. Mental retardation manifests before 18. (American Association on Mental Retardation, 1992, p. 8)

There are three important components to the definition. First, the individual must demonstrate significant intellectual impairment. The current definition specifies IQ scores of 75 on the WISC–III and 73 on the SBIS as the cutoffs. This represents a change from the earlier definition where 2 standard deviations below the mean constituted the cutoff. Second, relating to adaptive functioning, the individual must display deficits in adaptive skills in at least two of the identified areas. This also represents a change from the earlier definition, which was based on an index of global adaptive functioning. Third, the developmental delay must have manifested itself prior to 18 years of age.

An additional change from the earlier 1983 definition involves the elimination of the four categories of severity of developmental delay: mild, moderate, severe, and profound. This system has been replaced by a categorization based on the amount of environmental supports required by the individual. This is represented as a continuum ranging from intermittent to pervasive support.

The *DSM–IV* (American Psychiatric Association, 1994) definition of mental retardation is also widely used as a basis for diagnosis. The general definition is as follows:

The essential feature of Mental Retardation is significantly subaverage general intellectual function (Criterion A) that is accompanied by significant limitations in adaptive functioning in at least two of the following skill areas: communication, self-care, home living, social/interpersonal skills, use of community resources, self-direction, functional academic skills, work, leisure, health, and safety (Criterion B). The onset must occur before 18 years (Criterion C). Mental Retardation has many different etiologies and may be seen as a final common pathway of various psychologicial processes that affect the functioning of the central nervous system. (p. 39)

Note that the *DSM–IV* diagnosis is closer to the earlier 1983 American Association on Mental Deficiency (AAMD) definition than the more recent revision, with only the change to a multidimensional conceptualization of adaptive functioning incorporated into the definition. Also, the IQ cutoffs are different in the *DSM–IV* definition, and the levels of severity distinction is retained (see Table 11.4).

TABLE 11.4
*DSM–IV* Criteria for Degrees of Severity of Mental Retardation

| | |
|---|---|
| Mild mental retardation | IQ level 50–55 to approximately 70 |
| Moderate retardation | IQ level 35–40 to 50–55 |
| Severe mental retardation | IQ level 20–25 to 35–40 |
| Profound mental retardation | IQ level below 20 or 25 |

Source: American Psychiatric Association (1994).

Both the AAMD and *DSM–IV* definitions have been the subject of continuing criticism from experts such as Gresham, MacMillan, and Siperstein (1995), Hodapp (1995), Sattler (1992), and Zigler, Balla, and Hodapp (1984). These writers have, for example, emphasized difficulties associated with the definition and measurement of adaptive functioning. There has always been dissatisfaction with both the conceptualization and measurement of this construct. The problem is compounded with the new AAMR definition, which requires assessment of functioning in specific areas (the standardized measures of adaptive functioning currently available are all designed for assessing global functioning). Similar difficulties have been noted with efforts to define and measure the environmental supports construct. Finally, questions have been raised about the elimination of the severity categories (mild, moderate, severe, profound) in the 1992 revision of the AAMR definition. Many practitioners feel that discriminating on the basis of the level of cognitive deficit exhibited is essential for valid assessments. It would seem that most practitioners are continuing to employ the older categorization of severity of delay.

Both the AAMR and *DSM–IV* definitions of mental retardation require two types of assessment tools. The first requirement is assessment of cognitive functioning. The WISC–III and SBIS:4 individual intelligence tests discussed in chapter 5 are nearly always used and should form the basis of any battery for assessing developmental delays. Both Reschly (1997) and Sattler (1992) provided useful discussions of the applications of these tests to the assessment of developmental delays.

The second requirement is for measures of adaptive functioning and, reflecting the 1992 AAMD definition, degree of dependence on environmental supports. There are, however, no standardized tools available for assessing the latter construct and those assessments must be based for the time being on clinical judgment.

Although, as previously indicated, considerable difficulty has been encountered in defining and measuring the adaptive behavior construct, a wide range of assessment instruments have been developed for this purpose. These may be divided into two large groups. The first group includes criterion-referenced scales such as the Revised Independent Living Behavior Checklist (Walls, Zane, & Thvedt, 1991). These are nonnormative measures designed to provide a survey of areas of adaptive competence and incompetence. These measures are sometimes useful tools in training and rehabilitation settings, but because they are nonstandardized measures, they are not considered here.

The second group includes normative measures of adaptive functioning. These provide indexes of adaptation to life challenges based on data collected from representative samples of age-graded groups. Instruments appropriate for use with older children and adolescents generally focus on personal, social, academic, and occupational competencies. These measures vary in terms of complexity, with some reflecting a rating or checklist format and others providing for a more comprehensive assessment of functioning. Most of these instruments were originally developed for assessing developmentally delayed individuals, but they also have uses in assessing adaptive behaviors in children with physical disabilities or severe developmental disorders such as autism (see Sparrow & Cicchetti, 1987). Detailed reviews of these instruments were provided by Aman et al. (1993), Coates and Vietze (1996), and Sattler (1992). Some of the instruments most relevant to the assessment of adolescents are reviewed here (see Table 11.5).

## AAMD Adaptive Behavior Scale–School–Second Edition (AAMR–ABS:2)

This is the second edition (published in 1993) of a popular instrument for assessing adaptive behavior in developmentally delayed children, adolescents, and adults. The measure is in a sense the "official" instrument for assessing adaptive behaviors in developmentally delayed youths because it is published by the AAMR. The version of the instrument described here is suitable for evaluating individuals in the school setting, but there are versions available for assessment in residential facilities and for the physically challenged. The instrument may be used completed by an informant such as a parent, but it is more effectively used as an interview schedule completed by a professional familiar with the child or with access to extensive information about the child.

TABLE 11.5
Measures of Adaptive Functioning

| Measure | Source/Reference |
| --- | --- |
| AAMD Adaptive Behavior Scale–School | PRO-ED |
| Adaptive Behavior Inventory | PRO-ED |
| Comprehensive Test of Adaptive Behavior | Psychological Corporation |
| Scales of Independent Behavior–Revised | Riverside Publishing Company |
| Street Survival Skills Questionnaire | McCarron–Dial |
| Vineland Adaptive Behavior Scales | American Guidance Service |

Items within the scale are divided into two parts, with Part I focusing on adaptation to demands of daily living and Part II concentrating on maladaptive behaviors. Scores may be expressed in terms of the two domain scores or 16 subscale scores. Provision is also made for calculating five factor scores: Personal Self-Sufficiency, Community Self-Sufficiency, Personal-Social Responsibility, Social Adjustment, and Personal Adjustment. Scores are converted to percentiles or standard scores through normative data based on developmentally disabled and nondisabled samples.

Reviews of the previous edition of AAMR–ABS:2 by Mayfield, Forman, and Nagle (1984) and Sattler (1992) acknowledged that the instrument is a useful alternative to collecting information about adaptive behavior through a completely unstructured format, but they also noted some serious problems with the normative samples and with the reliability and validity of the measure. Some improvements in those areas are evident in the manual for the newest edition, but the cautions about using the instrument for placement decisions remain.

### Adaptive Behavior Inventory (ABI)

This is a measure of adaptive functioning using a rating scale format. It is designed for assessing competencies in educational settings and may be completed by a teacher or another professional familar with the youth. The administration and scoring guidelines for the instrument are quite clear, but caution should be observed in allowing inexperienced personnel to interpret the scores. The ABI may be used for evaluating individuals between the ages of 6 and 19.

The ABI consists of five scales: Communication Skills (32 items), Occupational Skills (28 items), Self-Care (30 items), Academic (30 items), and Social Skills (30 items). A 50-item short form of the scale is also available. The instrument yields a composite adaptive behavior quotient. Two normative samples are presented: The first is based on 1,296 nondisabled students and the second on a sample of 1,076 mentally retarded individuals. Care has been taken to ensure that the samples are representative of the U.S. population.

Hughes (1988) reviewed the available psychometric data and concluded that satisfactory levels of reliability and validity have been reported. However, it is clear that additional information about the construct validity of the instrument is required, as is more research on links between ABI scores and actual functioning in educational and other settings.

### Comprehensive Test of Adaptive Behavior (CTAB)

This is a 529-item rating scale designed for completion by a teacher or other professional acquainted with the youth and with access to other sources of information about his or her functioning. It provides both descriptive and prescriptive information relevant to the individual's adaptive behaviors.

CTAB items are divided into six skill categories: self-help, home living, independent living, social, sensory/motor, and language/academic. Each of the six categories is in turn divided into a number of subscales. The instrument also yields a total score that represents a composite of the six skill categories. Raw score conversions are based on a large and representative normative sample.

A review of the CTAB by Swartz (1986) noted adequate support for the internal consistency and test–retest reliability of the scale, but he also concluded that at that time only limited validity evaluations were available. This must still be regarded as a weakness, and, although the instrument has some attractive features, it should be used with this limitation in mind.

### Scales of Independent Behavior–Revised (SIB–R)

This composite measure provides for a comprehensive assessment of individuals in 14 areas of adaptive behavior and 8 areas of problem behavior. It has been developed for identifying developmentally handicapped individuals, for guiding placement and intervention decisions, and for evaluating the impact of training or rehabilitation efforts. This is one of the most widely used instruments for assessing developmentally delayed individuals, suitable for use across the entire age range.

The scale is administered individually and is designed for use by teachers, counselors, and other such professionals who are provided special training in the adminstration and scoring of the instrument. The instrument could, however, be completed by a psychologist or other mental health provider on the basis of information collected from respondents and direct observations.

Table 11.6 provides an outline of the 14 adaptive behavior and 8 problem behavior clusters contained in the instrument and the skill areas represented in those clusters. Items within the clusters are based on concrete behaviors. The scoring methods differ somewhat for the adaptive and problem behavior items. Adaptive behavior items are scored on a 4-point scale reflecting a judgment made about the frequency with which an act is performed, the quality of its performance, and the initiative displayed in performing the act. The items from the behavior problem cluster receive two separate ratings, one based on the frequency with which the behavior is displayed and the second based on its severity.

The SIB–R yields a variety of standardized scores, including age-equivalent and percentile scores for each of the adaptive and problem behavior clusters and a composite adaptive functioning score. The latter is termed the broad independence or support score. It represents a

TABLE 11.6
Subscales for the Scales of Independent Behavior–Revised

---

I. Adaptive Behavior Clusters
Motor skills
  Gross motor
  Fine motor
Social interaction and communication skills
  Social interaction
  Language comprehension
  Language expression
Personal living skills
  Eating and meal preparation
  Toileting
  Dressing
  Personal self-care
  Domestic skills
Community living skills
  Time and punctuality
  Money and value
  Work skills
  Home/community orientation
II. Problem Behavior Clusters
Internalized maladaptive
  Hurtful to self
  Unusual or repetitive habits
  Withdrawal or inattentive behavior
Asocial maladaptive
  Socially offensive behavior
  Uncooperative behavior
Externalized maladaptive
  Hurtful to others
  Destructive to property
  Disruptive behavior

---

*Note.* Based on Bruininks, R. H., Woodcock, R. W., Weatherman, R. F., & Hill, B. K. (1996), *Manual for the Scales of Independent Behavior–Revised*. Chicago: Riverside Publishing Co.

weighted measure of the adaptive and maladaptive behaviors and may be used to categorize the individual by the level of supervision required: pervasive, extensive, frequent, limited, intermittent, and infrequent. The latter is, of course, relevant to the level of support provision of the new AAMD definition of mental retardation. It is also possible to directly compare the SIB–R scores with scores from the Woodcock–Johnson Psychoeducational Battery–Revised so that adaptive functioning can be evaluated with reference to cognitive ability.

Reviews of the immediately preceding edition of SIB–R by Heifetz (1989) and Sattler (1992) note the considerable efforts that have been devoted to the development of the measure and accompanying manuals and other supporting material. Adequate procedures have also been followed in forming the normative sample. Reported levels of internal consistency and test–retest and interrater agreement reliabilities are judged moderate to adequate. The reviewers also indicated that some evidence in support of the construct and criterion-related validity of the measure had been reported. These studies have generally involved relating SIB–R scores to scores from alternative measures of adaptive functioning or clinically based groupings of individuals according to the nature and severity of their disability. Both reviewers concluded, however, that additional support for the validity of the cluster scores would be desirable.

## Street Survival Skills Questionnaire (SSSQ)

Unlike the other instruments reviewed in this section, the SSSQ is designed for direct administration to the client. It involves a multiple-choice format in which the client is presented with a series of pictorial items reflecting various aspects of everyday living. These might involve identifying familiar objects such as a bus or interpreting actions such as counting change. The SSSQ is designed to assess the individual's competency in performing everyday tasks. It is presented as a useful measure of adaptive behavior for use in placement and treatment planning decisions and for evaluating the effects of intervention efforts. It has also seen some use in research and evaluation studies of rehabilitation programs.

The SSSQ is composed of nine subscales: Basic Concepts, Functional Signs, Tool Identification, Domestic Management, Health/First Aid/Safety, Public Services, Time, Money, and Measurement. Each subscale is composed of 24 items, and the total scale requires approximately 1 hour to administer. The administration and scoring are relatively simple, and instructions are clearly presented in the manual. Two types of standardized scores may be derived: (a) scores for each of the nine subtests, and (b) an overall score, the survival skill quotient. Several normative groups are available for converting raw to standardized scores; the latter include groups of developmentally and normal individuals.

DeStefano (1992) and Haring's (1992) reviews of the SSSQ note the care with which the instrument has been constructed and the fact that support has been provided for the reliability and content validity of the measure. There are, on the other hand, some weaknesses noted with the instrument. First, although the authors present some information supporting the construct and criterion-related validity of the scale, the evaluations have generally not involved relating scores to actual performance in real-life situations. This is a serious drawback in an instrument designed to have a role in referral and placement decisions. Second, the normative groups are relatively small and the distributions of subjects by age are not reported. The normative data are particularly weak for those under 15 years of age. Finally, the direct administration format means that there are many important areas of adaptive functioning that are not assesssed by the instrument. In sum, the SSSQ does have a role to play as a direct measure of adaptive functioning in developmentally delayed youths, but it should constitute only one part of a larger battery of instruments.

## Vineland Adaptive Behavior Scales (VABS)

This is among the most widely used instruments for assessing adaptive functioning in developmentally delayed children and adolescents. The instrument is designed for providing information relevant to the youth's personal and social functioning in a variety of environments.

Two versions of the instrument are appropriate for use with adolescents and both utilize a semistructured interview format. The Interview Edition, Survey Form contains 297 items surveying adaptation in four domains: communication, daily living skills, socialization, and motor skills. Each of the domains is, in turn, divided into subdomains. For example, the daily living domain is divided into the subdomains personal, domestic, and community. A maladaptive behavior score is also calculated. The interview is completed on the basis of information provided by a parent or caregiver. The second version is termed the Interview Edition, Expanded Form. This is composed of a total of 577 items, including the 297 items of the Survey Form. This version is designed to provide more detailed information about functioning in the four domains and it is also structured to yield program planning guidance. A shorter version of the scale (Classroom Edition) is also available for completion by teachers.

The VABS yield scores for the four domain areas, a maladaptive behavior score, and a composite adaptive behavior score. Standardized scores are based on a large and representative sample of children between birth and 19 years old. Supplementary norms are also provided for retarded, emotionally disturbed, and physically challenged individuals.

Reviews of the VABS by Sattler (1992) and Silverstein (1986) stress a number of positive features of the scales. They are carefully developed instruments with clear administration and scoring procedures. Normative samples are more than adequate and strong support has been presented for the reliability and validity of the scales. Test–retest and interrater agreement values are particularly impressive.

However, the reviewers noted two cautions. First, the validity of scores depends very directly on the quality of the information provided to the interviewer by the parent or other observer. The respondent must have a thorough knowledge of the functioning of the youth. This must always be kept in mind in evaluating the scores. Second, there is a problem created by the fact that means and standard deviations are not uniform across the age levels. This creates problems, for example, in attempting to track changes in an individual over time.

## PARENT AND FAMILY ENVIRONMENT MEASURES

The interactionist models reviewed in chapters 1 and 2 emphasize the importance of considering the broad range of individual and situational factors confronting the individual in efforts to understand his or her behavior and the impact of interventions on behavior. This view was represented, for example, in Bronfenbrenner's (1979, 1986) ecological model of development, which views development in terms of interacting factors operating at various levels: (a) psychological processes within the individual; (b) forces within the immediate environment relating, for example, to parental and family influences; (c) interactions among the immediate environmental factors; and (d) forces within the larger community and society.

It follows from this conceptualization that efforts to assess individuals for placement, treatment, or other purposes should take into account not only processes operating at the individual level, but also the larger context in which they are functioning. Traditional psychological assessments have tended to employ standardized assessments for the individual psychological variables but have generally depended on more unsystematic procedures for assessing situational or contextual factors. For example, an assessment of an underachieving student might involve administration of standardized aptitude and achievement tests and a standardized teacher rating measure of maladaptive behaviors. However, important information about this student's experiences in the home and community setting would probably be collected through informal interviews or observations.

There are, on the other hand, a variety of standardized tools available for assessing these contextual variables. These are not always as refined or as thoroughly evaluated as the standardized aptitude and personality measures, but they are worthy of consideration when the goal is the systematic assessment of the environment confronting the youth. As so often noted here, the standardized procedures are, for all of their limitations, often more reliable and valid sources of information than the informal and unsystematic procedures often used in assessment situations.

The range of contextual variables relevant to adolescent development and behavior is very wide, as shown in the interactionist models. One of the most important of those environments is parenting and the family, and I focus in this section on a set of standardized procedures appropriate

TABLE 11.7
Parent and Family Environment Measures

| Measure | Source/Reference |
| --- | --- |
| Adolescent–Family Inventory of Life Events and Changes | Family Social Science |
| Family Adaptability and Cohesion Evaluation Scales–III | Family Social Science |
| Family Assessment Measure III | H. A. Skinner, Steinhauer, & Santa-Barbara (1983) |
| Family Environment Scale–Second Edition | Consulting Psychologists Press |
| Parent–Adolescent Communication Scale | Family Social Science |
| Stress Index for Parents of Adolescents | Bennett, Sheras, & Abidin (1997) |

for assessing factors operating in this context. The following section on composite risk measures includes some instruments providing for assessment of other contextual factors.

There are important conceptual and methodological problems associated with the measurement of family and parenting dynamics (see Tutty, 1995), but there are some potentially useful measures available. As we saw in chapter 8, some of the interview and observation schedules provide for the systematic collection of information on family functioning. Another type of measure is based on a rating scale or checklist format, and that forms the focus of this section. The review of these instruments is selective, and the reader is referred to Jacob and Tennenbaum (1988), L'Abate and Bagarozzi (1993), and Touliatos, Perlmutter, and Straus (1990) for comprehensive reviews of family and parenting assessment instruments. The instruments reviewed are listed in Table 11.7.

### Adolescent–Family Inventory of Life Events and Changes (A–FILE)

This instrument is designed for assessing the impact on the adolescent of life stressors and changes being experienced by his or her family. It is designed to detect both persistent stresses confronting the family (e.g., persistent illness or long-term unemployment) and unexpected changes or crises (e.g., death of a family member). The A-FILE represents an adaptation of the Family Inventory of Life Events and Changes (FILE; McCubbin & Patterson, 1991). The latter was developed from the ABCX model of family functioning under stress (Hill, 1958). That model attempts to explicate the various reactions families display toward persistent and unexpected stresses and the dynamics of coping mechanisms available to the family.

The A-FILE consists of 50 self-report items for which the individual indicates both positive and negative events and changes. Some items refer to events occuring during the past year and others relate to longer term stresses experienced by the family. Items are grouped into six rationally derived categories: transitions, sexuality, losses, responsibilities and strains, substance use, and legal conflict. The instrument yields a variety of scores: (a) six subscale scores, (b) total recent life change score, and (c) total past life changes score. It is also possible to derive weighted scores where the weights reflect the degree of readjustment required by the changes.

Busch-Rossnagel (1987) reviewed the A-FILE and concluded, first, that it does represent a potentially valuable clinical instrument. There is clearly a need for a standardized measure of the youth's perception of the stresses and changes confronting his or her family unit. On the other hand, she noted some important weaknesses with the instrument in its current form relating to inadequacies in the normative sample and with psychometric evaluations of the instrument. Although some psychometric information is presented in the manual, support for the validity of the measure is relatively weak, and considerably more work needs to be done, particularly with respect to construct and criterion-related validity. The measure may, therefore, have some use in a clinical context, but it should be employed with these reservations in mind. Similar observations could be made for the FILE instrument, which may have some utility in collecting information about family stresses and changes from parents.

### Family Adaptability and Cohesion Evaluation Scales–III (FACES–III)

This scale is based on the circumplex model of family systems developed by Olson and his colleagues (D. H. Olson, Russell, & Sprenkle, 1980, 1983). That model characterizes family dynamics in terms of three dimensions: cohesion, adaptability, and communication. *Cohesion* refers to the extent of bonding within the family unit, *adaptability* refers to the ability of the family to change to meet new circumstances, and *communication* refers to the nature and quality of communication patterns within the family. The FACES–III instrument is designed to assess the first two of those dimensions; communication is assessed with the Parent–Adolescent Communication Scale, described later. The model also identifies 16 family types and rates those types with respect to stability or healthiness.

The FACES–III instrument is composed of 20 items. This includes two items for each of five subscales for the cohesion dimension: Emotional Bonding, Supportiveness, Family Boundaries, Time and Friends, and Interest in Recreation. There are also two items for each of the four subscales of adaptability: Leadership, Control, Discipline, and Rules. Provision is made for two administrations of the scale. The first asks the respondent to describe his or her family unit and in the second administration the respondent is to indicate the ideal family situation.

The FACES–III instrument is extremely easy to administer and score, but interpretation of the scores may present some problems. The instrument may be administered to all family members and a composite index of cohesion and adaptability can be derived for the family unit. Alternatively, scores for individual family members can be compared to assess discrepancies in perceptions. Comparisons may also be made between the ratings of the actual family situation and the ideal ratings as a measure of satisfaction with the family situation. Raw scores from the instrument may be interpreted in light of normative data, with the latter provided for a variety of family types, including families with adolescents. With the aid of norms, families can be described in terms of the dimensions of the circumplex model of family functioning.

FACES–III represents the third version of this instrument and includes a number of improvements over earlier versions. Considerable reliability and validity data have been reported (D. H. Olson, Portner, & Lavee, 1985) that are generally supportive of the psychometric properties of the instrument. However, Camara (1988) noted several cautions to be observed with the instrument in her evaluation of the measure. First, practitioners must keep in mind that this represents a self-report measure and therefore alternative sources of information about family functioning should be considered. Second, it has not been shown that the measure is relevant for nontraditional family structures or for all ethnic and cultural groups. Certainly these are not necessarily represented in the normative samples. The functioning of families changes with the developmental level of members of the family, and this is also difficult to represent in normative data. Finally, Camara noted that indexes of family functioning based on a combining of the responses of individual family members may provide misleading information about the actual functioning of the family unit.

### Family Assessment Measure III (FAM III)

This measure of family functioning was developed from the McMaster model of family functioning (N. B. Epstein, Baldwin, & Bishop, 1983). Table 11.8 outlines the seven clinical and two validity scales on which the instrument is based. The FAM III is designed to provide information about general and specific aspects of family functioning and about the differential perceptions of family members regarding family functioning. The instrument is somewhat unique in that it assesses both family strengths and weaknesses.

FAM III consists of three forms: (a) the 50-item general scale provides information about general family functioning; (b) the 42-item self-rating Scale assesses the individual's perceptions of his or her role in the family; and (c) the 42-item dyadic relationships scale assesses relations between

TABLE 11.8
Scales of the Family Assessment Measure III

Clinical scales
  Task Accomplishment
  Communication
  Involvement
  Values and Norms
  Role Performance
  Affective Expression
  Control
Validity Scales
  Social Desirability
  Defensiveness

*Note.* Based on Skinner, H., Steinhauer, P., & Santa-Barbara, J. (1983). The Family Assessment Measure. *Canadian Journal of Community Mental Health, 2,* 91–105.

individual family members. The validity scales are useful in assessing socially desirable and defensive responding. Scoring is based on normative data collected from nonclinical families with adolescents.

Considerable research has been reported in connection with the three versions of the instrument, and the reliability and validity data reported in the manual are generally supportive of the measure. Tutty (1995) concluded in her review that the instrument can be recommended for clinical application at the present time, although additional reliability and validity investigations are still required.

## Family Environment Scale–Second Edition (FES–2)

This instrument was developed by Moos, one of the most prolific researchers in the area of environmental assessment. He and other members of his team have been responsible for the development of 10 standardized instruments for assessing aspects of what he termed the *social climate* (Moos, 1987). These include, in addition to the FES, instruments for assessing work, educational, and other institutional environments.

The FES–2 is a 90-item scale designed for assessing aspects of the family environment that is presumably appropriate for any type of family structure. It may be completed by any family member or any combination of members. Items are divided into three domains that are, in turn, divided into 10 subscales (see Table 11.9). Scoring of the instrument may be based on the 10 subscales and the three overall domain scores. Billings and Moos (1982) also developed a typology for categorizing families. The seven family types are as follows: independence oriented, achievement oriented, moral-religious oriented, intellectual-cultural oriented, support oriented, conflict oriented, and disorganized. Finally, an index of family

TABLE 11.9
Family Environment Scale Subscales

| | |
|---|---|
| Cohesion | Expressiveness |
| Conflict | Independence |
| Achievement Orientation | Intellectual-Cultural Orientation |
| Active-Recreational Orientation | Moral-Religious Emphasis |
| Organization | Control |

*Note.* Based on Moos, R. H., & Moos, B. S. (1986), *Manual for the Family Environment Scale.* Palo Alto, CA: Consulting Psychologists Press.

incongruence can be calculated to reflect the extent of agreement or disagreement among family members regarding their perceptions of the family environment. Scoring is based on representative samples of distressed and nondistressed families.

An interesting feature of the instrument is its three separate forms. The Real Form (Form R) assesses people's perceptions of their actual family environments, the Ideal Form (Form I) assesses their perceptions of the ideal family environment, and the Expectations Form (Form E) solicits information about the respondent's expectations for any changes in the family environment. Most of the psychometric information for the measure relates to Form R, and the others, although they have some utility in clinical settings, should be regarded as experimental.

The FES–2 is one of the most widely researched and evaluated of all family assessment measures. Critical reviews of this literature were reported by Allison (1995) and Loyd (1995), who both concluded that reliability and validity support for the measure are adequate and sufficient to justify its use for research and clinical purposes. On the other hand, Tutty (1995) raised some questions about the construct validity of the measure and suggested that the scoring format may produce misleading information about family dynamics. In any case, it should be kept in mind that family dynamics constitute a very complex phenomenon and the interpretation and use of scores from this sort of instrument should always be approached with caution.

## Parent–Adolescent Communication Scale (PACS)

This instrument must be regarded as experimental because relatively little reliability and validity information has been reported. However, it does represent an effort to systematically assess an important aspect of adolescent–parent relationships, and it may find a role in an applied assessment setting when used with care.

The PACS is designed to assess the third dimension of D. H. Olson et al.'s (1983) circumplex model of family systems. The other two dimensions of that model are, as we saw earlier, adaptability and cohesion. This 20-item self-report measure may be completed by the adolescent, father, mother, or any combination. Three scores are derived: (a) total communication score, (b) openness of family communication, and (c) problems of family communication.

The PACS measure has been widely used in research studies, but evaluative reviews by A. J. Edwards (1995), Goldenthal (1988), and Pfeiffer (1995) observe that the measure should be used with caution in clinical settings, because very limited information exists regarding the reliability and validity of the measure.

### Stress Index for Parents of Adolescents (SIPA)

This instrument is in the very early stages of development, but it is included here because it could potentially provide very useful information in clinical settings. It is also worth noting that the instrument is based on the more established Parenting Stress Index (Abidin, 1993), an instrument for assessing stress in parents of children under 12 years of age.

The SIPA is composed of three domains. The Parent domain is composed of six subscales: Attachment, Parental Competence, Restriction of Parental Role, Depression, Social Isolation, and Health Concerns. The Adolescent domain consists of 10 subscales: Adjustment of Social Norms, Sociality, Passivity, Achievement, Mood, Delinquency, Peer Influence, Norm Violations, Aggression, and Reinforces Parent. The third domain, Life Stress, contains items reflecting life stresses and changes. Several different scores may be derived: subscores from the first two domains, an overall total score arrived at by combining the Parent and Adolescent domain scores, and an overall Life Stress score.

It is important to note that normative data are not yet available for the SIPA and only limited reliability and validity data have been reported to this point (see Bennett, Sheras, & Abidin, 1997). On the other hand, the instrument does have potential, and practitioners are advised to follow developments with the measure.

## BROAD-BASED RISK MEASURES

The material reviewed thus far demonstrates that significant advances have been made in the development of measuring instruments for assessing a wide range of aptitude, personality, attitudinal, and behavioral dimensions of adolescent functioning. Some progress is also being made in creating tools for assessing aspects of the youth's environment. On the other hand, the integration of information across dimensions or across multiple sources of information within a dimension continues to depend largely on clinical judgments. For example, practitioners confronted with information from the WISC–III, the BPI, and both teacher and parent ratings from the CBCL will normally integrate that information in an informal manner, depending on their clinical judgments.

However, as shown in earlier chapters, the exercise of clinical judgment is highly fallible. Further, wherever clinical judgments are directly compared with judgments arrived at through standardized or actuarial procedures, the latter have generally proven superior. This is the case when inferences are being formed from a single source of information or from multiple sources of information.

A major theme of this volume is that the judgmental and decision processes represented in psychological assessments will be improved to the extent that standardized procedures are introduced. We have applied this point to the assessment of specific constructs with individual measuring instruments, but it also applies to the formation of inferences from a variety of sources of information. To some extent this process is facilitated by the use of a battery of assessment instruments, but even in those cases the final integration of the information from the battery depends on clinical inferences. The ideal, on the other hand, would be a means whereby the various sources of information could be combined in some standardized form.

Unfortunately, there are relatively few examples of such efforts. An exception, however, are efforts to develop composite or broad-based risk measures. These generally involve standardized schedules designed for completion by a mental health professional with access to a wide range of information about the individual from a variety of sources. Most of this work has been conducted at the adult level and has focused on the development of instruments for assessing risk for criminal and violent actions on the part of convicted offenders and mental health patients. Theoretical and methodological advances in this area have been discussed by Borum (1996), Champion (1994), Monohan and Steadman (1994), and Rice (1997). The Level of Supervision Inventory (Andrews & Bonta, 1995), Psychopathy Checklist (Hare, 1991), and Risk Assessment Guide (C. D. Webster, Harris, Rice, Cormier, & Quinsey, 1994) are examples of broad-based risk assessment instruments appropriate for use with adult offenders or psychiatric patients.

Standardized measures of risk for antisocial behaviors would, of course, be of great value in dealing with adolescents. In many cases, decisions are required about institutionalization or incarceration or about the level of supervision or intervention to be provided when the youth's risk for criminal or violent activity is involved. There have been fewer efforts to develop such instruments at the adolescent level, but as reviews by

TABLE 11.10
Broad-Based Risk Measures

| Measure | Source/Reference |
| --- | --- |
| Child and Adolescent Functional Assessment Scale | Hodges (1989) |
| Psychopathy Checklist: Youth Version | Hare, Forth, & Kosson (1994) |
| Youth Level of Service/Case Management Inventory | Hoge & Andrews (1994) |

Champion (1994), Hoge and Andrews (1996b), and Wiebush, Baird, Krisberg, and Onek (1995) indicate, some advances are being made in this area. Three of these instruments are described in this section (see Table 11.10). Two of the measures have been specifically developed for application in forensic settings, whereas the third, the Child and Adolescent Functional Assessment Scale, was designed for more general application. It should be stressed again, however, that all of these measures are in the early stages of development.

## Child and Adolescent Functional Assessment Scale (CAFAS)

This is a relatively complex instrument that provides for a broad assessment of risk and protective factors in youths aged 7 to 17. It is specifically designed for guiding initial therapeutic decisions and for assessing therapeutic progress. The CAFAS is completed on the basis of all information available about the client. The latter might include interviews with the student, parent, or teachers; medical and school files; and clinical ratings. The instrument is designed for use by mental health workers, and the manual contains detailed instructions for administration and scoring.

Items are divided into 10 subscales identified in Table 11.11. Responses to the items are on the basis of four levels of impairment: severe, moderate, mild, and minimal or none. The instrument yields 10 subscores corresponding to the categories shown in Table 11.11. In addition, an overall personal impairment score is arrived at by summing across the first eight subscales. Separate ratings are provided for assessing risk to self and others. Another useful feature of the scale is that the impairment scores are directly linked with recommendations for supervision and intervention levels.

Limited reliability and validity data for the CAFAS are presented in the manual and elsewhere (Hodges & Wong, 1996, 1997). Support has been provided for the internal consistency of the scales and for validity where assessed by relating CAFAS scores to alternative impairment measures, clinical groupings of subjects, and service utilization indexes. This

TABLE 11.11
Scales of the Child and Adolescent Functional Assessment Scale

---

Role Performance
  School/Work
  Home
  Community
Behavior Toward Others
Moods/Self-Harm
  Moods/Emotions
  Self-Harmful Behavior
Substance Abuse
Thinking

---

Note. Based on K. Hodges (1989). *Manual for the Child and Adolescent Functional Assessment Scale.* Ypsilanti: Eastern Michigan University, Department of Psychology.

is, however, a new instrument, and we may expect to see additional evaluations in the near future.

### Psychopathy Checklist: Youth Version (PCL:YV)

This represents an adaptation of the Psychopathy Checklist–Revised (PCL–R; Hare, 1991), a widely used and well-researched instrument for assessing psychopathic characteristics in adults. Considerable evidence has been presented in support of the reliability, construct validity, and criterion-related validity of this measure. Particularly important are demonstrations that PCL–R scores are predictive of antisocial behaviors, including violent criminal activity.

The PCL:YV is in the form of a semistructured interview and it is designed for completion on the basis of interviews with the client, other respondents with information about the client, and available file information. Instructions stress that information collected in the client interview should be confirmed through collateral information where possible. The 20 items of the instrument parallel those of the PCL–R, but with some changes to make them suitable for the adolescent level. These items refer to aspects of psychopathic personality (e.g., pathological lying, grandiose sense of self-worth) and psychopathic lifestyle (e.g., parasitic lifestyle, many short-term relationships). Paralleling the PCL–R, the PCL:YV yields a total psychopathy score (summing across all items) and two factor scores: Factor 1 is based on items reflecting interpersonal and affective characteristics of psychopathy, and Factor 2 is based on behavioral characteristics. These are termed the Callous/Deceitful and Conduct Problems factors in the youth version.

Forth (1995) presented some preliminary normative, reliability, and validity data for the PCL:YV. The data are based on relatively small samples of offender and nonoffender adolescents and should be considered preliminary. Moderate to strong levels of internal consistency and interrater agreement values are reported for the total score and two factor scores. Construct validity analyses support the integrity of the two-factor solution and demonstrate the ability of PCL:YV scores to discriminate between offender and nonoffender samples. The scores were also shown to relate to a variety of other criteria, including antisocial activities and disrupted home environments. It must be stressed again, however, that these analyses are preliminary and any use of the PCL:YV must take account of this fact.

## Youth Level of Service/Case Management Inventory (YLS/CMI)

This is an adaptation of a well-established instrument for assessing risk factors in adult criminal offenders, the Level of Service Inventory (Andrews & Bonta, 1995). The latter is widely used in criminal justice and correctional systems throughout the world as an aid in disposition and release decisions.

Like the Level of Supervision Inventory, the YLS/CMI is in the form of a checklist designed for completion by a mental health professional on the basis of all information available about the client. It is composed of the six sections identified in Table 11.12. Part I contains a set of 42 items reflecting the range of risk and need factors identified in research as relevant to criminal activity in young people. Thus, it includes both static risk factors (e.g., criminal history) and need factors, identified as risk factors amenable to change, and, if changed, reduce the chances of future criminal activity. Examples include inadequate parental supervision and negative peer associations. The 42 items of Part I are divided into eight subscales: Offense History, Family/Parent Circumstances, Education, Peer Relations, Substance Abuse, Leisure/Recreation, Personality/Behavior, and Attitudes. An opportunity is also provided for recording the presence of protective factors in the categories. Part II provides, then, for

TABLE 11.12
Components of the Youth Level of Service/Case Management Inventory

| | |
|---|---|
| Part I | Assessment of risk and need factors |
| Part II | Summary of total and subscale risk and need scores |
| Part III | Other needs and special considerations |
| Part IV | Case manager's assessment of risk and need levels |
| Part V | Goals and case plan |

*Note.* Based on R. D. Hoge & D. A. Andrews (1994). *Manual for the Youth Level of Service/Case Management Inventory.* Ottawa, Canada: Carleton University, Department of Psychology.

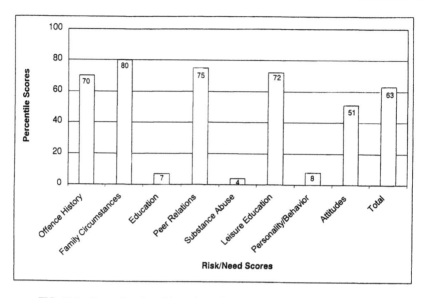

FIG. 11.1. Example of a risk and need profile from the Youth Level of Service/Case Management Inventory.

a graphic summary of the subscale and total scores. Figure 11.1 presents an example of a risk and need profile plotted against percentile scores based on a normative sample of youthful offenders.

Part III of the instrument allows for the assessment of a variety of other factors descriptive of the adolescent and his or her circumstances. These represent factors that, although not directly associated with criminal activity, should be taken into account in case planning. Part IV represents an effort to incorporate a professional override into the instrument: Here the mental health professional is to indicate his or her own estimate of the level of risk and need represented in the youth. Part V provides for recording the level of intervention or supervision recommended for the youth and Part VI the recording of the case plan. The manual and training program that accompany the instrument stress that the latter two decisions should be tied directly to the risk and need asssessment.

As indicated, the YLS/CMI is designed for completion by a mental health professional on the basis of all sources of information available about the client. This might include interviews, file information, and standardized test scores. That information, however, should derive from standardized measures as much as possible.

Considerable psychometric support has accumulated for the Level of Supervision instrument (see Andrews & Bonta, 1995), and some preliminary data have been provided for the risk and need subscales of the YLS/CMI by Hoge and Andrews (1996a) and Jung and Rawana (1997).

Adequate levels of internal consistency for the risk and need subscales have been reported. Some support has been provided for validity by demonstrating that subscale scores significantly discriminate offender and nonoffender samples and are predictive of future criminal activity. However, these data are preliminary and research on the instrument is continuing.

## GENERAL CONSIDERATIONS

The instruments reviewed in this chapter are diverse, but all are designed for assessing relatively specific aspects of functioning or environmental conditions. They included measures of neuropsychological functioning, adaptive functioning, risk for antisocial behaviors, and family and parental dynamics. A notable feature of some of the measures, particularly those relevant to assessing neuropsychoical impairments and risk for antisocial behavior, is that they provide for integrating information from a variety of sources. This is important because, as we have seen, validity is generally enhanced when the assessment is based on multiple sources of information.

Also noteworthy are the efforts within the three measures of risk for antisocial behavior to integrate into a single measure the assessment of a broad range of individual and circumstantial variables. The YLS/CMI, for example, includes items ranging from criminal history through family dynamics to personality and attitudinal characteristics. Efforts to develop these broad-based risk and need assessment tools is seen as consistent with the integrated models of child development and pathology reviewed in chapters 1 and 2. Decisons about adolescents cannot be based on information about isolated individual or circumstantial variables but must take account of the full range of forces impacting the youth.

There is also an important caution to be observed about the measures reviewed in this chapter relating to the constructs being assessed by the measures. Neurological impairment, mental retardation, family functioning, and risk for antisocial behavior all represent very complex constructs that are not always clearly defined and about which there remains considerable theoretical controversy. This is reflected, for example, in the continuing debate over the appropriate definition of mental retardation, but similar debates are taking place regarding the definition of neuropsychological impairment, family functioning, and risk for antisocial behaviors. Anastasi (1986) and Messick (1989a, 1995) long argued over the necessity for basing assessments on clearly defined constructs. Considerable progress is being made in the explication of these constructs, but the users of these instruments must remain sensitive to this issue.

# 12

## Conclusions and Recommendations

This final chapter summarizes the major themes and draws together recommendations emerging from the previous discussions.

Assessments of adolescents have been shown to be important in screening, placement and referral, instructional and treatment planning, and outcome evaluation contexts. Table 12.1 provides some examples of the wide range of decisions about young people made in these contexts. The importance of these decisions should not be underestimated. Placing a young person in a special opportunity class, deciding to provide a program of substance abuse counseling, or directing a youth to a secure custody facility are examples of the kinds of decisions having short- and long-term implications for the young people, their families, and society.

A key assumption developed at the beginning of this volume is that the quality of decisions made about the adolescent depends very directly on the quality of the assessments on which they are based. The examples provided there are worth repeating. A decision to provide a youth with a program of behavior modification for depression would be appropriate to the extent that the initial assessment of depression is valid. Similarly, the ultimate success of a decision to counsel a student to follow an academic stream in secondary school would be limited by the accuracy of the initial assessment of the student's aptitudes and interests. There are many examples of adolescents being deprived of needed services because of faulty assessments and inappropriate decisions of both sorts are often very costly to the individual and to society.

A second key assumption is that standardized psychological assessments have the potential to yield more valid and useful assessments than

TABLE 12.1
Examples of Decisions Relating to Youths

| |
| --- |
| School placement to: |
|   Learning disability class |
|   Enriched program |
|   Class for emotionally or behaviorally disordered youths |
|   Class for developmentally delayed youths |
|   Psychological counseling program |
|   After-school recreation program |
| Referral to: |
|   Residential treatment program |
|   Outpatient treatment program |
|   Foster home |
|   Juvenile custody facility |
|   Family counseling program |
|   Gang prevention program |

the informal and unstandardized procedures so often employed in applied assessment situations. This applies to the information collected in the assessments and the inferences or judgments derived from the information.

## ARGUMENTS IN FAVOR OF STANDARDIZED PSYCHOLOGICAL ASSESSMENTS

We have seen that standardized psychological assessments vary considerably in format. They also vary in the extent to which they satisfy standardization criteria. Some tools or procedures are more highly structured than others, and the extent and quality of psychometric support vary. Nevertheless, there are some potential strengths that generally characterize these measures, particularly in contrast to unstructured clinical procedures.

### Psychometric Soundness

Reliability and validity data have been presented for all of the standardized measures reviewed in this volume. It must be acknowledged that the results of the psychometric research have sometimes been mixed, and, further, that very few instruments have met the strict standards of psychometric evaluation outlined in the *Standards for Educational and Psychological Testing* (American Psychological Association, 1985). Nevertheless, the psychometric qualities are known; in contrast, in unstructured clinical assessments there is generally no information about psychometric properties.

There are two other relevant points. First, as we saw in chapter 4, where direct comparisons have been made between standardized and clinical assessments, the former have almost always proven superior.

Second, nearly all of the standardized instruments reviewed in this book are the focus of continuing research activity. Methods for constructing and evaluating psychological assessments are becoming increasingly sophisticated. We may expect, then, that the reliability and validity of these measures will continue to improve.

### Explicitness of Constructs

There is often ambiguity and controversy over the constructs underlying assessment tools. Intelligence, conduct disorder, risk for criminal activity, and giftedness are a few examples of the kinds of constructs that are the subject of continuing debate. Using standardized psychological assessments does not solve this problem, but it does offer two advantages. First, our efforts to evaluate the construct validity of our measures force us to examine the constructs. Second, the content of the measures represents explicit operational definitions of the construct.

The point is perhaps most easily illustrated with intelligence tests. The literature continues to show lively and intense controversies over the nature of that construct. However, although the nature of the construct remains elusive, we can at least describe the aptitudes being assessed in a particular instrument such as the WISC–III and use those as operational definitions of the construct of intelligence represented in that particular measure. Another example may also be useful. There are many situations in which an assessment of risk for violent criminal activity is required. There is, however, considerable debate about this risk construct and a number of different theories regarding the determinants of criminal activity. As well, as we saw in chapter 11, there are a number of different instruments for assessing risk levels. Those instruments do not resolve the conflicts over definitions of the risk construct, but each does provide an explicit operational definition of the construct through its items and scoring procedures.

We may contrast this situation with that of the informal and unsystematic assessments so often used in applied settings, including clinical interviews. We rarely have access to the basis for the inferences resulting from those assessments. The school psychologists providing an assessment of learning disability on the basis of their informal observations or the clinicians diagnosing an adolescent as emotionally disturbed on the basis of a clinical interview would probably have difficulty fully articulating the bases for their judgments.

The use of assessment instruments with explicit operational referents is very important for explaining and defending our assessments. We have seen that our assessments are often linked with labels and decisions having significant consequences for the individual. It is important for us to be able to justify our labeling and decision making. If, for example, we are going to categorize a youth as developmentally delayed on the basis of a standardized test and place him or her in a special education class, then we should be able to fully explain the basis for the assessment. Similarly, if we judge a youth at high risk for continuing criminal activity on the basis of a standardized risk assessment and recommend placement in a secure custody facility, then we should be able to explain the way in which the assessment was derived. This point has also been made by Messick (1980, 1989b) in his discussion of the concept of the evidential basis for test interpretation.

## Promoting Consistency

Equity of treatment is an important goal in most assessment and decision situations. We want to ensure as far as possible that decisions are based on consistent criteria, consistently applied. If a school board is going to identify some students as gifted and place them in special enriched classes, it is important to ensure that all students are exposed to the same assessment procedures and eligibility criteria. Similarly, if evaluations of risk levels of juvenile offenders are used to recommend dispositions, it is important that consistent procedures be used.

We generally do not observe high levels of consistency in decision situations in which informal and unstandardized procedures are employed. If each school psychologist is allowed to use his or her own assessment tools and decision procedures for identifying students eligible for a special education class, there will probably be considerable variability in the selection criteria employed. Some of the specific limits associated with unstructured clinical assessments were discussed in chapters 4 and 8.

A related advantage of standardized assessments is control for biasing factors. There is considerable room for the operation of individual biases when assessment and decision procedures are unstructured and informal. For example, research on personnel selection interviews shows variability across experienced interviewers in biasing factors (see M. M. Harris, 1989; McDaniel et al., 1994).

The use of standardized psychological assessments will, of course, not eliminate inequity and bias in assessment and decision activities. As noted briefly in chapter 5, biases may be built into the assessment tools. Still, to the extent that the standardized procedures represent consistently applied explicit procedures, the possibility for these errors is reduced.

## System Efficiency

The arguments in favor of standardized psychological assessments have focused largely on benefits to the individual of more effective assessments and decisions. It is important to also note that there may be significant benefits to organizations. Schools, hospitals, community clinics, juvenile justice systems, and voluntary community agencies are just some of the types of public and private organizations involved in providing services to young people. One hopes that these organizations place the welfare of the young person at the top of their hierarchy of goals. Reality also dictates, however, that they must be concerned with the efficient use of their resources. The demand for accountability seems to be increasing, particularly in the case of publicly supported agencies, where politicians and policymakers continue to insist on evidence of efficient use of resources.

The argument developed here is that the efficient use of resources depends in part on effective decisions about service needs, which in turn, as we have seen, depend on accurate assessments of the client, or to use the terminology introduced earlier, on a careful matching of the risk and need levels of the client with the services offered.

The point can be illustrated by provision of special education services in the schools. Special remedial classes are expensive. It would be a waste of money to offer them to students who really have no need for them. Similarly, no program that did not match the actual need of the young person would be effectively used. The other side of this equation must also be acknowledged. Denying services to youths who actually need them would be costly to the youths, and perhaps ultimately to the school and society.

Another example may be drawn from the treatment of youths in juvenile justice systems. The role of incarceration programs in these systems is widely debated, but it is generally agreed that the programs should be reserved for the highest risk clients. The effective utilization of the programs depends, then, on valid assessments of risk levels. Wiebush et al. (1995) cited several studies demonstrating that the use of standardized assessment procedures can result in improvements in the use of resources within juvenile justice systems.

## LIMITATIONS ON THE USE OF STANDARDIZED PSYCHOLOGICAL ASSESSMENTS

It is important to note some potential problems associated with the use of standardized psychological assessments. Many of these problems are not inherent in the instruments and procedures, but, rather, arise from their misuse. Recommendations to help avoid these misapplications are made in a later section.

## Limited Reliability and Validity

It has already been acknowledged that there are limits to the reliability and validity of all of the instruments reviewed here. None of the measures satisfies all of the psychometric criteria designated in the *Standards for Educational and Psychological Testing*. Any use of a measure must take account of the limits of that measure in the situation in which it is being employed. It also follows that a decision should never be based solely on the results of a single assessment instrument. The dangers associated with the misuse of psychological measures highlight the importance of ensuring that only qualified individuals administer and interpret the instruments. That issue was addressed in chapter 5 and is raised again later in this chapter.

Two earlier points are also relevant. First, although there are psychometric limitations associated with these standardized measures, at least those limits are known and may be taken into account in interpretation. Second, significant advances are being made in the development of new standardized tools and the refinement of existing ones. Our ability to use these tools with confidence should only increase in the future.

## Unavailability of Instruments

It must be acknowledged that there are dimensions that we might want to assess but for which there are no assessment tools, or, at any rate, no adequate tools. In these cases we are generally forced to employ clinical assessment procedures. Assessing risk for suicide or risk for violent activity are two examples. We saw in previous chapters that some efforts have been made to develop measures in these areas, but those efforts are preliminary, at least with respect to adolescents. As we also saw, assessing environmental factors continues to depend largely on informal and unstructured assessment procedures.

Integrating information from a variety of sources to derive an inference is another endeavor in which we are generally forced to employ clinical procedures. We saw some beginning efforts to derive composite measures in chapter 11, but, generally speaking, developing a diagnosis from multiple sources of information still depends on clinical judgment. It is here, of course, where there is a real need for the development of actuarial formulas to integrate multiple types of information.

## Narrowness of Focus

Another common complaint about standardized psychological assessments is that they focus too narrowly on psychological processes and do not devote enough attention to other variables that might affect the behavior and functioning of the individual. There is considerable truth in this criticism. This book reflects the reality that the majority of psychological assessment tools focus on aptitudes, performance levels, personality traits, cognitions, attitudes, and overt behaviors. Fewer efforts have been made to develop procedures for assessing family, peer, school, or other external environments that influence adolescents.

The latest developments in the analysis of adolescent behavior discussed in chapters 2 and 3, however, suggest the need to broaden this narrow focus on psychological variables. Recent theoretical and empirical work reflects the assumption that the functioning of the individual is a product of complex interactions among variables operating at the levels of the individual and of the larger social environment; for example, Bronfenbrenner's (1979, 1986) ecological model of development presented in chapter 2. If we want a comprehensive assessment of risk and need levels in clients, we must assess a broader range of variables.

There are signs that this problem is being addressed. Awareness is the first important step. We saw in chapter 11 that efforts are being made to develop tools for the systematic assessment of environments, particularly family environments. The composite measures described in chapter 11 are also designed to provide a means for incorporating a broad range of individual and environmental variables into a single standardized measure. Those efforts must be regarded as preliminary at present, but we can expect rapid advances in the future.

## Removing the "Human Equation"

Critics have cited a variety of dangers of expanding the role of standardized assessments that are associated with removing the "human equation" from the process. One suggestion is that an overdependence on standardized assessments removes the opportunity for the examiner to establish a rapport with the client. The system becomes highly mechanical. There is, however, no need for this to occur. Highly structured assessment procedures can be administered in a sensitive and responsive manner just as easily as clinical assessments are sometimes made in an uncaring and insensitive manner.

It is also sometimes argued that dependence on standardized assessments removes the opportunity for the examiner to demonstrate the flexibility and professional discretion so important when dealing with clients. This is a danger when the results of the assessment are applied in a mechanical manner and the outcome of the assessment is allowed to dictate a decision. However, the professional override principle (Andrews et al., 1990) emphasizes that final decisions about individuals should depend on the judgment of those ultimately responsible for the decisions.

Standardized psychological assessments are designed to assist in the decision-making process, not to dictate outcomes.


## RECOMMENDATIONS

Chapter 5 provided a discussion of a number of issues relevant to the use of psychological assessments in applied settings. I return to some of those issues in this section and consider their implications for professionals, practitioners, and researchers.

### Professional Regulation

Professional regulation is the key to the ethical and effective use of psychological assessments. This regulation should extend to the distribution of psychological tools, the control of those who utilize them, and the ways in which they are applied in specific situations. The integrity of the psychological profession and its public image depend very directly on the success of these regulatory efforts. Matarazzo (1990), Resnick and Resnick (1982), and Tyler (1986) are just three of the many experts in assessment who argued strongly for more effective regulation of psychological assessment activities.

We saw in chapter 5 that progress is being made in this respect. Professional organizations such as the American Psychological Association, the Canadian Psychological Association, and the American Educational Research Association have been very active in the development of standards for the conduct of assessments and in encouraging their memberships to observe the guidelines. The American Psychological Association's (1992) *Ethical Principles of Psychologists and Code of Conduct* and the *Standards for Educational and Psychological Testing* (American Psychological Association, 1985) constitute, as we saw, the primary sources of these standards. We are seeing, however, an increasing number of guidelines relevant to more specific areas of application. The *Ethical Guidelines for Forensic Psychology* (American Psychological Association, 1991) and *Guidelines for Child Custody Evaluations in Divorce Proceedings* (American Psychological Association, 1994) are two examples.

The ability of these organizations to regulate assessment activities is limited, however, because membership is voluntary. It is the legally established psychology regulatory bodies that play a more direct role in this respect. These are established by state or provincial legislatures to regulate the profession of psychology in their jurisdiction. The nature of these bodies varies somewhat from one jurisdiction to another, but in most cases they possess legislative mandates to establish and enforce standards for the delivery of psychological services. These mandates are largely fulfilled through licensing and certification procedures, but the bodies also play a role in monitoring the delivery of services, including assessment services.

Another level of regulation concerns the distribution of the psychological instruments. As we have seen, most tests and other tools must be purchased from commercial publishers. The majority of these publishers have voluntarily subscribed to a code whereby assessment tools are made available only to those qualified to administer them. The classification system within this code was described in chapter 5 but as we saw there, there is considerable debate about the effectiveness of that system (Fremer et al., 1989; Oles & Davis, 1977). One problem is that the publishers generally use academic degrees or certification by a body such as the American Board of Professional Psychology as evidence of qualification. However, those qualifications are not necessarily relevant to the conduct of specific assessments. A more effective procedure for evaluating examiner qualifications is described in a later section.

One important development in efforts to improve the provision of psychological assessments that bears mention was the creation in 1984 of a Joint Committee on Testing Practices. This committee is composed of representatives of the American Psychological Association, the American Educational Research Association, the National Council on Measurement in Education, and the Canadian Psychological Association. It is continuing to work toward the development of meaningful assessment standards and procedures for ensuring enforcement of the standards, and to promote public awareness of assessment issues. This committee has been responsible for some significant advances in improving the delivery of assessment services.

## Professional Expertise

Both the *Standards for Educational and Psychological Testing* and the *Ethical Principles of Psychologists and Code of Conduct* contain general guidelines regarding the competencies required for the administration and interpretation of psychological assessments. Those documents also make clear that psychologists should administer only those instruments within their areas of competence; that is, they must possess expertise in using the instrument in question as well as general competence in measurement and assessment.

Moreland, Eyde, Robertson, Primoff, and Most (1995) recently reported an effort to develop a research-based procedure for assessing the general competence of professionals in measurement and assessment. Their job analysis methodology led to the identification of 86 test user competencies.

Factor analysis was then used to reduce these to seven factors of assessment competence, which in turn yielded 12 minimum competencies associated with test use. These are outlined in Table 12.2. The authors have also developed a test purchaser qualification form that could be used by test publishers to determine whether an individual possesses the qualifications for administering a particular assessment instrument. That form is potentially more effective than the procedures currently used to monitor test distribution.

The expertise required for administering psychological instruments may also be discussed in terms of three more general categories. First, as we saw in chapter 5, a general background in assessment and measurement is essential. This is clearly true for the more complex instruments, but true for the easily administered and scored paper-and-pencil tests as well. The effective use of all of the measures reviewed in this book requires knowledge about reliability, validity, and normative data, and the way in which those constructs bear on the interpretation of individual scores.

The need for a solid knowledge base in assessment and measurement is not negated by the increasing availability of computer-based scoring and interpretation procedures. The professional must have this knowledge to use the outcomes of those programs intelligently. Eyde et al. (1993) discussed a number of examples of unethical test use based on unsophisticated uses of computer-based assessments.

TABLE 12.2
12 Minimum Competencies for Proper Use of Tests

1. Avoiding errors in scoring and recording.
2. Refraining from labeling people with personally derogatory terms like *dishonest* on the basis of a test score that lacks perfect validity.
3. Keeping scoring keys and test materials secure.
4. Seeing that every examinee follows directions so that test scores are accurate.
5. Using settings for testing that allow for optimum performance by test takers (e.g., adequate room).
6. Refraining from coaching or training individuals or groups on test items, which results in misrepresentation of the person's abilities and competencies.
7. Willingness to give interpretation and guidance to test takers in counseling situations.
8. Not making photocopies of copyrighted material.
9. Refraining from using homemade answer sheets that do not align properly with scoring keys.
10. Establishing rapport with examinees to obtain accurate scores.
11. Refraining from answering questions from test takers in greater detail than the test manual permits.
12. Not assuming that a norm for one job applies to a different job (and not assuming that norms for one group automatically apply to other groups).

*Note.* Adapted from "Assessment of Test User Qualifications: A Research-Based Measurement Procedure," by K. L. Moreland, L. D. Eyde, G. J. Robertson, E. S. Primoff, & R. B. Most, 1995, *American Psychologist, 50.* Reproduced with permission.

Second, specialized knowledge in administering, scoring, and interpreting individual instruments is required. Many of the instruments reviewed present few challenges; some of the rating scales and checklists are indeed quite simple to use. Other instruments, however, require specialized training. These include all of the individually administered standardized aptitude tests such as the WISC–III, some of the personality tests, and the composite measures discussed in chapter 11. These instruments should only be used by practitioners with appropriate training.

Third, an understanding of adolescent functioning and development and a sensitivity to the needs of this group are necessary. Professionals working with adolescents sometimes lack this understanding and sensitivity, and it is not surprising that these individuals often experience frustration and failure in their efforts.

Aiken et al. (1990), Byrne (1996b), and Meir (1993) are among the writers who called attention to a general weakness in measurement and assessment technical skills on the part of psychologists. They attributed these deficiencies to the failure of graduate programs to emphasize measurement and assessment. Unfortunately, not only general degree programs fail, but so do specialized programs in counseling, clinical, and school psychology preparing students for positions in which assessment demands are very heavy. More attention to needs for solid education about assessment and measurement will go far toward improving the delivery of assessment services. It should be emphasized, though, that the ultimate responsibility for acquiring the expertise to conduct assessments is the individual practitioner's.

### Selecting and Using Psychological Assessments

Chapter 5 discussed a number of practical issues relevant to the use of psychological assessments.

*Clarifying Goals.* Clear identification of goals is one of the most important challenges of the assessment process. It is essential to begin by specifying the dimensions we wish to assess and the uses to be made of the assessment. Too often this stage is treated in a haphazard or ad hoc fashion, and it is no wonder that assessments are often considered irrelevant or misguided.

Some examples of problem situations might be useful. There are many cases of special enriched programs created for students with exceptional academic competencies. Very often, however, there is little connection between the goals and activities of the program and the procedures used to select individuals for the programs (Hoge, 1988, 1989). The programs may be designed, for example, to emphasize creative academic work and to expect independent and enthusiastic efforts from the student. The selection procedures, though, may be based on standardized aptitude tests that provide virtually no information about creativity or motivation level.

Another example is programs designed for youths with serious substance abuse problems. The selection of students for these programs is often via procedures that do not assess the dysfunctional attitudes and behaviors that the programs are designed to address. In many of these cases too little thought has gone into the dimensions relevant to the programs.

Our ability to clarify the goals of the assessment process is, of course, limited by our imperfect knowledge about adolescent functioning and the effects of alternative treatment strategies. We discussed those limits in chapters 2 and 3. Still, the problem is complicated by this common failure to think through the goals of an assessment process and explain them as clearly as possible.

*Selecting and Applying Assessment Instruments.* Once the goals of the assessment process have been identified, the next task is to select the most appropriate tools and procedures for achieving them.

This involves, first, a thorough familiarity with available materials. Chapter 5 reviewed a wide range of reference publications and periodicals that represent important sources of information about tests and other assessment instruments. The *Mental Measurements Yearbook* and *Test Critiques* series provide objective reviews of measuring tools, but many other sources of information about current developments were cited as well. Unfortunately, many professionals persist in using older instruments simply because they are familiar with them. Ours is a rapidly developing field, and it is important that practitioners remain current.

As we saw in chapter 5, the actual selection of measuring instruments should take into account the goals of the assessment process, the characteristics of the individual being assessed (including gender and ethnic and cultural group membership), and the values of the organization in which the assessment is being conducted. The task, then, is to select the most psychometrically sound instruments satisfying those criteria.

We have also had many occasions to note the dangers of depending on a limited source of information. None of our instruments is perfect. There are limits on the reliability and validity of all of the measures, and they affect the degree of confidence we can feel in inferences. Nearly all the instruments also present a limited view of the functioning of the youth. Some focus on aptitudes, some on personality traits, others on attitudes, and so forth. Finally, as demonstrated by Achenbach et al. (1987), different informants may bring different perspectives to the assessment of similar dimensions. For example, teachers and parents sometimes provide different ratings for aggressive tendencies in a student. Such differences may, however, reflect variability in that student's behavior across situations, and both sets of ratings may represent valuable information.

It follows that in most assessment situations we are required to employ a battery of assessment tools. Ideally, we would have actuarial formulas for integrating the information from the various sources. As we saw in chapter 11, some efforts are being made to develop composite assessment tools, but only slow progress has been made in this respect. We are generally forced, then, to depend on clinical judgment in our integration of information. I return to this point when I offer research recommendations.

The rules regarding the formation of assessment batteries parallel those for selecting individual instruments: The batteries should be composed of psychometrically sound instruments consistent with the purposes of the assessment. Tables 12.3 and 12.4 present two model assessment batteries, one for the assessment of attention deficit disorders and the second for the assessment of youthful offenders. Both batteries include standardized instruments encompassing the entire range of variables associated with the phenomena in question.

It may also be useful to review the basic rules for administering psychological assessment discussed in chapter 5. These involve (a) carefully preparing materials for the assessment, (b) establishing a positive rapport with the youth, and (c) carefully observing the youth's behavior in the assessment situation. The importance of carefully preparing and delivering the assessment report was also emphasized.

## Future Research Directions

Some suggestions about research needs are discussed under three headings.

TABLE 12.3
Model Intake Assessment Battery for the
Diagnosis of Attention Deficit Disorder

---

Structured interview—Parent
  Revised Diagnostic Interview Schedule for Children and Adolescents
Aptitude and achievement measures
  Wechsler Intelligence Scale for Children–III/ Wechsler Adult Intelligence Scale Diagnostic
    Achievement Test for Adolescents–2
Measure of memory processes
  Wide Range Assessment of Memory and Learning
Measures of behavioral pathology—Parent
  Child Behavior Checklist
Measures of attention deficit disorder symptoms—Parent and teacher
  Conner's Rating Scale–Revised: Long
Composite risk and need assessment
  Child and Adolescent Functional Assessment Scale

---

TABLE 12.4
Model Intake Assessment Battery for Diagnosing
Risk and Need Factors in a Youthful Offender

---

Structured interview–Youth
  Revised Diagnostic Interview Schedule for Children and Adolescents Aptitude measure
  Aptitude test
  The Cognitive Abilities Test
Personality tests
  Minnesota Multiphasic Personality Inventory–Adolescent
  Multidimensional Self-Concept Scale
Attitudinal measure
  Criminal Sentiments Scale
Measure of behavioral pathology—Parent
  Child Behavior Checklist
Measure of behavioral pathology and school performance—Teacher
  Child Behavior Checklist–Teacher Report Form
Composite risk and need assessment
  Youth Level of Service/Case Management Inventory

---

*Adolescent Development.* One theme of this book is that the quality of psychological assessments of adolescents depends very directly on an understanding of the dynamics of adolescent behavior and development. For example, our ability to conduct valid assessments of depression in adolescents is limited by our knowledge about the factors affecting this condition and its developmental course. Similarly, the success of our assessment-based predictions of future conduct disorders depends on our understanding of the factors that affect the development of those behaviors over time.

There is often a lag between advances in knowledge about behavior and the translation of those advances into practical assessment instruments. A good example may be found in the area of aptitude testing. We saw in chapters 2 and 6 that significant advances are being made in our understanding of cognitive processes and what we generally term intelligence. However, those advances have yet to be translated into practical instruments. Still, that is only a question of time, and aptitude assessment will eventually benefit from these knowledge advances (see also Matarazzo, 1992).

We saw in chapters 2 and 3 that significant theoretical and research advances are being made as we seek to learn more about adolescent development. Here are some directions for future research of particular relevance to psychological assessment activities.

First, we need more information about the meaningfulness of the various aptitude, personality, behavioral, and attitudinal constructs applied to adolescents. Examples of relevant research include Sternberg's (1985, 1988, 1997) efforts to refine the concept of intelligence, Achenbach's (1991, 1994, 1995) work on the constructs of behavioral pathology in children and adolescents, and the efforts to more fully explicate the self-concept construct (see Byrne, 1996a). The utility of our measures is limited by their construct validity, and improvements in the latter depend directly on the quality of our understanding of the constructs.

Second, we need more information about the developmental course of the conditions we are attempting to assess. The nature of self-concept seems to change with developmental level, and it is important to understand those changes if we want to meaningfully assess the construct. We also require research on the extent to which the course of development in different domains varies with factors such as gender and ethnic and cultural group membership. Loeber's (Loeber & Hay, 1997; Loeber et al., 1993) efforts to describe the developmental course of the conduct disorders is a good example of the type of work needed.

Third, we need more theory and research concerning family and social influences on development during the adolescent years. We have seen that many counseling and therapeutic interventions depend on knowledge of the larger environment of the adolescent. Assessments for purposes of referral and treatment planning should, then, take account of these other variables. Similarly, many program evaluation efforts require assessments of a broad range of variables, including aspects of the youth's social environment. Conger et al.'s (1995) efforts to explore the way in which the family system affects the development of the adolescent represents a good example of the type of research needed in this area.

*Instrument Development.* The preceding chapters have documented the progress that has been made in the development and refinement of assessment instruments and procedures appropriate for use with adolescents. Still, considerable work needs to be done. There are two general needs: Existing instruments must be refined and new instruments and procedures must be developed.

Research on current measuring instruments must be done. Virtually none of the instruments reviewed satisfies the stringent psychometric criteria presented in the *Standards for Educational and Psychological Testing*. In some cases construct validity remains a major issue. This is true, for example, for some of the personality tests, for which there are serious questions about the meaningfulness of dimensions such as sociability, impulse control, or conscientiousness. Similarly, predictive validity has not always been well established, even for instruments used for making future projections. We saw cases, for example, of vocational interest inventories used to predict future job satisfaction that lacked information about predictive validity. Finally, there are cases in which instruments are used to assess changes in the client that lack treatment validity support.

There is often an absence of information about reliability and validity for different gender and ethnic and cultural groups. The *Standards for*

*Educational and Psychological Testing* make clear that instruments should not be used with individuals from groups for which the instrument has not been evaluated. Unfortunately, many of the instruments reviewed in this book have been evaluated only for a narrow range of ethnic, cultural, and special needs groups. A similar problem exists with respect to normative data. Considerably more work needs to be done with some of the measures to extend the generality of the norms on which their scoring is based.

Continuing psychometric evaluations of the computer-based delivery, scoring, and interpretive assessment systems are also required. We saw in chapter 4 that writers such as Lanyon (1984) and Matarazzo (1983, 1986) expressed concern about the poor research base for many of the computer-based systems, and those problems appear to persist. The American Psychological Association (1986) also acknowledged these serious issues in their *Guidelines for Computer-Based Tests and Interpretations*.

Efforts to develop actuarial formulas for existing assessment tools must continue. Too often information about the client is collected through standardized assessment procedures, but the inferences from the results rely on clinical judgment. For example, a standardized personality test may be used to describe certain traits in the youth, but the examiner's intuitions are involved in translating that information into a prediction about future performance or the effectiveness of a particular treatment. This inferential or judgmental phase can also be standardized as we have seen. The Personality Inventory for Children–Revised was earlier presented as an example of an instrument for which actuarial formulas are being developed. It is, however, the exception, and considerably more work of this sort is needed.

Conducting psychometric research is not always exciting or particularly easy. Predictive validity studies are especially time consuming and expensive. Nevertheless, the utility of our measures is directly dependent on our ability to demonstrate their reliability and validity for the situations in which they are being employed, and this type of basic psychometric research is essential.

There are several directions that work to develop new instruments and procedures should take. First, more efforts should be made to translate findings from basic research into practical assessment instruments. We have already seen one example, in the cognitive area. Some research has targeted general cognitive processes; other research, more specific activities, for example, mathematical reasoning. However, very little has yet led to usable instruments for assessing aptitudes or achievement levels.

It would be helpful if we could expand the range of assessment tools, and add in particular instruments focusing on situational and environmental variables. We have a wide selection of instruments for assessing characteristics of the individual, but we have a real lack of standardized measures of family dynamics, peer group experiences, school factors, or aspects of the larger social environment. As we have seen, we are forced to depend on clinical assessments in evaluating these important influences, and that is a situation that needs to be changed.

Finally, we must increase our efforts to develop standardized tools and procedures with which to integrate information from a variety of sources or measures. Here, too, we are almost always forced to depend on clinical judgment in processing information. A few efforts to develop composite measures for combining information from a variety of sources in the prediction of conduct disorders were described in chapter 11. Those efforts are still preliminary, but represent the kind of work that is needed.

*The Assessment Process.* There are a number of aspects of the assessment process that would benefit from continuing research attention. The first has to do with the basic constructs underlying assessment activities. This book has reflected the traditional psychometric model with its emphasis on the concepts of reliability and validity. There have, however, been frequent attacks on that model, particularly from more behaviorally oriented psychologists (see, e.g., Cone & Hawkins, 1977). The criticisms have focused largely on assumptions of the existence of stable underlying traits and of the relative neglect of situational factors. However, some adjustments are being made in both the traditional and behaviorist approaches to assessment, and there does appear to be some convergence (Mash & Terdal, 1997). Still, ongoing analysis of the nature of the assessment process and of the best means for evaluating the resulting assessments will be important.

Research on the technology of assessments must also continue. Some very promising developments have been reported in connection with item response theory, and it is likely that research in that area will continue to lead to improvements in test format. Efforts to improve the technology of rating scales and checklists are also worthy of note (see Aiken, 1996b). One specific issue that requires additional research attention is the operation and control of response distortions in self-report measures.

Improvements in assessment technology may also be expected from attempts to expand the use of computer technology in assessments. We have seen that computerizing assessments has created some problems, but it is likely that future research will eventually lead to more effective assessments. Applications involving individualized aptitude testing have already proven very promising (Britton & Tidwell, 1995). Also noteworthy is Matarazzo's (1990, 1992) projection that computer technology will permit the more effective integration of both clinical and standarized information:

> I predict that these highly computerized assessments will start by combining, into a meaningful whole, salient information from the individual's educational, occupational, social and medical histories, and then add to and integrate into that whole equally relevant input consisting of observational-interview data plus the findings from a battery of tests (including biological) that tap intellectual, attitudinal, interest, personality, neuropsychological, adaptive behavior, and quality of life functions. (Matarazzo, 1992, p. 1016)

This is an exciting suggestion in light of the serious problems discussed regarding the integration of information from multiple sources.

More work is also needed on the processes used by the professional in forming an assessment. We saw earlier that some work has been done on the clinical inference process, particularly in clinical and employment interviews (see Lanyon & Goodstein, 1997; Murphy & Davidshofer, 1994). That research has given us some insights into how individuals approach the assessment task and the kinds of errors in information collection and processing that they make. Continuing study is necessary. Garb's (1984, 1986, 1989) explorations of the factors affecting the accuracy of clinical judgments is representative of the kind of research needed in this area. We will undoubtedly be depending for a long time on clinical judgments, and it is important to achieve ways of refining the processes involved in them.

Continuing efforts to address and resolve ethical issues in assessment are also crucial. These relate more to policy than to research, but important questions are being raised about the operation of bias in assessments, invasion of privacy, confidentiality, and access to assessment services that require continuing attention from the profession.

Finally, psychological professionals would benefit from a fuller understanding of the general public's beliefs and attitudes about psychological assessments. T. B. Rogers (1995) traced the history of the antitest movement and showed that it has sometimes been a powerful force. We need current information about the extent of negative attitudes toward assessment as well as about the bases for these attitudes. Such information is extremely important for educating the public regarding positive contributions of psychological assessments.

We also require more information about the beliefs and attitudes toward assessment of the groups of other professionals with whom we work. Grisso (1987) and Hoge and Andrews (1996b), for example, talked about the importance of educating judges, attorneys, and police about the contributions of psychological assessments to judicial and correctional systems. A similar point can be made about physicians, teachers, educational administrators, and other professionals who represent the "consumers" of our assessments. Our outreach efforts will be most effective when they are based on knowledge about the beliefs and attitudes of these groups.

# Appendix

Addresses for Major Test Publishers

| Publisher | Address |
|---|---|
| American Guidance Service | 4201 Woodland Rd. |
| | Circle Pines, MN 55014–1796 |
| Consulting Psychologist Press | 3803 East Bayshore Rd. |
| | Palo Alto, CA 94303 |
| CTB/Macmillan/McGraw-Hill | 20 Ryan Ranch Rd. |
| | Monterey, CA 93940–5703 |
| Family Social Science | 290 McNeil Hall |
| | University of Minnesota |
| | St. Paul, MN 55108 |
| Guidance Centre | 712 Gordon Baker Rd. |
| | Toronto, ON M2H 3R7 |
| Hawthorne Educational Services | 800 Gray Oak Dr. |
| | Columbia, MO 65201 |
| Houghton-Mifflin | 222 Berkeley St. |
| | Boston, MA 02116 |
| Institute for Personality and Ability Testing | P.O. Box 1188 |
| | Champaign, IL 61824–1188 |
| Jastak Associates, Inc. | P.O. Box 3410 |
| | Wilmington, DE 19804 |
| Multi-Health Systems | 908 Niagara Falls Blvd. |
| | North Tonawanda, NY 14120–2060 |
| Multi-Health Systems (Canada) | 5 Overlea Blvd., Suite 210 |
| | Toronto, ON M4H 1P1 |

*(Continued)*

| Publisher | Address |
| --- | --- |
| National Computer Systems | P.O. Box 1416 |
| | Minneapolis, MN 55440 |
| PRO-ED | 8700 Shoal Creek Blvd. |
| | Austin, TX 78757–6897 |
| Psychological Assessment Resources | P.O. Box 998 |
| | Odessa, FL 33556 |
| Psychological Corporation | 555 Academic Ct. |
| | San Antonio, TX 78204–2498 |
| Reitan Neuropsychology Laboratories | 2920 South 4th Ave. |
| | Tucson, AZ 85713–4819 |
| Research Psychologists Press | P.O. Box 3292, Station B |
| | London, ON N6A 4K3 |
| Riverside Publishing Company | 3 O'Hare Towers |
| | 8420 Bryn Mawr Ave. |
| | Chicago, IL 60631 |
| Sigma Assessment Systems | 511 Fort St., #435 |
| | P.O. Box 610984 |
| | Port Huron, MI 48061–0984 |
| Slosson Educational Publications | P.O. Box 280 |
| | East Aurora, NY 14052 |
| United States Employment Service | Testing Directorate |
| | U.S. Department of Labor |
| | 601 D St., N.W. |
| | Washington, DC 20213 |
| University Associates in Psychiatry | Department of Psychiatry |
| | University of Vermont |
| | Burlington, VT 05401 |
| Western Psychological Services | 12031 Wilshire Blvd. |
| | Los Angeles, CA 90025 |

# References

Abidin, R. R. (1993). *Parenting Stress Index Manual—Third edition.* Odessa, FL: Psychological Assessment Resources.

Abramson, L. Y., Seligman, M. E. P., & Teasdale, J. (1978). Learned helplessness in humans: Critique and reformulation. *Journal of Abnormal Psychology, 87,* 49–74.

Achenbach, T. M. (1991). *Integrative guide for the 1991 CBCL/4-18, YSR, and TRF profiles.* Burlington: University of Vermont, Department of Psychiatry.

Achenbach, T. M. (1993). *Empirically based taxonomy: How to use syndromes and profile types derived from the CBCL/4-18, TRF, and YSR.* Burlington, VT: University of Vermont, Department of Psychiatry.

Achenbach, T. M. (1994). Child Behavior Checklist and related instruments. In M. E. Maruish (Ed.), *The use of psychological testing for treatment planning and outcome assessment* (pp. 517–549). Hillsdale, NJ: Lawrence Erlbaum Associates.

Achenbach, T. M. (1995). Diagnosis, assessment, and comorbidity in psychosocial treatment research. *Journal of Abnormal Child Psychology, 23,* 45–66.

Achenbach, T. M., & McConaughy, S. H. (1987). *Empirically based assessment of child and adolescent psychopathology: Practical applications.* Newbury Park, CA: Sage.

Achenbach, T. M., McConaughy, S. H., & Howell, C. T. (1987). Child/adolescent behavioral and emotional problems: Implications of cross-informant correlations for situational specificity. *Psychological Bulletin, 101,* 213–232.

Adwere-Boamah, J., & Curtis, D. A. (1993). A confirmatory factor analysis of a four-factor model of adolescent concerns revisited. *Journal of Youth and Adolescence, 22,* 297–312.

Aiken, L. R. (1996a). *Personality assessment: Methods and practices* (2nd ed.). Seattle, WA: Hogrefe & Huber.

Aiken, L. R. (1996b). *Rating scales and checklists: Evaluating behavior, personality, and attitudes.* New York: Wiley.

Aiken, L. R. (1997). *Psychological testing and assessment* (9th ed.). Boston: Allyn & Bacon.

Aiken, L. S., West, S. G., Sechrest, L., & Reno, R. R. (1990). Graduate training in statistics, methodology, and measurement in psychology: A survey of Ph.D. programs in North America. *American Psychologist, 45,* 721–734.

Allison, J. A. (1995). Review of the Family Environment Scale. *Mental Measurements Yearbook, 12,* 384–385.

Allport, G. W. (1968). *The person in psychology: Selected essays*. Boston: Beacon.

Aman, M. G., Hammer, D., & Rojahn, J. (1993). Mental retardation. In T. Ollendick & M. Hersen (Eds.), *Handbook of child and adolescent assessment* (pp. 321–345). Boston: Allyn & Bacon.

American Association on Mental Retardation (1992). *Mental retardation: Definition, classification, and systems of support*. Washington, DC: Author.

American Psychiatric Association. (1994). *Diagnostic and statistical manual of mental disorders* (4th ed.). Washington, DC: Author.

American Psychological Association. (1954). *Technical recommendations for psychological tests and diagnostic techniques*. Washington, DC: Author.

American Psychological Association. (1985). *Standards for educational and psychological testing*. Washington, DC: Author.

American Psychological Association. (1986). *Guidelines for computer-based tests and interpretations*. Washington, DC: Author.

American Psychological Association. (1988). *Code of fair testing practices in education*. Washington, DC: Author.

American Psychological Association. (1991). *Ethical guidelines for forensic psychology*. Washington, DC: Author.

American Psychological Association. (1992). *Ethical principles of psychologists and code of conduct*. Washington, DC: Author.

American Psychological Association. (1993). Record keeping guidelines. *American Psychologist*, *48*, 984–986.

American Psychological Association. (1994). Guidelines for child custody evaluations in divorce proceedings. *American Psychologist*, *49*, 677–680.

Anastasi, A. (1986). Evolving concepts of test validation. *Annual Review of Psychology*, *37*, 1–15.

Anastasi, A., & Urbina, S. (1997). *Psychological testing* (9th ed.). Upper Saddle River, NJ: Prentice-Hall.

Andrews, D. A., & Bonta, J. (1995). *Level of Service Inventory–Revised*. Toronto: Multi-Health Systems.

Andrews, D. A., Bonta, J., & Hoge, R. D. (1990). Classification for effective rehabilitation: Rediscovering psychology. *Criminal Justice and Behavior*, *17*, 19–52.

Ansorge, C. J. (1985). Review of the Cognitive Abilities Test. *Mental Measurements Yearbook*, *9*, 351–352.

Archambault, F. X. (1995). Review of the Multidimensional Self Concept Scale. *Mental Measurements Yearbook*, *12*, 647–649.

Archer, R. P. (1992). *MMPI-A: Assessing adolescent psychopathology*. Hillsdale, NJ: Lawrence Erlbaum Associates.

Archer, R. P. (1994). Minnesota Multiphasic Personality Inventory–Adolescent. In M. Maruish (Ed.), *The use of psychological testing for treatment planning and outcome assessment* (pp. 423–452). Hillsdale, NJ: Lawrence Erlbaum Associates.

Archer, R. P. (1997). *MMPI-A: Assessing adolescent psychopathology* (2nd ed.). Mahwah, NJ: Lawrence Erlbaum Associates.

Archer, R. P., Maruish, M., Imhof, E. A., & Piotrowski, C. (1991). Psychological test usage with adolescent clients: 1990 survey findings. *Professional Psychology: Research and Practice*, *22*, 247–252.

Arkowitz, H. (1992). Integrative theories of therapy. In D. K. Freedheim (Ed.), *History of psychotherapy: A century of change* (pp. 261–303). Washington, DC: American Psychological Association.

Armacost, R. L. (1989). Perceptions of stressors by high school students. *Journal of Adolescent Research*, *4*, 443–461.

Ash, P. (1995). Review of the Eating Disorder Inventory-2. *Mental Measurements Yearbook*, *12*, 334–335.

Association of State and Provincial Psychology Boards. (1993). *Handbook of licensing and certification requirements.* Montgomery, AL: Author.

Attkinson, C. C., Roberts, R. E., & Pascoe, G. C. (1983). The Evaluation Ranking Scale: Clarification of methodological problems. *Evaluation and Program Planning, 6,* 349–358.

Auld, R. (1994). Review of the Beck Hopelessness Scale. *Test Critiques, 10,* 82–90.

Austin, G. W., Leschied, A. W., Jaffe, P. G., & Sas, L. (1986). Factor structure and construct validity of the Basic Personality Inventory with juvenile offenders. *Canadian Journal of Behavioural Science, 18,* 238–247.

Ayers, M., & Burns, L. (1991). Review of the Luria–Nebraska Neuropsychological Battery: Children's revision. *Test Critiques, 8,* 358–373.

Bandura, A. (1977). *Social learning theory.* Englewood Cliffs, NJ: Prentice-Hall.

Bandura, A. (1986). *Social foundations of thought and action: A social cognitive theory.* Englewood Cliffs, NJ: Prentice-Hall.

Bandura, A. (1989). Regulation of cognitive processes through perceived self-efficacy. *Developmental Psychology, 25,* 729–735.

Bardwell, R. (1985). Review of the Suicide Probability Scale. *Test Critiques, 4,* 649–655.

Barnes, L. B. (1995). Review of the Occupational Aptitude Survey and Interest Schedule. *Mental Measurements Yearbook, 12,* 698–699.

Bascue, L. O. (1991). Review of the Suicidal Ideation Questionnaire. *Test Critiques, 8,* 663–667.

Beck, A. T. (1967). *Depression: Clinical, experimental, and theoretical aspects.* New York: Harper & Row.

Beck, A. T. (1976). *Cognitive theory and the emotional disorders.* New York: International Universities Press.

Beck, A. T., Brown, G., Steer, R. A., & Weissman, A. N. (1991). Factor analysis of the Dysfunctional Attitude Scale in a clinical population. *Psychological Assessment, 3,* 478–483.

Beere, C. A., King, D. W., Beere, D. B., & King, L. A. (1984). The Sex-Role Egalitarianism Scale: A measure of attitudes toward equality between the sexes. *Sex Roles, 10,* 563–576.

Belsky, J. (1981). Early human experience: A family perspective. *Developmental Psychology, 17,* 3–23.

Belsky, J. (1984). The determinants of parenting: A process model. *Child Development, 55,* 83–96.

Belsky, J., Lerner, R. M., & Spanier, G. B. (1984). *The child in the family.* Reading, MA: Addison-Wesley.

Benes, K. M. (1992). Review of the Peabody Individual Achievement Test–Revised. *Mental Measurements Yearbook, 11,* 649–652.

Bennett, E., Sheras, P., & Abidin, R. (1997, August). *Analyses of the reliability and validity of the Stress Index for Parents of Adolescents.* Presentation at the Annual Conference of the American Psychological Association, Chicago.

Bernal, G., Bonilla, J., & Bellido, C. (1995). Ecological validity and cultural sensitivity for outcome research: Issues for the cultural adaptation and development of prosocial treatments for Hispanics. *Journal of Abnormal Child Psychology, 23,* 67–82.

Bersoff, D. N. (1995). *Ethical conflicts in psychology.* Washington, DC: American Psychological Association.

Bettelheim, B. (1966). *The empty fortress.* New York: Macmillan.

Beutler, L. E. (1979). Toward specific psychological therapies for specific conditions. *Journal of Consulting and Clinical Psychology, 47,* 882–897.

Beutler, L. E., & Clarkin, J. (1990). *Systematic treatment selection: Toward targeted therapeutic interventions.* New York: Brunner/Mazel.

Beutler, L. E., Wakefield, P., & Williams, R. E. (1994). Use of psychological tests/instruments for treatment planning. In M. Maruish (Ed.), *The use of psychological testing for treatment planning and outcome assessment* (pp. 55–74). Hillsdale, NJ: Lawrence Erlbaum Associates.

Billings, A., & Moos, R. (1982). Family environments and adaptation: A clinically applicable typology. *American Journal of Family Therapy, 10,* 26–38.

Bird, H. R., Gould, M. S., & Staghezza, B. (1992). Aggregating data from multiple informants in child psychiatry epidemiological research. *Journal of the American Academy of Child and Adolescent Psychiatry, 31,* 78–85.

Blashfield, R. K. (1984). *The classification of psychopathology.* New York: Plenum.

Block, J. (1995). A contrarian view of the five-factor approach to personality description. *Psychological Bulletin, 117,* 187–213.

Borum, R. (1996). Improving the clinical practice of violence risk assessment: Technology, guidelines, and training. *American Psychologist, 51,* 945–956.

Boswell, D. L., Tarver, P. J., & Simoneaux, J. C. (1994). The Psychological Screening Inventory's usefulness as a screening instrument for adolescent inpatients. *Journal of Personality Assessment, 62,* 262–268.

Boyle, G. J. (1994). Review of Self-Description Questionnaire II. *Test Critiques, 10,* 632–643.

Boyle, M. H., Offord, D. R., Racine, Y., Sanford, M., Szatmari, P., Fleming, J. E., & Prince-Munn, N. (1993). Evaluation of the Diagnostic Interview for Children and Adolescents for use in general population samples. *Journal of Abnormal Child Psychology, 21,* 663–682.

Bracken, B. A. (1992). *Multidimensional Self Concept Scale.* Austin, TX: PRO-ED.

Bracken, B. A. (1996). *Handbook of self-concept: Developmental, social, and clinical considerations.* New York: Wiley.

Braden, J. P. (1995). Review of the Wechsler Intelligence Scale for Children–III. *Mental Measurements Yearbook, 12,* 1090–1102.

Braithwaite, V. A., & Scott, W. C. (1991). Values. In J. P. Robinson, P. R. Shaver, & L. S. Wrightsman (Eds.), *Measures of personality and social psychological attitudes* (Vol. I, pp. 661–753). New York: Academic Press.

Britton, B. K., & Tidwell, P. (1995). Cognitive structure testing: A computer system for diagnosis of expert-novice differences. In P. D. Nichols, S. F. Chipman, & R. L. Brennon (Eds.), *Cognitively diagnostic assessment* (pp. 251–278). Hillsdale, NJ: Lawrence Erlbaum Associates.

Brodsky, S. L., & Smitherman, H. W. (1983). *Handbook of scales for research in crime and delinquency.* New York: Plenum.

Bronfenbrenner, U. (1979). *The ecology of human development.* Cambridge, MA: Harvard University Press.

Bronfenbrenner, U. (1986). Ecology of the family as a context for human development: Research perspectives. *Developmental Psychology, 22,* 723–742.

Brookhart, S. M. (1995). Review of the Rokeach Value Survey. *Mental Measurements Yearbook, 12,* 878–884.

Brookings, J. B. (1994). Review of the Eating Disorder Inventory–2. *Test Critiques, 10,* 226–233.

Brooks-Gunn, J. (1987). Pubertal processes and girls' psychological adaptation. In R. M. Lerner & T. Foch (Eds.), *Biological-psychosocial interaction in early adolescence* (pp. 123–153). Hillsdale, NJ: Lawrence Erlbaum Associates.

Brooks-Gunn, J., & Reiter, E. O. (1990). The role of pubertal processes. In S. S. Feldman & G. R. Elliott (Eds.), *At the threshold: The developing adolescent* (pp. 89–112). Cambridge, MA: Harvard University Press.

Brooks-Gunn, J., & Warren, M. P. (1985). Measuring physical status and timing in early adolescence: A developmental perspective. *Journal of Youth and Adolescence, 14,* 163–189.

Broughton, J. (1983). The cognitive-developmental theory of adolescent self and identity. In B. Lee & G. Moam (Eds.), *Developmental approaches to self* (pp. 215–266). New York: Plenum.

Brown, D. T. (1989). Review of the Jackson Vocational Interest Survey. *Mental Measurements Yearbook, 10,* 401–403.

Bruininks, R. H., Woodcock, R. W., Weatherman, R. F., & Hill, B. K. (1996). *Manual for the Scales of Independent Behavior–Revised*. Chicago, IL: Riverside Publishing Co.

Burgess, E., & Haaga, D. A. F. (1994). The Positive Automatic Thoughts Questionnaire (ATQ-P) and the Automatic Thoughts Questionnaire–Revised (ATQ-R): Equivalent measures of positive thinking. *Cognitive Therapy and Research, 18*, 15–23.

Busch, J. C. (1995). Review of the Strong Interest Inventory. *Mental Measurements Yearbook, 12*, 997–999.

Busch-Rossnagel, N. A. (1987). Review of the Adolescent-Family Inventory of Life Events and Changes. *Test Critiques, 6*, 16–20.

Butcher, J. N. (Ed.). (1987). *Computerized psychological assessment: A practitioner's guide*. New York: Basic.

Butcher, J. N., & Rouse, S. V. (1996). Personality: Individual differences and clinical assessment. *Annual Reviews of Psychology, 47*, 87–111.

Butcher, J. N., Williams, C. L., Graham, J. R., Archer, R. P., Tellegen, R. P., Ben-Porath, Y. S., & Kaemmer, B. (1992). *MMPI-A: Manual for administration, scoring, and interpretation*. Minneapolis: University of Minnesota Press.

Byrne, B. M. (1996a). *Measuring self-concept across the life span: Issues and instrumentation*. Washington, DC: American Psychological Association.

Byrne, B. M. (1996b). The status and role of quantitative methods in psychology: Past, present, and future perspectives. *Canadian Psychology, 37*, 76–80.

Camara, J. (1988). Review of the Family Adaptability and Cohesion Evaluation Scales. *Test Critiques, 7*, 209–219.

Campbell, D. T., & Fiske, D. W. (1959). Convergent and discriminant validation by the multitrait-multimethod matrix. *Psychological Bulletin, 56*, 81–105.

Canadian Psychological Association. (1987). *Guidelines for educational and psychological testing*. Ottawa, Canada: Author.

Canadian Psychological Association. (1991). *Canadian code of ethics for psychologists*. Ottawa, Canada: Author.

Cane, D. B., Olinger, L. J., Gotlib, I. H., & Kuiper, N. A. (1986). Factor structure of the Dysfunctional Attitude Scale in a student population. *Journal of Clinical Psychology, 42*, 307–309.

Caplan, G. (1964). *Principles of preventive psychiatry*. London: Tavistock.

Carey, M. P., Faulstich, M. E., Carey, T. L. (1994). Assessment of anxiety in adolescents: Concurrent and factorial validities of the trait anxiety scale of Spielberger's State-Trait Anxiety Inventory for Children. *Psychological Reports, 75*, 331–338.

Cattell, R. B. (1940). A culture free intelligence test, Part I. *Journal of Educational Psychology, 31*, 161–179.

Cattell, R. B. (1968). Trait-view theory and perturbations in ratings and self-ratings: Its application to obtaining pure trait score estimates in questionnaires. *Psychological Review, 75*, 90–103.

Cattell, R. B., & Cattell, M. D. (1975). *Handbook for the Jr.-Sr. High School Personality Questionnaire*. Champaign, IL: Institute for Personality and Ability Testing.

Champion, D. J. (1994). *Measuring offender risk: A criminal justice sourcebook*. Westport, CT: Greenwood.

Clark, E. (1987). Review of the Child Assessment Schedule. *Test Critiques, 6*, 91–96.

Clark, E., & Gardner, M. K. (1988). Review of the Henmon–Nelson Test of Intelligence. *Test Critiques, 7*, 228–233.

Coates, D. L., & Vietze, P. M. (1996). *Manual of diagnostic and professional practices in mental retardation*. Washington, DC: American Psychological Association.

Cohen, D. (1995). Prosocial therapies for children and adolescents: Overview and future directions. *Journal of Abnormal Child Psychology, 23*, 141–156.

Coie, J. D., Wall, N. F., West, S. G., Hawkins, J. D., Asarnow, J. R., Markman, H. J., Ramey, S. L., Shure, M. B., & Long, B. (1993). The science of prevention: A conceptual framework and some directions for a national research program. *American Psychologist, 48*, 1013–1022.

Collins, D. (1995). Review of the Attention Deficit Disorders Evaluation Scale. *Mental Measurements Yearbook, 12*, 95–96.

Compas, B. E. (1987). Stress and life events during childhood and adolescence. *Clinical Psychology Review, 98*, 310–357.

Compas, B. E., Hinden, B. R., & Gerhardt, C. A. (1995). Adolescent development: Pathways and processes of risk and resilience. *Annual Review of Psychology, 46*, 265–293.

Cone, J. D., & Hawkins, R. P. (Eds.). (1977). *Behavior assessment: New directions in clinical psychology*. New York: Brunner/Mazel.

Conger, R. D., Patterson, G. R., & Ge, X. (1995). It takes two to replicate: A mediational model for the impact of parenting stress on adolescent development. *Child Development, 66*, 80–97.

Conners, C. K. (1969). A teacher rating scale for use in drug studies with children. *American Journal of Psychiatry, 126*, 884–888.

Conners, C. K. (1989). *Manual for the Conners Rating Scales*. Toronto, ONT: Multihealth Systems.

Conners, C. K. (1995). *Manual for the Conners–Wells' Adolescent Self-Report Scale*. North Tonawanda, NY: Multi-Health Systems.

Conoley, J. C., & Impara, J. C. (1995). *The 12th mental measurements yearbook*. Lincoln: University of Nebraska and Buros Institute of Mental Measurement.

Costa, P. T., & McCrae, R. R. (1988). Personality in adulthood: A six-year longitudinal study of self-reports and spouse ratings on the NEO Personality Inventory. *Journal of Personality and Social Psychology, 54*, 853–863.

Costa, P. T. Jr., & McCrae, R. R. (1992). *Manual for the Revised NEO Personality Inventory (NEO–PI–R) and NEO Five-Factor Inventory (NEO–FFI)*. Odessa, FL: Psychological Assessment Resources.

Costello, E. J., Edelbrock, L. S., Dulcan, M. K., Kalas, R., & Klaric, S. H. (1984). *Report on the NIMH Diagnostic Interview Schedule for Children (DISC)*. Washington, DC: National Institute of Mental Health.

Crockett, L. J., & Crouter, A. C. (Eds.). (1995). *Pathways through adolescence: Individual development in relation to social contexts*. Mahwah, NJ: Lawrence Erlbaum Associates.

Cronbach, L. J. (1990). *Essentials of psychological testing* (5th ed.). Cambridge, MA: Harper & Row.

Cronbach, L. J., & Meehl, P. E. (1955). Construct validity in psychological tests. *Psychological Bulletin, 52*, 281–302.

Cummings, J. A. (1995). Review of the Woodcock–Johnson Psycho-Educational Battery–Revised. *Mental Measurements Yearbook, 12*, 1113–1116.

Dahmus, S., Bernardin, H. J., & Bernardin, K. (1992). Personal Experience Inventory. *Measurement and Evaluation in Counseling and Development, 25*, 91–94.

Daniel, M. H. (1997). Intelligence testing: Status and trends. *American Psychologist, 52*, 1038–1045.

Daniels, M. H. (1989). Review of the Self-Directed Search. *Mental Measurements Yearbook, 10*, 735–738.

Dawes, R. M., Faust, D., & Meehl, P. E. (1989). Clinical vs. actuarial judgments. *Science, 243*, 1668–1674.

Dean, R. S. (1985). Neuropsychological assessment. In J. D. Cavenar, R. Michels, H. K. H. Brodie, A. M. Cooper, S. B. Guz, L. L. Judd, G. L. Klerman, & A. J. Solnit (Eds.), *Psychiatry* (pp. 1–16). Philadelphia: Lippincott.

Dean R. S., & Gray, J. W. (1990). Traditional approaches to neuropsychological assessment. In C. R. Reynolds & R. W. Kamphaus (Eds.), *Handbook of psychological and educational assessment of children: Intelligence and achievement* (pp. 371–389). New York: Guilford.

Delaney, E. A., & Hopkins, T. F. (1987). *Examiner's handbook: An expanded guide for fourth edition users*. Chicago: Riverside.

Delis, D. C., & Kaplan, E. (1983). Hazards of a standardized neuropsychological test with low content validity. *Journal of Consulting and Clinical Psychology, 51*, 396–398.

Derogatis, L. R., & DellaPietra, L. (1994). Psychological tests in screening for psychiatric disorder. In M. E. Maruish (Ed.), *The use of psychological testing for treatment planning and outcome assessment* (pp. 22–54). Hillsdale, NJ: Lawrence Erlbaum Associates.

Derogatis, L. R., & Lazarus, L. (1994). SCL–90–R, Brief Symptom Inventory, and matching clinical rating scales. In M. E. Maruish (Ed.), *The use of psychological testing for treatment planning and outcome assessment* (pp. 217–248). Hillsdale, NJ: Lawrence Erlbaum Associates.

DeStefano, L. (1992). Review of Street Survival Skills Questionnaire. *Test Critiques, 9*, 526–533.

Diamond, G. S., Serrano, A. C., Dickey, M., & Sonis, W. A. (1996). Current status of family-based outcome and process research. *Journal of the American Academy of Child and Adolescent Psychiatry, 35*, 6–16.

Dinero, T. E. (1995). Review of the Occupational Aptitude Survey and Interest Schedule–Second edition. *Mental Measurements Yearbook, 12*, 699–700.

Dodge, K. A. (1993). Social-cognitive mechanisms in the development of conduct disorders and depression. *Annual Review of Psychology, 44*, 559–584.

Dodge, K. A., & Newman, J. P. (1981). Biased decision making processes in aggressive boys. *Journal of Abnormal Psychology, 90*, 375–379.

Dodge, K. A., Price, J. M., Bachorowski, J., & Newman, J. P. (1990). Hostile attributional biases in severely aggressive adolescents. *Journal of Abnormal Psychology, 99*, 385–392.

Doll, E. J. (1989). Review of the Kaufman Test of Educational Achievement. *Mental Measurements Yearbook, 10*, 410–412.

Donlon, T. F. (1995). Review of the Adolescent Drinking Index. *Mental Measurements Yearbook, 12*, 44–47.

Dreger, R. M. (1982). The classification of children and their emotional problems: An overview: II. *Clinical Psychology Review, 2*, 349–385.

Drummond, R. J. (1986). Review of the Jesness Behavior Checklist. *Test Critiques, 5*, 226–229.

Drummond, R. J. (1987). Review of the Learning Style Inventory. *Test Critiques, 6*, 308–312.

Dryfoos, J. G. (1990). *Adolescents at risk: Prevalence and prevention*. New York: Oxford University Press.

Dunn, R. (1989). Individualizing instruction for mainstreamed gifted students. In R. M. Milgram (Ed.), *Teaching gifted and talented learners in regular classrooms* (pp. 63–111). Springfield, IL: Thomas.

Dunn, R., & Dunn, K. (1978). *Teaching students through individual learning styles*. Reston, VA: Reston.

Dwyer, C. A. (1996). Cut scores and testing: Statistics, judgment, truth, and error. *Psychological Assessment, 8*, 360–362.

Eccles, J. S., Lord, S., & Midgley, C. (1991). What are we doing to early adolescents? The impact of educational contexts on early adolescents. *American Journal of Education, 99*, 521–542.

Eccles, J. S., Midgley, C., Wigfield, A., Buchanan, C. M., Reuman, D., Flanagan, C., & MacIver, D. (1993). Development during adolescence: The impact of stage-environment fit on young adolescents' experiences in schools and in families. *American Psychologist, 48*, 90–101.

Edelbrock, C. S. (1987). Psychometric research on children and adolescents. In C. G. Last & M. Hersen (Eds.), *Issues in diagnostic research* (pp. 219–240). New York: Plenum.

Edelbrock, C. S. (1988). Informant reports. In E. S. Shapiro & T. R. Kratchowill (Eds.), *Behavioral assessment in schools: Conceptual foundations and practical applications* (pp. 351–383). New York: Guilford.

Edelbrock, C. S., & Costello, A. J. (1988). Structured psychiatric interview for children. In M. Rutter, H. Tuma, & I. Lann (Eds.), *Assessment and diagnosis in child psychopathology* (pp. 87–112). New York, NY: Guilford.

Edwards, A. J. (1995). Review of the Parent–Adolescent Communication Scale. *Mental Measurements Yearbook, 12,* 733–735.

Edwards, H. P. (1994). Regulation and accreditation in professional psychology: Facilitators? Safeguards? Threats? *Canadian Psychology, 35,* 66–69.

Elder, G. G. (1980). Adolescence in historical perspective. In J. Adelson (Ed.), *Handbook of adolescent psychology* (pp. 3–46). New York: Wiley.

Elliott, S. N., & Busse, R. T. (1993). Effective treatments with behavioral consultation. In J. E. Zins, T. R. Kratochwill, & S. N. Elliott (Eds.), *Handbook of consultation services for children* (pp. 179–203). San Francisco: Jossey-Bass.

Elliott, S. N., Busse, R. T., & Gresham, F. M. (1993). Behavior rating scales: Issues of use and development. *School Psychology Review, 22,* 313–321.

Ellis, A. (1962). *Reason and emotion in psychotherapy.* New York: Stuart.

Ellis, A. (1971). *Growth through reason.* Hollywood, CA: Wilshire.

Elmen, J., & Offer, D. (1993). Normality, turmoil, and adolescence. In P. Tolan & B. Cohler (Eds.), *Handbook of clinical research and practice with adolescents* (pp. 5–19). New York: Wiley.

Endicott, J., & Spitzer, R. L. (1978). A diagnostic interview: The Schedule for Affective Disorders and Schizophrenia. *Archives of General Psychiatry, 35,* 837–844.

Epstein, N. B., Baldwin, L. M., & Bishop, D. S. (1983). The McMaster Family Assessment Device. *Journal of Marital and Family Therapy, 9,* 171–180.

Epstein, S. (1973). The self-concept revisited: Or a theory of a theory. *American Psychologist, 28,* 404–416.

Erikson, E. H. (1963). *Childhood and society* (2nd ed.). New York: Norton.

Erikson, E. H. (1982). *The life cycle completed: A review.* New York: Norton.

Evans, E. D. (1988). Review of Reynolds Adolescent Depression Scale. *Test Critiques, 10,* 485–495.

Eyde, L. D. (Ed.). (1993). *Responsible test use: Case studies for assessing human behavior.* Washington, DC: American Psychological Association.

Eysenck, H. J. (1982). Development of a theory. In C. D. Spielberger (Ed.), *Personality, genetics and behavior* (pp. 1–38). New York: Praeger.

Fairbank, D. W. (1995). Review of the Behavior Disorders Identification Scale. *Mental Measurements Yearbook, 12,* 116–117.

Farrington D. P., Loeber, R., & Van Kammen, W. B. (1990). Long-term criminal outcomes of hyperactivity-impulsivity-attention-deficit and conduct problems in childhood. In L. N. Robins & M. Rutter (Eds.), *Straight and devious pathways from childhood to adulthood* (pp. 62–81). Cambridge, UK: Cambridge University Press.

Feazell, D. M., Quay, H. C., & Murray, E. J. (1991). The validity and utility of Lanyon's Psychological Screening Inventory in a youth services agency sample. *Criminal Justice and Behavior, 18,* 166–179.

Felner, R. D., & Aden, A. M. (1988). The School Transitional Environment Project: An ecological intervention and evaluation. In R. H. Price, E. L. Cowen, R. P. Lorion, & J. Ramos-McKay (Eds.), *Fourteen ounces of prevention: A casebook for practitioners.* Washington, DC: American Psychological Association.

Fergusson, D. M., Lynskey, M. T., & Horwood, J. (1996). Factors associated with continuity and changes in disruptive behavior patterns between childhood and adolescence. *Journal of Abnormal Child Psychology , 24,* 533–553.

Fisher, P., Blouin, A., & Shaffer, D. (1993, January). *The C-DISC: A computerized version of the NIMH Diagnostic Interview Schedule for Children, Version 2.3.* Poster presentation at the Annual Meeting of the Society for Research in Child and Adolescent Psychopathology, Santa Fe, NM.

Flanagan, D. P. (1995). Review of the Kaufman Adolescent and Adult Intelligence Test. *Mental Measurements Yearbook, 12,* 527–530.

Flavell, J. H. (1963). *The developmental psychology of Jean Piaget.* New York: Van Nostrand Reinhold.

Flavell, J. H. (1985). *Cognitive development* (2nd ed.). Englewood Cliffs, NJ: Prentice-Hall.

Forth, A. E. (1995). Psychopathy and young offenders: Prevalence, family background, and violence. Ottawa, Canada: Ministry of the Solicitor General.

Frances, A., Clarkin, J., & Perry, S. (1984). *Differential therapeutics in psychiatry.* New York: Brunner/Mazel.

Frank, R. G., Sullivan, M. J., & DeLeon, P. H. (1994). Health care reform in the states. *American Psychologist, 49,* 855–867.

Franzen, M. D. (1992). Review of the Wide Range Assessment of Memory and Learning. *Test Critiques, 9,* 653–659.

Fremer, J., Diamond, E. E., & Camara, W. J. (1989). Developing a code of fair testing practices in education. *American Psychologist, 44,* 1062–1067.

Freud, A. (1958). *The ego and the mechanism of defence.* New York: International Universities Press.

Freud, S. (1938). *The basic writings of Sigmund Freud.* New York, NY: The Modern Library.

Fristad, M. A., Emery, B. L., & Beck, S. J. (1997). Use and abuse of the Children's Depression Inventory. *Journal of Consulting and Clinical Psychology, 65,* 699–702.

Fromm, E. (1965). *Escape from freedom.* New York, NY: Avon.

Garb, H. N. (1984). The incremental validity of information used in personality assessment. *Clinical Psychology Review, 4,* 641–655.

Garb, H. N. (1986). The appropriateness of confidence ratings in clinical judgment. *Journal of Clinical Psychology, 42,* 190–197.

Garb, H. N. (1989). Clinical judgment, clinical training, and professional experience. *Psychological Bulletin, 105,* 387–396.

Gardner, E. F., & Slocum, M. O. (1978). Review of the Henmon–Nelson Test of Intelligence. *Mental Measurements Yearbook, 8,* 273–274.

Gardner, H. (1983). *Frames of mind: The theory of multiple intelligences.* New York: Basic.

Gardner, H. (1993). *Multiple intelligences: The theory in practice.* New York: Basic.

Garmezy, N. (1985). Stress-resistant children: The search for protective factors. In J. E. Stevenson (Ed.), *Recent research in developmental psychopathology* (pp. 213–233). Oxford, England: Oxford University Press.

Garner, D. M. (1991). *The Eating Disorder Inventory–2 professional manual.* Odessa, FL: Psychological Assessment Resources.

Garner, D. M. (1996). The Eating Disorder Inventory–2. In L. I. Sederer & B. Dickey (Eds.), *Outcomes assessment in clinical practice* (pp. 92–96). Baltimore: Williams & Wilkins.

Gendreau, P., Grant, B. A., Leipciger, M., & Collins, C. (1979). Norms and recidivism rates for the MMPI and selected experimental scales on a Canadian delinquent sample. *Canadian Journal of Behavioural Science, 11,* 21–31.

Ghiselli, E. E., Campbell, J. P., & Zedek, S. (1981). *Measurement theory for the behavioral sciences.* San Francisco: Freeman.

Gibbins, K., & Walker, I. (1993). Multiple interpretations of the Rokeach Value Survey. *Journal of Social Psychology, 133,* 797–805.

Gilligan, C. (1982). *In a different voice: Psychological theory and women's development.* Cambridge, MA: Harvard University Press.

Glanz, L. M., Haas, G. L., & Sweeney, J. A. (1995). Assessment of hopelessness in suicidal patients. *Clinical Psychology Review, 15,* 49–64.

Glasser, W. (1965). *Reality therapy: A new approach to psychiatry.* New York: Harper & Row.

Glasser, W. (1969). *Schools without failure.* New York: Harper & Row.

Golden, C. J. (1981). The Luria–Nebraska Neuropsychological Battery: Theory and research. *Advances in Psychological Assessment, 5,* 191–235.

Golden, C. J. (1987). *The Luria–Nebraska Neuropsychological Inventory: Children's revision.* Los Angeles, CA: Western Psychological Services.

Golden, C. J., Purich, A. D., & Hammeke, T. A. (1980). *Manual for the Luria–Nebraska Neuropsychological Battery.* Los Angeles, CA: Western Publishing Co.

Goldenberg, I., & Goldenberg, H. (1980). *Family therapy: An overview.* Monterey, CA: Brooks/Cole.

Goldenthal, P. (1988). Review of the Parent–Adolescent Communication Scale. *Test Critiques, 7,* 417–422.

Gordon, L. V. (1975). *The measurement of interpersonal values.* Chicago: Science Research Associates.

Gough, H. G. (1957). *California Psychological Inventory manual.* Palo Alto, CA: Consulting Psychologists Press.

Gough, H. G. (1968). *An interpreter's syllabus for the California Psychological Inventory.* Palo Alto, CA: Consulting Psychologists Press.

Gough, H. G. (1987). *California Psychological Inventory administrator's guide.* Palo Alto, CA: Consulting Psychologists Press.

Gresham, F. M. (1984). Behavioural interviews in school psychology: Issues in psychometric adequacy and research. *School Psychology Review, 13,* 17–25.

Gresham, F. M., & Little, S. G. (1993). Peer-referenced assessment strategies. In T. H. Ollendick & M. Hersen (Eds.), *Handbook of child and adolescent assessment* (pp. 165–179). Boston: Allyn & Bacon.

Gresham, F. M., MacMillan, D. L., & Siperstein, G. N. (1995). Critical analysis of the 1992 AAMR definition: Implications for school psychology. *School Psychology Quarterly, 10,* 1–19.

Griggs, S. A. (1991). Counseling gifted children with different learning style preferences. In R. N. Milgram (Ed.), *Counseling gifted and talented children: A guide for teachers, counselors, and parents* (pp. 53–74). Norwood, NJ: Ablex.

Grisso, T. (1987). The economic and scientific future of forensic assessment. *American Psychologist, 42,* 831–839.

Gronlund, N. E. (1973). *Preparing criterion-referenced tests for classroom instruction.* New York: Macmillan.

Group for the Advancement of Psychiatry. (1966). *Psychopathological disorders in childhood: Theoretical considerations and a proposed classification.* Washington, DC: Author.

Gudjonsson, G. H. (1995). The Standard Progressive Matrices: Methodological problems associated with the administration of the 1992 adult standardization sample. *Personality and Individual Differences, 18,* 441–442.

Guerra, N. G. (1989). Consequential thinking and self-reported delinquency in high school youth. *Criminal Justice and Behavior, 16,* 440–454.

Gutterman, E. M., O'Brien, J. D., & Young, J. G. (1987). Structured diagnostic interviews for children and adolescents: Current status and future directions. *Journal of the American Academy of Child and Adolescent Psychiatry, 26,* 621–630.

Hafkenscheid, A. (1993). Psychometric evaluation of the Symptom Checklist (SCL–90) in psychiatric patients. *Personality and Individual Differences, 14,* 751–756.

Hall, G. S. (1904). *Adolescence: Its psychology and its relations to physiology, anthropology, sociology, sex, crime, religion, and education* (Vol. 1). New York: Appleton-Century-Crofts.

Hallahan, D. P., Kauffman, J. M., & Lloyd, J. W. (1985). *Introduction to learning disabilities* (2nd ed.). Englewood Cliffs, NJ: Prentice-Hall.

Hammill, D. D., Brown, L., & Bryant, B. R. (1992). *A consumer's guide to tests in print* (2nd ed.). Austin, TX: PRO-ED.

Hare, R. D. (1991). *The Psychopathy Checklist–Revised.* Toronto: MHS Publishing.

Hare, R. D., Forth, A. E., & Kosson, D. S. (1994). *The Psychopathy Checklist: Youth Version.* Vancouver, Canada: University of British Columbia, Department of Psychology.

Haring, T. G. (1992). Review of the Street Survival Skills Questionnaire. *Mental Measurements Yearbook, 11,* 11–14.

Harris, K. R. (1985). Conceptual, methodological, and clinical issues in cognitive-behavioral assessment. *Journal of Abnormal Child Psychology, 13,* 373–390.

Harris, M. M. (1989). Reconsidering the employment interview: A review of recent literature and suggestions for future research. *Personnel Psychology, 42,* 691–726.

Harter, S. (1985). *Manual for the Self-Perception Profile for Children.* Denver, CO: University of Denver, Department of Psychology.

Harter, S. (1988). *Manual for the Self-Perception Profile for Adolescents.* Denver, CO: University of Denver, Department of Psychology.

Hattrup, K. (1995). Review of the Differential Aptitude Tests–Fifth edition. *Mental Measurements Yearbook, 12,* 302–304.

Heifetz, L. J. (1989). Review of the Scales of Independent Behavior. *Mental Measurements Yearbook, 10,* 713–718.

Henggeler, S. W., Melton, G. B., & Smith, L. A. (1992). Family preservation using multisystemic therapy: An effective alternative to incarcerating serious juvenile offenders. *Journal of Consulting and Clinical Psychology, 60,* 953–961.

Henggeler, S. W., Melton, G. B., Smith, L. A., Schoenwald, S. K., & Hanley, J. H. (1993). Family preservation using multisystematic treatment: Long term follow-up to a clinical trial with serious juvenile offenders. *Journal of Child and Family Studies, 2,* 283–293.

Henson, F. O., & Bennett, L. M. (1985). Review of the Kaufman Test of Educational Achievement. *Test Critiques, 4,* 368–375.

Hersen, M., & Ammerman, R. T. (Eds.). (1995). *Advanced abnormal child psychology.* Mahwah, NJ: Lawrence Erlbaum Associates.

Hersen, M., & Bellack, A. S. (Eds.). (1988). *Dictionary of behavioral assessment techniques.* Oxford, UK: Pergamon.

Hersen, M., & Van Hasselt, V. B. (Eds.). (1998). *Basic interviewing: A practical guide for counselors and clinicians.* Mahwah, NJ: Lawrence Erlbaum Associates.

Highlin, P. S., & Hill, C. E. (1984). Factors affecting client change in individual counselling: Current status and theoretical speculations. In S. D. Brown & R. W. Lent (Eds.), *Handbook of counseling psychology* (pp. 334–396). New York: Wiley.

Hill, R. (1958). Generic features of families under stress. *Social Casework, 49,* 139–150.

Hoagwood, K., Jensen, P. S., Petti, T., & Burns, B. J. (1996). Outcomes of mental health care for children and adolescents: I. A comprehensive conceptual model. *Journal of the American Academy of Child and Adolescent Psychiatry, 35,* 1055–1063.

Hodapp, R. M. (1995). Definitions in mental retardation: Effects on research, practice, and perceptions. *School Psychology Quarterly, 10,* 24–28.

Hodges, K. (1987). Assessing children with a clinical research interview: The Child Assessment Schedule. In R. J. Prinz (Ed.), *Advances in behavioral assessment of children and families* (Vol. 3, pp. 203–234). Greenwich, CT: JAI.

Hodges, K. (1989). *Child and Adolescent Functional Assessment Scale.* Ypsilanti: Eastern Michigan University, Department of Psychology.

Hodges, K. (1993). Structured interviews for assessing children. *Journal of Child Psychology and Psychiatry, 34,* 49–68.

Hodges, K. (1997). *Manual for the Child Assessment Schedule.* Ypsilanti: Eastern Michigan University, Department of Psychology.

Hodges, K., & Wong, M. M. (1996). Psychometric characteristics of a multidimensional measure to assess impairment: The Child and Adolescent Functional Assessment Scale. *Journal of Child and Family Studies, 5,* 445–467.

Hodges, K., & Wong, M. M. (1997). Use of the Child and Adolescent Functional Assessment Scale to predict service utilization and cost. *Journal of Mental Health Administration, 24,* 278–290.

Hodges, K., & Zeman, J. (1993). Interviewing. In T. H. Ollendick & M. Hersen (Eds.), *Handbook of child and adolescent assessment* (pp. 65–81). Boston: Allyn & Bacon.

Hogan, R., & Nicholson, R. A. (1988). The meaning of personality test scores. *American Psychologist, 43,* 621–626.

Hoge, R. D. (1988). Issues in the definition and measurement of the giftedness construct. *Educational Researcher, 17,* 12–16.

Hoge, R. D. (1989). An examination of the giftedness construct. *Canadian Journal of Education, 14,* 6–16.

Hoge, R. D., & Andrews, D. A. (1986). A model for conceptualizing interventions in social service agencies. *Canadian Psychology, 27,* 332–341.

Hoge, R. D., & Andrews, D. A. (1992). Assessing conduct problems in the classroom. *Clinical Psychology Review, 12,* 1–20.

Hoge, R. D., & Andrews, D. A. (1994). *The Youth Level of Service/Case Management Inventory and manual.* Ottawa, Canada: Carleton University, Department of Psychology.

Hoge, R. D., & Andrews, D. A. (1996a, August). *Assessing risk and need factors in the youthful offender.* Presentation at the Annual Conference of the American Psychological Association, Toronto.

Hoge, R. D., & Andrews, D. A. (1996b). *Assessing the youthful offender: Issues and techniques.* New York: Plenum.

Hoge, R. D., Andrews, D. A., & Leschied, A. W. (1994). Tests of three hypotheses regarding the predictors of delinquency. *Journal of Abnormal Child Psychology, 22,* 547–559.

Hoge, R. D., Andrews, D. A., Robinson, D., & Hollett, J. (1988). The construct validity of interview-based assessments in family counseling. *Journal of Clinical Psychology, 44,* 563–572.

Holden, R. R. (1985). Review of the Carlson Psychological Survey. *Test Critiques, 4,* 144–148.

Holland, J. L. (1985). *Making vocational choices: A theory of vocational choices and work environments* (2nd ed.). Englewood Cliffs, NJ: Prentice-Hall.

Hollon, S. D., & Kendall, P. C. (1980). Cognitive self-statements in depression: Development of an automatic thoughts questionnaire. *Cognitive Therapy and Research, 4,* 383–395.

Hong, E., Perkins, P. G., & Milgram, R. M. (1993). Learning styles of gifted adolescents with in-school versus out-of-school accomplishments in literature. *Perceptual and Motor Skills, 76,* 1099–1102.

Horn, J. L., & Cattell, R. B. (1966). Refinement and test of the test of fluid and crystallized intelligence. *Journal of Educational Psychology, 57,* 253–270.

Hufano, L. D. (1985). Review of the Devereux Adolescent Behavior Rating Scale. *Test Critiques, 3,* 221–225.

Huffcutt, A. E., & Arthur, W., Jr. (1994). Hunter and Hunter (1984) revisited: Interview validity for entry-level jobs. *Journal of Applied Psychology, 79,* 184–190.

Hughes, S. (1988). Review of the Adaptive Behavior Inventory. *Test Critiques, 7,* 3–9.

Hunter, J. E. (1994). General Aptitude Test Battery. In R. J. Sternberg (Ed.), *Encyclopedia of human intelligence* (pp. 120–146). New York: Macmillan.

Hunter, J. E., & Schmidt, F. L. (1990). *Methods of meta-analysis.* Newbury Park, CA: Sage.

Hutton, J. B. (1994). Review of Conners' Parent and Teacher Rating Scales. *Test Critiques, 10,* 172–182.

Hynd, G. W., & Willis, W. G. (1988). *Pediatric neuropsychology.* New York: Grune & Stratton.

Ingram, R. E., Kendall, P. C., Siegle, G., Guarino, J., & McLaughlin, S. C. (1995). Psychometric properties of the Positive Automatic Thoughts Questionnaire. *Psychological Assessment, 7,* 495–507.

Ingram, R. E., Smith, T. W., & Brehm, S. S. (1983). Depression and information processing: Self-schemata and the encoding of self-referent information. *Journal of Personality and Social Psychology, 45,* 412–420.

Ingram, R. E., & Wisnicki, K. S. (1988). Assessment of positive automatic cognition. *Journal of Consulting and Clinical Psychology, 56,* 898–902.

Jackson, D. N. (1996). *The Basic Personality Inventory manual.* Port Huron, MI: Sigma Assessment Systems.

Jackson, D. N., & Messick, S. (1958) Content and style in personality assessment. *Psychological Bulletin, 55,* 243–252.

Jackson, S., & Rodriquez-Tome, H. (Eds.). (1995). *Adolescence and its social worlds.* Mahwah, NJ: Lawrence Erlbaum Associates.

Jacob, T., & Tennenbaum, D. L. (1988). *Family assessment: Rationale, methods, and future directions.* New York: Plenum.

Jensen, P. S., Hoagwood, K., & Petti, T. (1996). Outcomes of mental health care for children and adolescents: II. Literature review and application of a comprehensive model. *Journal of the American Academy of Child and Adolescent Psychiatry, 35,* 1064–1077.

Jesness, C. F. (1996). *The Jesness Inventory manual.* Toronto: Multi-Health Systems.

Jesness, C. F., & Wedge, R. F. (1984). Validity of a revised Jesness Inventory I-Level classification with delinquents. *Journal of Consulting and Clinical Psychology, 52,* 997–1010.

Jesness, C. F., & Wedge, R. F. (1985). *Jesness Inventory classification system: Supplementary manual.* Palo Alto, CA: Consulting Psychologists Press.

Jessor, R. (1992). Risk behavior in adolescence: A psychosocial framework for understanding and action. In D. E. Rogers & E. Ginsberg (Eds.), *Adolescents at risk: Medical and social perspectives* (pp. 19–34). Boulder, CO: Westview.

Jessor, R. (1993). Successful adolescent development among youth in high risk settings. *American Psychologist, 48,* 117–126.

Jirsa, J. E. (1994). Review of the Kaufman Brief Intelligence Test. *Test Critiques, 10,* 340–349.

John, K. R., & Rattan, G. (1992). Review of the Shipley Institute of Living Scale–Revised. *Test Critiques, 9,* 490–495.

Johnson, J. H. (1986). *Life events as stressors in childhood and adolescence.* Newbury Park, CA: Sage.

Johnson, O. (1976). *Tests and measurement in child development* (Vols. 1 & 2). San Francisco: Jossey-Bass.

Johnson, R. G. (1986). Review of the Shipley Institute of Living Scales. *Test Critiques, 5,* 425–443.

Johnston, C. S. (1995). The Rokeach Value Survey: Underlying structure and multidimensional scaling. *Journal of Psychology, 129,* 583–597.

Jolly, J. B., & Wiesner, D. C. (1996). Psychometric properties of the Automatic Thoughts Questionnaire–Positive with inpatient adolescents. *Cognitive Therapy and Research, 20,* 481–498.

Joseph, S. (1994). Subscales of the Automatic Thoughts Questionnaire. *Journal of Genetic Psychology, 155,* 367–368.

Jung, C. (1933). *Modern man in search of a soul.* New York, NY: Harcourt Brace Jovanovich.

Jung, S., & Rawana, E. P. (1997, August). *Risk and need factors of offending and nonoffending youths.* Presentation at the Annual Conference of the American Psychological Association, Chicago.

Kagan, J. (1988). The meaning of personality predicates. *American Psychologist, 43,* 614–620.

Kaslow, N. J., Brown, R. T., & Mee, L. L. (1994). Cognitive and behavioral correlates of childhood depression: A developmental perspective. In W. M. Reynolds & H. F. Johnston (Eds.), *Handbook of depression in children and adolescents* (pp. 97–122). New York: Plenum.

Kaslow, N. J., & Nolen-Hoeksema, S. (1991). *Children's Attributional Style Questionnaire.* Atlanta, GA: Emory University, Department of Psychology.

Kaufman, A. S. (1979). *Intelligent testing with the WISC–R.* New York: Wiley.

Kaufman, A. S. (1994). *Intelligent testing with the WISC–III.* New York: Wiley.

Kaufman, A. S., & Kaufman, N. L. (1990). *Manual for the Kaufman Brief Intelligence Test.* Circle Pines, MN: American Guidance Service.

Kaufman, J., Birmaher, B., Brent, D., Rao, U., Flynn, C., Moreci, P., Williamson, D., & Ryan, N. (1997). Schedule for Affective Disorders and Schizophrenia for School-Age Children–Present and Lifetime Version (K–SADS–PL): Initial reliability and validity data. *Journal of the American Academy of Child and Adolescent Psychiatry, 36,* 980–988.

Kazdin, A. E. (1988). *Child psychotherapy: Developing and identifying effective treatments.* New York: Pergamon.

Kazdin, A. E. (1990). Evaluation of the Automatic Thoughts Questionnaire: Negative cognitive processes and depression among children. *Psychological Assessment, 2,* 73–79.

Kazdin, A. E. (1993). Adolescent mental health: Prevention and treatment programs. *American Psychologist, 48,* 127–141.

Keane, E. M., Eick, R. W., Bechtold, D. W., & Manson, S. M. (1996). Predictive and concurrent validity of the Suicidal Ideation Questionnaire among American Indian adolescents. *Journal of Abnormal Child Psychology, 24,* 735–747.

Kehoe, J. F. (1992). Review of the Career Assessment Inventory. *Mental Measurements Yearbook, 11,* 149–151.

Keith, T. Z. (1995). Review of the Kaufman Adolescent and Adult Intelligence Test. *Mental Measurements Yearbook, 12,* 530–532.

Kellerman, H., & Burry, A. (1997). *Handbook of psychodiagnostic testing: Analysis of personality in the psychological report.* Boston: Allyn & Bacon.

Kelley, M. L. (1985). Review of the Child Behavior Checklist. *Mental Measurements Yearbook, 9,* 301–303.

Kendall, P. C. (1985). Toward a cognitive-behavioral model of child psychopathology and a critique of related interventions. *Journal of Abnormal Child Psychology, 13,* 357–372.

Kendall, P. C. (1991). Guiding theory for treating children and adolescents. In P. C. Kendall (Ed.), *Child and adolescent therapy: Cognitive-behavioral procedures* (pp. 3–22). New York: Guilford.

Kendall, P. C. (1993). Cognitive-behavioral therapies with youth: Guiding theory, current status, and emerging developments. *Journal of Consulting and Clinical Psychology, 61,* 235–247.

Kendall, P. C., Hollon, S. D., Beck, A. T., Hammen, C. L., & Ingram, R. E. (1987). Issues and recommendations regarding use of the Beck Depression Inventory. *Cognitive Therapy and Research, 11,* 289–299.

Kendall, P. C., Howard, B. L., & Hays, R. C. (1989). Self-reference speech and psychopathology: The balance of positive and negative thinking. *Cognitive Therapy and Research, 13,* 583–598.

Keyser, D. J., & Sweetland, R. C. (1994). *Test critiques.* Austin, TX: PRO-ED.

King, C. A., Katz, S. H., Ghaziuddin, N., & Brand, E. (1997). Diagnosis and assessment of depression and suicidaility using the NIMH Diagnostic Interview Schedule for Children (DISC–2.3). *Journal of Abnormal Child Psychology, 25,* 173–181.

King, L. A., & King, D. W. (1997). Sex-Role Egalitarianism Scale: Development, psychometric properties, and recommendations for future research. *Psychology of Women Quarterly, 21,* 71–87.

Kirman, J. P., & Geisinger, K. F. (1986). Review of the General Aptitude Battery. *Test Critiques, 5,* 222–225.

Klein, N. C., Alexander, J. F., & Parsons, B. V. (1977). Impact of family systems intervention on recidivism and sibling delinquency: A model of primary prevention and program evaluation. *Journal of Consulting and Clinical Psychology, 45,* 469–474.

Koch, W. R. (1984). Review of the Culture Fair Intelligence Test. *Test Critiques, 1,* 233–238.

Kohlberg, L. (1969). Stage and sequence: The cognitive-developmental approach to socialization. In D. A. Goslin (Ed.), *Handbook of socialization theory and research* (pp. 347–480). Chicago: Rand McNally.

Kohlberg, L. (1984). *The psychology of moral development.* New York: Harper & Row.

Kohn, P. M., & Milrose, J. A. (1993). The Inventory of High-School Students' Recent Life Experiences: A decontaminated measure of adolescents' hassles. *Journal of Youth and Adolescence, 22,* 43–55.

Kohut, H., & Elsen, M. (1987). *The Kohut seminar on self-psychology and psychotherapy with adolescents and young adults.* New York: Norton.

Kovacs, M., & Lohr, W. D. (1995). Research on psychotherapy with children and adolescents: An overview of evolving trends and current issues. *Journal of Abnormal Child Psychology, 23,* 11–30.

Kranzler, J. H. (1991). The construct validity of the Multidimensional Aptitude Battery: A word of caution. *Journal of Clinical Psychology, 47,* 691–697.

Kratochwill, T. R., & Morris, R. J. (Eds.). (1993). *Handbook of psychotherapy with children and adolescents.* Boston: Allyn & Bacon.

Krieshok, T. S., & Harrington, R. G. (1985). Review of the Multidimensional Aptitude Battery. *Journal of Counseling and Development, 64,* 87–89.

L'Abate, L., & Bagarozzi, D. A. (1993). *Sourcebook of marriage and family evaluation.* New York: Brunner/Mazel.

Lachar, D. (1982). *Personality Inventory for Children–Revised (PIC-R).* Los Angeles, CA: Western Psychological Services.

Lachar, D., & Gdowski, C. L. (1979). *Actuarial assessment of child and adolescent personality: An interpretive guide for the Personality Inventory for Children.* Los Angeles: Western Psychological Services.

Lachar, D., & Gruber, C. P. (1993). Development of the Personality Inventory for Youth: A self-report companion to the Personality Inventory for Children. *Journal of Personality Assessment, 61,* 81–98.

Lachar, D., & Gruber, C. P. (1994). *A manual for the Personality Inventory for Youth (PIY): A self-report companion to the Personality Inventory for Children (PIC).* Los Angeles, CA: Western Psychological Services.

Lachar, D., & Kline, R. B. (1994). Personality Inventory for Children and Personality Inventory for Youth. In M. E. Maruish (Ed.), *The use of psychological testing for treatment planning and outcome assessment* (pp. 479–516). Hillsdale, NJ: Lawrence Erlbaum Associates.

LaCombe, J. A., Kline, R. B., & Lachar, D. (1991). Clinical case record correlates of Personality Inventory for Children (PIC) profile types for referred children and adolescents. *Psychological Assessment, 3,* 678–687.

Lahey, B. B., Applegate, B., Barkley, R. A., Garfindel, B., McBurnett, K., Kerdyck, L., Greenhill, L., Hynd, G. W., Frick, P. J., Newcorn, J., Biederman, I., & Ollendick, T., Hart, E. L., Perez, D., Waldman, I., & Shaffer, D. (1994). DSM-IV field trials for oppositional defiant disorder and conduct disorder in children and adolescents. *American Journal of Psychiatry, 151,* 1163–1171.

Lahey, B. B., & Piacentini, J. C. (1985). An evaluation of the Quay–Peterson Revised Behavior Problem Checklist. *Journal of School Psychology, 23,* 285–289.

Lambert, M. J. (1994). Use of psychological tests for outcome assessment. In M. E. Maruish (Ed.), *The use of psychological testing for treatment planning and outcome assessment* (pp. 75–97). Hillsdale, NJ: Lawrence Erlbaum Associates.

Landy, F. J. (1986). Stamp collecting vs. science: Validation as hypothesis testing. *American Psychologist, 41,* 1183–1192.

Lanyon, R. I. (1984). Personality assessment. *Annual Review of Psychology, 35,* 667–701.

Lanyon, R. I. (1993). Development of scales to assess specific deception strategies on the Psychological Screening Inventory. *Psychological Assessment, 5,* 324–329.

Lanyon, R. I., & Goldstein, L. D. (1997). *Personality assessment* (3rd ed.). New York: Wiley.

Larzelere, R. E., Smith, G. L., Batenhorst, L. M., & Kelly, D. B. (1996). Predictive validity of the Suicide Probability Scale among adolescents in group home treatment. *Journal of the American Academy of Child and Adolescent Psychiatry, 35,* 166–172.

LaVoie, A. L. (1989). Review of the Basic Personality Inventory. *Test Critiques, 8,* 38–43.

LaVoie, A. L. (1994). Review of the Jesness Inventory. *Test Critiques, 10,* 322–326.

Lazarus, R. S., & Folkman, S. (1984). *Stress, appraisal and coping.* New York: Springer-Verlag.

Leckliter, I. N., & Forster, A. A. (1994). The Halstead-Reitan Neuropsychological Test Battery for Older Children: The need for standardization. *Developmental Neuropsychology, 10,* 455–471.

Lee, S., & Stefany, E. F. (1995). Review of the Woodcock–Johnson Psycho-Educational Battery–Revised. *Mental Measurements Yearbook, 12,* 1116–1117.

Lee, M. S., Wallbrown, F. H., & Blaha, J. (1990). Note on the construct validity of the Multidimensional Aptitude Battery. *Psychological Reports, 67,* 1219–1222.

Leong, F. T., & Dollinger, S. J. (1990). Review of NEO Personality Inventory. *Test Critiques, 8,* 527–539.

Lerner, R. M. (Ed.). (1993). *Early adolescence: Perspectives on research, policy, and intervention.* Mahwah, NJ: Lawrence Erlbaum Associates.

Lewinsohn, P. M., Rohde, P., & Seeley, J. R. (1993). Psychosocial characteristics of adolescents with a history of suicide attempt. *Journal of the American Academy of Child and Adolescent Psychiatry, 32,* 60–68.

Lezak, M. D. (1995). *Neuropsychological assessment.* New York: Oxford University Press.

Lilienfeld, S. O., Waldman, I. D., & Israel, A. C. (1994). A critical examination of the use of the term and concept of comorbidity in psychotherapy research. *Clinical Psychology Science and Practice, 1,* 71–83.

Linn, R. L. (1980). Test design and analysis for measurement of educational achievement. *New Directions for Testing and Measurement, 5,* 81–92.

Lipsey, M. W., & Wilson, D. B. (1993). The efficacy of psychological, educational, and behavioral treatment: Confirmation from meta-analysis. *American Psychologist, 48,* 1181–1209.

Little, S. G. (1992). The WISC–III: Everything old is new again. *School Psychology Quarterly, 7,* 148–154.

Loeber, R., & Dishion, T. J. (1983). Early predictors of male delinquency: A review. *Psychological Bulletin, 94,* 68–99.

Loeber, R., Dishion, T. J., & Patterson, G. R. (1984). Multiple gating: A multistage assessment procedure for identifying youths at risk for delinquency. *Journal of Research in Crime and Delinquency, 21,* 7–32.

Loeber, R., & Hay, D. (1997). Key issues in the development of aggression and violence from childhood to early adulthood. *Annual Review of Psychology, 48,* 371–410.

Loeber, R., Keenan, K., Lahey, B. B., Green, S. M., & Thomas, C. (1993). Evidence for developmentally based diagnoses of oppositional defiant disorder and conduct disorder. *Journal of Abnormal Child Psychology, 21,* 377–410.

Lowman, R. L. (1991). *The clinical practice of career assessment.* Washington, DC: American Psychological Association.

Loyd, B. H. (1995). Review of the Family Environment Scale. *Mental Measurements Yearbook, 12,* 385–386.

Luria, A. R. (1973). *The working brain.* Harmondsworth, UK: Penguin.

Luthar, S. S. (1993). Annotation: Methodological and conceptual issues in research on childhood resilience. *Journal of Child Psychology and Psychiatry, 14,* 441–453.

Maguire, K., Pastore, A. L., & Flanagan, T. J. (Eds.). (1992). *Bureau of Justice Statistic sourcebook of justice statistics.* Washington, DC: United States Department of Justice.

Manuele-Adkins, C. (1989). Review of the Self-Directed Search. *Mental Measurements Yearbook, 10,* 738–740.

Marcia, J. E. (1989). Identify and intervention. *Adolescence, 12,* 401–410.

Marsh, H. W. (1990). A multidimensional, hierarchical model of self-concept: Theoretical and empirical justification. *Educational Psychology Review, 2,* 77–172.

Marsh, H. W. (1993a). Academic self-concept: Theory, measurement and research. In J. Suls (Ed.), *Psychological perspectives on the self: The self in social perspective* (Vol. 4, pp. 59–98). Hillsdale, NJ: Lawrence Erlbaum Associates.

Marsh, H. W. (1993b). *Physical Self-Description Questionnaire.* Macarthur, Australia: University of Western Sydney, Faculty of Education.

Marsh, H. W., Byrne, B. M., & Shavelson, R. J. (1988). A multifaceted self-concept: Its hierarchical structure and its relation to academic achievement. *Journal of Educational Psychology, 80,* 366–380.

Martin, R. D. (1988). *Assessment of personality and behavior problems: Infancy through adolescence.* New York: Guilford.

Mash, E. J., & Terdal, L. G. (Eds.). (1997). *Assessment of childhood disorders* (3rd ed.). New York: Guilford.

Masterson, J. (1985). *The treatment of the borderline adolescent: A developmental approach.* New York: Brunner-Mazel.

Matarazzo, J. D. (1983). Computerized psychological testing. *Science, 221,* 333.

Matarazzo, J. D. (1986). Computerized clinical psychological test interpretations: Unvalidated plus all mean and no sigma. *American Psychologist, 41,* 14–24.

Matarazzo, J. D. (1990). Psychological assessment versus psychological testing: Validation from Binet to the school, clinic, and courtroom. *American Psychologist, 45,* 999–1017.

Matarazzo, J. D. (1992). Psychological testing and assessment in the 21st century. *American Psychologist, 47,* 1007–1018.

Mayfield, K. L., Forman, S., & Nagle, R. J. (1984). Reliability of the AAMD Adaptive Behavior Scale–Public School Version. *Journal of Personality and Social Psychology, 22,* 53–61.

McCarthy, K. J., & Dralle, P. W. (1995). Review of the Adolescent Drinking Index. *Mental Measurements Yearbook, 12,* 46–47.

McCrae, R. R., & Costa, P. T., Jr. (1987). Validation of the five-factor model of personality across instruments and observers, *52,* 81–90.

McCubbin, H. I., & Patterson, J. (1983). The family stress process: The double ABCX model of adjustment and adaptation. *Marriage and Family Review, 6,* 7–37.

McDaniel, M. A., Whetzel, D. L., Schmidt, F. L., & Maurer, S. D. (1994). The validity of employment interviews: A comprehensive review and meta-analysis. *Journal of Applied Psychology, 79,* 599–616.

McGough, J., & Curry, J. F. (1992). Utility of the SCL–90–R with depressed and conduct disordered adolescent inpatients. *Journal of Personality Assessment, 59,* 552–563.

McHugh, M. C., & Frieze, I. H. (1997). The measurement of gender-role attitudes: A review and commentary. *Psychology of Women Quarterly, 21,* 1–16.

McManus, I. C., & Richards, P. (1992). *Psychology in medicine.* Boston: Butterworth Heinemann.

McNulty, J. L., Harkness, A. R., Ben-Porath, Y. S., & Williams, C. L. (1997). Assessing the Personality Psychopathology Five (PSY-5) in adolescents: New MMPI-A scales. *Psychological Assessment, 9,* 250–259.

McReynolds, P. (1989). Diagnosis and clinical assessment: Current status and major issues. *Annual Review of Psychology, 40,* 83–108.

Meehl, P. E. (1954). *Clinical vs. statistical prediction.* Minneapolis: University of Minnesota Press.

Meehl, P. E. (1957). When shall we use our heads instead of formula? *Journal of Counseling Psychology, 4,* 268–273.

Meehl, P. E. (1965). Seer over sign: The first good example. *Journal of Experimental Research in Personality, 1,* 27–32.

Meehl, P. E. (1986). Causes and effects of my disturbing little book. *Journal of Personality Assessment, 50,* 370–375.

Mehrens, W. A. (1995). Review of the Detroit Tests of Learning Aptitudes–Third edition. *Mental Measurements Yearbook, 12,* 275–277.

Meichenbaum, D. (1977). *Cognitive-behavior modification: An integrative approach.* New York: Plenum.

Meir, S. T. (1993). Revitalizing the measurement curriculum: Four approaches for emphasis in graduate education. *American Psychologist, 48,* 886–891.

Melton, G. B., Petrila, J., Poythress, N. G., & Slobogin, C. (1987). *Psychological evaluations for the court: A handbook for mental health professionals and lawyers.* New York: Guilford.

Messick, S. (1980). Test validity and the ethics of assessment. *American Psychologist, 35,* 1012–1027.

Messick, S. (1989a). Meaning and values in test validation: The science and ethics of assessment. *Educational Researcher, 18,* 5–11.

Messick, S. (1989b). Validity. In R. L. Linn (Ed.), *Educational measurement* (3rd ed., pp. 13–103). Washington, DC: American Council on Education and National Council on Measurement in Education.

Messick, S. (1995). Validity of psychological assessment: Validation of inferences from persons' responses and performances as scientific inquiry into score meaning. *American Psychologist, 50,* 741–749.

Miller, M. D. (1995). Review of the Kaufman Brief Intelligence Test. *Mental Measurements Yearbook, 12,* 533–534.

Millon, T. (1987). *Manual for the MCMI–II* (2nd ed.). Minneapolis, MN: National Computer Systems.

Millon T. (1990). *Toward a new personology: An evolutionary model.* New York: Wiley.

Millon, T., Green, C. J., & Meagher, R. B. (1982). *Millon Adolescent Personality Inventory manual.* Minneapolis, MN: National Computer Systems.

Millon, T., Millon, C., & Davis, R. (1993). *Millon Adolescent Clinical Inventory manual.* Minneapolis, MN: National Computer Systems.

Mills, C. J., Ablard, K. E., & Brody, L. E. (1993). The Raven's Progressive Matrices: Its usefulness for identifying gifted/talented students. *Roeper Review, 15,* 183–186.

Mills, J. F., & Kroner, D. G. (1996). The Criminal Sentiments Scale: Predictive validity in a sample of violent and sex offenders. *Journal of Clinical Psychology, 53,* 399–404.

Millstein, S. G., Petersen, A. C., & Nightingale, E. O. (Eds.). (1993). *Promoting the health of adolescents: New directions for the twenty-first century.* New York: Oxford University Press.

Minuchin, S. (1974). *Families and family therapy.* Cambridge, MA: Harvard University Press.

Mischel, W. (1984). Convergences and challenges in the search for consistency. *American Psychologist, 39,* 351–364.

Moffitt, T. E. (1993). Adolescence-limited and life-course-persistent antisocial behavior: A developmental taxonomy. *Psychological Review, 100,* 674–701.

Moilanen, D. L. (1995). Validity of Beck's cognitive theory of depression with nonreferred adolescents. *Journal of Counseling and Development, 73,* 438–442.

Monohan, J., & Steadman, H. J. (1994). *Violence and mental disorder: Developments in risk assessment.* Chicago: University of Chicago Press.

Moos, R. H. (1987). *Social Climate Scales: A users guide.* Palo Alto, CA: Consulting Psychologists Press.

Moos, R. H., & Moos, B. S. (1986). *Manual for the Family Environment Scale.* Palo Alto, CA: Consulting Psychologists Press.

Moreland, K. L. (1985). Validation of computer-based test interpretations: Problems and prospects. *Journal of Consulting and Clinical Psychology, 53,* 816–825.

Moreland, K. L., Eyde, L. D., Robertson, G. J., Primoff, E. S., & Most, R. B. (1995). Assessment of test user qualifications: A research-based measurement procedure. *American Psychologist, 50,* 14–23.

Moses, J. A. (1992). Review of the State–Trait Anger Expression Inventory, Research edition. *Test Critiques, 9,* 510–525.

Mueller, D. J. (1985). Review of the Survey of Interpersonal Values. *Test Critiques, 2,* 759–764.

Murphy, K. R. (1992). Review of the Test of Nonverbal Intelligence–Second Edition. *Mental Measurements Yearbook, 11,* 969–970.

Murphy, K. R., & Davidshofer, C. O. (1994). *Psychological testing: Principles and applications* (3rd ed.). Englewood Cliffs, NJ: Prentice-Hall.

Murray, H. A. (1938). *Explorations in personality: A clinical and experimental study of fifty men of college age.* New York: Oxford University Press.

Newcomer, P. L., & Bryant, B. R. (1993). *Manual for the Diagnostic Achievement Test for adolescents.* Austin, TX: PRO-ED.

Nichols, M. (1984). *Family therapy: Concepts and methods.* Boston: Allyn & Bacon.

Nolen-Hoeksema, S., Girgus, J. S., & Seligman, M. E. P. (1986). Learned helplessness in children: A longitudinal study of depression, achievement, and explanatory style. *Journal of Personality and Social Psychology, 51,* 435–442.

Nolen-Hoeksema, S., Girgus, J. S., & Seligman, M. E. P. (1992). Predictors and consequences of childhood depressive symptoms: A 5-year longitudinal study. *Journal of Abnormal Psychology, 101,* 405–422.

Nurius, P. S. (1990). A review of automated assessment. *Computers in Human Services, 6,* 265–281.

Offord, D. R., Boyle, M. H., Szatmari, P., Rae-Grant, N. I., Links, P. S., Cadman, D. T., Byles, J. A., Crawford, J. W., Blum, H. M., Byrne, C., Thomas, H., & Woodward, C. A. (1987). Ontario Child Health Study: Six month prevalence of disorder and rates of service utilization. *Archives of General Psychiatry, 44,* 832–836.

Olejnik, S. (1995). Review of the Attention Deficit Disorders Evaluation Scale. *Mental Measurements Yearbook, 12,* 96–97.

Oles, H. J., & Davis, G. D. (1977). Publishers violate APA standards of test distribution. *Psychological Reports, 41,* 713–714.

Oliver, W. (1989). Sexual conquest and patterns of Black-on-Black violence: A structural-cultural perspective. *Violence and Victims, 4,* 257–273.

Olson, D. H., Portner, J., & Lavee, Y. (1985). *FACES III.* St. Paul: University of Minnesota Publications.

Olson, D. H., Russell, C. S., & Sprenkle, D. H. (1980). Marital and family therapy: A decade review. *Journal of Marriage and Family, 42,* 973–993.

Olson, D. H., Russell, C. S., & Sprenkle, D. H. (1983). Circumplex model of marital and family systems: VI. Theoretical update. *Family Process, 22,* 69–83.

Olson, J. M., & Zanna, M. P. (1993). Attitudes and attitude change. *Annual Review of Psychology, 44,* 117–154.

Osborne, A. G. (1996). *Legal issues in special education.* Boston: Allyn & Bacon.

Paikoff, R. L., & Brooks-Gunn, J. (1991). Do parent–child relationships change during puberty? *Psychological Bulletin, 110,* 47–66.

Paludi, M. A. (1987). Review of the Child and Adolescent Adjustment Profile. *Test Critiques, 6,* 87–90.

Panak, W. F., & Garber, J. (1992). Role of aggression, rejection, and attributions in the prediction of depression in children. *Development and Psychopathology, 4,* 145–165.

Patterson, G. R., DeBaryshe, B. D., & Ramsey, E. (1989). A developmental perspective on antisocial behavior. *American Psychologist, 44,* 329–335.

Paulhus, D. L. (1984). Two-component models of socially desirable responding. *Journal of Personality and Social Psychology, 46,* 598–609.

Paulhus, D. L. (1994). *Balanced Inventory of Desirable Responding: Reference manual for BIDR version 6.* Vancouver, Canada: University of British Columbia, Department of Psychology.

Pena, L. M., Megargee, E. I., & Brody, E. (1996). MMPI-A patterns of male juvenile delinquents. *Psychological Assessment, 8,* 388–397.

Pfeiffer, S. I. (1995). Review of the Parent–Adolescent Communication Scale. *Mental Measurements Yearbook, 12,* 734–735.

Phelps, L., & Wilczenski, F. (1993). Eating Disorders Inventory–2: Cognitive-behavioral dimensions with nonclinical adolescents. *Journal of Clinical Psychology, 49,* 508–515.

Piaget, J. (1950). *The psychology of intelligence.* San Diego, CA: Harcourt Brace Jovanovich.

Piaget, J. (1965). *The moral judgment of the child.* New York: The Free Press.

Pinto, A., Whisman, M. A., & McCoy, K. J. (1997). Suicidal ideation in adolescents: Psychometric properties of the Suicidal Ideation Questionnaire in a clinical sample. *Psychological Assessment, 9,* 63–66.

Pope, M. (1995). Review of the Kuder General Interest Survey. *Mental Measurements Yearbook, 12,* 543–545.

Poteat, G. M. (1995). Review of the Detroit Tests of Learning Aptitude–Third Edition. *Mental Measurements Yearbook, 12,* 277–278.

Prewett, P. N. (1992). The relationship between the Kaufman Brief Intelligence Test (K–BIT) and the WISC–R with referred students. *Psychology in the Schools, 29,* 25–27.

Quay, H. C. (1987). Patterns of delinquent behavior. In H. C. Quay (Ed.), *Handbook of juvenile delinquency* (pp. 118–138). New York: Wiley.

Quay, H. C., & Peterson, D. R. (1979). *Manual for the Behavior Problem Checklist.* Miami, FL: University of Miami.

Quay, H. C., & Peterson, D. R. (1987). *Manual for the Revised Behavior Problem Checklist.* Miami, FL: University of Miami.

Quay, H. C., Routh, D. K., & Shapiro, S. K. (1987). Psychopathology of childhood: From description to evaluation. *Annual Review of Psychology, 38,* 491–532.

Rabian, B. (1994). Review of Revised Children's Manifest Anxiety Scale. *Test Critiques, 10,* 593–600.

Reich, W., & Welner, Z. (1988). *Revised version of the Diagnostic Interview for Children and Adolescents.* St. Louis, MO: Washington University School of Medicine, Department of Psychiatry.

Reitan, R. M., & Wolfson, D. (1985). *Manual for the Halstead-Reitan Neuropsychological Test Battery for Older Children.* Tuscon, AZ: Neuropsychology Press.

Reschly, D. J. (1997). Diagnostic and treatment utility of intelligence tests. In D. P. Flanagan, J. L. Genshaft, & P. L. Harrison (Eds.), *Contemporary intelligence assessment: Theories, tests, and issues* (pp. 437–456). New York: Guilford.

Resnick, L. B., & Resnick, D. P. (1982). Testing in America: The current challenge. *International Review of Applied Psychology, 31,* 75–90.

Retzlaff, P. (1995). Review of the Millon Adolescent Clinical Inventory. *Mental Measurements Yearbook, 12,* 620–622.

Reynolds, C. R. (1985). Review of the Personality Inventory for Children. *Mental Measurements Yearbook, 9,* 1154–1157.

Reynolds, C. R., & Fletcher-Janzen, E. (1997). *Handbook of clinical child neuropsychology* (2nd ed.). New York: Plenum.

Reynolds, C. R., & Kamphaus, R. W. (Eds.). (1990). *Handbook of psychological and educational assessment of children: Intelligence and achievement.* New York: Guilford.

Reynolds, C. R., & Richmond, B. O. (1997). What I think and feel: A revised measure of children's manifest anxiety. *Journal of Abnormal Child Psychology, 25,* 15–20.

Rice, M. E. (1997). Violent offender research and implications for the criminal justice system. *American Psychologist, 52,* 414–423.

Riggio, R. E., & Porter, L. W. (1996). *Introduction to industrial/organizational psychology* (2nd ed.). New York: HarperCollins.

Roberts, M. C., Koocher, G. P., Routh, D. K., & Willis, D. J. (Eds.). (1993). *Readings in pediatric psychology.* New York: Plenum.

Roberts, R., Solovitz, B. L., Chen, Y., & Casat, C. (1996). Retest stability of DSM–III–R diagnoses among adolescents using the Diagnostic Interview Schedule for Children (DIS–2.1C). *Journal of Abnormal Child Psychology, 24,* 349–362.

Roberts, T. (1986). Review of the Revised Behavior Problem Checklist. *Test Critiques, 5,* 371–377.

Robinson, J. P., Shaver, P. R., & Wrightsman, L. S. (Eds.). (1991). *Measures of personality and social psychological attitudes* (Vol. 1). New York: Academic Press.

Robinson, N. S., Garber, J., & Hilsman, R. (1995). Cognition and stress: Direct and mediating effects on depressive versus externalizing symptoms during the junior high school transition. *Journal of Abnormal Psychology, 104,* 453–463.

Rogers, B. G. (1992). Review of the Peabody Individual Achievement Test–Revised. *Mental Measurements Yearbook, 11,* 652–654.

Rogers, C. (1951). *Client-centered therapy.* Boston: Houghton-Mifflin.

Rogers, R., & Mitchell, C. N. (1991). *Mental health experts and the criminal courts.* Toronto: Carswell.

Rogers, T. B. (1995). *The psychological testing enterprise: An introduction.* Pacific Grove, CA: Brooks/Cole.

Rokeach, M. (1968). *Beliefs, attitudes, and values.* San Francisco: Jossey-Bass.

Rokeach, M. (1973). *The nature of human values.* New York: The Free Press.

Rotter, J. B. (1982). *The development and applications of social learning theory: Selected papers.* New York: Praeger.

Rourke, B. P., Bakker, D. J., Fisk, J. L., & Strang, J. D. (1983). *Child neuropsychology: An introduction to theory, research, and practice.* New York: Guilford.

Rourke, B. P., & Del Dotto, J. E. (1994). *Learning disabilities: A neuropsychological perspective.* Thousand Oaks, CA: Sage.

Rourke, B. P., Fisk, J. L., & Strang, J. D. (1986). *Neuropsychological assessment of children: A treatment oriented approach.* New York: Guilford

Rourke, B. P., & Fuerst, D. R. (1991). *Learning disabilities and psychosocial functioning: A neuropsychological perspective.* New York: Guilford.

Rozensky, R. H., Sweet, J. J., & Tovian, S. M. (Eds.). (1997). *Psychological assessment in medical settings.* New York: Plenum.

Rubio-Stipec, M., Shrout, P. E., Canino, G., Bird, H. R., Jensen, P., Dulcan, M., & Schwab-Stone, M. (1996). Empirically defined symptom scales using the DISC 2.3. *Journal of Abnormal Child Psychology, 24,* 67–84.

Rutter, M., & Rutter, M. (1993). *Developing minds: Challenge and continuity across the life span.* New York: Basic.

Saklofske, D. H., & Zeidner, M. (Eds.). (1995). *International handbook of personality and intelligence: Perspectives on individual differences.* New York: Plenum.

Salvia, J., & Ysseldyke, J. E. (1991). *Assessment* (5th ed.). Boston: Houghton-Mifflin.

Sandoval, J. (1995). Review of the Wechsler Intelligence Scale for Children–Third Edition. *Mental Measurements Yearbook, 12,* 1103–1104.

Sandoval, J. (1998). Review of the Behavior Assessment System for Children. *Mental Measurements Yearbook, 13,* 128–131.

Sanford, E. E. (1995). Review of the Rokeach Value Survey. *Mental Measurements Yearbook, 12,* 879–880.

Sattler, J. M. (1992). *Assessment of children* (3rd ed., rev.). San Diego, CA: Author.

Sattler, J. M. (1997). *Clinical and forensic interviewing of children and families.* San Diego, CA: Author.

Sawyer, J. (1966). Measurement and prediction, clinical and statistical. *Psychological Bulletin*, 66, 178–200.

Sbordone, R. J. (1991). *Neuropsychology for the attorney*. Orlando, FL: Paul M. Deutsch.

Schmitt, N. (1995). Review of the Differential Aptitude Tests–Fifth edition. *Mental Measurements Yearbook*, 12, 304–305.

Schwab-Stone, M. E., Shaffer, D., Dulcan, M. K., Jensen, P. S., Fisher, P., Bird, H. R., Goodman, S. H., Lahen, B. B., Lichtman, J. H., Canino, G., Rubio-Stipec, M., & Rae, D. S. (1996). Criterion validity of the NIMH Diagnostic Interview Schedule for Children Version 2.3 (DISC–2.3). *Journal of the American Academy of Child and Adolescent Psychiatry*, 35, 878–888.

Scotti, J. R., Morris, T. L., McNeil, C. B., & Hawkins, R. P. (1996). DSM–IV and disorders of childhood and adolescence: Can structural criteria be functional? *Journal of Consulting and Clinical Psychology*, 64, 1177–1191.

Seligman, L. (1994). *Developmental career counseling and assessment*. Thousand Oaks, CA: Sage.

Seligman, M. E. P. (1975). *Helplessness, on depression, development and death*. San Francisco: Freeman.

Seligman, M. E. P., Peterson, C., Kaslow, N. J., Tanenbaum, R. L., Alloy, L. B., & Abramson, L. Y. (1984). Attributional style and depressive symptoms among children. *Journal of Abnormal Psychology*, 93, 235–238.

Selman, R. (1980). *The growth of interpersonal understanding*. New York: Academic Press.

Shaffer, D., Fisher, P., Dulcan, M. K., Davies, M., Piacentini, J., Schwab-Stone, M. E., Lahey, B. B., Bourdon, K., Jensen, P. S., Bird, H. R., Canino, G., & Regier, D. A. (1996). The NIMH Diagnostic Interview Schedule for Children Version 2.3 (DISC–2.3): Description, acceptability, prevalence rates, and performance in the MECA study. *Journal of the American Academy of Child and Adolescent Psychiatry*, 35, 865–877.

Shaffer, D., Schwab-Stone, M., Fisher, P., Cohen, P., Piacentini, J., Davies, M., Conners, C. K., & Regier, D. (1993). The Diagnostic Interview Schedule for Children Revised Versions (DISC–R): Preparation, field testing, inter-rater reliability and acceptability. *Journal of the American Academy of Child and Adolescent Psychiatry*, 32, 643–650.

Shavelson, R. J., Hubner, J. J., & Stanton, G. C. (1976). Self-concept: Validation of construct interpretations. *Review of Educational Research*, 46, 407–441.

Shaw, M. W., & Wright, M. (1967). *Scales for the measurement of attitudes*. New York: McGraw-Hill.

Shepard, J. W. (1989). Review of the Jackson Vocational Interest Survey. *Mental Measurements Yearbook*, 10, 403–404.

Shields, I. W., & Simourd, D. J. (1991). Predicting predatory behavior in a population of young offenders. *Criminal Justice and Behavior*, 18, 180–194.

Shields, I. W., & Whitehall, G. C. (1994). Neutralization and delinquency among teenagers. *Criminal Justice and Behavior*, 21, 223–235.

Shure, M. P., & Spivack, G. (1978). *Problem-solving techniques in childrearing*. San Francisco: Jossey-Bass.

Siddique, C. M., & D'Arcy, C. (1984). Adolescence, stress, and psychological well-being. *Journal of Youth and Adolescence*, 13, 459–473.

Siegel, L. J. (1986). Review of The Children's Depression Inventory. *Test Critiques*, 5, 65–72.

Silverstein, A. B. (1986). Nonstandard standard scores on the Vineland Adaptive Behavior Scales: A cautionary note. *American Journal of Mental Deficiency*, 91, 1–4.

Simourd, D. J. (1997). The Criminal Sentiments Scale–Modified and Pride in Delinquency Scale: Psychometric properties and construct validity of two measures of criminal attitudes. *Criminal Justice and Behavior*, 24, 52–70.

Skinner, B. F. (1953). *Science and human behavior*. New York: Macmillan.

Skinner, H., Steinhauer, P., & Santa-Barbara, J. (1983). The Family Assessment Measure. *Canadian Journal of Community Mental Health*, 2, 91–105.

Slaby, R. G., & Guerra, N. A. (1988). Cognitive mediators of aggression in adolescent offender: I. Assessment. *Developmental Psychology, 24,* 580–588.

Snow, J. H. (1992). Review of the Luria–Nebraska Neuropsychological Battery: Forms I and II. *Mental Measurements Yearbook, 11,* 484–486.

Sparrow, S. S., & Cicchetti, D. V. (1987). Adaptive behavior and the psychologically disturbed child. *Journal of Special Education, 21,* 89–100.

Spielberger, C. D. (1988). *State-Trait Anger Expression Inventory, Research Edition: Professional manual.* Odessa, FL: Psychological Assessment Resources.

Spielberger, C. D., Krasner, S. S., & Solomon, E. P. (1988). The experience, expression, and control of anger. In M. P. Janisse (Ed.), *Health psychology: Individual differences and stress* (pp. 479–516). New York: Springer.

Spitzer, D., & Levinson, E. M. (1988). A review of selected vocational interest inventories for use by school psychologists. *School Psychology Review, 17,* 673–692.

Spivack, G., Haimes, P. E., & Spotts, J. (1967). *Devereux Adolescent Behavior Rating Scale.* Devon, PA: The Devereux Foundation.

Spivack, G., & Shure, M. B. (1974). *Social adjustment of young children: A cognitive approach to solving real-life problems.* Washington, DC: Jossey-Bass.

Spivack, G., & Swift, M. (1972). *Hahnemann High School Behavior Rating Scale.* Philadelphia: Hahnemann Medical College.

Spruill, J. (1987). Review of the Stanford–Binet Intelligence Scale–Fourth edition. *Test Critiques, 6,* 544–559.

Steinberg, L., & Thissen, D. (1995). Item response theory in personality research. In P. E. Shrout & S. T. Fiske (Eds.), *Personality research, methods, and theory: A festschrift honoring Donald W. Fiske* (pp. 161–181). Hillsdale, NJ: Lawrence Erlbaum Associates.

Steiner, D. L. (1985). Review of the Psychological Screening Inventory. *Test Critiques, 4,* 509–515.

Sternberg, R. J. (1985). *Beyond IQ: A triarchic theory of human intelligence.* Cambridge, UK: Cambridge University Press.

Sternberg, R. J. (1988). *The triarchic mind: A new theory of human intelligence.* New York: Cambridge University Press.

Sternberg, R. J. (Ed.). (1994). *Intelligence.* San Diego, CA: Academic Press.

Sternberg, R. J. (1997). The concept of intelligence and its role in lifelong learning and success. *American Psychologist, 52,* 1030–1037.

Stientjes, H. J. (1995). Review of the Behavior Disorders Identification Scale. *Mental Measurements Yearbook, 12,* 117.

Stoddard, A. H. (1994). Review of the Culture-Fair Intelligence Test. *Test Critiques, 10,* 188–194.

Stoloff, M. L., & Couch, J. V. (Eds.). (1992). *Computer use in psychology: A directory of software* (Vol. 3). Washington, DC: American Psychological Association.

Stuart, R. B. (1995). Review of the Millon Adolescent Clinical Inventory. *Mental Measurements Yearbook, 12,* 622–623.

Stuempfig, D. W. (1988). Review of the Diagnostic Achievement Test for Adolescents. *Test Critiques, 7,* 177–184.

Sullivan, H. S. (1953). *The interpersonal theory of psychiatry.* New York, NY: Norton.

Sundberg, N. D. (1992). Review of the Beck Depression Inventory. *Mental Measurements Yearbook, 11,* 79–80.

Swartz, J. D. (1986). Review of the Comprehensive Test of Adaptive Behavior. *Test Critiques, 5,* 73–75.

Sweetland, R. C., & Keyser, D. J. (1991). *Tests* (3rd ed.). Austin, TX: PRO-ED.

Swenson, L. C. (1993). *Psychology and law for the helping professions.* Pacific Grove, CA: Brooks/Cole.

Szulecka, T., Springett, N., & De Pauw, K. (1986). Psychiatric morbidity in first-year undergraduates and the effect of brief psychiatric intervention. *British Journal of Psychiatry, 149*, 75–80.

Tallent, N. (1993). *Psychological report writing* (4th ed.). Englewood Cliffs, NJ: Prentice-Hall.

Tanner, J. M. (1989). *Foetus into man: Physical growth from conception to maturity* (2nd ed.). Ware, UK: Castlemead.

Tanner, J. M. (1991). Menarche, secular trend in age of. In R. M. Lerner, A. C. Peterson, & J. Brooks-Gunn (Eds.), *Encyclopoedia of adolescence* (Vol. 2, pp. 637–641). New York: Garland.

Tatman, S. M., Greene, A. L., & Karr, L. C. (1993). Use of the suicide probability scale with adolescents. *Suicide and Life Threatening Behavior, 23*, 188–203.

Taylor, H. G., & Fletcher, J. M. (1990). Neuropsychological assessment of children. In G. Goldstein & M. Hersen (Eds.), *Handbook of psychological assessment* (2nd ed., pp. 228–255). New York: Pergamon.

Thompson, D. (1995). Review of the Kuder General Interest Survey. *Mental Measurements Yearbook, 12*, 545–546.

Thorndike, R. L., & Hagen, E. P. (1997). *Manual for the Cognitive Abilities Test*. Chicago, IL: Riverside Publishing Co.

Tinsley, H. E. A. (1994). Review of the NEO Personality Inventory–Revised. *Test Critiques, 10*, 443–455.

Tolan, P. H., & Cohler, B. J. (Eds.). (1993). *Handbook of clinical research and practice with adolescents*. New York: Wiley.

Tolan, P. H., & Gorman-Smith, D. (1997). Families and the development of urban children. In H. J. Walberg, O. Reyes, & R. P. Weissberg (Eds.), *Children and youth: Interdisciplinary perspectives* (Vol. 7). Thousand Oaks, CA: Sage.

Toneatto, T. (1992). Review of the Adolescent Diagnostic Interview. *Mental Measurements Yearbook, 12*, 42–43.

Touliatos, J., Perlmutter, B. F., & Straus, M. A. (1990). *Handbook of family measurement techniques*. Newbury Park, CA: Sage.

Tuma, J. M. (1985). Review of the Personality Inventory for Children. *Mental Measurements Yearbook, 9*, 1157–1159.

Tutty, L. M. (1995). Theoretical and practical issues in selecting a measure of family functioning. *Research on Social Work Practice, 5*, 80–106.

Tyler, B. (1986). Responsibility in practice: Some implications of the BPS Survey on test use—A postcript. *Bulletin of the British Psychological Society, 39*, 410–413.

Umberger, F. G. (1985). Review of the Peabody Picture Vocabulary Test–Revised. *Test Critiques, 3*, 488–495.

Vacc, N. A. (1992). Review of the Career Assessment Inventory. *Mental Measurements Yearbook, 11*, 150–151.

Van Gorp, W. (1992). Review of Luria–Nebraska Neuropsychological Battery: Forms I and II. *Mental Measurements Yearbook, 11*, 486–488.

Vieweg, B. W., & Hedlund, J. L. (1984). Psychological Screening Inventory: A comprehensive review. *Journal of Clinical Psychology, 40*, 1382–1393.

Violato, C., & Holden, W. B. (1988). A confirmatory factor analysis of a four-factor model of adolescent concerns. *Journal of Youth and Adolescence, 17*, 101–113.

Wakefield, J. C. (1992). Disorder as harmful dysfunction: A conceptual critique of DSM–III–R's definition of mental disorder. *Psychological Review, 99*, 232–247.

Waldman, I. D., Lilienfield, S. O., & Lahey, B. B. (1995). Toward construct validity in the childhood disruptive behavior disorders: Classification and diagnosis in DSM–IV and beyond. *Advances in Clinical Child Psychology, 17*, 323–363.

Walls, R. T., Zane, T., & Thvedt, J. E. (1991). Review of the Independent Living Behavior Checklist. *Test Critiques, 8*, 301–307.

Watkins, C. E., Campbell, V. L., & Nieberding, R. (1994). The practice of vocational assessment by counseling psychologists. *Counseling Psychology, 22,* 115–128.

Watson, T. S. (1992). Review of the Test of Nonverbal Intelligence. *Mental Measurements Yearbook, 11,* 970–972.

Webster, C. D., Harris, G. T., Rice, M. E., Cormier, C., & Quinsey, V. L. (1994). *The violence prediction scheme: Assessing dangerousness in high risk men.* Toronto: Centre of Criminology, University of Toronto.

Webster, R. E. (1994). Review of the Woodcock–Johnson Psycho-Educational Test Battery–Revised. *Test Critiques, 10,* 804–815.

Wechsler, D. (1991). *Wechsler Intelligence Scale for Children–III.* San Antonio, TX: Psychological Corporation.

Wegner, K. W. (1988). Review of the California Psychological Inventory–1987 Revised edition. *Test Critiques, 7,* 66–75.

Weissman, A. N., & Beck, A. T. (1978, November). *Development and validation of the Dysfunctional Attitude Scale: A preliminary investigation.* Paper presented at the meeting of the Association for the Advancement of Behavior Therapy, Chicago.

Weisz, J. R., Donenberg, G. R., Han, S. S., & Kauneckis, D. (1995). Child and adolescent psychotherapy outcomes in experiments vs. clinics: Why the disparity? *Journal of Abnormal Child Psychology, 23,* 83–106.

Weisz, J. R., & Weiss, B. (1993). *Effects of psychotherapy with children and adolescents.* Newbury Park, CA: Sage.

Weisz, J. R., Weiss, B., Alicke, M. D., & Klotz, M. L. (1987). Effectiveness of psychotherapy with children and adolescents: A meta-analysis for clinicians. *Journal of Consulting and Clinical Psychology, 55,* 542–549.

Weisz, J. R., Weiss, B., Han, S. S., Granger, D. A., & Morton, T. (1995). Effects of psychotherapy with children and adolescents revisited: A meta-analysis of treatment outcome studies. *Psychological Bulletin, 117,* 450–468.

Wiebush, R. G., Baird, C., Krisberg, B., & Onek, D. (1995). Risk assessment and classification for serious, violent, and chronic juvenile offenders. In J. C. Howell, B. F. Krisberg, J. D. Hawkins, & J. J. Wilson (Eds.), *A sourcebook: Serious, violent, and chronic juvenile offenders* (pp. 171–212). Thousand Oaks, CA: Sage.

Wiesner, W. H., & Cronshaw, S. F. (1988). A meta-analytic investigation of the impact of interview format and degree of structure on the validity of the employment interview. *Journal of Occupational Psychology, 61,* 275–290.

Williams, C. L., Ben-Porath, Y. S., & Weed, N. C. (1990). Ratings of behavior problems in adolescents hospitalized for substance abuse. *Journal of Adolescent Chemical Dependency, 1,* 95–112.

Williams, C. L., Butcher, J. N., Ben-Porath, Y. S., & Graham, J. R. (1992). *MMPI–A content scales: Assessing psychopathology in adolescents.* Minneapolis: University of Minnesota Press.

Winters, K. C., & Henly, G. A. (1991). *Manual for the Personal Experience Inventory.* Los Angeles, CA: Western Psychological Services.

Winters, K. C., Stinchfield, R. D., Fulkerson, J., & Henly, G. A. (1993). Measuring alcohol and cannabis use disorders in an adolescent clinical sample. *Psychology of Addictive Behaviors, 7,* 185–196.

Wirt, R. D., Lachar, D., Klinedinst, J. E., Seat, P. D., & Broen, W. E. (1990). *Manual for the Personality Inventory for Children–Revised format.* Los Angeles: Western Psychological Services.

Witt, J. C. (1998). Review of the Behavior Assessment System for Children. *Mental Measurements Yearbook, 13,* 131–133.

Woodward, M. J., Goncalves, A. A., & Millon, T. (1994). Millon Personality Inventory and Millon Adolescent Clinical Inventory. In M. E. Maruish (Ed.), *The use of psychological testing for treatment planning and outcome assessment* (pp. 453–478). Hillsdale, NJ: Lawrence Erlbaum Associates.

Wormith, J. S., & Andrews, D. A. (1995, June). *The development and validation of three measures of criminal sentiments and their role in the assessment of offender attitudes.* Paper presented at the annual convention of the Canadian Psychological Association, Charlottetown, Canada.

Worthen, B. R., & Sailor, P. (1995). Review of the Strong Interest Inventory. *Mental Measurements Yearbook, 12,* 999–1002.

Wright, L., Ford, D., & Kiser, K. (1992). Review of the Adolescent Diagnostic Interview. *Mental Measurements Yearbook, 12,* 43–44.

Yong, F. L., & McIntyre, J. D. (1992). A comparative study of the learning style preferences of students with learning disabilities and students who are gifted. *Journal of Learning Disabilities, 25,* 124–132.

Young, J. G., O'Brien, J. D., Gutterman, E. M., & Cohen, P. (1987). Research on the clinical interview. *Journal of the American Academy of Child and Adolescent Psychiatry, 26,* 613–620.

Young, J. W. (1995). Review of the Kaufman Brief Intelligence Test. *Mental Measurements Yearbook, 12,* 534–536.

Zaslow, J., & Takanishi, R. (1993). Priorities for research in adolescent development. *American Psychologist, 48,* 185–192.

Zigler, E., Balla, D., & Hodapp, R. (1984). On the definition and classification of mental retardation. *American Journal of Mental Deficiency, 89,* 215–230.

# Author Index

## A

Abiden, R. R., 239
Ablard, K. E., 123
Abramson, L. Y., 206, 207
Achenbach, T. M., 47, 71, 77, 101, 136, 180, 181, 182, 194, 257, 259
Aden, A. M., 53
Adwere-Boamah, J., 49
Aiken, L. R., 65, 71, 100, 110, 136, 178, 194, 196, 199, 256, 262
Alexander, J. F., 58
Alicke, M. D., 58
Allison, J. A., 238
Alloy, L. B., 207
Allport, G. W., 26
Aman, M. G., 224, 227
American Asociation on Mental Retardation, 225
American Psychiatric Association, 27, 43, 45, 46, 225, 261
American Psychological Association, 73, 94, 95, 134, 247, 253
Ammerman, R. T., 41
Anastasi, A., 46, 76, 103, 134, 245
Andrews, D. A., 24, 47, 59, 60, 86, 89, 94, 172, 195, 199, 200, 240, 241, 243, 244, 252, 263
Ansorge, C. J., 119
Applegate, B., 168
Archambault, F. X., 148
Archer, R. P., 8, 143
Arkowitz, H., 60, 88
Armacost, R. L., 49
Arthur, W., Jr., 159
Asarnow, J. R., 50
Ash, P., 192
Association of State and Provincial Psychology Boards, 97

## B

Attkinson, C. C., 91
Auld, R., 206
Austin, G. W., 138
Ayers, M., 223

Bachorowski, J., 23, 204
Bagarozzi, D. A., 234
Baird, C., 241, 250
Bakker, D. J., 220
Baldwin, L. M., 236
Balla, D., 226
Bandura, A., 23, 27, 34, 199
Bardwell, R., 210
Barkley, R. A., 169
Barnes, L. B., 128
Bascue, L. O., 209
Batenhorst, L. M., 210
Bechtold, D. W., 210
Beck, A. T., 151, 152, 206, 207, 208
Beck, S. J.
Beere, C. A., 203
Beere, D. B., 203
Bellack, A., 178
Bellido, C., 60
Belsky, J., 29, 35
Benes, K. M., 131
Bennett, E., 239
Bennett, L. M., 130
Ben-Porath, Y. S., 143, 185
Bernal, G., 60
Bernardin, H. J., 193
Bernardin, K., 193
Bersoff, D. N., 96, 98
Bettelheim, B., 54
Beutler, L. E., 60, 88, 89, 90
Biederman, I., 168
Bird, H. R., 101, 164, 168, 169, 173

# Subject Index

www.ingramcontent.com/pod-product-compliance
Ingram Content Group UK Ltd.
Pitfield, Milton Keynes, MK11 3LW, UK
UKHW020434010325